The Humanities in the Western Tradition

The Humanities in the Western Tradition

Readings in Literature and Thought

VOLUME I

Marvin Perry
Baruch College, City University of New York

J. Wayne Baker
The University of Akron

Pamela Pfeiffer Hollinger
The University of Akron

WADSWORTH
CENGAGE Learning™

Australia • Brazil • Japan • Korea • Mexico • Singapore • Spain • United Kingdom • United States

WADSWORTH
CENGAGE Learning

The Humanities in the Western Tradition: Readings in Literature and Thought: Volume I
Marvin Perry, J. Wayne Baker, Pamela Pfeiffer Hollinger

Senior Sponsoring Editor: Nancy Blaine

Development Editor: Julie Dunn

Senior Project Editor: Bob Greiner

Editorial Assistant: Wendy Thayer

Production/Design Assistant: Bethany Schlegel

Manufacturing Manager: Florence Cadran

Senior Marketing Manager: Sandra McGuire

Cover Image: Museo Archeologico Nazionale, Naples, Italy/Canali. PhotoBank Milan/Superstock

For product information and technology assistance, contact us at
Cengage Learning Customer & Sales Support, 1-800-354-9706

For permission to use material from this text or product, submit all requests online at **www.cengage.com/permissions**
Further permissions questions can be emailed to
permissionrequest@cengage.com

ISBN-13: 978-0-395-84814-2

ISBN-10: 0-395-84814-8

Wadsworth
25 Thomson Place
Boston, MA 02210
USA

Cengage Learning is a leading provider of customized learning solutions with office locations around the globe, including Singapore, the United Kingdom, Australia, Mexico, Brazil, and Japan. Locate your local office at **international.cengage.com/region**

Cengage Learning products are represented in Canada by Nelson Education, Ltd.

To learn more about Wadsworth, visit **www.cengage.com/wadsworth**

Purchase any of our products at your local college store or at our preferred online store **www.ichapters.com**

Printed in the United States of America
3 4 5 6 7   16 15 14 13 12

FD227

Contents

PART II

THE MIDDLE AGES:
THE CHRISTIAN CENTURIES   133

Preface

The Humanities in the Western Tradition: Readings in Literature and Thought surveys thought and literature from antiquity to the present with an assortment of sources. Instructors in Humanities courses have long recognized the pedagogical value of primary sources in exploring the profound questions of human experience and understanding the historical stages of the Western tradition. These selections have been carefully chosen and edited to fit the needs of a survey of the Humanities and to supplement standard textbooks in literature and histories of the West.

We have based our choice of readings for the two volumes on several criteria. As an aid for understanding the dominant ideals of the Western tradition this reader emphasizes primarily the foremost thinkers and authors who shaped the Western tradition. In their choice of readings, the editors hope to convey to students that the Western heritage is a living, vital tradition and that studying these primary sources in literature and thought will enrich their lives. Even though the reader focuses on great thinkers, the great ideas, and great works of literature, it also includes a sampling of works that capture the social, political, and economic outlook of an age so that students derive a sense of movement and development in Western history. While some readings are included in their entirety, such as Sophocles' *Oedipus the King* and Chaucer's "The Nun's Priest's Tale," the other readings are of sufficient length to convey their essential meaning and main ideas.

An important feature of the reader is the use of the constellation, the grouping of several related documents illuminating a single theme; such constellations reinforce the student's understanding of important themes and invites comparison, analysis, and interpretation. For example, in Volume I, Chapter 3, Section 3, the constellation "Humanism" contains three interrelated readings: "The Pursuit of Excellence" by Pindar, "Lauding Human Talents" by Sophocles, and "The Funeral Oration of Pericles" by Thucydides. In Volume II, Chapter 15, Section 8, the constellation "American Realism" contains three readings: *The Adventures of Huckleberry Finn* by Mark Twain, *Leaves of Grass* by Walt Whitman, and "Selected Poems" by Emily Dickinson.

An overriding concern for the editors in preparing this compilation was to make the documents accessible—to enable students to comprehend and to interpret both literary works and historical documents on their own. To facilitate this aim, we have provided several pedagogical features. Introductions of three types explain the historical setting, the authors' intents, and the meaning and significance of the readings. First, introductions to each chapter provide comprehensive overviews to each period considered. Second, introductions to each numbered section or grouping treat the historical background for the reading(s) that follow(s). Third, each reading has a brief headnote that provides specific details about that reading.

Within some readings, interlinear notes, clearly set off from the text of the document, serve as transitions and suggest the main themes of the passage that follow. Used primarily in longer extracts, these interlinear notes help to guide students through the readings. Moreover, to assist students' comprehension, brief, bracketed editorial definitions or notes that explain unfamiliar or foreign terms or phrases are inserted into the running text. When terms or concepts in the documents require fuller explanations, these appear at the bottom of the pages as editors' footnotes. Where helpful, we have retained the notes of authors, translators, or editors from whose works the documents were acquired.

For ancient sources, we have generally selected recent translations that are both faithful to the text and readable. For some seventeenth- and eighteenth-century English documents, the archaic spelling has been retained, when this does not preclude comprehension, to demonstrate to students how the English language has evolved over time.

It is our hope that this reader enhances the appreciation of Western literature and thought and enriches the study of the Humanities. The selection and compilation of sources is not an easy task and the authors wish to thank the following instructors for their helpful suggestions and advice:

Robert Eisner, *San Diego State University*

David Fenimore, *University of Nevada, Reno*

Sandi S. Landis, *St. Johns River Community College, Orange Park Campus*

Charlie McAllister, *Catawba College*

Merry Ovnick, *California State University, Northridge*

Richard A. Voeltz, *Cameron University*

M. P.

J. W. B.

P. P. H.

PART I

THE BIRTH OF THE WEST: THE GRECO-ROMAN AND JUDEO-CHRISTIAN HERITAGE

CHAPTER 1

The Ancient Near East

The world's first civilizations arose some five thousand years ago in the river valleys of Mesopotamia (later Iraq) and Egypt. In these Near Eastern lands people built cities, organized states with definite boundaries, invented writing, engaged in large-scale trade, practiced specialization of labor, and erected huge monuments: all activities that historians associate with civilization. Scholars emphasize the fact that civilizations emerged in the river valleys—the Tigris and Euphrates in Mesopotamia and the Nile in Egypt. When they overflowed their banks, these rivers deposited fertile soil, which could provide a food surplus required to sustain life in cities. The early inhabitants of these valleys drained swamps and built irrigation works, enabling them to harness the rivers for human advantage. In the process they also strengthened the bonds of cooperation, a necessary ingredient of civilization.

Religion and myth were the central forces in these early civilizations. They pervaded all phases of life, providing people with satisfying explanations for the operations of nature and the mystery of death and justifying traditional rules of morality. Natural objects—the sun, the river, the mountain—were seen either as gods or as the abodes of gods. The political life of the Near East was theocratic: that is, people regarded their rulers as either divine or as representatives of the gods and believed that law originated with the gods. Near Eastern art and literature were dominated by religious themes.

The Sumerians, founders of urban life in Mesopotamia, developed twelve city-states in the region of the lower Euphrates near the Persian Gulf. Each city-state included a city and the farmland around it; each had its own government and was independent of the other city-states. In time the Sumerians were conquered, and their cities were incorporated into kingdoms and empires. However, as Akkadians, Elamites, Babylonians, and other peoples of the region adopted and built upon Sumerian religion, art, and literary forms, the Sumerian achievement became the basis of a coherent Mesopotamian civilization that lasted some three thousand years.

Early in its history, Egypt became a centralized state under the rule of a pharaoh, who was viewed as both a man and a god. The pharaoh's authority was all-embracing, and all Egyptians were subservient to him. Early in their history, the Egyptians developed cultural patterns that were to endure for three thousand years; the ancient Egyptians looked to the past, seeking to maintain the ways of their ancestors.

Although the cultural patterns of both civilizations were similar—in both, religion and theocratic kingship played a dominant role—there were significant differences between the two. Whereas in Egypt the pharaoh was considered divine, rulers in Mesopotamia were regarded as exceptional human beings whom the gods had selected to act as their agents. Second, the natural environment of the Egyptians fostered a sense of security and an optimistic outlook toward life. Natural barriers—deserts, the Mediterranean Sea, and cataracts in the Nile—protected Egypt from invasion, and the overflowing of the Nile was regular and predictable, ensuring a good harvest. In contrast, Mesopotamia, without natural barriers, suffered from frequent invasions, and the Tigris and Euphrates rivers were unpredictable. Sometimes there was insufficient overflow, and the land was afflicted with drought; at other times, rampaging floods devastated the fields. These conditions promoted a pessimistic outlook, which pervaded Mesopotamian civilization.

After 1500 B.C., the Near East entered a period of empire building. In the late sixth century B.C., the Persians, the greatest of the empire builders, conquered all the lands from the Nile River to the Indus River in India. Persia united Egypt, Mesopotamia, and other Near Eastern lands into a world-state and brought together the region's various cultural traditions. In the first half of the fifth century B.C., the Persians tried to add the city-states of Greece to their empire; the ensuing conflict was of critical importance for the history of Western civilization.

Egyptians, Mesopotamians, and other Near Eastern peoples developed a rich urban culture and made important contributions to later civilizations. They established bureaucracies, demonstrated creativity in art and literature, fashioned effective systems of mathematics, and advanced the knowledge of architecture, metallurgy, and engineering. The wheel, the plow, the phonetic alphabet, and the calendar derive from the Near East. Both the Hebrews and the Greeks, the principal sources of Western civilization, had contact with these older civilizations and adopted many of their cultural forms. But, as we shall see, even more important for the shaping of Western civilization was how the Hebrews and the Greeks broke with the essential style of Near Eastern society and conceived new outlooks, new points of departure for the human mind.

1 Mesopotamian Protest Against Death and the Flood

The *Epic of Gilgamesh,* the greatest work of Mesopotamian literature, was written about 2000 B.C. It utilized legends about Gilgamesh, probably a historical figure who ruled the city of Uruk about 2600 B.C. The story deals with a profound theme—the human protest against death. In the end, Gilgamesh learns to accept reality: there is no escape from death. While the *Epic of Gilgamesh* is an expression of the pessimism that pervaded Mesopotamian life, it also reveals the Mesopotamians' struggle to come to terms with reality.

Epic of Gilgamesh[1]

The *Epic of Gilgamesh* involves the gods in human activities. Because King Gilgamesh, son of a human father and the goddess Ninsun, drives his subjects too hard, they appeal to the gods for help. The gods decide that a man of Gilgamesh's immense vigor and strength requires a rival with similar attributes with whom he can contend. The creation goddess, Aruru, is instructed to create a man worthy of Gilgamesh. From clay she fashions Enkidu in the image of Anu, the god of the heavens and father of all the gods. Enkidu is a powerful man who roams with the animals and destroys traps set by hunters, one of whom appeals

---

[1] Throughout the text, titles original to the source appear in italics. Titles added by the editors are not italicized.

to King Gilgamesh. The two of them, accompanied by a harlot, find Enkidu at a watering place frequented by animals. The harlot removes her clothes and seduces Enkidu, who spends a week with her, oblivious to everything else. After this encounter, the bond between Enkidu and the animals is broken. He now enters civilization and is befriended by Gilgamesh, with whom he slays the terrible monster Humbaba.

Returning to Uruk after the encounter with Humbaba, Gilgamesh washes away the grime of battle and dons his royal clothes; thus arrayed he attracts the goddess of love, Ishtar, patroness of Uruk, who proposes marriage, but because of Ishtar's previous marriages and infidelities, Gilgamesh refuses. Ishtar falls into a bitter rage and appeals to her father, the god Anu, to unleash the fearful Bull of Heaven on Gilgamesh. However, Gilgamesh and Enkidu together slay the beast. To avenge the deaths of Humbaba and the Bull of Heaven, the gods decide that Enkidu shall die. In the following passage, Enkidu dreams of his impending death and the House of Darkness, from which no one returns.

When the daylight came Enkidu got up and cried to Gilgamesh, "O my brother, such a dream I had last night. Anu, Enlil, Ea and heavenly Shamash took counsel together, and Anu said to Enlil, 'Because they have killed the Bull of Heaven, and because they have killed Humbaba who guarded the Cedar Mountain one of the two must die.' . . ."

So Enkidu lay stretched out before Gilgamesh: his tears ran down in streams and he said to Gilgamesh, "O my brother, so dear as you are to me, brother, yet they will take me from you." Again he said, "I must sit down on the threshold of the dead and never again will I see my dear brother with my eyes."

. . . In bitterness of spirit he poured out his heart to his friend. "It was I who cut down the cedar, I who levelled the forest, I who slew Humbaba and now see what has become of me. Listen, my friend, this is the dream I dreamed last night. The heavens roared, and earth rumbled back an answer; between them stood I before an awful being, the sombre-faced man-bird; he had directed on me his purpose. His was a vampire face, his foot was a lion's foot, his hand was an eagle's talon. He fell on me and his claws were in my hair, he held me fast and I smothered; then he transformed me so that my arms became wings covered with feathers. He turned his stare towards me, and he led me away to the palace of Irkalla, the Queen of Darkness, to the house from which none who enters ever returns, down the road from which there is no coming back.

"There is the house whose people sit in darkness; dust is their food and clay their meat. They are clothed like birds with wings for covering, they see no light, they sit in darkness. I entered the house of dust and I saw the kings of the earth, their crowns put away for ever; rulers and princes, all those who once wore kingly crowns and ruled the world in the days of old. They who had stood in the place of the gods like Anu and Enlil, stood now like servants to fetch baked meats in the house of dust, to carry cooked meat and cold water from the water-skin. In the house of dust which I entered were high priests and acolytes, priests of the incantation and of ecstasy; there were servers of the temple, and there was

Etana, that king of Kish whom the eagle carried to heaven in the days of old. I saw also Samuqan, god of cattle, and there was Ereshkigal the Queen of the Underworld; and Belit-Sheri squatted in front of her, she who is recorder of the gods and keeps the book of death. She held a tablet from which she read. She raised her head, she saw me and spoke: 'Who has brought this one here?' Then I awoke like a man drained of blood who wanders alone in a waste of rushes; like one whom the bailiff has seized and his heart pounds with terror."

Gilgamesh had peeled off his clothes, he listened to his words and wept quick tears, Gilgamesh listened and his tears flowed. . . .

This day on which Enkidu dreamed came to an end and he lay stricken with sickness. One whole day he lay on his bed and his suffering increased. He said to Gilgamesh, the friend on whose account he had left the wilderness, "Once I ran for you, for the water of life, and I now have nothing." A second day he lay on his bed and Gilgamesh watched over him but the sickness increased. A third day he lay on his bed, he called out to Gilgamesh, rousing him up. Now he was weak and his eyes were blind with weeping. Ten days he lay and his suffering increased, eleven and twelve days he lay on his bed of pain. Then he called to Gilgamesh, "My friend, the great goddess cursed me and I must die in shame. I shall not die like a man fallen in battle; I feared to fall, but happy is the man who falls in the battle, for I must die in shame." And Gilgamesh wept over Enkidu. With the first light of dawn he raised his voice and said to the counsellors of Uruk:

"Hear me, great ones of Uruk,
I weep for Enkidu, my friend,
Bitterly moaning like a woman mourning
I weep for my brother.
O Enkidu, my brother,
You were the axe at my side,
My hand's strength, the sword in my belt,
The shield before me,
A glorious robe, my fairest ornament;
An evil Fate has robbed me.

. . .

All the people of Eridu
Weep for you Enkidu.

. . .

What is this sleep which holds you now?
You are lost in the dark and cannot hear me."

He touched his heart but it did not beat, nor did he lift his eyes again. When Gilgamesh touched his heart it did not beat. So Gilgamesh laid a veil, as one veils the bride, over his friend. He began to rage like a lion, like a lioness robbed of her whelps. This way and that he paced round the bed, he tore out his hair and strewed it around. He dragged off his splendid robes and flung them down as though they were abominations.

In the first light of dawn Gilgamesh cried out, "I made you rest on a royal bed, you reclined on a couch at my left hand, the princes of the earth kissed your feet. I will cause all the people of Uruk to weep over you and raise the dirge of the dead. The joyful people will stoop with sorrow; and when you have gone to the earth I will let my hair grow long for your sake, I will wander through the wilderness in the skin of a lion." The next day also, in the first light, Gilgamesh lamented; seven days and seven nights he wept for Enkidu, until the worm fastened on him. Only then he gave him up to the earth, for the Anunnaki, the judges [of the dead],[2] had seized him. . . .

In his despair, Gilgamesh is confronted with the reality of his own death. Yearning for eternal life, he seeks Utnapishtim, legendary king of the city of Shurrupak, a man to whom the gods had granted everlasting life.

Bitterly Gilgamesh wept for his friend Enkidu; he wandered over the wilderness as a hunter, he roamed over the plains; in his bitterness he cried, "How can I rest, how can I be at peace? Despair is in my heart. What my brother is now, that shall I be when I am dead. Because I am afraid of death I will go as best I can to find Utnapishtim whom they call the Faraway, for he has entered the assembly of the gods." So Gilgamesh travelled over the wilderness, he wandered over the grasslands, a long journey, in search of Utnapishtim, whom the gods took after the deluge; and they set him to live in the land of Dilmun, in the garden of the sun; and to him alone of men they gave everlasting life. . . .

In the garden of the gods, Gilgamesh speaks with Siduri, the divine winemaker, who tells him that his search for eternal life is hopeless.

". . . My friend who was very dear to me and who endured dangers beside me, Enkidu my brother, whom I loved,

the end of mortality has overtaken him. I wept for him seven days and nights till the worm fastened on him. Because of my brother I am afraid of death, because of my brother I stray through the wilderness and cannot rest. But now, young woman, maker of wine, since I have seen your face do not let me see the face of death which I dread so much."

She answered, "Gilgamesh, where are you hurrying to? You will never find that life for which you are looking. When the gods created man they allotted to him death, but life they retained in their own keeping. As for you, Gilgamesh, fill your belly with good things; day and night, night and day, dance and be merry, feast and rejoice. Let your clothes be fresh, bathe yourself in water, cherish the little child that holds your hand, and make your wife happy in your embrace; for this too is the lot of man."

But Gilgamesh said to Siduri, the young woman, "How can I be silent, how can I rest, when Enkidu whom I love is dust, and I too shall die and be laid in the earth. You live by the sea-shore and look into the heart of it; young woman, tell me now, which is the way to Utnapishtim, the son of Ubara-Tutu? What directions are there for the passage; give me, oh, give me directions, I will cross the Ocean if it is possible; if it is not I will wander still farther in the wilderness." . . .

Siduri instructs Gilgamesh how to reach Utnapishtim. Ferried across the "waters of death" by a boatman, Gilgamesh meets Utnapishtim. But he, too, cannot give Gilgamesh the eternal life for which he yearns.

. . . "Oh father Utnapishtim, you who have entered the assembly of the gods, I wish to question you concerning the living and the dead, how shall I find the life for which I am searching?"

Utnapishtim said, "There is no permanence. Do we build a house to stand for ever, do we seal a contract to hold for all time? Do brothers divide an inheritance to keep for ever, does the flood-time of rivers endure? It is only the nymph of the dragon-fly who sheds her larva and sees the sun in his glory. From the days of old there is no permanence. The sleeping and the dead, how alike they are, they are like a painted death. What is there between the master and the servant when both have fulfilled their doom? When the Anunnaki, the judges, come together, and Mammetun the mother of destinies, together they decree the fates of men. Life and death they allot but the day of death they do not disclose." . . .

The tale concludes with one of the many ancient stories of a great flood. In the West, the best known of these stories is the Hebrew account of Noah and his ark in Genesis (chapters 6–9). However, the *Epic of Gilgamesh* contains quite possibly an older version of the story—one that is quite similar to the Genesis account. The two accounts have several similarities: Both were worldwide floods that destroyed all the animals and humans except those who were saved in a huge boat built by a single righteous man,

---

Noah in Genesis and Utnapishtim in *Gilgamesh*; both boats landed on a mountaintop; and both men sent out birds to find out whether the waters had subsided. There are also differences: in the Genesis account, God sent the forty-day flood as a punishment for human sinfulness, whereas in *Gilgamesh*, a council of the gods decided to destroy humanity with a six-day flood because humans had become too numerous and noisy. In the Gilgamesh account, it was Enlil, the god of the earth, who proposed the idea of the flood, and his plan was approved by the other gods, even by his father, Anu, the chief of the Sumerian gods. The only opposition came from Enlil's brother Ea, the god of fresh water and the creator of humans. Ea warned Utnapishtim of the impending flood and told him to build a boat. Enlil's flood was made even more destructive by the Annunaki, the gods of the underworld, and by Niurta, the god of war. After the flood, Ishtar, goddess of love and the daughter of Anu, placated the gods and made possible the reconciliation between Enlil and Utnapishtim.

... "You know the city Shurrupak, it stands on the banks of Euphrates? That city grew old and the gods that were in it were old. There was Anu, lord of the firmament, their father, and warrior Enlil their counsellor, Ninurta the helper, and Ennugi watcher over canals; and with them also was Ea. In those days the world teemed, the people multiplied, the world bellowed like a wild bull, and the great god was aroused by the clamour. Enlil heard the clamour and he said to the gods in council, 'The uproar of mankind is intolerable and sleep is no longer possible by reason of the babel.' So the gods agreed to exterminate mankind. Enlil did this, but Ea because of his oath warned me in a dream. He whispered their words to my house of reeds, 'Reed-house, reed-house! Wall, O wall, hearken reed-house, wall reflect; O man of Shurrupak, son of Ubara-Tutu; tear down your house and build a boat, abandon possessions and look for life, despise worldly goods and save your soul alive. Tear down your house, I say, and build a boat. These are the measurements of the barque as you shall build her: let her beam equal her length, let her deck be roofed like the vault that covers the abyss; then take up into the boat the seed of all living creatures.'

"When I had understood I said to my lord, 'Behold, what you have commanded I will honour and perform, but how shall I answer the people, the city, the elders?' Then Ea opened his mouth and said to me, his servant, 'Tell them this: I have learnt that Enlil is wrathful against me, I dare no longer walk in his land nor live in his city; I will go down to the Gulf to dwell with Ea my lord. But on you he will rain down abundance, rare fish and shy wild-fowl, a rich harvest-tide. In the evening the rider of the storm will bring you wheat in torrents.

"In the first light of dawn all my household gathered round me, the children brought pitch and the men whatever

was necessary. On the fifth day I laid the keel and the ribs, then I made fast the planking. The ground-space was one acre, each side of the deck measured one hundred and twenty cubits, making a square. I built six decks below, seven in all, I divided them into nine sections with bulkheads between. I drove in wedges where needed, I saw to the punt-poles, and laid in supplies. The carriers brought oil in baskets, I poured pitch into the furnace and asphalt and oil; more oil was consumed in caulking, and more again the master of the boat took into his stores. I slaughtered bullocks for the people and every day I killed sheep. I gave the shipwrights wine to drink as though it were river water, raw wine and red wine and oil and white wine. There was feasting then as there is at the time of the New Year's festival; I myself anointed my head. On the seventh day the boat was complete.

"Then was the launching full of difficulty; there was shifting of ballast above and below till two thirds was submerged. I loaded into her all that I had of gold and of living things, my family, my kin, the beast of the field both wild and tame, and all the craftsmen. I sent them on board, for the time that Shamash had ordained was already fulfilled when he said, 'In the evening, when the rider of the storm sends down the destroying rain, enter the boat and batten her down.' The time was fulfilled, the evening came, the rider of the storm sent down the rain. I looked out at the weather and it was terrible, so I too boarded the boat and battened her down. All was now complete, the battening and the caulking; so I handed the tiller to Puzur-Amurri the steersman, with the navigation and the care of the whole boat.

"With the first light of dawn a black cloud came from the horizon; it thundered within where Adad, lord of the storm was riding. In front over hill and plain Shullat and Hanish, heralds of the storm, led on. Then the gods of the abyss rose up; Nergal pulled out the dams of the nether waters, Ninurta the war-lord threw down the dykes, and the seven judges of hell, the Annunaki, raised their torches, lighting the land with their livid flame. A stupor of despair went up to heaven when the god of the storm turned daylight to darkness, when he smashed the land like a cup. One whole day the tempest raged, gathering fury as it went, it poured over the people like the tides of battle; a man could not see his brother nor the people be seen from heaven. Even the gods were terrified at the flood, they fled to the highest heaven, the firmament of Anu; they crouched against the walls, cowering like curs. Then Ishtar the sweet-voiced Queen of Heaven cried out like a woman in travail: 'Alas the days of old are turned to dust because I commanded evil; why did I command this evil in the council of all the gods? I commanded wars to destroy the people, but are they not my people, for I brought them forth? Now like the spawn of fish they float in the ocean.' The great gods of heaven and of hell wept, they covered their mouths.

"For six days and six nights the winds blew, torrent and tempest and flood overwhelmed the world, tempest and flood raged together like warring hosts. When the seventh day dawned the storm from the south subsided, the sea grew calm, the flood was stilled; I looked at the face of the world and there was silence, all mankind was turned to clay. The surface of the sea stretched as flat as a roof-top; I opened a hatch and the light fell on my face. Then I bowed low, I sat down and I wept, the tears streamed down my face, for on every side was the waste of water. I looked for land in vain, but fourteen leagues distant there appeared a mountain, and there the boat grounded; on the mountain of Nisir the boat held fast, she held fast and did not budge. One day she held, and a second day on the mountain of Nisir she held fast and did not budge. A third day, and a fourth day she held fast on the mountain and did not budge; a fifth day and a sixth day she held fast on the mountain. When the seventh day dawned I loosed a dove and let her go. She flew away, but finding no resting-place she returned. Then I loosed a swallow, and she flew away but finding no resting-place she returned. I loosed a raven, she saw that the waters had retreated, she ate, she flew around, she cawed, and she did not come back. Then I threw everything open to the four winds, I made a sacrifice and poured out a libation on the mountain top. Seven and again seven cauldrons I set up on their stands, I heaped up wood and cane and cedar and myrtle. When the gods smelled the sweet savour, they gathered like flies over the sacrifice. Then, at last, Ishtar also came, she lifted her necklace with the jewels of heaven that once Anu had made to please her. 'O you gods here present, by the lapis lazuli round my neck I shall remember these days as I remember the jewels of my throat; these last days I shall not forget. Let all the gods gather round the sacrifice, except Enlil. He shall not approach this offering, for without reflection he brought the flood; he consigned my people to destruction.'

"When Enlil had come, when he saw the boat, he was wrath and swelled with anger at the gods, the host of heaven, 'Has any of these mortals escaped? Not one was to have survived the destruction.' Then the god of the wells and canals Ninurta opened his mouth and said to the warrior Enlil, 'Who is there of the gods that can devise without Ea? It is Ea alone who knows all things.' Then Ea opened his mouth and spoke to warrior Enlil, 'Wisest of gods, hero Enlil, how could you so senselessly bring down the flood?

> Lay upon the sinner his sin,
> Lay upon the transgressor his transgression,
> Punish him a little when he breaks loose,
> Do not drive him too hard or he perishes;
> Would that a lion had ravaged mankind
> Rather than the flood,
> Would that a wolf had ravaged mankind
> Rather than the flood,
> Would that famine had wasted the world
> Rather than the flood,
> Would that pestilence had wasted mankind
> Rather than the flood.

It was not I that revealed the secret of the gods; the wise man learned it in a dream. Now take your counsel what shall be done with him.

"Then Enlil went up into the boat, he took me by the hand and my wife and made us enter the boat and kneel down on either side, he standing between us. He touched our foreheads to bless us saying, 'In time past Utnapishtim was a mortal man; henceforth he and his wife shall live in the distance at the mouth of the rivers.' Thus it was that the gods took me and placed me here to live in the distance, at the mouth of the rivers."

2   A Pessimistic View of Life

Uncertainty and danger filled life in Mesopotamia. Sometimes, the unpredictable waters of the rivers broke through dikes, flooding fields, ruining crops, and damaging cities. At other times, an insufficient overflow deprived the land of water, causing crops to fail. Great windstorms left the countryside covered with a layer of sand, and heavy thunderstorms turned fields into a sea of mud that made travel impossible. Unlike Egypt, which was protected by vast deserts, Mesopotamia had no natural barriers to invasion. Feeling themselves surrounded by unfathomable and often hostile forces, Mesopotamians lived in an atmosphere of anxiety, which permeated their civilization.

Contributing to this sense of insecurity was the belief that the gods behaved capriciously, malevolently, and vindictively. What do the gods demand of me? Is it ever possible to please them? To these questions Mesopotamians had no reassuring answers, for the gods' behavior was a mystery to mere human beings.

MESOPOTAMIAN WISDOM LITERATURE

The following selection reveals the pessimism that pervaded Mesopotamian life. The sufferer tries to do everything that he believes the gods want of him but cannot escape misfortune.

I survived to the next year; the appointed time passed.
I turn around, but it is bad, very bad;
My ill luck increases and I cannot find what is right.
I called to my god, but he did not show his face,
I prayed to my goddess, but she did not raise her head.
Even the diviner with his divination could not make a prediction,
And the interpreter of dreams with his libation could not elucidate my case.
I sought the favor of the . . . spirit, but he would not enlighten me;
The exorcist with his ritual could not appease the divine wrath against me.
What strange conditions everywhere!
When I look behind (me), there is persecution, trouble.
Like one who has not made libations to his god,
Nor invoked his goddess when he ate,
Does not make prostrations nor recognize (the necessity of) bowing down,
In whose mouth supplication and prayer are lacking,
Who has even neglected holy days, and ignored festivals,
Who was negligent and did not observe the gods' rites,
Did not teach his people reverence and worship,
But has eaten his food without invoking his god,
And abandoned his goddess by not bringing a flour offering,
Like one who has gone crazy and forgotten his lord,
Has frivolously sworn a solemn oath by his god, (like such a one) do I appear.
For myself, I gave attention to supplication and prayer:
My prayer was discretion, sacrifice my rule.
The day for worshipping the god was a joy to my heart;
The day of the goddess's procession was profit and gain to me.
The king's blessing—that was my joy,
And the accompanying music became a delight for me.
I had my land keep the god's rites,
And brought my people to value the goddess's name.
I made the praise for the king like a god's,
And taught the people respect for the palace.
I wish I knew that these things would be pleasing to one's god!
What is good for oneself may be offense to one's god,
What in one's own heart seems despicable may be proper to one's god.
Who can know the will of the gods in heaven?
Who can understand the plans of the underworld gods?
Where have humans learned the way of a god?

He who was alive yesterday is dead today.
One moment he is worried, the next he is boisterous.
One moment he is singing a joyful song,
A moment later he wails like a professional mourner.
Their condition changes (as quickly as) opening and shutting (the *eyes*).
When starving they become like corpses,
When full they oppose their god.
In good times they speak of scaling heaven,
When they are troubled they talk of going down to hell.
I am *perplexed* at these things; I have not been able to understand their significance.
As for me, exhausted, a windstorm is driving me on!
Debilitating Disease is let loose upon me:
An Evil Wind has blown (from the) horizon,
Headache has sprung up from the surface of the underworld. . . .
(They all joined in) and came on me together.
(They *struck*) my head, they enveloped my skull;
(My) face is gloomy, my eyes flow.
They have wrenched my neck muscles and made (my) neck limp.
They struck (my chest,) beat my breast.
They affected my flesh and made me shake,
(In) my epigastrium [abdomen] they kindled a fire.
They churned up my bowels, . . . (they) . . . my . . .
Causing the discharge of phlegm, they tired out my (lungs).
They tired out my limbs and made my *fat* quake.
My upright stance they knocked down like a wall,
My robust figure they laid down like a rush [a grasslike plant]. . . .

My eyes stare straight ahead, but cannot see,
My ears are open, but cannot hear.
Feebleness has overcome my whole body,
An attack of illness has fallen upon my flesh.
Stiffness has taken over my arms,
Weakness has come upon my knees,
My feet forget their motion.
(A stroke) has got me; I choke like someone prostrate.
Death has (*approached*) and has covered my face.
If someone is concerned about me, I am not even able to answer the one who inquires.
(My . . .) weep, but I cannot control myself.
A snare is laid on my mouth,
And a bolt keeps my lips barred. . . .

My malady is indeed protracted.
Through not eating, my looks have become strange,
My flesh is flaccid, and my blood has ebbed away.
My bones look separated, and are covered (only) with my
    skin.
My flesh is inflamed, and the . . . -disease has afflicted me.
I have taken to a bed of *bondage;* going out is a pain;
My house has become my prison. . . .

I spent the night in my dung like an ox,
And wallowed in my excrement like a sheep.
My symptoms are beyond the exorcist,
And my omens have confused the diviner.
The exorcist could not diagnose the nature of my sickness,
Nor could the diviner set a time limit on my illness.
My god has not come to the rescue nor taken me by the hand;
My goddess has not shown pity on me nor gone by my side.

3 Mesopotamian Concepts of Justice

A significant source of information about the life of the ancient peoples of Mesopotamia is a code of laws issued about 1750 B.C. by the Babylonian king Hammurabi (1792–1750 B.C.). Discovered by archaeologists in 1901, the code was inscribed on a stone that shows the king accepting the laws from the sun god, Shamash, who was also the Babylonian god of justice.

These laws offer striking insights into the moral values, class structure, gender relationships, and roles of kingship and religion in Babylonian society. The 282 laws cover a range of public and private matters: marriage and family relations, negligence, fraud, commercial contracts, duties of public officials, property and inheritance, crimes and punishments, and techniques of legal procedure. The prologue to the code reveals the Mesopotamian concept of the priest-king—a ruler chosen by a god to administer his will on earth. In it, Hammurabi asserted that he had a divine duty to uphold justice in the land, to punish the wicked, and to further the welfare of the people.

CODE OF HAMMURABI

Two distinct approaches to choice of punishment for crime are found in Hammurabi's code with its numerous laws. In some instances, the guilty party is required to pay a monetary compensation to the victim, a tradition traceable to the earliest known Sumerian laws. Another approach, also found in the later Hebrew codes of law, is the principle of exact retaliation: "an eye for an eye, a tooth for a tooth."

Another feature of Hammurabi's code is that the penalties vary according to the social status of the victim. Three classes are represented: free men and women (called *patricians* in the reading here); commoners (or *plebeians*), not wholly free, but dependents of the state or perhaps serfs on landed estates; and slaves. The patricians are protected by the law of retaliation. People of the lower classes receive only monetary compensation if they are victims of a crime.

196. If a man has knocked out the eye of a patrician, his eye shall be knocked out.

197. If he has broken the limb of a patrician, his limb shall be broken.

198. If he has knocked out the eye of a plebeian or has broken the limb of a plebeian, he shall pay one mina[1] of silver.

199. If he has knocked out the eye of a patrician's servant, or broken the limb of a patrician's servant, he shall pay half his value.

200. If a patrician has knocked out the tooth of a man that is his equal, his tooth shall be knocked out.

201. If he has knocked out the tooth of a plebeian, he shall pay one-third of a mina of silver. . . .

209. If a man has struck a free woman with child, and has caused her to miscarry, he shall pay ten shekels[2] for her miscarriage.

210. If that woman die, his daughter shall be killed.

211. If it be the daughter of a plebeian, that has miscarried through his blows, he shall pay five shekels of silver.

212. If that woman die, he shall pay half a mina of silver.

213. If he has struck a man's maid and caused her to miscarry, he shall pay two shekels of silver.

214. If that woman die, he shall pay one-third of a mina of silver.

Many laws relating to business transactions show the importance of trade in Mesopotamian society and the willingness of the government to intervene in order to regulate the practices of the marketplace.

---

218. If a surgeon has operated with the bronze lancet on a patrician for a serious injury, and has caused his death, or has removed a cataract for a patrician, with the bronze lancet, and has made him lose his eye, his hands shall be cut off.

219. If the surgeon has treated a serious injury of a plebeian's slave, with the bronze lancet, and has caused his death, he shall render slave for slave.

220. If he has removed a cataract with the bronze lancet, and made the slave lose his eye, he shall pay half his value.

221. If a surgeon has cured the limb of a patrician, or has doctored a diseased bowel, the patient shall pay five shekels of silver to the surgeon.

222. If he be a plebeian, he shall pay three shekels of silver.

223. If he be a man's slave, the owner of the slave shall give two shekels of silver to the doctor. . . .

228. If a builder has built a house for a man, and finished it, he shall pay him a fee of two shekels of silver, for each SAR[3] built on.

229. If a builder has built a house for a man, and has not made his work sound, and the house he built has fallen, and caused the death of its owner, that builder shall be put to death.

230. If it is the owner's son that is killed, the builder's son shall be put to death.

231. If it is the slave of the owner that is killed, the builder shall give slave for slave to the owner of the house.

232. If he has caused the loss of goods, he shall render back whatever he has destroyed. Moreover, because he did not make sound the house he built, and it fell, at his own cost he shall rebuild the house that fell. . . .

271. If a man has hired oxen, a wagon, and its driver, he shall pay one hundred and sixty KA[4] of corn daily. . . .

275. If a man has hired a boat, its hire is three ŠE[5] of silver daily.

The outcome of some procedures depended upon the will of the gods: for example, an accused woman could place her fate in the hands of a god by plunging into a river, canal, or reservoir; if she did not drown, she was declared innocent. In other cases, legal culpability could be removed by invoking a god to bear witness to the truth of one's testimony. The law was particularly harsh on perjurers and those who made grave charges that they could not prove in court.

---

1. If a man has accused another of laying a nêrtu (death spell?) upon him, but has not proved it, he shall be put to death.

2. If a man has accused another of laying a kišpu (spell) upon him, but has not proved it, the accused shall go to the sacred river, he shall plunge into the sacred river, and if the sacred river shall conquer him, he that accused him shall take possession of his house. If the sacred river shall show

---

[1]The mina was a weight of silver used to express monetary value. (Throughout the text, the editors' notes carry numbers, whereas notes from the original sources are indicated by asterisks, daggers, et cetera. An exception is made for editorial notes pertaining to Scriptures, which have symbols rather than numbers.)

[2]The shekel, also a weight of monetary value, was worth far less than the mina.

[3]SAR was a measure of land.

[4]KA stood for a bulk measure.

[5]ŠE was another monetary weight of silver.

his innocence and he is saved, his accuser shall be put to death. He that plunged into the sacred river shall appropriate the house of him that accused him.

3. If a man has borne false witness in a trial, or has not established the statement that he has made, if that case be a capital trial, that man shall be put to death.

4. If he has borne false witness in a civil law case, he shall pay the damages in that suit. . . .

9. If a man has lost property and some of it be detected in the possession of another, and the holder has said, "A man sold it to me, I bought it in the presence of witnesses"; and if the claimant has said, "I can bring witnesses who know it to be property lost by me"; then the alleged buyer on his part shall produce the man who sold it to him and the witnesses before whom he bought it; the claimant shall on his part produce the witnesses who know it to be his lost property. The judge shall examine their pleas. The witnesses to the sale and the witnesses who identify the lost property shall state on oath what they know. Such a seller is the thief and shall be put to death. The owner of the lost property shall recover his lost property. The buyer shall recoup himself from the seller's estate.

The laws concerned with family relationships placed great power in the hands of husbands and fathers, yet the code tried to protect women and children from neglect and mistreatment. Divorce initiated by either husband or wife was permitted under specific circumstances.

---

141. If a man's wife, living in her husband's house, has persisted in going out, has acted the fool, has wasted her house, has belittled her husband, he shall prosecute her. If her husband has said, "I divorce her," she shall go her way; he shall give her nothing as her price of divorce. If her husband has said, "I will not divorce her," he may take another woman to wife; the wife shall live as a slave in her husband's house.

142. If a woman has hated her husband and has said, "You shall not possess me," her past shall be inquired into, as to what she lacks. If she has been discreet, and has no vice, and her husband has gone out, and has greatly belittled her, that woman has no blame, she shall take her marriage-portion and go off to her father's house.

143. If she has not been discreet, has gone out, ruined her house, belittled her husband, she shall be drowned. . . .

148. If a man has married a wife and a disease has seized her, if he is determined to marry a second wife, he shall marry her. He shall not divorce the wife whom the disease has seized. In the home they made together she shall dwell, and he shall maintain her as long as she lives. . . .

168. If a man has determined to disinherit his son and has declared before the judge, "I cut off my son," the judge shall inquire into the son's past, and, if the son has not committed a grave misdemeanor such as should cut him off from sonship, the father shall (not) disinherit his son.

169. If he has committed a grave crime against his father, which cuts him off from sonship, for the first offence he shall pardon him. If he has committed a grave crime a second time, the father shall cut off his son from sonship. . . .

195. If a son has struck his father, his hands shall be cut off.

One of the most unusual features of the law dealt with the failure of the government officials of a city or a district to prevent banditry. The code held the governor responsible for the breach of the peace and required him to compensate the bandit's victim. Government officials found guilty of extortion, bribery, or use of public employees for private purposes were severely punished.

---

23. If the highwayman has not been caught, the man that has been robbed shall state on oath what he has lost and the city or district governor in whose territory or district the robbery took place shall restore to him what he has lost.

24. If a life (has been lost), the city or district governor shall pay one mina of silver to the deceased's relatives. . . .

34. If either a governor, or a prefect, has appropriated the property of a levymaster,[6] has hired him out, has robbed him by high-handedness at a trial, has taken the salary which the king gave to him, that governor, or prefect, shall be put to death. . . .

---

[6]A levymaster was a military official.

4 Religious Inspiration of Akhenaten

Pharaoh Amenhotep IV (1369–1353 B.C.) was a religious mystic who conceived of divinity in a manner approaching monotheism. He suppressed the worship of the many gods of Egypt and insisted that only Aton—the sun god—and himself, the king and son of Aton, be worshiped by the Egyptians. Aton was viewed as the creator of the world, a god of love, peace, and justice. To promote the exclusive worship of Aton, Amenhotep changed his name to Akhenaten ("It is well with Aton"), and near modern Tell El-Amarna he built a new capital city, Akhetaten, which became the center of the new religious cult. The new religion perished quickly after Akhenaten's death. There is no evidence that this step toward a monotheistic conception of the divine had any later influence on the Hebrews.

The masses of Egypt were not influenced by Akhenaten's religious inspiration, and he was resisted by the priests, who clung to traditional beliefs. His immediate successors abandoned the new capital and had the monuments to Aton destroyed.

Hymn To Aton

Akhenaten's religious outlook inspired remarkable works of art and literature. In the following hymn, Akhenaten glorifies Aton in words that are reminiscent of Psalm 104.

Thou appearest beautifully on the horizon of heaven,
Thou living Aton, the beginning of life!
When thou art risen on the eastern horizon,
Thou hast filled every land with thy beauty.
Thou art gracious, great, glistening, and high over every
    land;
Thy rays encompass the lands to the limit of all that thou
    hast made. . . .
At daybreak, when thou arisest on the horizon,
When thou shinest as the Aton by day,
Thou drivest away the darkness and givest thy rays.
The Two Lands[1] are in festivity *every day,*
Awake and standing upon (their) feet,
For thou hast raised them up.
Washing their bodies, taking (their) clothing,
Their arms are (raised) in praise at thy appearance.
All the world, they do their work.

All beasts are content with their pasturage;
Trees and plants are flourishing.
The birds which fly from their nests,

Their wings are (stretched out) in praise to thy *ka.*[2]
All beasts spring upon (their) feet.
Whatever flies and alights,
They live when thou hast risen (for) them.
The ships are sailing north and south as well,
For every way is open at thy appearance.
The fish in the river dart before thy face;
Thy rays are in the midst of the great green sea.

Creator of seed in women,
Thou who makest fluid into man,
Who maintainest the son in the womb of his mother,
Who soothest him with that which stills his weeping,
Thou nurse (even) in the womb,
Who givest breath to sustain all that he had made!
When he descends from the womb to *breathe*
On the day when he is born,
Thou openest his mouth completely,
Thou suppliest his necessities.
When the chick in the egg speaks within the shell,
Thou givest him breath within it to maintain him.

---

[1]The Two Lands were the two political divisions of Egypt, Upper and Lower Egypt. They were usually governed by the same king.

[2]The *ka* was a protective and guiding spirit, which each person was thought to have.

When thou hast made him his fulfillment within the egg, to
    break it,
He comes forth from the egg to speak at his completed
    (time);
He walks upon his legs when he comes forth from it.

How manifold it is, what thou hast made!
They are hidden from the face (of man).
O sole god, like whom there is no other!
Thou didst create the world according to thy desire,
Whilst thou wert alone:
All men, cattle, and wild beasts,
Whatever is on earth, going upon (its) feet,
And what is on high, flying with its wings.

The countries of Syria and Nubia,[3] the *land* of Egypt,
Thou settest every man in his place,

---

[3]Syria was an ancient country, larger than modern Syria, north of modern Israel and Jordan; Nubia was a kingdom located south of the first cataract of the Nile. It is now in Sudan.

Thou suppliest their necessities:
Everyone has his food, and his time of life is reckoned.
Their tongues are separate in speech,
And their natures as well;
Their skins are distinguished,
As thou distinguishest the foreign peoples.
Thou makest a Nile in the underworld,[4]
Thou bringest it forth as thou desirest
To maintain the people (of Egypt)
According as thou madest them for thyself,
The lord of all of them, wearying (himself) with them,
The lord of every land, rising for them,
The Aton of the day, great of majesty.

---

[4]The Egyptians believed that the source of their Nile was in a huge body of water, which they called Nun, under the earth.

5 Love, Passion, and Misogyny in Ancient Egypt

As in most ancient societies, Egyptian women were concerned principally with marriage, children, and household. But in comparison to other societies, Egyptian women suffered fewer disabilities. They had legal rights, could enter the priesthood, a truly prestigious position, and like men, were thought to have access to the other world after death.

Both men and women came under love's power, and the Egyptians wrote numerous poems that expressed both the joy and pain of love.

LOVE POETRY

In the first selection, a young man admires his loved one's beauty. In this instance, the word "sister"[1] is probably not to be taken literally; it is intended as an expression of endearment.

The *One,* the sister without peer,
The handsomest of all!
She looks like the rising morning star
At the start of a happy year.
Shining bright, fair of skin,
Lovely the look of her eyes,
Sweet the speech of her lips,
She has not a word too much.

Upright neck, shining breast,
Hair true lapis lazuli;
Arms surpassing gold,
Fingers like lotus buds.
Heavy thighs, narrow waist,
Her legs parade her beauty;
With graceful step she treads the ground,
Captures my heart by her movements.

---

[1]Since Egyptians were interested in maintaining pure bloodlines, incestuous relationships, including brother and sister, were not uncommon. Therefore, the word "sister," when used by a lover, may be taken figuratively or literally, depending on the circumstances.

She causes all men's necks
To turn about to see her;
Joy has he whom she embraces,
He is like the first of men!

Without his love the young man suffers.

Seven days since I saw my sister,
And sickness invaded me;
I am heavy in all my limbs,
My body has forsaken me.
When the physicians come to me,
My heart rejects their remedies;
The magicians are quite helpless,
My sickness is not discerned.
To tell me "She is here" would revive me!
Her name would make me rise;
Her messenger's coming and going,
That would revive my heart!
My sister is better than all prescriptions,
She does more for me than all medicines;
Her coming to me is my amulet,
The sight of her makes me well!
When she opens her eyes my body is young,
Her speaking makes me strong;

Embracing her expels my malady—
Seven days since she went from me!

Egyptian women also experience love and vent their feelings.

My heart *flutters* hastily,
When I think of my love of you;
It lets me not act sensibly,
It leaps (from) its place.
It lets me not put on a dress,
Nor wrap my scarf around me;
I put no paint upon my eyes,
I'm even not anointed.

"Don't wait, go there," says it to me,
As often as I think of him;
My heart, don't act so stupidly,
Why do you play the fool?
Sit still, the brother comes to you,
And many eyes as well!
Let not the people say of me:
"A woman fallen through love!"
Be steady when you think of him,
My heart, do not *flutter!*

THE INSTRUCTION OF ANKHSHESHONQ

Some Egyptian men held unflattering views of women. In his advice to his son, the priest Ankhsheshonq, who lived sometime between 300 B.C. and 50 B.C., expresses such misogynist views.

Do not take to yourself a woman whose husband is alive, lest he become your enemy. . . .
Let your wife see your wealth; do not trust her with it. . . .
Do not open your heart to your wife or to your servant.
Open it to your mother; she is a woman of discretion. . . .
Instructing a woman is like having a sack of sand whose side is split open.
Her savings are stolen goods.
What she does with her husband today she does with another man tomorrow. . . .
Do not rejoice in your wife's beauty; her heart is set on her lover. . . .
A woman lets herself be loved according to the character of her husband. . . .
He who violates a married woman on the bed will have his wife violated on the ground. . . .

He who makes love to a woman of the street will have his purse cut open on its side. . . .
He who makes love to a married woman is killed on her doorstep. . . .
Do not marry an impious woman, lest she give your children an impious upbringing.
If a woman is at peace with her husband they will never fare badly.
If a woman whispers about her husband [they will never] fare well.
If a woman does not desire the property of her husband she has another man [in her] heart. . . .
If a wife is of nobler birth than her husband he should give way to her.

The Hebrews

Two ancient peoples, the Hebrews (Jews) and the Greeks, are the principal founders of Western civilization. From the Hebrews derives the concept of *ethical monotheism*—the belief in one God who demands righteous behavior from his human creations—which is an essential element of the Western tradition.

The Hebrews originated in Mesopotamia and migrated to Canaan (Palestine). Some Hebrews who journeyed to Egypt to become farmers and herdsmen were forced to labor for the Egyptian state. In the thirteenth century B.C., Moses, who believed that he was doing God's bidding, led the Hebrews from Egypt—the biblical Exodus. While wandering in the Sinai Desert, the Hebrews were uplifted and united by a belief in Yahweh, the One God. In the eleventh century B.C., some two hundred years after they had begun the conquest of Canaan, the Hebrews were unified under the leadership of Saul, their first king. Under Solomon (d. 922 B.C.) the kingdom of Israel reached the height of its power and splendor.

The Hebrews borrowed elements from the older civilizations of the Near East. Thus there are parallels between Babylonian literature and biblical accounts of the Creation, the Flood, and the Tower of Babel. Nevertheless, Israelite religion marks a profound break with the outlook of the surrounding civilizations of the Near East.

There are two fundamental characteristics of ancient Near Eastern religion. First, the Near Eastern mind saw gods everywhere in nature: the moon and stars, rivers and mountains, thunder and wind storms were either gods or the dwelling places of gods. The Near Eastern mind invented myths—stories about the gods' birth, deeds, death, and resurrection. Second, Near Eastern gods were not fully sovereign. They were not eternal but were born or created; their very existence and power depended on some prior realm. They grew old, became ill, required food, and even died—all limitations on their power. The gods were subject to magic and destiny—forces that preceded them in time and surpassed them in power—and if the gods did wrong, destiny, or fate, punished them.

Hebrew religious thought evolved through the history and experience of the Jewish people. Over the centuries the Hebrew view of God came to differ markedly from Near Eastern ideas about the gods and the world. For the Hebrews, God was not only one, he was also *transcendent*—above nature. This means that natural objects were not divine, holy, or alive, but were merely God's creations. In contrast to the Near Eastern gods, Yahweh was fully sovereign, absolutely free; there were no limitations whatsoever on his power. He was eternal and the source of all in the universe; he did not answer to fate but he himself determined the consequences of wrongdoing; he was not subject to any primordial power or to anything outside or above him.

The Hebrew conception of God led to a revolutionary view of the human being. The Hebrews believed that God had given the individual moral autonomy—the capacity to choose between good and evil. Therefore, men and women had to measure their actions by God's laws and were responsible for their own behavior. Such an outlook led people to become aware of themselves—their moral potential and personal worth. From the Hebrews came a fundamental value of the Western tradition—the inviolable worth and dignity of the individual.

1 Hebrew Cosmogony and Anthropology

The Hebrew Scriptures, which form the Old Testament of the Christian Bible, are a collection of thirty-nine books written over several centuries by several authors. It is a record of more than a thousand years of ancient Jewish history and religious development. Among the topics treated in Genesis, the first book of the Bible, are God's creation of the universe and human beings, the original human condition in the Garden of Eden, and the origin of evil with Adam and Eve's disobedience of God and their resultant expulsion from Eden.

Genesis

The first two chapters from the book of Genesis follow. The first chapter presents the *cosmogony* and *anthropology* of the Jews. Hebrew cosmogony—that is, their view of the generation of the universe and all that is in it—exemplifies God's majesty and power. Although Genesis is similar to other Near Eastern creation myths, it also sharply breaks with the essential outlook of the time. In Genesis, nature is no longer inhabited by mythical gods, and inanimate objects are not suffused with life. The Hebrews did not worship the moon and stars and mountains and rivers, but they regarded nature as the orderly creation of one supreme and eternal being.

How the Hebrews conceived of the creation of men and women and their position in the universe—the anthropology of the Jews—is dealt with in verses 26–31. The Hebrews' conception of the individual created in God's image and subordinate to nothing except God is as revolutionary as their idea of God, for this conception confers great power and dignity upon human beings.

1 [1]In the beginning God created the heaven and the earth. [2]Now the earth was unformed and void, and darkness was upon the face of the deep; and the spirit of God hovered over the face of the waters. [3]And God said: "Let there be light," And there was light. [4]And God saw the light, that it was good; and God divided the light from the darkness. [5]And God called the light Day, and the darkness He called Night. And there was evening and there was morning, one day.

[6]And God said: "Let there be a firmament in the midst of the waters, and let it divide the waters from the waters." [7]And God made the firmament, and divided the waters which were under the firmament from the waters which were above the firmament; and it was so. [8]And God called the firmament Heaven. And there was evening and there was morning, a second day.

[9]And God said: "Let the waters under the heaven be gathered together unto one place, and let the dry land appear." And it was so. [10]And God called the dry land Earth, and the gathering together of the waters called He Seas; and God saw that it was good. [11]And God said: "Let the earth put forth grass, herb yielding seed, and fruit tree bearing fruit after its kind, wherein is the seed thereof, upon the earth." And it was so. [12]And the earth brought forth grass, herb yielding seed after its kind, and tree bearing fruit, wherein is the seed thereof, after its kind; and God saw that it was good. [13]And there was, evening and there was morning, a third day.

[14]And God said: "Let there be lights in the firmament of the heaven to divide the day from the night; and let them be for signs, and for seasons, and for days and years; [15]and let them be for lights in the firmament of the heaven to give light upon the earth." And it was so. [16]And God made the two great lights; the greater light to rule the day, and the lesser light to rule the night; and the stars. [17]And God set them in the firmament of the heaven to give light upon the earth, [18]and to rule over the day and over the night, and to divide the light from the darkness; and God saw that it was good. [19]And there was evening and there was morning, a fourth day.

[20]And God said: "Let the waters swarm with swarms of living creatures, and let fowl fly above the earth in the open firmament of heaven." [21]And God created the great sea-monsters, and every living creature that creepeth, wherewith

the waters swarmed, after its kind, and every winged fowl after its kind; and God saw that it was good. [22]And God blessed them, saying: "Be fruitful, and multiply, and fill the waters in the seas, and let fowl multiply in the earth." [23]And there was evening and there was morning, a fifth day.

[24]And God said: "Let the earth bring forth the living creature after its kind, cattle, and creeping thing, and beast of the earth after its kind." And it was so. [25]And God made the beast of the earth after its kind, and the cattle after their kind, and every thing that creepeth upon the ground after its kind; and God saw that it was good. [26]And God said: "Let us make man in our image, after our likeness; and let them have dominion over the fish of the sea, and over the fowl of the air, and over the cattle, and over all the earth, and over every creeping thing that creepeth upon the earth." [27]And God created man in His own image, in the image of God created He him; male and female created He them. [28]And God blessed them; and God said unto them: "Be fruitful, and multiply, and replenish the earth, and subdue it; and have dominion over the fish of the sea, and over the fowl of the air, and over every living thing that creepeth upon the earth." [29]And God said: "Behold, I have given you every herb yielding seed, which is upon the face of all the earth, and every tree, in which is the fruit of a tree yielding seed—to you it shall be for food; [30]and to every beast of the earth and to every fowl of the air, and to every thing that creepeth upon the earth, wherein there is a living soul, [I have given] every green herb for food." And it was so. [31]And God saw every thing that He had made, and, behold, it was very good. And there was evening and there was morning, the sixth day.

The second chapter of Genesis contains a retrospective view of the creation of the universe; a second account of man's creation from "the dust of the ground"; a description of the Garden of Eden, into which man was placed, with the injunction that he may eat freely of every tree in the garden, except the tree of the knowledge of good and evil; and an account of God's creation of woman from the rib of man as a companion for him. In Genesis, Eden was an idyllic garden, a paradise, in which the first human beings lived. It has been compared with the mythic land of the blessed, Dilmun, described in the Babylonian epic *Gilgamesh*. In Eden, human beings were free of death, illness, pain, and a consciousness of evil, or sin.

2 [1]And the heaven and the earth were finished, and all the host of them. [2]And on the seventh day God finished His work which He had made; and He rested on the seventh day from all His work which He had made. [3]And God blessed the seventh day, and hallowed it; because that in it He rested from all His work which God in creating had made.

[4]These are the generations of the heaven and of the earth when they were created, in the day that the LORD God made earth and heaven.

[5]No shrub of the field was yet in the earth, and no herb of the field had yet sprung up; for the LORD God had not caused it to rain upon the earth, and there was not a man to till the ground; [6]but there went up a mist from the earth, and watered the whole face of the ground. [7]Then the LORD God formed man of the dust of the ground, and breathed into his nostrils the breath of life; and man became a living soul. [8]And the LORD God planted a garden eastward, in Eden; and there He put the man whom He had formed. [9]And out of the ground made the LORD God to grow every tree that is pleasant to the sight, and good for food; the tree of life also in the midst of the garden, and the tree of the knowledge of good and evil. [10]And a river went out of Eden to water the garden; and from thence it was parted, and became four heads. [11]The name of the first is Pishon; that is it which compasseth the whole land of Havilah, where there is gold; [12]and the gold of that land is good; there is bdellium and the onyx stone. [13]And the name of the second river is Gihon; the same is it that compasseth the whole land of Cuski. [14]And the name of the third river is Tigris; that is it which goeth toward the east of Asshur. And the fourth river is the Euphrates. [15]And the LORD God took the man, and put him into the garden of Eden to dress it and to keep it. [16]And the LORD God commanded the man, saying "Of every tree of the garden thou mayest freely eat; [17]but of the tree of the knowledge of good and evil, thou shalt not eat of it; for in the day that thou eatest thereof thou shalt surely die."

[18]And the LORD God said: "It is not good that the man should be alone; I will make him a help meet for him." [19]And out of the ground the LORD God formed every beast of the field, and every fowl of the air; and brought them unto the man to see what he would call them; and whatsoever the man would call every living creature, that was to be the name thereof. [20]And the man gave names to all cattle, and to the fowl of the air, and to every beast of the field; but for Adam there was not found a help meet for him. [21]And the LORD God caused a deep sleep to fall upon the man, and he slept; and He took one of his ribs, and closed up the place with flesh instead thereof. [22]And the rib, which the LORD God had taken from the man, made He a woman, and brought her unto the man. [23]And the man said: "This is now bone of my bones, and flesh of my flesh; she shall be called Woman, because she was taken out of Man." [24]Therefore shall a man leave his father and his mother, and shall cleave unto his wife, and they shall be one flesh. [25]And they were both naked, the man and his wife, and were not ashamed.

2 The Covenant and the Ten Commandments

Central to Hebrew religious thought was the covenant that the Hebrews believed had been made between God and themselves at Mount Sinai. The Hebrews believed that God had chosen them to be the first recipients of his law. They did not hold that this honor was bestowed on them because they were better than other nations or that they had done something special to earn it. Rather they viewed the covenant as an awesome responsibility; God had chosen them to set an example of righteous behavior to the other nations.

Exodus
THE COVENANT

As described in the nineteenth chapter of Exodus, the Israelite leader Moses received the covenant on Mount Sinai at the time of the Hebrews' flight from Egypt and wanderings in the wilderness of the Sinai Desert.

19 ³And Moses went up unto God, and the LORD called unto him out of the mountain, saying: "Thus shalt thou say to the house of Jacob, and tell the children of Israel: ⁴Ye have seen what I did unto the Egyptians, and how I bore you on eagles' wings, and brought you unto Myself. ⁵Now therefore, if ye will hearken unto My voice indeed, and keep My covenant, then ye shall be Mine own treasure from among all peoples; for all the earth is Mine; ⁶and ye shall be unto Me a kingdom of priests, and a holy nation. These are the words which thou shalt speak unto the children of Israel." ⁷And Moses came and called for the elders of the people, and set before them all these words which the LORD commanded him. ⁸And all the people answered together, and said: "All that the LORD hath spoken we will do." And Moses reported the words of the people unto the LORD. ⁹And the LORD said unto Moses. "Lo, I come unto thee in a thick cloud, that people may hear when I speak with thee, and may also believe thee for ever."

Exodus
THE TEN COMMANDMENTS

Together with the covenant, Moses received the Ten Commandments, which specified God's moral laws. Chapter 20 sets forth the Ten Commandments.

19 ¹⁷And Moses brought forth the people out of the camp to meet God; and they stood at the nether part of the mount. ¹⁸Now mount Sinai was altogether on smoke, because the LORD descended upon it in fire; and the smoke thereof ascended as the smoke of a furnace, and the whole mount quaked greatly. ¹⁹And when the voice of the horn waxed louder and louder, Moses spoke, and God answered him by a voice. ²⁰And the LORD came down upon mount Sinai, to the top of the mount; and the LORD called Moses to the top of the mount; and Moses went up.

20 ¹And God spoke all these words, saying: ²I am the LORD thy God, who brought thee out of the land of Egypt, out of the house of bondage. ³Thou shalt have no other gods before Me. ⁴Thou shalt not make unto thee a graven image, nor any manner of likeness, of any thing that is in heaven above, or that is in the earth beneath, or that is in the water under the earth; [5]thou shalt not bow down unto them, nor serve them; for I the LORD thy God am a jealous God, visiting the iniquity of the fathers upon the children unto the third and fourth generation of them that hate Me; [6]and showing mercy unto the thousandth generation of them that love Me and keep My commandments.

[7]Thou shalt not take the name of the LORD thy God in vain; for the LORD will not hold him guiltless that taketh His name in vain.

[8]Remember the sabbath day, to keep it holy. [9]Six days shalt thou labour, and do all thy work; [10]but the seventh day is a sabbath unto the LORD thy God, in it thou shalt not do any manner of work, thou, nor thy son, nor thy daughter, nor thy man-servant, nor thy maid-servant, nor thy cattle, nor thy stranger that is within thy gates; [11]for in six days the LORD made heaven and earth, the sea, and all that in them is, and rested on the seventh day; wherefore the LORD blessed the sabbath day, and hallowed it.

[12]Honour thy father and thy mother, that thy days may be long upon the land which the LORD thy God giveth thee.

[13]Thou shalt not murder.

Thou shalt not commit adultery.

Thou shalt not steal.

Thou shalt not bear false witness against thy neighbour.

[14]Thou shalt not covet thy neighbour's house; thou shalt not covet thy neighbour's wife, nor his man-servant, nor his maid-servant, nor his ox, nor his ass, nor anything that is thy neighbour's.

[15]And all the people perceived the thunderings, and the lightnings, and the voice of the horn, and the mountain smoking; and when the people saw it, they trembled, and stood afar off. [16]And they said unto Moses: "Speak thou with us, and we will hear; but let not God speak with us, lest we die." [17]And Moses said unto the people: "Fear not; for God is come to prove you, and that His fear may be before you, that ye sin not." [18]And the people stood afar off; but Moses drew near unto the thick darkness where God was.

3 Humaneness of Hebrew Law

The new awareness of the individual that was produced by the Hebrew concept of God found expression in Hebrew law, which was recorded in the Torah, the first five books of the Scriptures. For the Hebrews, the source of law was, of course, God, and because God is good, his law must be concerned with human welfare. Israelite law incorporated the legal codes and oral traditions of the older civilizations of the Near East. In contrast to the other law codes of the Near East, however, Hebrew laws were more concerned with people than with property; they expressed a humane attitude toward slaves and rejected the idea (so clearly demonstrated in the Code of Hammurabi) of one law for nobles and another for commoners.

Leviticus
NEIGHBOR AND COMMUNITY

To the Hebrews, laws governing economic, social, and political relationships gave practical expression to God's universal standards of morality. Leviticus, the third book in the Scriptures, contains laws governing actions dealing with neighbors and the community.

19 [9]And when ye reap the harvest of your land, thou shalt not wholly reap the corner of thy field, neither shalt thou gather the gleaning of thy harvest. [10]And thou shalt not glean thy vineyard, neither shalt thou gather the fallen fruit of thy vineyard; thou shalt leave them for the poor and for the stranger: I am the LORD your God. [11]Ye shall not steal; neither shall ye deal falsely, nor lie one to another. [12]And ye shall not swear by My name falsely, so that thou profane the name of thy God: I am the LORD. [13]Thou shalt not oppress thy neighbour, nor rob him; the wages of a hired servant shall not abide with thee all night until the morning. [14]Thou shalt not curse the deaf, nor put a stumbling-block before the blind, but thou shalt fear thy God: I am the LORD. [15]Ye shall do no unrighteousness in judgment; thou shalt not respect the person of the poor, nor favour the person of the mighty; but in righteousness shalt thou judge thy neighbour. [16]Thou shalt not go up and down as a tale-bearer among thy people; neither shalt thou stand idly by the blood of thy neighbour: I am the LORD. [17]Thou shalt not hate thy brother in thy heart; thou shalt surely rebuke thy neighbour, and not bear sin because of him. . . . [33]And if a stranger sojourn with thee in your land, ye shall not do him wrong. [34]The stranger that sojourneth with you shall be unto you as the home-born among you, and thou shalt love him as thyself. . . .

Deuteronomy
JUDGES, WITNESSES, AND JUSTICE

The book of Deuteronomy was composed in the seventh century B.C., some six centuries after the exodus from Egypt. Written as though it were a last speech of Moses advising the people how to govern themselves as they entered the land of Canaan, Deuteronomy reflects the new problems faced by the Hebrews who had already established a kingdom and lived in a settled urban society. In presenting their reform program, the authors of Deuteronomy linked their message to the authority of Moses. The central theme of these verses is the attainment of justice.

16 [18]Judges and officers shalt thou make thee in all thy gates, which the LORD thy God giveth thee, tribe by tribe; and they shall judge the people with righteous judgment. [19]Thou shalt not wrest judgment; thou shalt not respect persons; neither shalt thou take a gift; for a gift doth blind the eyes of the wise, and pervert the words of the righteous. [20]Justice, justice shalt thou follow, that thou mayest live, and inherit the land which the LORD thy God giveth thee.

---

19 [15]One witness shall not rise up against a man for any iniquity, or for any sin, in any sin that he sinneth; at the mouth of two witnesses, or at the mouth of three witnesses, shall a matter be established. [16]If an unrighteous witness rise up against any man to bear perverted witness against him; [17]then both the men, between whom the controversy is, shall stand before the LORD, before the priests and the judges that shall be in those days. [18]And the judges shall inquire diligently; and, behold, if the witness be a false witness, and hath testified falsely against his brother; [19]then shall ye do unto him, as he had purposed to do unto his brother; so shalt thou put away the evil from the midst of thee.

---

23 [16]Thou shalt not deliver unto his master a bondman that is escaped from his master unto thee; [17]he shall dwell with thee, in the midst of thee, in the place which he shall choose within one of thy gates, where it liketh him best; thou shalt not wrong him.

---

24 [14]Thou shalt not oppress a hired servant that is poor and needy, whether he be of thy brethren, or of thy strangers that are in thy land within thy gates. [15]In the same day thou shalt give him his hire, neither shall the sun go down upon it; for he is poor, and setteth his heart upon it lest he cry against thee unto the LORD and it be sin in thee.

[16]The fathers shall not be put to death for the children, neither shall the children be put to death for the fathers; every man shall be put to death for his own sin.

[17]Thou shalt not pervert the justice due to the stranger, or to the fatherless; nor take the widow's raiment to pledge. [18]But thou shalt remember that thou wast a bondman in Egypt, and the LORD thy God redeemed thee thence; therefore I command thee to do this thing.

[19]When thou reapest thy harvest in thy field, and hast forgot a sheaf in the field, thou shalt not go back to fetch it; it shall be for the stranger, for the fatherless, and for the widow; that the LORD thy God may bless thee in all the work of thy hands.

[20]When thou beatest thine olive-tree, thou shalt not go over the boughs again; it shall be for the stranger, for the fatherless, and for the widow. [21]When thou gatherest the grapes of thy vineyard, thou shalt not glean it after thee; it shall be for the stranger, for the fatherless, and for the widow. [22]And thou shalt remember that thou wast a bondman in the land of Egypt; therefore I command thee to do this thing.

4 Human Sinfulness

The Hebrews defined sin as a violation of God's laws and a breach of his covenant. This offense against God corrupts his created order, which was intended to be beneficial to human beings, and brings suffering into the world. Biblical writers regarded sin as a universal phenomenon, an ever-present menace to both individual and group life, deserving of God's punishment. Yet, even when God inflicts terrible pain on the Hebrews for violating his law, he still remains compassionate and merciful, an inducement to sinners to renew their commitment to God's teachings.

Genesis
THE ORIGINS OF SIN

The third chapter of Genesis deals with the origin of evil. When Adam and Eve disobeyed God by eating from the tree of knowledge, they were driven from the Garden of Eden. For the Hebrews the expulsion from paradise marks the beginning of human history, suffering, and death. This passage provides one of the fundamental explanations of evil in the Western tradition, the Judaic conception, later to be refashioned by the Apostle Paul into the Christian notion of original sin. The language of the biblical narrative is naive and framed in mythic imagery, but the ideas that it presents are timeless.

3 [1]Now the serpent was more subtle than any beast of the field which the LORD God had made. And he said unto the woman: "Yea, hath God said: Ye shall not eat of any tree of the garden?" [2]And the woman said unto the serpent: "Of the fruit of the trees of the garden we may eat; [3]but of the fruit of the tree which is in the midst of the garden, God hath said: Ye shall not eat of it, neither shall ye touch it, lest ye die." [4]And the serpent said unto the woman: "Ye shall not surely die; [5]for God doth know that in the day ye eat thereof, then your eyes shall be opened, and ye shall be as God, knowing good and evil." [6]And when the woman saw that the tree was good for food, and that it was a delight to the eyes, and that the tree was to be desired to make one wise, she took of the fruit thereof, and did eat; and she gave also unto her husband with her, and he did eat. [7]And the eyes of them both were opened, and they knew that they were naked; and they sewed fig-leaves together, and made themselves girdles. [8]And they heard the voice of the LORD God walking in the garden toward the cool of the day; and the man and his wife hid themselves from the presence of the LORD God amongst the trees of the garden. [9]And the LORD God called unto the man, and said unto him: "Where art thou?" [10]And he said: "I heard Thy voice in the garden, and I was afraid, because I was naked; and I hid myself." [11]And He said: "Who told thee that thou wast naked? Hast thou eaten of the tree, whereof I commanded thee that thou shouldest not eat?" [12]And the man said: "The woman whom Thou gavest to be with me, she gave me of the tree, and I did eat." [13]And the LORD God said unto the woman: "What is this thou hast done?" And the woman said: "The serpent beguiled me, and I did eat." [14]And the LORD God said unto the serpent: "Because thou hast done this, cursed art thou from among all cattle, and from among all beasts of the field; upon thy belly shalt thou go, and dust shalt thou eat all the days of thy life. [15]And I will put enmity between thee and the woman, and between thy seed and her seed; they shall bruise thy head, and thou shalt bruise their heel."

[16]Unto the woman He said: "I will greatly multiply thy pain and thy travail; in pain thou shalt bring forth children; and thy desire shall be to thy husband, and he shall rule over thee."

[17]And unto Adam He said: "Because thou hast hearkened unto the voice of thy wife, and hast eaten of the tree, of which I commanded thee, saying: "Thou shalt not eat of it; cursed is the ground for thy sake; in toil shalt thou eat of it all the days of thy life. [18]Thorns also and thistles shall it bring forth to thee; and thou shalt eat the herb of the field. [19]In the sweat of thy face shalt thou eat bread, till thou return unto the ground; for out of it wast thou taken; for dust thou art, and

unto dust shalt thou return." [20]And the man called his wife's name Eve; because she was the mother of all living. [21]And the LORD God made for Adam and for his wife garments of skins, and clothed them.

[22]And the LORD God said: "Behold, the man is become as one of us, to know good and evil; and now, lest he put forth his hand, and take also of the tree of life, and eat, and live for ever." [23]Therefore the LORD God sent him forth from the garden of Eden, to till the ground from whence he was taken. [24]So He drove out the man; and He placed at the east of the garden of Eden the cherubim, and the flaming sword which turned every way, to keep the way to the tree of life.

Job
THE PROBLEM OF UNDESERVED SUFFERING

Written sometime between the seventh and the fourth centuries B.C., the Book of Job is one of the best examples of Hebrew wisdom literature. It is concerned with profound questions. Why do the righteous often suffer and the wicked prosper? And why does God permit such injustice? The Book of Job does not provide conclusive answers to these questions, but it does impel us to ponder them and to think about our relationship to God.

In the prologue, the first two chapters of the book, God tells Satan[1] that there is none like his servant Job, "a whole-hearted and an upright man that feareth God and shunneth evil." Satan replies that Job is loyal only because God has protected him from misfortune. Put an end to his good fortune, says Satan, and Job "will blaspheme Thee to Thy face." Accepting the challenge, God permits Satan to destroy Job's children, take away his possessions, and afflict him with painful boils all over his body. Still Job does not curse God.

So far Job has accepted his fate uncomplainingly. But then in the company of three friends, Eliphaz, Bildad, and Zophar, he laments his misfortune and protests that God has treated him unjustly. Why is this happening, he asks, since he has not knowingly sinned? And why does a merciful God continue to make him suffer?

3 [1]After this opened Job his mouth, and cursed his day. [2]And Job spoke and said:
[3]Let the day perish wherein I was born,
And the night wherein it was said: "A man-child is brought forth."
[4]Let that day be darkness. . . .
[11]Why died I not from the womb?
Why did I not perish at birth? . . .

---

7 [11]Therefore I will not refrain my mouth;
I will speak in the anguish of my spirit;
I will complain in the bitterness of my soul.

[12]Am I a sea, or a sea-monster,
That Thou settest a watch over me?
[13]When I say: "My bed shall comfort me,
My couch shall ease my complaint";
[14]Then Thou scarest me with dreams,
And terrifest me through visions;
[15]So that my soul chooseth strangling,
And death rather than these my bones.
[16]I loathe it; I shall not live alway;
Let me alone; for my days are vanity.
[17]What is man, that Thou shouldest magnify him,
And that thou shouldst set thy heart upon him,
[18]And that Thou shouldest remember him every morning,

---

[1]At this stage in Jewish thought, Satan is simply a member of God's court; he is not the enemy of God and the leader of the forces of evil as he is later depicted, particularly at the time of Jesus and in early Christian writings.

And try him every moment?
¹⁹How long wilt Thou not look away from me,
Nor let me alone till I swallow down my spittle?
²⁰If I have sinned, what do I unto Thee, O Thou watcher of
   men?
Why hast Thou set me as a mark for Thee,
So that I am a burden to myself?
²¹And why dost Thou not pardon my transgression,
And take away mine iniquity?
For now shall I lie down in the dust;
And Thou wilt seek me, but I shall not be. . . .

9²²It is all one—therefore I say:
He destroyeth the innocent and the wicked.
²³If the scourge slay suddenly,
He will mock at the calamity of the guiltless.
²⁴The earth is given into the hand of the wicked;
He coverth the faces of the judges thereof;
If it be not He, who then is it?
²⁵Now my days are swifter than a runner;
They flee away, they see no good.

Job's friends take the orthodox position that "God
will not cast away an innocent man,/Neither will he
uphold the evil-doers. . . ." But Job replies that God
is destroying an innocent man.

16²²God delivereth me to the ungodly,
And casteth me into the hands of the wicked.
¹²I was at ease, and He broke me asunder;
Yea, He hath taken me by the neck, and dashed me to pieces;
He hath also set me up for His mark.
¹³His archers compass me round about,
He cleaveth my reins asunder, and doth not spare;
He poureth out my gall upon the ground.
¹⁴He breaketh me with breach upon breach;
He runneth upon me like a giant.
¹⁵I have sewed sackcloth upon my skin,
And have laid my horn in the dust.
¹⁶My face is reddened with weeping,
And on my eyelids is the shadow of death;
¹⁷Although there is no violence in my hands,
And my prayer is pure. . . .

19⁶Know now that God hath subverted my cause,
And hath compared me with His net.
⁷Behold, I cry out: "Violence!" but I am not heard;
I cry aloud, but there is no justice.
⁸He hath fenced up my way that I cannot pass,
And hath set darkness in my paths.
⁹He hath stripped me of my glory,
And taken the crown from my head.
¹⁰He hath broken me down on every side, and I am gone;

And my hope hath He plucked up like a tree.
¹¹He hath also kindled His wrath against me,
And He counteth me unto Him as one of His adversaries. . . .

Job protests that the wicked often go unpunished,
while he who aspired to righteousness is made to
suffer.

21⁷Wherefore do the wicked live,
Become old, yea, wax mighty in power?
⁸Their seed is established in their sight with them,
And their offspring before their eyes.
⁹Their houses are safe, without fear,
Neither is the rod of God upon them.
¹⁰Their bull gendereth, and faileth not;
Their cow calveth, and casteth not her calf.
¹¹They send forth their little ones like a flock,
And their children dance.
¹²They sing to the timbrel and harp,
And rejoice at the sound of the pipe.
¹³They spend their days in prosperity,
And peacefully they go down to the grave.
¹⁴Yet they said unto God: "Depart from us;
For we desire not the knowledge of Thy ways.
¹⁵What is the Almighty, that we should serve Him?
And what profit should we have, if we pray unto Him?" . . .

29¹²Because I delivered the poor that cried,
The fatherless also, that had none to help him.
¹³The blessing of him that was ready to perish came upon me;
And I caused the widow's heart to sing for joy.
¹⁴I put on righteousness, and it clothed itself with me;
My justice was as a robe and a diadem.
¹⁵I was eyes to the blind,
And feet was I to the lame.
¹⁶I was a father to the needy;
And the cause of him that I knew not I searched out.
¹⁷And I broke the jaws of the unrighteous,
And plucked the prey out of his teeth.

Elihu, a young man, joins the symposium. He is angry with Job for his self-righteousness, for trying to
justify himself rather than God, and with Job's
friends, for having found no answer to Job's
dilemma. But in proclaiming God's justice, Elihu essentially repeats the friends' arguments.

30¹⁶And now my soul is poured out within me;
Days of affliction have taken hold upon me.
¹⁷In the night my bones are pierced, and fall from me,
And my sinews take no rest.
¹⁸By the great force [of my disease] is my garment disfigured;
It bindeth me about as the collar of my coat.
¹⁹He hath cast me into the mire,

And I am become like dust and ashes.
²⁰I cry onto Thee, and Thou dost not answer me;
I stand up, And Thou lookest at me.
²¹Thou art turned to be cruel to me;
With the might of Thy hand Thou hatest me.
²²Thou liftest me up to the wind,
Thou causest me to ride upon it;
And Thou dissolvest my substance.
²³For I know that Thou wilt bring me to death,
And to the house appointed for all living.

34¹⁰Therefore hearken unto me, ye men of understandin
Far be it from God, that He should do wickedness;
And from the Almighty, that He should commit iniquity.
For the work of a man will He requite unto him,
And cause every man to find according to his ways.
¹²Yea, of a surety, God will not do wickedly,
Neither will the Almighty pervert justice.
¹³Who gave Him a charge over the earth?
Or who hath disposed the whole world?
¹⁴If He set His heart upon man,
If He gather unto Himself his spirit and his breath;
¹⁵All flesh shall perish together,
And man shall return unto dust.
¹⁶If now thou hast understanding, hear this;
Hearken to the voice of my words. . . .
³¹For hath any said unto God:
"I have borne chastisement, though I offend not;
³²That which I see not teach Thou me;
If I have done iniquity, I will do it no more"?
³³Shall His recompense be as thou wilt? For thou loathest it,
So that thou must choose, and not I;
Therefore speak what thou knowest.
³⁴Men of understanding will say unto me,
Yea, every wise man that heareth me:
³⁵"Job speaketh without knowledge,
And his words are without discernment."

³⁶Would that Job were tried unto the end,
Because of his answering like wicked men.
³⁷For he addeth rebellion unto his sin,
He clappeth his hands among us,
And multiplieth his words against God.

36⁵Behold, God is mighty, yet He despiseth not any;
He is mighty in strength of understanding.
⁶He preserveth not the life of the wicked;
But giveth to the poor their right.
⁷He withdraweth not His eyes from the righteous;
But with kings upon the throne
He setteth them for ever, and they are exalted.
⁸And if they be bound in fetters,
And be holden in cords of affliction;
⁹Then He declareth unto them their work,
And their transgressions, that they have behaved themselves
   proudly.
¹⁰He openeth also their ear to discipline,
And commandeth that they return from iniquity.
¹¹If they hearken and save Him,
They shall spend their days in prosperity,
And their years in pleasures.
¹²But if they hearken not, they shall perish by the sword,
And they shall die without knowledge.

Then God, "out of the whirlwind," replies to Job. But in God's response, we do not find a clear answer to the problem of undeserved suffering. Instead, God, in a series of rhetorical questions, reminds Job that he alone is the creator and sustainer of the universe and that it is the obligation of Job, a mere mortal, to honor his creator and not find fault with him. Awed by God's majesty and power, a humbled Job declares, "I abhor my words and repent." In an epilogue, God responds by restoring Job's good fortune.

5 The Age of Classical Prophecy

Ancient Jewish history was marked by the rise of prophets—spiritually inspired persons who believed that God had chosen them to remind the Jews of their duties to God and his law. These prophets carried God's message to the leaders and the people and warned of divine punishments for disobedience to God's commandments.

The prophetic movement—the age of classical prophecy—which emerged in the eighth century B.C., creatively expanded Hebrew religious thought. Prophets denounced exploitation of the poor, the greed of the wealthy, and the oppressive behavior of the powerful as a betrayal of Yahweh, a violation of his moral laws. They insisted that the core of Hebrew faith was not ritual but morality. Their concern for the poor and their attack on injustice received reemphasis in the Christian faith and thus became incorporated into the Western ideal of social justice.

Amos and *Isaiah*
SOCIAL JUSTICE

By the eighth century B.C. a significant disparity existed between the wealthy and the poor. Small farmers in debt to moneylenders faced the loss of their land or even bondage. Amos, a mid-eighth-century prophet, felt a tremendous compulsion to speak out in the name of God against these injustices.

AMOS

5 [21]I hate, I despise your feasts,
And I will take no delight in your solemn assemblies.
[22]Yea, though ye offer me burnt-offerings and your meal-offerings,
I will not accept them;
Neither will I regard the peace-offerings of your fat beasts.
[23]Take thou away from Me the noise of thy songs;
And let Me not hear the melody of thy psalteries.
[24]But let justice well up as waters,
And righteousness as a mighty stream.

The prophets' insistence that rituals were not the essence of the law and their passion for righteousness are voiced in the Scriptures by Isaiah of Jerusalem, who lived in the mid-eighth century B.C. Scholars agree that Isaiah of Jerusalem did not write all sixty-six chapters that make up the Book of Isaiah. Some material appears to have been written by his disciples and interpreters, and Chapters 40 to 55, composed two centuries later, are attributed to a person given the name Second Isaiah. The following verses come from Isaiah of Jerusalem.

ISAIAH

1 [11]To what purpose is the multitude of your sacrifices unto Me?
Saith the LORD;
I am full of the burnt-offerings of rams,
And the fat of fed beasts;
And I delight not in the blood
Of bullocks, or of lambs, or of he-goats.

[12]When ye come to appear before Me,
Who hath required this at your hand,
To trample My courts?
[13]Bring no more vain oblations;
It is an offering of abomination unto Me;
New moon and sabbath, the holding of convocations—
I cannot endure iniquity along with the solemn assembly.
[14]Your new moons and your appointed seasons
My soul hateth;
They are a burden unto Me;
I am weary to bear them.
[15]And when ye spread forth your hands,
I will hide Mine eyes from you;
Yea, when ye make many prayers,
I will not hear;
Your hands are full of blood.
[16]Wash you, make you clean,
Put away the evil of your doings
From before Mine eyes,
Cease to do evil;
[17]Learn to do well;
Seek justice, relieve the oppressed,
Judge the fatherless, plead for the widow.

Isaiah denounced the rich and the powerful for exploiting the poor.

3 [13]The LORD standeth up to plead,
And standeth to judge the peoples.
[14]The LORD will enter into judgment
With the elders of His people, and the princes thereof.
"It is ye that have eaten up the vineyard;
The spoil of the poor is in your houses;
[15]What mean ye that ye crush My people,
And grind the face of the poor?"
Saith the Lord, the GOD of hosts.

Isaiah
PEACE AND HUMANITY

Isaiah of Jerusalem envisioned the unity of all people under God. This universalism drew out the full implications of Hebrew monotheism. In Isaiah's vision all peoples would live together in peace and harmony. Some of these lines are inscribed on the building that houses the United Nations in New York City.

2 [2]And it shall to pass in the end of days,
That the mountain of the LORD's house shall be established as the top of the mountains,
And shall be exalted above the hills;
And all nations shall flow unto it.
[3]And many peoples shall go and say:
  "Come ye, and let us go up to the mountain of the LORD,
To the house of the God of Jacob;
And He will teach us of His ways,

And we will walk in His paths."
For out of Zion shall go forth the law,
And the word of the LORD from Jerusalem.
[4]And He shall judge between the nations,
And shall decide for many peoples;
And they shall beat their swords into plowshares,
And their spears into pruning-hooks;
Nation shall not lift up sword against nation,
Neither shall they learn war any more.

3

Hellenic Civilization

Hebrew ethical monotheism, which gave value to the individual, is one source of Western civilization. Another source derives from the ancient Greeks, who originated scientific and philosophic thought, created democracy, and developed a humanistic outlook. From about 750 B.C. to 338 B.C. the Greek world consisted of small, independent, and self-governing city-states. Within this political-social context, the Greeks made their outstanding contributions to civilization.

In contrast to the Egyptians and Mesopotamians, the Greeks developed rational-scientific, rather than mythical, interpretations of nature and the human community. In trying to understand nature, Greek philosophers proposed physical explanations: that is, they gradually omitted the gods from their accounts of how nature came to be the way it is. Greek intellectuals also analyzed government, law, and ethics in logical and systematic ways. It was the great achievement of Greek thinkers to rise above magic, miracles, mystery, and custom and to assert that reason was the avenue to knowledge. The emergence of rational attitudes did not, of course, end traditional religion, particularly for the peasants, who remained devoted to their ancient cults, gods, and shrines. But what distinguishes the Greeks is that alongside an older religious-mythical tradition arose a philosophic-scientific view of the natural world and human culture.

The Greeks, who defined human beings by their capacity to use reason, also defined the principle of political liberty. Egyptians and Mesopotamians were subject to the authority of god-kings and priest-kings; the common people did not participate in political life, and there was no awareness of individual liberty. In contrast, many Greek city-states, particularly Athens, developed democratic institutions and attitudes. In the middle of the fifth century B.C., when Athenian democracy was at its height, adult male citizens were eligible to hold public office and were equal before the law; in the assembly, which met some forty times a year, they debated and voted on the key issues of state. Whereas Mesopotamians and Egyptians believed that law had been given to them by the gods, the Greeks came to understand that law was a human creation, a product of human reason. The Athenians abhorred rule by absolute rulers and held that people can govern themselves. While expressing admiration for the Greek political achievement, modern critics also point out several limitations of Greek democracy, notably slavery and the inability of women to participate in political life.

The Greeks originated the Western humanist tradition. They valued the human personality and sought the full cultivation of human talent. In the Greek view, a man of worth pursued excellence, that is, he sought to mold himself in accordance with the highest standards and ideals. Greek art, for example, made the human form the focal point of attention and exalted the nobility, dignity, self-assurance, and beauty of the human being.

Greek culture has a distinctive style that enables us to see it as an organic whole. To the English classicist H. D. F. Kitto, the common thread that runs through Greek philosophy, literature, and art is "a sense of the wholeness of things"—the conviction that the universe contains an inherent order, that law governs both nature and human affairs, and that this law can be comprehended by human reason.

Although the Greek city-states shared a common culture, they frequently warred with each other. Particularly ruinous was the Peloponnesian War (431–404 B.C.)

between Athens and Sparta and their allies. The drawn-out conflict, marked by massacres and civil wars within city-states, shattered the Greek world spiritually. Increasingly, a narrow individualism and worsening factional disputes weakened the bonds of community within the various city-states. Moreover, learning little from the Peloponnesian War, the Greeks continued their internecine conflicts. Finally, by 338 B.C. the weakened city-states were conquered by Philip II of Macedonia, a kingdom to the north of Greece. Although the Greek cities continued to exist, they had lost their political independence; Greek civilization was entering a new phase.

1 Homer: The Educator of Greece

The poet Homer, who probably lived during the eighth century B.C., helped shape the Greek outlook. His great epics, the *Iliad* and the *Odyssey,* contain the embryo of the Greek humanist tradition: the concern with man and his achievements. "To strive always for excellence and to surpass all others"—in these words lies the essence of the Homeric hero's outlook. In the warrior-aristocratic world of Homer, excellence is primarily interpreted as bravery and skill in battle. The Homeric hero is driven to demonstrate his prowess, to assert himself, to win honor, and to earn a reputation.

The *Iliad* deals in poetic form with the Trojan War, which probably was waged in the thirteenth century B.C., between the Mycenaean Greeks and the Trojans of Asia Minor. At the outset Homer states his theme: the wrath of Achilles that brought so much suffering to the Greeks. Agamemnon, their king, has deprived the great warrior Achilles of his rightful prize, the captive girl Briseis. Achilles will not submit to this grave insult to his honor and refuses to join the Greeks in combat against the Trojans. In this way he intends to make Agamemnon pay for his arrogance, for without the Greeks' greatest warrior, Agamemnon will have no easy victories. With Achilles on the sidelines, the Greeks suffer severe losses.

Destiny is at work: the "wicked arrogance" of Agamemnon and the "ruinous wrath" of Achilles have caused suffering and death among the Greek forces. For Homer, human existence has a pattern—a universal plan governs human affairs. People, even the gods, operate within a certain unalterable framework; their deeds are subject to the demands of destiny or necessity. Later Greek thinkers would express this idea of a universal order in philosophic and scientific terms.

Homer

Iliad

The following passages from the *Iliad* illustrate the Homeric ideal of excellence. In the first, Hector of Troy, son of King Priam, prepares for battle. Hector's wife Andromache pleads with him to stay within the city walls, but Hector, in the tradition of the Homeric hero, feels compelled to engage in combat to show his worth and gain honor.

Hector looked at his son and smiled, but said nothing. Andromache, bursting into tears, went up to him and put her hand in his. "Hector," she said, "you are possessed. This bravery of yours will be your end. You do not think of your little boy or your unhappy wife, whom you will make a widow soon. Some day the Achaeans [Greeks] are bound to kill you in a massed attack. And when I lose you I might as well be dead. There will be no comfort left, when you have met your doom—nothing but grief. I have no father, no mother, now. My father fell to the great Achilles when he sacked our lovely town, Cilician Thebe[1] of the High Gates. . . . I had seven brothers too at home. In one day all of them went down to Hades' House.[2] The great Achilles of the swift feet killed them all. . . ."

"So you, Hector, are father and mother and brother to me, as well as my beloved husband. Have pity on me now; stay here on the tower; and do not make your boy an orphan and your wife a widow. . . ."

"All that, my dear," said the great Hector of the glittering helmet, "is surely my concern. But if I hid myself like a coward and refused to fight, I could never face the Trojans and the Trojan ladies in their trailing gowns. Besides, it would go against the grain, for I have trained myself always, like a good soldier, to take my place in the front line and win glory for my father and myself. . . ."

As he finished, glorious Hector held out his arms to take his boy. But the child shrank back with a cry to the bosom of his girdled nurse, alarmed by his father's appearance. He was frightened by the bronze of the helmet and the horsehair plume that he saw nodding grimly down at him. His father and his lady mother had to laugh. But noble Hector quickly took his helmet off and put the dazzling thing on the ground. Then he kissed his son, dandled him in his arms, and prayed to Zeus [the chief god] and the other gods: "Zeus, and you other gods, grant that this boy of mine may be, like me, pre-eminent in Troy; as strong and brave as I; a mighty king of Ilium [Troy]. May people say, when he comes back from battle, 'Here is a better man than his father.' Let him bring home the bloodstained armour of the enemy he has killed, and make his mother happy."

Hector handed the boy to his wife, who took him to her fragrant breast. She was smiling through her tears, and when her husband saw this he was moved. He stroked her with his hand and said: "My dear, I beg you not to be too much distressed. No one is going to send me down to Hades before my proper time. But Fate is a thing that no man born of woman, coward or hero, can escape. Go home now, and attend to your own work, the loom and the spindle, and see that the maidservants get on with theirs. War is men's business; and this war is the business of every man in Ilium, myself above all."

Many brave Greek warriors die in battle, including Achilles' best friend Patroclus, slain by the Trojan Hector. Torn by grief and rage, Achilles now sets aside his quarrel with Agamemnon (who has appealed to Achilles) and joins the battle.

---

[1] In the *Iliad* the Cilices lived in southern Asia Minor.
[2] Hades refers both to the god of the underworld and to the underworld itself.

Nestor's son halted before him with the hot tears pouring down his cheeks and gave him the lamentable news: "Alas, my royal lord Achilles! I have a dreadful thing to tell you—I would to God it were not true. Patroclus has been killed. They are fighting round his naked corpse and Hector of the flashing helmet has your arms."

When Achilles heard this he sank into the black depths of despair. He picked up the dark dust in both his hands and poured it on his head. He soiled his comely face with it, and filthy ashes settled on his scented tunic. He cast himself down on the earth and lay there like a fallen giant, fouling his hair and tearing it out with his own hands. The maidservants whom he and Patroclus had captured caught the alarm and all ran screaming out of doors. They beat their breasts with their hands and sank to the ground beside their royal master. On the other side, Antilochus shedding tears of misery held the hands of Achilles as he sobbed out his noble heart, for fear that he might take a knife and cut his throat.

Suddenly Achilles gave a loud and dreadful cry, and his lady Mother heard him where she sat in the depths of the sea beside her ancient Father. Then she herself took up the cry of grief, and there gathered round her every goddess, every Nereid that was in the deep salt sea. . . . "Ah misery me, the unhappy mother of the best of men! I brought into the world a flawless child to be a mighty hero and eclipse his peers. I nursed him as one tends a little plant in a garden bed, and he shot up like a sapling. I sent him to Ilium with his beaked ships to fight against the Trojans; and never again now shall I welcome him to Peleus' house. And yet he has to suffer, every day he lives and sees the sun; and I can do no good by going to his side. But I *will* go, none the less, to see my darling child and hear what grief has come to him, although he has abstained from fighting."

With that she left the cave. The rest went with her, weeping, and on either side of them the surging sea fell back. When they reached the deep-soiled land of Troy, they came up one by one onto the beach, where the Myrmidon ships were clustered round the swift Achilles. His lady Mother went up to him as he lay groaning there, and with a piercing cry took her son's head in her hands and spoke to him in her compassion. "My child," she asked him, "why these tears? What is it that has grieved you? Tell me and do not keep your sorrow to yourself. Some part, at any rate, of what you prayed for when you lifted up your hands to Zeus has been fulfilled by him. The Achaeans have been penned in at the ships for want of you, and have suffered horribly."

Achilles of the nimble feet gave a great sigh. "Mother," he said, "it is true that the Olympian has done that much in my behalf. But what satisfaction can I get from that, now that my dearest friend is dead, Patroclus, who was more to me than any other of my men, whom I loved as much as my own life? I have lost Patroclus. And Hector, who killed him, has stripped him of my splendid armour, the huge and wonderful arms that the gods gave Peleus as a wedding-present on the day when they married you off to a mortal man. Ah, how I wish that you had stayed there with the deathless salt-sea Nymphs and that Peleus had taken home a mortal wife! But you became my mother; and now, to multiply *your* sorrows too, you are going to lose your son and never welcome him at home again. For I have no wish to live and linger in the world of men, unless, before all else, Hector is felled by my spear and dies, paying the price for slaughtering Menoetius' son."

Thetis wept. She said: "If that is so, my child, you surely have not long to live; for after Hector's death you are doomed forthwith to die."

"Then *let* me die forthwith," Achilles said with passion, "since I have failed to save my friend from death. He has fallen, far from his motherland, wanting my help in his extremity. So now, since I shall never see my home again, since I have proved a broken reed to Patroclus and all my other comrades whom Prince Hector killed, and have sat here by my ships, an idle burden on the earth, I, the best man in all the Achaean force, the best in battle, defeated only in the war of words . . . Ah, how I wish that discord could be banished from the world of gods and men, and with it anger, insidious as trickling honey, anger that makes the wisest man flare up and spreads like smoke through his whole being, anger such as King Agamemnon roused in me that day! However, what is done is better left alone, though we resent it still, and we must curb our hearts perforce. I will go now and seek out Hector, the destroyer of my dearest friend. As for my death, when Zeus and the other deathless gods appoint it, let it come. . . . But for the moment, glory is my aim. I will make these Trojan women and deep-bosomed daughters of Dardanus wipe the tears from their tender cheeks with both their hands as they raise the dirge, to teach them just how long I have been absent from the war. And you, Mother, as you love me, do not try to keep me from the field. You will never hold me now."

"Indeed, my child," said Thetis of the Silver Feet, "it could not be an evil thing for you to rescue your exhausted comrades from destruction. But your beautiful burnished armour is in Trojan hands. Hector of the flashing helmet is swaggering about in it himself—not that he will enjoy it long, for he is very near to death. So do not think of throwing yourself into the fight before you see me here again. I will come back at sunrise to-morrow with a splendid set of armour from the Lord Hephaestus." . . .

All night long the Achaeans wept and wailed for Patroclus. The son of Peleus was their leader in the melancholy dirge. He laid his man-killing hands on his comrade's breast and uttered piteous groans, like a bearded lion when a huntsman has stolen his cubs from a thicket and he comes back too late, discovers his loss and follows the man's trail through glade after glade, hoping in his misery to track him down. Thus Achilles groaned among his Myrmidons. He thought with a pang of the idle words he had let fall one day at home in his attempts to reassure Patroclus' noble father. "I told Menoetius," he said, "that I would bring him back his son to Opus from the sack of Ilium, covered with glory and laden with his share of plunder. But Zeus makes havoc of the schemes of men; and now the pair of us are doomed to redden with our blood one patch of earth, here in the land of Troy. For I shall never see my home again, nor be welcomed there by Peleus the old charioteer and my Mother Thetis, but shall be swallowed by the earth I stand on. So then, Patroclus, since I too am going below, but after you, I shall not hold your funeral till I have brought back here the armour and the head of Hector, who slaughtered you, my noble-hearted friend. And at your pyre I will cut the throats of a dozen of the highborn youths of Troy, to vent my wrath on them for killing you. Till then, you shall lie as you are by my beaked ships, wailed and wept for day and night by the Trojan women and the deep-bosomed daughters of Dardanus whom we captured after much toil, with our own hands and our long spears, when we sacked rich cities full of men."

Prince Achilles then told his followers to put a big three-legged cauldron on the fire and make haste to wash the clotted gore from Patroclus' body. They put a large cauldron on the glowing fire, filled it with water, and brought faggots, which they kindled beneath it. The flames began to lick the belly of the cauldron and the water grew warm. When it came to the boil in the burnished copper, they washed the corpse, anointed it with olive oil and filled the wounds with an unguent nine years old. Then they laid it on a bier and covered it from head to foot with a soft sheet, over which they spread a white cloak. And for the rest of the night the Myrmidons with the great runner Achilles wept and wailed for Patroclus.

King Priam urges his son not to fight the mighty Achilles, but Hector, despite his fears, resolves to face Achilles.

"Hector!" the old man called, stretching out his arms to him in piteous appeal. "I beg you, my dear son, not to stand up to that man alone and unsupported. You are courting defeat and death at his hands. He is far stronger than you, and he is savage. The dogs and vultures would soon be feeding on his corpse (and what a load would be lifted from my heart!) if the gods loved him as little as I do—the man who has robbed me of so many splendid sons, killed them or sold them off as slaves to the distant isles. Even to-day there are two of them I cannot find among the troops that have taken refuge in the town, Lycaon and Polydorus, children of mine by the Princess Laothoe. If the enemy have taken them alive, we will ransom them presently with bronze and gold, of which she has plenty, for Altes, the honourable old man, gave his daughter a fortune. But if they are dead by now and in the Halls of Hades, there will be one more sorrow for me and their mother who brought them into the world, even though the rest of Ilium will not mourn for them so long—unless you join them and also fall to Achilles. So come inside the walls, my child, to be the saviour of Troy and the Trojans; and do not throw away your own dear life to give a triumph to the son of Peleus. Have pity too on me, your poor father, who is still able to feel. Think of the hideous fate that Father

Zeus has kept in store for my old age, the horrors I shall have to see before I die, the massacre of my sons, my daughters mauled, their bedrooms pillaged, their babies dashed on the ground by the brutal enemy, and my sons' wives hauled away by foul Achaean hands. Last of all my turn will come to fall to the sharp bronze, and when someone's javelin or sword has laid me dead, I shall be torn to pieces by ravening dogs at my own street door. The very dogs I have fed at table and trained to watch my gate will loll about in front of it, maddened by their master's blood. Ah, it looks well enough for a young man killed in battle to lie there with his wounds upon him: death can find nothing to expose in him that is not beautiful. But when an old man is killed and dogs defile his grey head, his grey beard and his privy parts, we plumb the depths of human degradation."

As he came to an end, Priam plucked at his grey locks and tore the hair from his head; but he failed to shake Hector's resolution. And now his mother in her turn began to wail and weep. Thrusting her dress aside, she exposed one of her breasts in her other hand and implored him, with the tears running down her cheeks. "Hector, my child," she cried, "have some regard for this, and pity me. How often have I given you this breast and soothed you with its milk! Bear in mind those days, dear child. Deal with your enemy from within the walls, and do not go out to meet that man in single combat. He is a savage; and you need not think that, if he kills you, I shall lay you on a bier and weep for you, my own, my darling boy; nor will your richly dowered wife; but far away from both of us, beside the Argive ships, you will be eaten by the nimble dogs."

Thus they appealed in tears to their dear son. But all their entreaties were wasted on Hector, who stuck to his post and let the monstrous Achilles approach him. As a mountain snake, who is maddened by the poisonous herbs he has swallowed, allows a man to come up to the lair where he lies coiled, and watches him with a baleful glitter in his eye, Hector stood firm and unflinching, with his glittering shield supported by an outwork of the wall. But he was none the less appalled, and groaning at his plight he took counsel with his indomitable soul. He thought: "If I retire behind the gate and wall, Polydamas will be the first to cast it in my teeth that, in this last night of disaster when the great Achilles came to life, I did not take his advice and order a withdrawal into the city, as I certainly ought to have done. As it is, having sacrificed the army to my own perversity, I could not face my countrymen and the Trojan ladies in their trailing gowns. I could not bear to hear some commoner say: 'Hector trusted his own right arm and lost an army.' But it *will* be said, and then I shall know that it would have been a far better thing for me to stand up to Achilles, and either kill him and come home alive or myself die gloriously in front of Troy."

When Achilles approaches Hector brandishing a "formidable . . . spear . . . and the bronze on his body glowed like a blazing fire, . . . Hector looked up, saw him, and began to tremble. He no longer had the heart to stand his ground . . . and ran away in terror." Achilles relentlessly pursues the fleeing Hector. But then Hector stops and addresses Achilles.

"My lord Achilles, I have been chased by you three times round the great city of Priam without daring to stop and let you come near. But now I am going to run away no longer. I have made up my mind to fight you man to man and kill you or be killed. But first let us make a bargain, you with your gods for witness, I with mine—no compact could have better guarantors. If Zeus allows me to endure, and I kill you, I undertake to do no outrage to your body that custom does not sanction. All I shall do, Achilles, is to strip you of your splendid armour. Then I will give up your corpse to the Achaeans. Will you do that same for me?"

Achilles of the nimble feet looked at him grimly and replied: "Hector, you must be mad to talk to me about a pact. Lions do not come to terms with men nor does the wolf see eye to eye with the lamb—they are enemies to the end. It is the same with you and me. Friendship between us is impossible, and there will be no truce of any kind till one of us has fallen and glutted the stubborn god of battles with his blood. So summon any courage you may have. This is the time to show your spearmanship and daring. Not that anything is going to save you now, when Pallas Athene is waiting to fell you with my spear. This moment you are going to pay the full price for all you made me suffer when your lance mowed down my friends."

With this Achilles poised and hurled his long-shadowed spear. But illustrious Hector was looking out and managed to avoid it. He crouched, with his eye on the weapon; and it flew over his head and stuck in the ground. But Pallas Athene snatched it up and brought it back to Achilles.

Hector the great captain, who had not seen this move, called across to the peerless son of Peleus: "A miss for the godlike Achilles! It seems that Zeus gave you the wrong date for my death! You were too cocksure. But then you're so glib, so clever with your tongue—trying to frighten me and drain me of my strength. Nevertheless, you will not make me run, or catch me in the back with your spear. Drive it through my breast as I charge—if you get the chance. But first you will have to dodge this one of mine. And Heaven grant that all its bronze may be buried in your flesh! This war would be an easier business for the Trojans, if you, their greatest scourge, were dead."

With that he swung up his long-shadowed spear and cast. And sure enough he hit the centre of Achilles' shield, but his spear rebounded from it. Hector was angry at having made so fine a throw for nothing, and he stood there discomfited, for he had no second lance. He shouted aloud to Deiphobus of the white shield, asking him for a long spear. But Deiphobus was nowhere near him; and Hector, realizing what had happened, cried: "Alas! So the gods did beckon me to my death! I thought the good Deiphobus was at my side; but he is in the town, and Athene has fooled me. Death is no longer far away; he is staring me in the face and there is no escaping him. Zeus and his Archer Son must long have been resolved on this, for all their goodwill and the help they gave me. So now I meet my doom. Let me at least sell my life dearly and have a not inglorious end, after some feat of arms that shall come to the ears of generations still unborn."

Hanging down at his side, Hector had a sharp, long and weighty sword. He drew this now, braced himself, and swooped like a high-flying eagle that drops to earth through the black clouds to pounce on a tender lamb or a crouching hare. Thus Hector charged, brandishing his sharp sword. Achilles sprang to meet him, inflamed with savage passion. He kept his front covered with his decorated shield; his glittering helmet with its four plates swayed as he moved his head and made the splendid golden plumes that Hephaestus had lavished on the crest dance round the top; and bright as the loveliest jewel in the sky, the Evening Star when he comes out at nightfall with the rest, the sharp point scintillated on the spear he balanced in his right hand, intent on killing Hector, and searching him for the likeliest place to reach his flesh.

Achilles saw that Hector's body was completely covered by the fine bronze armour he had taken from the great Patroclus when he killed him, except for an opening at the gullet where the collar bones lead over from the shoulders to the neck, the easiest place to kill a man. As Hector charged him, Prince Achilles drove at this spot with his lance; and the point went right through the tender flesh of Hector's neck, though the heavy bronze head did not cut his windpipe, and left him able to address his conqueror. Hector came down in the dust and the great Achilles triumphed over him. "Hector," he said, "no doubt you fancied as you stripped Patroclus that you would be safe. You never thought of me: I was too far away. You were a fool. Down by the hollow ships there was a man far better than Patroclus in reserve, the man who has brought you low. So now the dogs and birds of prey are going to maul and mangle you, while we Achaeans hold Patroclus' funeral."

"I beseech you," said Hector of the glittering helmet in a failing voice, "by your knees, by your own life and by your parents, not to throw my body to the dogs at the Achaean ships, but to take a ransom for me. My father and my lady mother will pay you bronze and gold in plenty. Give up my body to be taken home, so that the Trojans and their wives may honour me in death with the ritual of fire."

The swift Achilles scowled at him. "You cur," he said, "don't talk to me of knees or name my parents in your prayers. I only wish that I could summon up the appetite to carve and eat you raw myself, for what you have done to me. But this at least is certain, that nobody is going to keep the dogs from you, not even if the Trojans bring here and weigh out a ransom ten or twenty times your worth, and promise more besides; not if Dardanian Priam tells them to pay your weight in gold—not even so shall your lady mother lay you on a bier to mourn the son she bore, but the dogs and birds of prey shall eat you up."

Hector of the flashing helmet spoke to him once more at the point of death. "How well I know you and can read your mind!" he said. "Your heart is hard as iron—I have been wasting my breath. Nevertheless, pause before you act, in case the angry gods remember how you treated me, when your turn comes and you are brought down at the Scaean Gate in all your glory by Paris and Apollo."

Death cut Hector short and his disembodied soul took wing for the House of Hades, bewailing its lot and the youth and manhood that it left. But Prince Achilles spoke to him again though he was gone. "Die!" he said. "As for my own death, let it come when Zeus and the other deathless gods decide."

Then he withdrew his bronze spear from the corpse and laid it down. As he removed the bloodstained arms from Hector's shoulders, other Achaean warriors came running up and gathered round. They gazed in wonder at the size and marvellous good looks of Hector. And not a man of all who had collected there left him without a wound. As each went in and struck the corpse, he looked at his friends, and the jest went round: "Hector is easier to handle now than when he set the ships on fire."

After stripping Hector, the swift and excellent Achilles stood up and made a speech to the Achaeans. "My friends," he said, "Captains and Counsellors of the Argives; now that the gods have let us get the better of this man, who did more damage than all the rest together, let us make an armed reconnaissance round the city and find out what the Trojans mean to do next, whether they will abandon their fortress now that their champion has fallen, or make up their minds to hold it without Hector's help. But what am I saying? How can I think of anything but the dead man who is lying by my ships unburied and unwept—Patroclus, whom I shall never forget as long as I am still among the living and can walk the earth, my own dear comrade, whom I shall remember even though the dead forget their dead, even in Hades' Halls? So come now, soldiers of Achaea, let us go back to the hollow ships carrying this corpse and singing a song of triumph: 'We have won great glory. We have killed the noble Hector, who was treated like a god in Troy.'"

The next thing that Achilles did was to subject the fallen prince to shameful outrage. He slit the tendons at the back of both his feet from heel to ankle, inserted leather straps, and made them fast to his chariot, leaving the head to drag. Then he lifted the famous armour into his car, got in himself, and with a touch of his whip started the horses, who flew off with a will. Dragged behind him, Hector raised a cloud of dust, his black locks streamed on either side, and dust fell thick upon his head, so comely once, which Zeus now let his enemies defile on his own native soil.

Thus Hector's head was tumbled in the dust. When his mother saw what they were doing to her son, she tore her hair, and plucking the bright veil from her head cast it away with a loud and bitter cry. His father groaned in anguish, the people round them took up the cry of grief, and the whole city gave itself up to despair. They could not have lamented louder if Ilium had been going up in flames, from its frowning citadel to its lowest street. In his horror the old king made for the Dardanian Gate, bent on going out, and when his people had with difficulty stopped him, he grovelled in the dung and implored them all, calling on each man by his name. "Friends, let me be," he said. "You overdo your care for me. Let me go out of the town alone to the Achaean ships. I want to plead with this inhuman monster, who may perhaps be put to shame by Hector's youth and pity my old age. After all he too has a father of the same age as myself, Peleus, who gave him life and brought him up to be a curse to all the Trojans, though none of them has suffered at his hands so much as I, the father of so many sons butchered by him in the heyday of their youth. And yet, though I bewail them all, there is one for whom I mourn still more, with a bitter sorrow that will bring me to the grave; and that is Hector. Ah, if he could only have died in my arms! Then we could have wept and wailed for him to our hearts' content, I and the mother who brought him, to her sorrow, into the world."

Thus Priam, through his tears. The citizens of Troy added their moans to his; and now Hecabe led the Trojan women in a poignant lament. "My child!" she cried. "Ah, misery me! Why should I live and suffer now that you are dead? Night and day in Troy you were my pride, and to every man and woman in the town a saviour whom they greeted as a god. Indeed you were their greatest glory while you lived. Now, Death and Destiny have taken you away."

Thus Hecabe wailed and wept. But Hector's wife had not yet heard the news. No one in fact had even gone to tell her that her husband had remained outside the gates. She was at work, in a corner of her lofty house, on a purple web of double width, which she was decorating with a floral pattern. In her innocence, she had just called to the ladies-in-waiting in her house to put a big cauldron on the fire so that Hector could have a hot bath when he came home from the battle—never dreaming that far away from all baths he lay dead at the hands of Achilles and bright-eyed Athene. But now the keening and moaning at the battlements reached her ears. She trembled all over and dropped her shuttle on the floor. She called again to her ladies-in-waiting: "Come with me, two of you: I must see what has happened. That was my husband's noble mother that I heard; and as for me, my heart is in my mouth and I cannot move my legs. Some dreadful thing is threatening the House of Priam. Heaven defend me from such news, but I am terribly afraid that the great Achilles has caught my gallant husband by himself outside the town and chased him into the open; indeed that he may have put an end already to the headstrong pride that was Hector's passion. For Hector would never hang back with the crowd; he always sallied out in front of all the rest and let no one be as daring as himself."

As she finished, Andromache, with palpitating heart, rushed out of the house like a mad woman, and her maidservants went with her. When they came to the wall, where the men had gathered in a crowd, she climbed up on the battlements, searched the plain, and saw them dragging her husband in front of the town—the powerful horses were hauling him along at an easy canter towards the Achaean ships. The world went black as night before Andromache's eyes. She lost her senses and fell backward to the ground, dropping the whole of her gay headdress from her head, the coronet, the cap, the plaited snood and the veil that golden Aphrodite gave her on the day when Hector of the flashing helmet, having paid a princely dowry for his bride, came to fetch her from Eëtion's house. As she lay there in a dead faint, her husband's sisters and his brothers' wives crowded around her and supported her between them. When at length she recovered and came to herself, she burst out sobbing and made her lament to the ladies of Troy.

"Alas, Hector; alas for me!" she cried. "So you and I were born under the same unhappy star, you here in Priam's house and I in Thebe under wooded Placus in the house of Eëtion, who brought me up from babyhood, the unlucky father of a more unlucky child, who wishes now that she had never seen the light of day. For you are on your way to Hades and the unknown world below, leaving me behind in misery, a widow in your house. And your son is no more than a baby, the son we got between us, we unhappy parents. You, Hector, now that you are dead, will be no joy to him, nor he to you. Even if he escapes the horrors of the Achaen war, nothing lies ahead of him but hardship and trouble, with strangers eating into his estate. An orphaned child is cut off from his playmates. He goes about with downcast looks and tear-stained cheeks. In his necessity he looks in at some gathering of his father's friends and plucks a cloak here and a tunic there, till someone out of charity holds up a wine-cup to his mouth, but only for a moment, just enough to wet his lips and leave his palate dry. Then comes another boy, with both his parents living, who beats him with his fists and drives him from the feast and jeers at him. 'Out you go!' he shouts 'You have no father dining here.' So the child runs off in tears to his widowed mother—little Astyanax, who used to sit on his father's knees and eat nothing but marrow and mutton fat, and when he was sleepy and tired of play, slept in a bed, softly cradled in his nurse's arms, full of good cheer. But now, with his father gone, evils will crowd in on Astyanax, Protector of Troy, as the Trojans called him, seeing in you the one defence of their long walls and gates. And you, by the beaked ships, far from your parents, will be eaten by the wriggling worms when the dogs have had their fill, lying naked, for all the delicate and lovely clothing made by women's hands that you possess at home. All of which I am going to burn to ashes. It is of no use to you: you will never lie in it. But the men and women of Troy shall accord you that last mark of honour."

Thus Andromache lamented through her tears, and the women joined in her lament.

In this passage, the grief-stricken Priam goes to Achilles and requests Hector's body. Achilles responds with compassion. This scene shows that although Homer sees the essence of life as the pursuit of glory, he is also sensitive to life's brevity and to the suffering that pervades human existence.

. . . Big though Priam was, he came in unobserved, went up to Achilles, grasped his knees and kissed his hands, the terrible, man-killing hands that had slaughtered many of his sons. Achilles was astounded when he saw King Priam, and so were all his men. . . .

But Priam was already praying to Achilles. "Most worshipful Achilles," he said, "think of your own father, who is the same age as I, and so has nothing but miserable old age ahead of him. No doubt his neighbours are oppressing him and there is nobody to save him from their depredations. Yet he at least has one consolation. While he knows that you are still alive, he can look forward day by day to seeing his beloved son come back from Troy; whereas my fortunes are completely broken. I had the best sons in the whole of this broad realm, and now not one, not one I say, is left. There were fifty when the Achaean expedition came. Nineteen of them were borne by one mother and the rest by other ladies in my palace. Most of them have fallen in action, and Hector, the only one I still could count on, the bulwark of Troy and the Trojans, has now been killed by you, fighting for his native land. It is to get him back from you that I have come to the Achaean ships, bringing this princely ransom with me. Achilles, fear the gods, and be merciful to me, remembering your own father, though I am even more entitled to compassion, since I have brought myself to do a thing that no one else on earth has done—I have raised to my lips the hand of the man who killed my son."

Priam had set Achilles thinking of his own father and brought him to the verge of tears. Taking the old man's hand, he gently put him from him; and overcome by their memories they both broke down. Priam, crouching at Achilles' feet, wept bitterly for man-slaying Hector, and Achilles wept for his father, and then again for Patroclus. The house was filled with the sounds of their lamentation. But presently, when he had had enough of tears and recovered his composure, the excellent Achilles leapt from his chair, and in compassion for the old man's grey head and grey beard, took him by the arm and raised him. Then he spoke to him from his heart: "You are indeed a man of sorrows and have suffered much. How could you dare to come by yourself to the Achaean ships into the presence of a man who has killed so many of your gallant sons? You have a heart of iron. But pray be seated now, here on this chair, and let us leave our sorrows, bitter though they are, locked up in our own hearts, for weeping is cold comfort and does little good. We men are wretched things, and the gods, who have no cares themselves, have woven sorrow into the very pattern of our lives."

2 Hesiod: A Plea for Justice

The poet Hesiod (c. 700 B.C.), who lived on a farm in Boetia, in central Greece, wrote two major poems: *Theogony,* which deals with the formation of the universe, and *Works and Days,* which depicts the life of peasants. Like Homer's epics, Hesiod's poems contain ideas that contributed to the shaping of the Greek outlook and the emergence of philosophy. For example, utilizing inherited ethical maxims and driven by his own deep concern for justice, Hesiod raised questions about the origin of evil, the existence of a moral order within nature, and what constitutes the good life that would greatly influence later Greek dramatists and philosophers.

Hesiod

Works and Days

While Homer's epics concentrate on heroes striving to win honor as defined by a chivalric aristocratic ideal, Hesiod's later poem, *Works and Days,* excerpted below, describes the daily ordeal of common folk struggling to feed their families.

A man of the soil, Hesiod also maintains that honest labor promotes the good life. For Hesiod, the farmer who perseveres in his daily labor demonstrates *areté* (excellence); heroes are not only made on the battlefield, but also on the farm in the farmer's confrontation with the land and nature.

But it is Hesiod's concern with justice that gives the poem stature. Cheated by his brother, Perses, out of part of their father's estate, Hesiod feels compelled to instruct Perses and others about the virtues of justice. He attributes the wretched condition of social life, including civil war and slaughter, to a break-down of moral standards. Hesiod believed that human beings could improve their lot if they embraced justice which is the best thing they have. An awareness of justice is what distinguishes human beings from other creatures. Human beings are faced with the choice between *Dikê* (straight judgment and justice) which safeguards society and *Hybris* (best defined here as insolence that is prone to violence) which destroys it. Honoring justice is what distinguishes a civilized society from a state of savagery.

Hesiod used the language and imagery of myth to express a concern for justice and an awareness of a universal moral order. In succeeding centuries, Greek thinkers would discuss these issues using the language and categories of philosophy.

But you, Perses, hearken to justice and don't honor Hybris.
Hybris is a bad thing for the poor man, for not even the rich man
easily bears it but staggers under its burdensome weight and
meets with calamity. Better it is to go on the road in
the other direction to Justice. Justice wins over Hybris,
finally coming in victor. The fool by suffering learns this.
For the oath-god Horkos runs after crooked injustice,
and there's an uproar when justice is dragged off, when she is seized by
gift-eating men who interpret the laws with crooked decisions.
Justice departs deploring the city, its people and ways,
being hidden in air and bringing evil to men
who would make her an exile and do not apportion her straightly.
But for those who give justice to stranger and native alike,
straight pronouncements of justice, and stray not at all from her path,
theirs is a flourishing city, a people who prosper and grow.
Peace, the nurse of the young, is over their land, and they are never afflicted with anguishing war by far-seeing Zeus.
Never do famine and ruin accompany men of straight justice,
but they enjoy in bountiful feasts the fruits of their labors.
Earth produces her plenty for them. The trees in the mountains
bear for them nuts on their outsides, swarms of bees in their centers.
Thick and soft is the wool which heavily covers their sheep.
And their wives are bearers of children resembling their fathers.
They abound in continuous plenty and have no need to
travel in ships, for the grain-giving earth provides them with food.

But upon those who are lovers of hybris and hard-hearted deeds
far-seeing Zeus, son of Kronos, dispenses his punishing justice.
Often even a whole city pays for the wrong of one person
who is a doer of evil and worker of ruinous folly.
Zeus, son of Kronos, sends terrible suffering from heaven upon them,
famine together with plague, and makes the people to perish.
Nor do their women bear children, but they have withering homes,
as the Olympian Zeus devises. And sometimes he makes them
pay by giving their broad army defeat or bringing their wall down,
or he, Zeus, son of Kronos, destroys their ships on the sea.
Kings, I beg you to take careful note of this punishing justice,
for there are here nearby among men immortal spirits
who take note of all who with crooked injustice trample
each other down, having no thought of divine retribution.
There are thirty thousand spirits on the bountiful earth,
immortal sentinels of Zeus, strict guardians of mortal men,
who keep a watch on cases at law and hard-hearted deeds,
being hidden in air and going all over the earth.
And there is also the virgin Justice, the daughter of Zeus,
who is honored and held in respect by the gods of Olympos.
When she is harmed by anyone scorning her, crookedly speaking,
she immediately goes to her seat by Zeus, son of Kronos, her father,
and informs on the unjust judge, so that the people
pay for the crimes of their kings who making baneful decisions

twist what is right into wrong with crooked pronouncements of justice.

Beware of these things, O Kings, and see that you straighten your verdicts,

eaters of gifts, and no longer think of crooked decisions.

He who devises harm for another is harming himself,

and from the plan that is harmful most harm comes to the planner.

The eye of Zeus that sees all things and observes all things

now, if only it so wills, sees this state of affairs, and

this sort of justice that our city harbors does not escape it.

Now neither would I myself be just in my dealings with men nor

hope that my son be, since it will be a bad thing to be just,

if the deviser of greater injustice will have greater justice.

But I hope Zeus of the Counsels will not yet bring this to pass.

Perses, I beg you carefully to ponder these things in your heart and

hearken to Justice and think not at all of insolent might.

For this law is allotted to men by Zeus, son of Kronos:

fish and beasts of the wild and birds that fly in the air

eat one another, since Justice has no dwelling among them;

but to men he gives Justice, which is the greatest of blessings.

If one is willing to speak what he sees to be justice, what he knows is the right thing, far-seeing Zeus grants him a blessed life.

But if he witnesses falsely and willfully perjures himself,

being a liar, a harmer of Justice, incurably blind,

he is leaving his family a gloomier future existence.

He who swears truly creates for his family future prosperity.

3 Humanism

The Greeks conceived the humanist outlook, one of the pillars of Western civilization. They urged human beings to develop their physical, intellectual, and moral capacities to the fullest, to shape themselves according to the highest standards, and to make their lives as harmonious as a flawless work of art. Such an aspiration required intelligence and self-mastery.

Pindar
THE PURSUIT OF EXCELLENCE

The poet Pindar (c. 518–438 B.C.) expressed the Greek view of excellence in his praise for a victorious athlete. Life is essentially tragic—triumphs are short-lived, misfortunes are many, and ultimately death overtakes everyone; still, human beings must demonstrate their worth by striving for excellence.

He who wins of a sudden, some noble prize
In the rich years of youth
Is raised high with hope; his manhood takes wings;
He has in his heart what is better than wealth
But brief is the season of man's delight.

Soon it falls to the ground;
Some dire decision uproots it.
—Thing of a day! such is man: a shadow in a dream.
Yet when god-given splendour visits him
A bright radiance plays over him, and how sweet is life!

Sophocles
LAUDING HUMAN TALENTS

In a famous passage from his play *Antigone,* Sophocles (c. 496–406 B.C.) lauded human talents.

Numberless wonders
terrible wonders walk the world but none the match for
    man—
that great wonder crossing the heaving gray sea,
    driven on by the blasts of winter
on through breakers crashing left and right,
    holds his steady course
and the oldest of the gods he wears away—
the Earth, the immortal, the inexhaustible—
as his plows go back and forth, year in, year out
    with the breed of stallions turning up the furrows.

And the blithe, lightheaded race of birds he snares,
    . . . the tribes of savage beasts, the life that
    swarms the depths—
    with one fling of his nets
woven and coiled tight, he takes them all,
    man the skilled, the brilliant!
He conquers all, taming with his techniques
the prey that roams the cliffs and wild lairs,
training the stallion, clamping the yoke across
    his shaggy neck, and the tireless mountain bull.

And speech and thought, quick as the wind
and the mood and mind for law that rules the city—
    all these he has taught himself
and shelter from the arrows of the frost
when there's rough lodging under the cold clear sky
and the shafts of lashing rain—
    ready, resourceful man!
    Never without resources
never an impasse as he marches on the future—
only Death, from Death alone he will find no rescue
but from desperate plagues he has plotted his escapes.
Man the master, ingenious past all measure
past all dreams, the skills within his grasp—
    he forges on, now to destruction
now again to greatness. When he weaves in
the laws of the land, and the justice of the gods
that binds his oaths together
    he and his city rise high—
    but the city casts out
that man who weds himself to inhumanity
thanks to reckless daring. Never share my hearth
never think my thoughts, whoever does such things.

Thucydides
THE FUNERAL ORATION OF PERICLES

The central figure in Athenian political life for much of the period after the Persian Wars was Pericles (c. 495–429 B.C.), a gifted statesman and military commander. In the opening stage of the Peloponnesian War between Athens and Sparta (431–404 B.C.), Pericles delivered an oration in honor of the Athenian war dead. In this speech, as reconstructed by the historian Thucydides, Pericles brilliantly described Athenian greatness.

Pericles contrasted Sparta's narrow conception of excellence with the Athenian ideal of the self-sufficiency of the human spirit. The Spartans subordinated all personal goals and interests to the demands of the Spartan state. As such, Sparta—a totally militarized society—was as close as the ancient Greeks came to a modern totalitarian society. The Athenians, said Pericles, did not require grinding military discipline in order to fight bravely for their city. Their cultivation of the mind and love of beauty did not make them less courageous.

To be sure, Pericles' "Funeral Oration," intended to bolster the morale of a people locked in a brutal war, idealized Athenian society. Athenians did not always behave in accordance with Pericles' high principles. Nevertheless, as both Pericles and Thucydides knew, Athenian democracy and humanist outlook were extraordinary achievements.

"Let me say that our system of government does not copy the institutions of our neighbours. It is more the case of our being a model to others, than of our imitating anyone else. Our constitution is called a democracy because power is in the hands not of a minority but of the whole people. When it is a question of settling private disputes, everyone is equal before the law; when it is a question of putting one person before another in positions of public responsibility, what counts is not membership of a particular class, but the actual ability which the man possesses. No one, so long as he has it in him to be of service to the state, is kept in political obscurity because of poverty. And, just as our political life is free and open, so is our day-to-day life in our relations with each other. We do not get into a state with our next-door neighbour if he enjoys himself in his own way, nor do we give him the kind of black looks which, though they do no real harm, still do hurt people's feelings. We are free and tolerant in our private lives; but in public affairs we keep to the law. This is because it commands our deep respect.

"We give our obedience to those whom we put in positions of authority, and we obey the laws themselves, especially those which are for the protection of the oppressed, and those unwritten laws which it is an acknowledged shame to break.

"And here is another point. When our work is over, we are in a position to enjoy all kinds of recreation for our spirits. There are various kinds of contests [in poetry, drama, music, and athletics] and sacrifices regularly throughout the year; in our own homes we find a beauty and a good taste which delight us every day and which drive away our cares. Then the greatness of our city brings it about that all the good things from all over the world flow in to us, so that to us it seems just as natural to enjoy foreign goods as our own local products.

"Then there is a great difference between us and our opponents, in our attitude towards military security. Here are some examples: Our city is open to the world, and we have no periodical deportations in order to prevent people observing or finding out secrets which might be of military advantage to the enemy. This is because we rely, not on secret weapons, but on our own real courage and loyalty. There is a difference, too, in our educational systems. The Spartans, from their earliest boyhood, are submitted to the most laborious training in courage; we pass our lives without all these restrictions, and yet are just as ready to face the same dangers as they are. Here is a proof of this: When the Spartans invade our land, they do not come by themselves, but bring all their allies with them; whereas we, when we launch an attack abroad, do the job by ourselves, and, though fighting on foreign soil, do not often fail to defeat opponents who are fighting for their

own hearths and homes. As a matter of fact none of our enemies has ever yet been confronted with our total strength, because we have to divide our attention between our navy and the many missions on which our troops are sent on land. Yet, if our enemies engage a detachment of our forces and defeat it, they give themselves credit for having thrown back our entire army; or, if they lose, they claim that they were beaten by us in full strength. There are certain advantages, I think, in our way of meeting danger voluntarily, with an easy mind, instead of with a laborious training, with natural rather than with state-induced courage. We do not have to spend our time practising to meet sufferings which are still in the future; and when they are actually upon us we show ourselves just as brave as these others who are always in strict training. This is one point in which, I think, our city deserves to be admired. There are also others:

"Our love of what is beautiful does not lead to extravagance; our love of the things of the mind does not make us soft. We regard wealth as something to be properly used, rather than as something to boast about. As for poverty, no one need be ashamed to admit it: the real shame is in not taking practical measures to escape from it. Here each individual is interested not only in his own affairs but in the affairs of the state as well: even those who are mostly occupied with their own business are extremely well-informed on general politics—this is a peculiarity of ours: we do not say that a man who takes no interest in politics is a man who minds his own business; we say that he has no business here at all. We Athenians, in our own persons, take our decisions on policy or submit them to proper discussions: for we do not think that there is an incompatibility between words and deeds; the worst thing is to rush into action before the consequences have been properly debated. And this is another point where we differ from other people. We are capable at the same time of taking risks and of estimating them beforehand. Others are brave out of ignorance; and, when they stop to think, they begin to fear. But the man who can most truly be accounted brave is he who best knows the meaning of what is sweet in life and of what is terrible, and then goes out undeterred to meet what is to come.

"Again, in questions of general good feeling there is a great contrast between us and most other people. We make friends by doing good to others, not by receiving good from them. This makes our friendship all the more reliable, since we want to keep alive the gratitude of those who are in our debt by showing continued goodwill to them: whereas the feelings of one who owes us something lack the same enthusiasm, since he knows that, when he repays our kindness, it will be more like paying back a debt than giving something spontaneously. We are unique in this. When we do kindnesses to others, we do not do them out of any calculations of profit or loss: we do them without afterthought, relying on our free liberality. Taking everything together then, I declare that our city is an education to Greece, and I declare that in my opinion each single one of our citizens, in all the manifold aspects of life, is able to show himself the rightful lord and owner of his own person, and do this, moreover, with exceptional grace and exceptional versatility. And to show that this is no empty boasting for the present occasion, but real

tangible fact, you have only to consider the power which our city possesses and which has been won by those very qualities which I have mentioned. Athens, alone of the states we know, comes to her testing time in a greatness that surpasses what was imagined of her. In her case, and in her case alone, no invading enemy is ashamed at being defeated, and no subject can complain of being governed by people unfit for their responsibilities. Mighty indeed are the marks and monuments of our empire which we have left. Future ages will wonder at us, as the present age wonders at us now."

4 The Climax of Lyric Poetry in Greece

During the seventh century B.C., lyric poetry began to supplant epic poetry. Greek lyric poetry was intended to be sung to the musical accompaniment of a lyre, a stringed instrument. In fact the word *lyric* means "accompanied by the lyre." Lyric poetry was much more concerned with a poet's own opinions and inner emotions than with the great deeds of heroes as recounted in epic poetry.

Sappho

LOVE, PASSION, AND FRIENDSHIP

The greatest female lyric poet in antiquity was Sappho, who lived around 600 B.C. on the island of Lesbos. She was a member of the aristocracy and married a man named Cercylas, with whom she had one daughter, Cleïs. Unfortunately, only one complete poem, of twenty-eight lines, still remains; the rest of her poems exist only in fragments. Nonetheless, Sappho is credited with creating the metric stanza that bears her name—*Sapphic.* She established a "finishing" school to teach music and singing to well-to-do girls and to prepare them for marriage. With great tenderness, she wrote poems of friendship and love. Although some of her poems are about love between women and men, a number of verses are addressed to women, suggesting a homoerotic interest. The sensual and erotic nature of these poems indicates that Sappho was bisexual. Such a sexual behavior was, however, tolerated in ancient Greece, for it did not deprive a woman of her status as a virgin, because it was nonprocreative.

In this first fragment, Sappho likens her absent friend, Anactoria, to a defiant Helen of Troy, who willingly left Sparta to sail away to Troy with her lover Paris, son of the Trojan King Priam—in spite of Homer's claims to the contrary.

Some an army on horseback, some an army on foot
and some say a fleet of ships is the loveliest sight
on this dark earth; but I say it is whatever you desire:

and it is perfectly possible to make this clear
to all; for Helen, the woman who by far surpassed

all others in her beauty, left her husband—
the best of all men—

behind and sailed far away to Troy; she did not spare
a single thought for her child nor for her dear parents
but [the goddess of love] led her astray
[to desire . . .]

[. . . which]
reminds me now of Anactoria
although far away,

whose long-desired footstep, whose radiant, sparkling face
I would rather see before me than the chariots
of Lydia[1] or the armour of men
who fight wars on foot . . .

The following poetic fragments also deal with the power of love. In the first one, Sappho frankly addresses passion between women.

. . . frankly I wish that I were dead:
she was weeping as she took her leave from me

and many times she told me this:
"Oh what sadness we have suffered,
Sappho, for I'm leaving you against my will."
So I gave this answer to her:
"Go, be happy but remember
me there, for you know how we have cherished you,

if not, then I would remind you
[of the joy we have known,] of all
the loveliness that we have shared together;

for many wreaths of violets,
of roses and of crocuses
. . . you wove around yourself by my side

. . . and many twisted garlands
which you had woven from the blooms
of flowers, you placed around your slender neck

. . . and you were anointed with
a perfume, scented with blossom,
. . . although it was fit for a queen

and on a bed, soft and tender
. . . you satisfied your desire . . ."

In this fragment, Sappho admits that Aphrodite, the goddess of love, has left her powerless to resist desire.

Mother dear, I simply cannot weave my cloth;
                    I'm overpowered
by desire for a slender youth—and it's all
                    Aphrodite's fault

Sappho loved her daughter dearly and speaks of her love for Cleïs in the following fragment.

I have a child; so fair
As golden flowers is she,
My Cleïs, all my care.

I'd not give her away
For Lydia's wide sway
Nor lands men long to see.

A lost love is the subject of this fragment, as Aphrodite responds to Sappho's plea for assistance.

Immortal Aphrodite, on your patterned throne,
daughter of Zeus, guile-weaver,
I beg you, goddess, don't subjugate my heart
with anguish, with grief

but come here to me now, if ever in the past
you have heard my distant pleas
and listened; leaving your father's golden house
you came to me then

with your chariot yoked; beautiful swift sparrows
brought you around the dark earth
with a whirl of wings, beating fast, from heaven
down through the mid-air

to reach me quickly; then you, my sacred goddess,
your immortal face smiling,
asked me what had gone wrong this time and this time
why was I begging

and what in my demented heart, I wanted most:
'Who shall I persuade this time
to take you back, yet once again, to her love;
who wrongs you, Sappho?

For if she runs away, soon she shall run after,
if she shuns gifts, she shall give,
if she does not love you, soon she shall even
against her own will.'

So come to me now, free me from this aching pain,
fulfil everything that
my heart desires to be fulfilled: you, yes you,
will be my ally.

Greek society mandated that women should marry and bear children, thus surrendering their symbol of female honor—virginity. In this poem, Sappho recounts the trauma a woman experiences when she loses her virginity.

FIRST VOICE
Virginity O my virginity!
Where will you go when I lose you?

SECOND VOICE
I'm off to a place I shall never come back from
Dear Bride!
I shall never come back to you
Never!

---

[1]Lydia was an ancient kingdom in the western part of Asia Minor.

5 Classical Greek Tragedy

Tragedy (*tragoidia*), which literally means "goat song," is an art form that originated in Greece in the religious festivals honoring Dionysos, the god of wine and
agricultural fertility during the sixth century B.C. It developed fully during the
height of Greek civilization, the Classical Age, which lasted from about 480 B.C.
to the death of Alexander the Great in 323 B.C. During the Great Dionysia, celebrated in March in Athens, a group called a *chorus* danced and sang hymns in
honor of Dionysos. In about 535 B.C., the first actor, Thespis, stepped away from
the chorus and engaged it in dialogue. However, with only one actor and a chorus, the possibilities for dramatic action and human conflicts were limited. Consequently, Aeschylus (525–456 B.C.), who is often called the father of tragedy,
introduced a second actor in his dramas, and then Sophocles (496–406 B.C.) a
third. By the middle of the fifth century B.C., tragedies were performed regularly
at religious and civic festivals. The plots, generally drawn from mythology, often
concerned royal families. The subject matter concentrated on grand themes of
the human condition—the sufferings, weaknesses, and triumphs of individuals.

Through the technique of dialogue, early dramatists first pitted human beings against the gods and destiny. Like the natural philosophers, Greek dramatists saw an inner logic to the social universe and called it Fate or Destiny. When
people were stubborn, narrow-minded, arrogant, or immoderate, they were punished. In being free to make decisions, the dramatist says, individuals have the
potential for greatness, but in choosing wrongly, unintelligently, they bring disaster on themselves and others. Tragic heroes were not passive victims of fate.
They were thinking human beings who felt a need to comprehend their position, explain the reasons for their actions, and analyze their feelings. The essence
of Greek tragedy lies in the tragic heroes' struggle against cosmic forces and insurmountable obstacles, which eventually crush them.

There were three great writers of tragedy. Aeschylus wrote more than
ninety plays, only seven of which remain. Euripides (480–406 B.C.) wrote ninety-
two plays, of which nineteen survive. Sophocles, perhaps the greatest author of
tragedy, wrote more than 100 plays. Only seven have survived, including his
masterpiece, *Oedipus the King,* which is generally recognized as the greatest of all
Greek tragedies.

Sophocles
Oedipus the King

The major characters of the play are Oedipus, king of Thebes; Jokasta, queen of
Thebes, mother and wife of Oedipus; and Kreon, brother of Jokasta. The plot of
the play revolves around two prophecies made by the oracle at Delphi. The first
one is made to his parents, Jokasta and Laios, before Oedipus was born: it pre-
dicted that their son would grow up to kill his father. The second prophecy,
made to Oedipus himself as an adult, foretold that he would kill his father and
marry his mother. Oedipus, in his futile attempt to avoid this fate, ended up ful-
filling both prophecies.

The play begins with a plague decimating Thebes. Oedipus agrees to send

Kreon to consult the oracle at Delphi about how to gain relief from the plague. The oracle tells Kreon that the killer of Laios is alive and living in Thebes, and that he must be found and punished to end the plague. Oedipus vows to punish the killer, but the blind prophet Teiresias tells him that he, Oedipus, had unknowingly killed Laios; Oedipus accuses Kreon of plotting with Teiresias to steal the throne. When Oedipus informs Jokasta about the prophet's words, she assures him that it cannot be true, for long ago when another prophet had made the prediction that the son of Laios would grow up to kill his father, she and Laios had exposed their son to the elements when he was three days old to make sure that the prophet's words could not become true.

Events do not turn out, as Oedipus discovers, the way a person thinks and desires that they should: the individual is impotent before a relentless fate, which governs human existence. It seems beyond imagining that Oedipus, whom all envied for his intelligence, courage, and good works, would suffer such dreadful misfortune.

But tragedy also gives Oedipus the strength to assert his moral independence. Although struck down by fate, Oedipus remains an impressive figure. In choosing his own punishment, self-inflicted blindness, Oedipus demonstrates that he still possesses the distinctly human qualities of choosing and acting, that he still remains a free man responsible for his actions. Despite his misery, Oedipus is able to confront a brutal fate with courage and to demonstrate nobility of character.

Thebes. Open space outside the palace.
A group of CITIZENS *is waiting. Enter* OEDIPUS.

OEDIPUS
Thebans. My people. Children.
What is it? Garlands, branches,
Cries, prayers, incense on every altar—
What d'you want of me? I'm here,
In person: here, children, here,
Your father, your saviour, your Oedipus.
You, sir. Speak for them. What is it?
Why are they here? Are they afraid?
In need? I'll help them, do what I can.
To ignore such a gathering, I'd be made of stone.

PRIEST
Majesty. Oedipus. Ruler of Thebes.
We're at your feet. Old, young, fledglings.
Priests—I of Zeus. Young men: warriors.
Others kneel in the marketplace,
In Athene's temple, in the fire-shrine.
We're drowning, Majesty. Storm, blood, death.
We're choking. Crops, parched.
Animals, dead in the fields. Women, barren.
Plague howls through the city, scours us.
The Underworld grows fat on us.
We're here, lord, not praying, you're not a god,
Begging: your children, our father, you'll help us,
We trust you, the storm of fate,
We trust you. You helped us before:
When the Sphinx was here,
Gulping our blood, you came,

You rescued us. A man, a mortal,
No different from the rest of us,
You knew what to do;
With God's help, you saved us.
Majesty, we're on our knees.
Help us, find a way now.
Ask the gods, ask mortals, act.
Your city, lord, save it, save it.
You helped us before, made us glad before,
Don't leave us now. "He saved them once.
Then stood and watched them die"—
Don't let that be your story.
Don't rule a desert.
Your kingdom, Majesty, your people:
Steer us full sail, full cargo, not a ship of ghosts.

OEDIPUS
Dear children, little ones,
I knew you'd come. You're sick, in pain—
And none of you feels pain like mine,
Your king. You weep individual tears,
Each for yourself; I weep for all—
For you, for Thebes, for me.
I wasn't asleep: this isn't new to us.
For weeks we've wept,
Cudgelled our brains, thought what to do.
There was one way, only one. We did it.
His Honour, her Majesty's own brother—
We sent him to Delphi, Apollo's oracle,
To ask what I must do or say to save us.
He should be here. I'm surprised.
He's been away for days. I swear to you,

Whatever the advice he brings, God's word,
I'll do it. I'll obey it. I'll never flinch.

PRIEST
Your words give us hope.
And look: he's here. His Honour: here.

OEDIPUS
Apollo! He's smiling.
God grant good news.

PRIEST
A laurel-crown, full berried.
That means—

OEDIPUS
We'll ask him.

As KREON *enters.*

Your Honour. Brother-in-law. Good news?

KREON
None better. If we obey,
If we do as Apollo says, we're saved.

OEDIPUS
If, lord? There's doubt?
What *does* he say?

KREON
Shall I tell your Majesty inside,
In private, or here, where everyone—

OEDIPUS
Let everyone hear.
Their pain's my pain. Their burden's mine.

KREON
God's words, then, Majesty.
Apollo's words. There's cancer in the city.
Malignant. Diagnosed.
We must root it out, or die.

OEDIPUS
How root it out? What cancer?

KREON
Death. Majesty. A man's death.
We must find the killer, and banish him
Or give death for death.

OEDIPUS
Whose death?

KREON
Laios, Majesty. Before you came,
Our lord before you came.

OEDIPUS
We know the name. Never knew the man.

KREON
We must find his killers and punish them. God's words.

OEDIPUS
Where, find? It's years ago.

KREON
Here, Majesty.
"Look carefully, you'll find": Apollo's words.

OEDIPUS
This Laios—where was he killed?
In Thebes? In the fields? Away?

KREON
He visited the oracle, they say,
And never came back.

OEDIPUS
No witnesses? Fellow-travellers?

KREON
One, Majesty. The rest are dead.
A poor witness, terrified.
Only one small clue.

OEDIPUS
What clue?

KREON
A band of men, he said.
Outlaws. Many hands. That's all.

OEDIPUS
Outlaws. The King?
They wouldn't dare. Unless—
Hired killers? Was this a plot?

KREON
We didn't pursue it.
Laios was dead. We'd problems.

OEDIPUS
Your king was murdered
And you did nothing. What problems?

KREON
The Sphinx, Majesty.
More urgent than Laios.
The riddle of the Sphinx.

OEDIPUS
I'll settle this. I'll find the truth.
God's orders, Apollo's words, I'll do it.
For Thebes, for Apollo. I'll hunt this down.
I must. This touches us ourselves.
The old king dead—we could be next.
By helping Laios, we help ourselves

Up, children.
Your garlands, your branches.
You: fetch the people. I'll do it.
With God's help, win or lose, I'll do it.

Exit.

PRIEST
We have what we asked.
He's promised. Apollo, fulfil your words.
Come down to us. Save us. Heal us.

Music. Enter CHORUS.

CHORUS
Sweet voice of God,
From Apollo's golden shrine,
What word for Thebes?
I shake, I cry.
Ee-AY-ee-e, DAH-lee-e, pe-AHN!
What's happening?
New pain? Old agony reborn?
Speak, child of golden Hope,
Immortal, speak!
Come down to us,
Athene, child of Zeus;
Bright Artemis,
Come down to us.
Apollo, archer, yoh! Come down,
Help us, save us now.
In the whirlwind of fate, of death,
You rescued us before—
Come, save us now.

Disaster, pain.
What's left for us?
No life, no green,
Dead children.
Our loved ones slip from us,
Shadows, smoke,
Ghosts in the dark of death.

Countless they lie,
Our city lies.
Dead corpses, weep for them
Wives, mothers.
Cry to the gods, cry, cry,
Help us, help,
Sweet gods, come help us now.

No clash of swords,
No hiss of spears—
Death, silent, stealthy,
He's here, he's here!
What darkness spares
Bright daylight snatches.
Zeus, father, strike him,
End him, the lightning-flash.

Apollo, come.
Bow springing,
Arrows dancing, dancing.
Artemis,

Bacchos lord of Thebes,
Dance him down,
Bright torches bring
And dance him, dance him down.

Dance. Music ends. Enter OEDIPUS.

OEDIPUS
Your prayers are answered.
If you hear my words, hear and obey,
Your prayers are answered.
I know nothing of this murder. It's news to me.
I came to Thebes afterwards. How could I know?
But now, concerning Laios son of Labdakos,
I make this proclamation: if anyone knows
How he met his death, who murdered him—
That person must speak, tell all.
No need for fear: no punishment,
Safe conduct from the city.
Was it a stranger, a foreigner?
Tell me the name, you'll be rewarded.
But if you say nothing—
To protect yourself perhaps,
Or one of your friends—be warned.
No one in Thebes, in all my lands,
Will speak to you, or shelter you,
Give water, food, a place at God's altar
On pain of death. Banishment.
You caused this plague.
God speaks; I speak God's words.
Hear and obey.

As for the murderer—
One man or a member of a gang
I curse him. Misery, life no-life.
And if he's mine,
If all unknowing I harbour him at home,
May all I pray for him be done to me.

Your task: obey. For me, for God, for Thebes.
Our country, torn, abandoned, cries out for this.
That such a man should die—your king—
And you do nothing! God orders it: find them.
I give my word, your king. I hold his throne,
His power, his wife (the mother of my heirs,
His own being dead, himself being . . . gone)
I'll fight for him as they would, as if he were
My own dead father. Laios, son of Labdakos,
Descendant of Kadmos, Agenor, Polydoros,
I'll find your murderer. I'll make him pay.

Solemn words. Heed them, or suffer.
Those who turn away: parched crops,
Dead children, barrenness—
All they suffer now, and more.
Those who help, good people of Thebes,
May Justice and all the gods be with you now.

CHORUS
Majesty, your curse . . . I'll say what I can.
I didn't kill him. I've no idea who did.
Apollo ordered this. Perhaps the oracle—

OEDIPUS
If it chooses.
Who can force a god to speak?

CHORUS
Unless—

OEDIPUS
Say it.

CHORUS
Teiresias, Majesty.
God's voice on earth.
Perhaps he knows.

OEDIPUS
His Honour suggested that.
I sent for the man. Urgent messengers.
Twice. He's still not here.

CHORUS
There's nothing else.
Rumours . . . guesses.

OEDIPUS
What rumours? Even they might help.

CHORUS
Some said he was killed by passers-by.

OEDIPUS
Said, yes. No witnesses.

CHORUS
They'll come forward.
They'll hear your curse, and speak.

OEDIPUS
But not the murderer. He'll not fear words.

CHORUS
If anything's known, Teiresias knows it.
He's here, Majesty. They're bringing him:
God's voice, the voice of truth.
                    Enter TEIRESIAS, *led by a* SERVANT.

OEDIPUS
Teiresias,
You know every secret, on earth, in heaven.
You're blind, but you see, you understand.
Our city's tottering; only you can save it.
Apollo's words—those, too, you'll know:
We'll die unless we find who murdered Laios,
And punish them. Speak, Eminence.
What secrets have you heard,
From birds or other messengers?

Tell us. Save yourself, your city, me.
Put an end to it, the pollution
We suffer for Laios' death.
You have us in your hands.
No finer work for a mortal than helping others.
Speak, Eminence.

TEIRESIAS
Feoo, feoo.
What use is knowledge,
When it makes bad worse?
I should have remembered.
I should have stayed away.

OEDIPUS
What's the matter?

TEIRESIAS
Send me home, before it's too late
For you, for me. Don't make me speak.

OEDIPUS
You know, and refuse to tell? You must.
Your own city, Eminence: your Thebes.

TEIRESIAS
You've spoken, Majesty.
Words of ill-omen.
I won't add to them.

OEDIPUS
We're on our knees, Eminence.

TEIRESIAS
Don't ask me to speak. I won't.

OEDIPUS
So Thebes must die. Your fault.

TEIRESIAS
My pain if I speak. Your pain. I won't.

OEDIPUS
Coward! Traitor!
You'd infuriate a stone!
What kind of man are you?

TEIRESIAS
What kind of man are you, my lord?
Your fury.

OEDIPUS
You spurn your own city, and I'm not to feel fury?

TEIRESIAS
It's coming; it'll happen;
My speaking won't stop it.

OEDIPUS
So, tell me. What difference does it make?

TEIRESIAS
Rage all you like, I'm dumb.

OEDIPUS
You go too far with me. I'll say what I think.
I think your Eminence, *you* had a hand in this.
You planned it, you set it up,
You'd have killed him yourself,
If you'd not been blind.

TEIRESIAS
Is that what you think?
You made a decree just now. Obey it.
Not another word, to me, to them.
The plague-bringer, polluter of Thebes,
Is you.

OEDIPUS
You'll suffer for this.

TEIRESIAS
I speak what I know.

OEDIPUS
Who told you? Birds?

TEIRESIAS
You forced me to speak.

OEDIPUS
Again. Say it again.

TEIRESIAS
You want it clearer still?

OEDIPUS
I want no doubt.

TEIRESIAS
You're hunting a murderer.
You've found him. You.

OEDIPUS
You'll feel pain for this.

TEIRESIAS
More fury, Majesty? Shall I say still more?

OEDIPUS
Say what you like. You're raving.

TEIRESIAS
Intimacy, hideous intimacy with her you love.
You're floundering, Majesty, you're drowning—

OEDIPUS
And you, your Eminence: you're dead.

TEIRESIAS
The power of truth.

OEDIPUS
You're blind.

TEIRESIAS
You'll remember that word, Majesty.
You'll hear it again. Then you, too, will see.

OEDIPUS
Night's all you know. Darkness.
You can't hurt me, hurt those with eyes.

TEIRESIAS
God hurts, Majesty. Not prophets.

OEDIPUS
His Honour. He planned this.
This work is his.

TEIRESIAS
Your work, Majesty.
Your own unaided work.

OEDIPUS
Money! Power! Fame!
How hobbled you are
With other people's envy!
They gave it me, this power I hold,
Gave it me freely, unasked, my city—
And now his Honour plots to steal it.
I trusted him, and he bribes this conjurer
To spirit it away, whose skill is blind,
Whose purse alone has eyes. You, tell me:
Who says you see so clearly?
Where were you then,
When the riddling Sphinx entwined our Thebes?
Your birds, your heavenly voices,
Where were they then?
When they needed a prophet,
A professional, *I* solved it.
Oedipus. I answered the riddle.
I alone. Native wit.
No birds, no magic. Brains.
And now you try to topple me.
You want to make his Honour king—
And bask in him.
You'll end this pollution? The pair of you?
If I didn't think you senile,
I'd teach you sense.

CHORUS
Your Eminence, he spoke out of turn.
You too, Majesty, your temper.
We need coolness, not fury,
To do what God commands.

TEIRESIAS
King you may be. But still I'll answer.
Point by point. I demand it
I serve Apollo, I'm not your slave,
And I owe his Honour no favours.
You taunt me with blindness. But what of you?
Where are your eyes, Majesty?
You did what should not be done,
You live where you should not live,
You're married where you should not be married.

You're drowning, Majesty.
Don't you understand? You cancer them all,
Your flesh and blood, the dead, the living.
Your father, your mother:
Their curse will bring you darkness
Where now there's light,
Will send you hurtling from Thebes,
Headlong from Thebes.
Where will they end,
What hills won't echo them,
Your shrieks, howls,
When you know at last
What parentage brought you here,
What harbour of pain after such fair sailing?
Agonies crowding, crowding,
Yourself and your children,
All one, all one.
Shout how you like, accuse his Honour, me—
No human being on Earth will match your fall.

OEDIPUS
Be quiet! Crawl home! Get out!

TEIRESIAS
You sent for me.

OEDIPUS
I sent for a prophet, not a madman.

TEIRESIAS
They'd not call me mad, your parents.

OEDIPUS
Now what does that mean? My parents?

TEIRESIAS
Today you were born, and today you die.

OEDIPUS
Another riddle.

TEIRESIAS
You boast you're good at them.

OEDIPUS
I earned this throne by them.

TEIRESIAS
And now you'll earn this pain.

OEDIPUS
I saved this city. You call that pain?

TEIRESIAS
I've no more to say. Boy, take me home.

OEDIPUS
Yes, take him. He scalds our ears.
Take him; dump him; make us clean of him.

TEIRESIAS
I'm not afraid. I'm safe from you.
I'll say it again, what I came to say.

The murderer, the man you're hunting
With all these oaths and threats,
The killer of Laios, is here in Thebes.
He thinks he's a foreigner. He's not.
He's a Theban, a native, and doesn't know.
He's drowning. He sees, and he'll be blind.
He's rich, he'll be poor. A proud man, a beggar.
He'll tap his way with a blind man's stick
In a foreign country. His children with him.
His sons his brothers,
His daughters his sisters,
His wife his mother,
His father his victim.
You asked for riddles. Solve these—
And then, if you can, say my prophecies are lies.

Exit. Exit OEDIPUS. *Music.*

CHORUS
God's word in sacred cave
Denounces him, criminal,
Crime of crimes, blood-hands,
Unspeakable. Who? Who?
Run, escape,
Galloping, galloping.
God's son pelts after him
In thunder, with lightning;
The Furies, untiring, hunt him down.

White snow on mountain peak—
A beacon, God's orders:
Track him down. Where? Where?
Bull, wild-eyed,
Snorting, high hills, forests,
Earth's deeps, far underground,
Cowering from heaven's eye
That hunts him, unsleeping, hunts him down.

Words of fear, fear them,
The prophet spoke:
How can we trust him?
We must, we must.
Hearts pound. We're blind.
Unheard-of—a quarrel? When?
Our Oedipus came from Corinth,
Rules Thebes, our Thebes.
We honour him. What does it mean?
Zeus knows, Apollo:
They understand.
Teiresias is mortal—
How can he know?
Proof, wait for proof,
Then believe it. The Sphinx,
When the Sphinx was here,
I saw it, he answered,
He knew. I won't condemn him now.

Music ends. Enter KREON.

KREON
People of Thebes, they say his Majesty
Is accusing me. I'm here, I'll answer.
If he thinks, as things now are in Thebes,
I've undermined him with words, or deeds,
If he offers proof, I'd rather die than live.
To be branded traitor—by his Majesty, by you,
By my own dear citizens! I'd rather die.

CHORUS
Wait, your Honour. Wait and see.
He was hot with fury.

KREON
I bribed that prophet to lie to him?
Is that what he said? And did he say why?

CHORUS
Your Honour, he gave no reasons.

KREON
But he meant it? He was . . . in control?

CHORUS
Your Honour: his Majesty. Ours not to question.
He's coming. Now.

Enter OEDIPUS.

OEDIPUS
You! Impudence!
You plot to kill me, steal
My throne from under me—and *visit* me?
Zeus above! D'you think I'm a fool?
Afraid? Did you think I wouldn't notice?
You dig a pit for me,
Under my nose, and think I'll fall?
That's not how kings are toppled, fool.
You need brains, money, accomplices,
To catch a king.

KREON
That's enough. Majesty.
You've made your charges.
Listen, now.
My turn to speak, to answer.

OEDIPUS
Speak, answer. You're good at that.
But I'm not good at listening—to traitors.

KREON
I said, listen.

OEDIPUS
I said, traitor.

KREON
You think no one's right but you,
No one else deserves hearing. You're mad.

OEDIPUS
You think you can undermine your king
And escape with your life. You're mad.

KREON
If that was true, I'd agree with you.
But what is it you say I've done?

OEDIPUS
You advised me, did you or didn't you,
To send for that . . . astrologer?

KREON
I'd do the same again.

OEDIPUS
How long ago did Laios . . . ?

KREON
What?

OEDIPUS
Meet his end?

KREON
Years ago.

OEDIPUS
And was that bird-interpreter in business then?

KREON
Highly respected, just as now.

OEDIPUS
So. *That* was when he mentioned me.

KREON
I never heard him.

OEDIPUS
This murder: you did enquire?

KREON
Of course we enquired.

OEDIPUS
So why did our learned friend say nothing?

KREON
I don't know. I can't explain.

OEDIPUS
You can. You know exactly.

KREON
What d'you mean?

OEDIPUS
He plotted this with you: to make this charge.

KREON
Is that what he says? Now, Majesty, *you* answer.

OEDIPUS
Your Honour, certainly. I didn't kill the king.

KREON
You married my sister?

OEDIPUS
Of course I did.

KREON
You share royal power with her?

OEDIPUS
Whatever she asks, is hers.

KREON
And I share that power, third among equals?

OEDIPUS
And first among traitors.

KREON
You don't know what you're saying.
I want to be king, you say? I want to exchange
A quiet life, easy sleep at night, royal rank,
For the panic and turbulence of being king?
Now, thanks to you, I've all I need.
His Honour, revered, respected, safe—
They smile to see me, they shake my hand,
If they want your favour, they come to me,
I bestow your bounty. All that you say I'd give
For a crown, for the hedged-in life of being a king?
A traitor? Ambitious? I'd not be such a fool.

It's easily proved.
Apollo, Delphi: go there, ask him.
Was the oracle I brought the one he gave me?
And as for Teiresias, that "astrologer"—
If you find any plot between his Eminence and me,
Kill me. Put me to death. I'll guide your hand.
But not on blind suspicion, Majesty. To know
Our friends is as vital as knowing our enemies.
When we drive out friends, we shrink our lives,
our own dear lives. To know an enemy,
One day's enough; to know a friend takes time.

CHORUS
Fair words, Majesty. Take time to ponder—

OEDIPUS
He's poised to strike, and you say take time?

KREON
You want me out of Thebes?

OEDIPUS
I want you dead.

KREON
For nothing?

OEDIPUS
For ambition.

KREON
You're mad.

OEDIPUS
For justice.

KREON
Except for me.

OEDIPUS
A traitor.

KREON
You've heard nothing.

OEDIPUS
I've heard enough.

KREON
Dictator.

OEDIPUS
Thebes is mine.

KREON
Yours alone? Not mine?

CHORUS
Lords. Someone's coming.
Her Majesty, Jokasta.
Let her help you. Settle this.

Enter JOKASTA.

JOKASTA
Fools!
The city's dying.
Aren't you ashamed?
Brawling like children.
Majesty, go in. Your Honour, home.
Have done with it.

KREON
Sister.
His Majesty, your husband,
Is trying to make up his royal mind:
Is he to banish me, or kill me?

OEDIPUS
Exactly.
His Honour, your brother
The schemer, the traitor. Trapped.

KREON
If this is true, if any of it's true,
Kill me. As God's my witness, kill me.

JOKASTA
Hear what he says, my lord.
For your sake, mine, the city's sake.

Music.

CHORUS
In God's name. Majesty—

OEDIPUS
What?

CHORUS
Respect his oath.
He called God's name.

OEDIPUS
You know what you ask?

CHORUS
I know what I ask.

OEDIPUS
Ask again.

CHORUS
An innocent man, a friend,
He swore in God's name.
Spare him.

OEDIPUS
And condemn myself?
To death? To exile?

CHORUS
No, Majesty.
By the Sun who sees all, knows all,
I don't mean that.
Our city's dying, tormented—
And now our princes quarrel, pain on pain.

Music ends.

OEDIPUS
So, spare him. And if I die of it,
If I'm driven out of the land I love,
On your head be it. Because you ask,
I do it. Not for him. Oh, not for him.

KREON
So merciful, so gracious!
You'll regret this. When your fury cools,
You'll regret it. You scald yourself.

OEDIPUS
In God's name, get out!

KREON
As you wish. They know I'm innocent.

Exit. Music.

CHORUS
Lady, go in.
Take his Majesty. Go in.

JOKASTA
First tell me what's happened.

CHORUS
Suspicion . . . accusation . . . unjust.

JOKASTA
From both?

CHORUS
From both.

JOKASTA
What words?

CHORUS
Lady, they're said.
As things now are,
They're best forgotten.

OEDIPUS
So old you are, so wise—
And all you do is blunt me.

CHORUS
Majesty, again I say it:
Fools only, madmen,
Would try to drag you down.
We were sinking before; you saved us,
You set us on course, you brought us home.
Now a second storm: we need you, need you.

Music ends.

JOKASTA
Husband,
Tell me. What is it?
This fury—why?

OEDIPUS
Wife,
I'll tell you.
His Honour's accusation.

JOKASTA
What accusation, to cause such rage?

OEDIPUS
Laios' murder. His Honour accuses me.

JOKASTA
There's evidence?

OEDIPUS
He spoke with another's mouth. A prophet.

JOKASTA
A prophet!
Husband, listen to me.
No human being on Earth
Need fear what prophets say.
I'll prove it.
A prophet came to Laios—
Not God, a prophet only—
And told him that one day his son,

His son and mine, would kill him.
But Laios was killed,
The whole world knows,
By strangers, at a crossroads,
Where three roads meet.
His son was exposed to die, at three days old:
We pegged his ankles and left him to die
Where no one ever went.
The prophecy was wrong.
The son never killed the father.
The father was not killed
By his own son's hand.
Ignore what prophets say!
What God wants us to know,
In his own good time, he'll tell us.

OEDIPUS
Wife.
What you said. I'm frightened.

JOKASTA
Husband.
What is it?

OEDIPUS
Where three roads meet, you said.
Laios was killed at a crossroads,
Where three roads meet.

JOKASTA
They said so at the time.
They'll say so still.

OEDIPUS
Where?
This crossroads, where?

JOKASTA
In Phokis.
Where the road from Daulia joins
The road from Delphi—

OEDIPUS
When?
When was he killed?

JOKASTA
A day or two before you came to Thebes.

OEDIPUS
O Zeus!
What will you do to me?

JOKASTA
Oedipus, what is it?

OEDIPUS
Laios. Tell me.
What did he look like?

JOKASTA
Tall. Greying hair. Like you.

OEDIPUS
Oee moee.
Myself. I cursed myself.

JOKASTA
What is it?
Husband. I'm frightened.

OEDIPUS
Not blind, the prophet.
He saw, he saw.
One more thing. Answer.

JOKASTA
If I can, I will.

OEDIPUS
Was he alone?
Or was there a bodyguard,
A royal bodyguard?

JOKASTA
Five men. One officer. The royal carriage.

OEDIPUS
Aee aee.
I knew it. Jokasta, who told you?
Who brought back news?

JOKASTA
The man who escaped. The only one.

OEDIPUS
He's here? Still in palace service?

JOKASTA
When he found you here,
On his master's throne,
He begged me on his knees
To send him away,
Up-country, mountain pastures,
As far as possible.
A good man, loyal—I did as he asked.

OEDIPUS
Can they find him?
Find him and bring him?

JOKASTA
Of course. But husband, why?

OEDIPUS
Jokasta,
I said . . . what I should not have said.
Too much. I have to see this man.

JOKASTA
They'll fetch him.
But what's the matter?

Husband. Majesty.
Who else should you tell but me?

OEDIPUS
As you say.
If what I fear is true,
Who else should I tell but you?
Listen, then.
My father was Polybos of Corinth,
My mother Merope.
I was high-born, well-regarded.
One day . . . a strange thing . . . nothing . . .
A drunk at dinner said I wasn't my father's son.
I was angry, but did nothing then.
Next day I asked them,
My father and mother. They dismissed it.
A drunken insult, no more. I believed them.
But it lay there, the accusation.
Nagged my mind. In the end,
Without a word to my parents,
I left for Delphi, consulted the oracle.
The god made no straight answer,
Told me instead a prophecy beyond belief . . .
I was to murder my father,
Mate with my mother
And sire a brood that would sicken all who saw it.

I never went home.
Between me and Corinth,
I put the stars.
To prevent the oracle, the foulness.
I wandered . . . anywhere.
I came to the place
Where that king of yours, you say,
Was killed. Listen, Jokasta.
I'll tell you exactly what happened.
There was a crossroads. Three roads.
Servants, an outrider, a carriage.
Exactly as you describe.
They ordered me out of the way.
The lord, the officer. The coachman jostled me.
I lost my temper, hit him—
And the lord in the carriage
Lashed out at me, whip in the face.
I dragged him out, killed him.
Left him lying, and dealt with the rest of them.
If that was Laios, if that old man was Laios,
There's no one on Earth more cursed than I.
They must turn me away, no words, no shelter,
The whole of Thebes. My own decree. I killed,
And I sleep in the bed of the man I killed.
God's curse is mine. I cancer all I touch.
Exile. How can I go home, to Corinth,
To kill my father Polybos and mate with Merope
My mother? God's curse. Fate treads me down.

Zeus, light of day, let me not live to see it.
Let me slip away, vanish, wiped from the earth,
And never see that day, that cancer.

CHORUS
Wait, Majesty.
Wait till you hear the witness.

OEDIPUS
The shepherd. My only hope.

JOKASTA
How, hope, my lord?

OEDIPUS
His story. If what he says
Is the same as yours. I'm safe.

JOKASTA
What was it I said?

OEDIPUS
A gang. Passers-by.
Not one man, many.
If he says "men", I'm safe. If not . . .

JOKASTA
He'll not change what he said.
He can't. I heard him, all Thebes heard him.
In any case, Majesty, even if Lord Laios
Was killed by a single man,
The prophecy still was wrong.
"His own son will kill him",
Apollo said. Laios' son, my son—
The baby we left to die.
Prophets, Majesty!
Don't give them the time of day!

OEDIPUS
I hear you.
But still, the shepherd,
Send someone to fetch the shepherd.

JOKASTA
As your Majesty pleases.
Now, husband, come inside.

Exeunt. Music.

CHORUS
God give us reverence,
In word and deed.
There are laws, enthroned,
High in Olympos,
God's laws, born of no mortal,
Unaging, eternal.

Pride breeds the tyrant.
Bloated, distended,
Climbing the high peaks,
Then falling, falling.

No cure. God send us honour,
For Thebes, protect us.

Those who march in pride,
Who fear no justice,
Laugh at gods—
Greed rules them,
Dishonour—
God's arrows, how will they dodge them?
And if they do, if they slip free of fate,
What use are these prayers, these dances?

If oracles lie
Why should we fear them?
Not Delphi,
Shrine of shrines,
Olympia—
Zeus, god of gods, do you hear us?
Your power, Apollo's ancient power, denied.
The age of the gods is over.

Music ends. Enter JOKASTA, with offerings.

JOKASTA
My lords, these garlands, these offerings:
We go to pray. His Majesty's mind
Is distracted, ragged with terror:
His judgement's gone, he ignores what's past.
Refuses to listen to common sense.
Hears only what feeds his fear.
Apollo, lord, come down,
Be near. Accept these offerings,
Give us peace, calm our fear,
Our helmsman's distracted,
Oh help us, lord.

Enter CORINTHIAN.

CORINTHIAN
Friends.
I'm a stranger here.
His Majesty's palace?
Please tell me.
Or better than that,
Lord Oedipus himself.

CHORUS
It's here. He's here, inside.
And this is her Majesty, the queen.

CORINTHIAN
Lady, all happiness,
Yours and his Majesty's, forever.

JOKASTA
We return your greeting.
You bring us news?

CORINTHIAN
I bring his Majesty good news.

JOKASTA
Where from, sir?

CORINTHIAN
Corinth. Joy mixed with tears.

JOKASTA
Explain.

CORINTHIAN
Your husband, Lord Oedipus:
They want to make him king.

JOKASTA
In Corinth? But Polybos—

CORINTHIAN
Dead, lady. He lies in his grave.

JOKASTA
Oedipus' father, dead?

CORINTHIAN
As I stand before you.

JOKASTA
Slave, fetch his Majesty. Now.
Oracles, prophecies, where are you now?
This king my lord shunned all these years,
For fear of killing him—he's dead. By Fate,
Not by his Majesty's hand at all, by Fate.

Enter OEDIPUS.

OEDIPUS
I grant your request, Jokasta.
As you ask, I'm here. What is it?

JOKASTA
Hear this man,
And then see what you think of oracles.

OEDIPUS
Who is he?

JOKASTA
He's from Corinth. Your father,
Lord Polybos, his Majesty—is dead.

OEDIPUS
Sir, is this true?

CORINTHIAN.
True, Majesty. Lord Polybos is dead.

OEDIPUS
Assassination? Sickness?

CORINTHIAN
It doesn't take much to end an old man's life.

OEDIPUS
Sickness, then.

CORINTHIAN
Old age, my lord.

OEDIPUS
Feoo, feoo.
Jokasta, so much for birds and omens.
I was to kill my father. They said so.
And now he's dead, buried,
And I was here all the time,
My sword undrawn—unless
My absence killed him, makes me a murderer.
All those oracles, they're dead,
He's bundled them up
And taken them to Hades. Worthless.

JOKASTA
I said exactly so.

OEDIPUS
Fear blocked my ears.

JOKASTA
There's nothing left to fear.

OEDIPUS
My mother . . . mating with my mother . . .

JOKASTA
You're still afraid of that?
Fate rules our lives, not prophecy.
Live each day as it comes.
You're afraid of mating with your mother
As thousands of men have done before you,
But in their dreams. Put it out of your mind,
Be easy.

OEDIPUS
Yes, if she'd died,
The mother who bore me.
But so long as she lives,
Whatever you say, I'll be afraid.

JOKASTA
Your father's dead.

OEDIPUS
It's her I fear.

CORINTHIAN
Excuse me, Majesty. Who is it you fear?

OEDIPUS
Merope, sir, the queen.

CORINTHIAN
Why, lord?

OEDIPUS
A fearful oracle.

CORINTHIAN
Can you tell a stranger?

OEDIPUS
"You'll kill your father
And mate with your mother"—
Apollo's words. Ever since
I heard them, I've kept from Corinth.
Years. I've kept from my parents;
I've prospered.

CORINTHIAN
That fear kept you away?

OEDIPUS
That and killing my father.

CORINTHIAN
Majesty,
If I ended these fears forever . . . ?

OEDIPUS
Undying gratitude.

CORINTHIAN
It was for that I came—
And to bring you home, my lord.

OEDIPUS
I won't go back to them, my parents.

CORINTHIAN
You still don't understand.

OEDIPUS
In God's name, tell me.

CORINTHIAN
You're afraid of *them?*

OEDIPUS
Because of the oracle.

CORINTHIAN
Afraid of double guilt?

OEDIPUS
The stain of it.

CORINTHIAN
Be easy, then.
Lord Polybos was no relation.

OEDIPUS
Not my father?

CORINTHIAN
No more than I am.

OEDIPUS
You? How?

CORINTHIAN
Neither of us.

OEDIPUS
I was his son.

CORINTHIAN
You were a gift to him. From me.

OEDIPUS
He loved me.

CORINTHIAN
Before you came, he was childless.

OEDIPUS
A "gift." You . . . gave me.
Did you buy me, or find me?

CORINTHIAN
I found you.
In the woods. On Mount Kithairon.

OEDIPUS
You were travelling there?

CORINTHIAN
Tending sheep, my lord.

OEDIPUS
A shepherd.

CORINTHIAN
—who rescued you.

OEDIPUS
From what?
What was wrong with me?

CORINTHIAN
Your ankles, Majesty—

OEDIPUS
They've been weak from birth.

CORINTHIAN
They were pinned together. I freed them.

OEDIPUS
I still have the scars.

CORINTHIAN
You were named for them, Majesty.
Oedipus: Swell-foot.

OEDIPUS
Who pinned them?
My father, my mother?

CORINTHIAN
The other man, perhaps.

OEDIPUS
What other man?

CORINTHIAN
The one who found you, gave you to me.

OEDIPUS
Who was it?

CORINTHIAN
He came from Thebes, he said.
One of Laios' men.

OEDIPUS
Laios!

CORINTHIAN
This man managed the royal flocks.

OEDIPUS
Can I speak to him? Is he still alive?

CORINTHIAN
Your people know that, not I.

OEDIPUS
You, sir. You . . . you.
Do any of you know
The man he means, the shepherd?
Is he here, still working?
This whole thing hangs on him.

CHORUS
Majesty, you sent for him just now.
It's the same man.
Her Majesty will tell you.
She knew him.

OEDIPUS
Jokasta?
This *is* the same man?

JOKASTA
Don't ask.
It's gossip. Not important.
Leave it.

OEDIPUS
It could tell me who I am.

JOKASTA
In God's name, stop.
For your own sake, stop now.
You'll kill us both.

OEDIPUS
She may have been a slave, my mother—
But why should that touch you?

JOKASTA
Majesty, on my knees, I beg you—

OEDIPUS
I'll know who I am.

JOKASTA
For your own sake, husband—

OEDIPUS
That's enough.

JOKASTA
Don't ask whose son you are.

OEDIPUS
Someone bring that shepherd.
Let her go in and enjoy her snobbery.

JOKASTA
Eeoo, eeoo,
THEES-teen-e
No more words.
No more. No more.

Exit

CHORUS
She's gone, Oedipus
Her Majesty. Storms of grief.
Silence. What's happening?

OEDIPUS
Storms, silence, I'll know who I am.
She's highborn, ashamed of me, a slave.
But I call myself Fate's child.
The son of Fate
Who gives all good to mortals.
I'm not ashamed.
My sisters are the seasons,
My life in step with theirs.
I am what I am,
And I will know what I am.

Music.

CHORUS
If I'm a prophet,
See what's to come,
Skilled in the ways of God,
Tomorrow Kithairon will fill our song.
Lord Oedipus is no one's son but yours:
You're his father, mother, nurse,
We'll dance for you, dance
Who gave us our our king.
Apollo ee-EH-i-e, hear us.

Who was your mother?
A mountain-nymph,
Immortal bride of Pan
Who walks the hills? Apollo loves our fields,
Our meadowland—was it he who fathered you?
Was it Hermes, who rules Kisthene,
Did Dionysos welcome you
From your mother's arms,
A nymph who dances on the hills?
            Dance. Music ends. Enter SHEPHERD, guarded.

OEDIPUS
My lords,
I never saw the shepherd,
The man we sent for.
But this must be him. He's old;
My guards are bringing him.
You've seen him before.
Look, and say: is this the man?

CHORUS
One of Laios' most trusted slaves.

OEDIPUS
You: Corinthian.
Is this the same man?

CORINTHIAN
Yes, Majesty.

OEDIPUS
Old man, come here.
Answer directly.
Were you once Laios' slave?

SHEPHERD
Yes, Majesty.
Born in the palace.

OEDIPUS
What were your duties?

SHEPHERD
I was a shepherd, Majesty.

OEDIPUS
On the plain, or far away?

SHEPHERD
Kithairon, sometimes.
Other places.

OEDIPUS
And this man here—

SHEPHERD
What man, Majesty?

OEDIPUS
D'you recognise him?

SHEPHERD
I . . . can't remember.

CORINTHIAN
It's hardly surprising, Majesty.
I'll remind him. Three summers
We spent together on Kithairon.
He had two flocks of sheep, I had one.
When winter came, we separated:
I drove my animals back to Corinth.
He brought his home, here,
To Laios' folds. Is this not true?

SHEPHERD
Years ago. I think so.

CORINTHIAN
And d'you remember the child,
The child you gave me,
To bring up as my own?

SHEPHERD
What child?
What d'you mean?

CORINTHIAN
He's grown up now.
This man: his Majesty.

SHEPHERD
You're lying.
Go to Hell. You're lying.

OEDIPUS
Control yourself.
You're lying.

SHEPHERD
Master, my dear, I'm not.

OEDIPUS
You deny what he says about the child?

SHEPHERD
It's nonsense.

OEDIPUS
Tell the truth, willingly, or—

SHEPHERD
Majesty

OEDIPUS
Take him.

SHEPHERD
Majesty, I'll tell you.

OEDIPUS
You gave him the child he speaks of?

SHEPHERD
Yes, Majesty.
I should have hanged myself.

OEDIPUS
Tell the truth, or you'll still be hanged.

SHEPHERD
Majesty,
If I tell what I know, I'm dead.

OEDIPUS
Take him away.

SHEPHERD
No, Majesty.
I told you: I gave him the child.

OEDIPUS
Where did you get it?
Was it your own? Someone else's?

SHEPHERD
Someone else's.

OEDIPUS
Whose?
Tell me.

SHEPHERD
Majesty, don't ask me.

OEDIPUS
Tell me. Whose child was it?

SHEPHERD
They say it was a child . . . of Laios' house.

OEDIPUS
A slave's? Someone else's? Answer!

SHEPHERD
Majesty, I daren't.

OEDIPUS
You must.

SHEPHERD
If I speak, I'll die.

OEDIPUS
And I if I hear. But hear I must.

SHEPHERD
They said it was . . .
His own son. His Majesty's son.
She'll tell you, her Majesty, inside.
She'll tell you.

OEDIPUS
She gave you the child?

SHEPHERD
Yes, Majesty.

OEDIPUS
With what orders?

SHEPHERD
Majesty, to kill.

OEDIPUS
His own mother?

SHEPHERD
There was an oracle.

OEDIPUS
Oracle?

SHEPHERD
That he would kill his parents.

OEDIPUS
You gave him to this old man?

SHEPHERD
I pitied him, Majesty.
I thought,
"I'll send him away, far away."
This man took him, saved him—
Doomed him.
If you're who he says you are,
Majesty, you're doomed.

OEDIPUS
Eeoo, eeoo.
Now I see, I know.
Born where I should not have been born,
Killing where I should not have killed,
Mating where I should not have mated:
Now at last, I see.

Exeunt all but CHORUS. Music.

CHORUS
Who lays true claim to happiness?
In the grey dawn we wake, we know
How all our joy was smoke, was dream.
Look now at Oedipus, at mortal fate.

How proud he stood, how high! He broke
The subtle Sphinx, he was a tower,
A lighthouse, in the agony of Thebes:
He was Majesty, master, lord of lords.

He strode the peaks, he fell.
Disaster, pain,
His mother's husband,
His children's brother—
Hidden, hidden in the dark.

Time found him out. Time saw.
Time brought him down.
Weep for his honour lost.
Who dazzled us, destroyed us.
The Majesty of Thebes.

Music ends. Enter SERVANT.

SERVANT
Lords, great ones,
It's happened, such things, such foulness,
The palace, inside, it's happened.
Rivers, washing, foulness,
It's there, it's there. They're hiding.
They're coming, we'll see them.
We'll shut our eyes, we'll see them
They did it.
They hurt themselves,
They did it, they did it.

CHORUS
We know what we know.
What could be worse than that?

SERVANT
I'll tell you. Tell you.
Her Majesty, Jokasta, her Majesty,
Is dead.

CHORUS
Poor lady. How?

SERVANT
Her own hand.
She did it. You haven't seen,
Don't know . . . I'll tell it,
Her agony, every detail.
She ran like a wild woman.
Hooks of hands, tearing at her hair.
Across the courtyard. Inside.
She barred the door.
She screamed at Laios.
His Majesty long dead.
His child, his son
Who was to kill the father
And mate with the mother,
Man-child, child-man, brother-father . . .
Silence.
Nothing else.
She died.
We didn't see.
His Majesty burst in, our eyes were on him,
Watching him, we didn't see her die.
He was shouting, running, room after room.
"A sword! Where is she?"
Wife no-wife. Mother-mistress.
Seedbed."
None of us moved.
Some god showed him the way.
He was howling, a hunting dog.
He smashed down the door,
Burst the bolt from the socket—
And there she was, dangling,
A pendulum.
He bellowed like a bull.
Unfastened her, laid her on the ground.
Then . . . There were pins,
Gold pins, fastening her dress.
He snatched them, stabbed his eyes,
Shouting "See nothing now. Not see
What I did, what they do to me,
Not see, not see.
Darkness. See dead. Not living see."
Each word, he stabbed and stabbed.
Blood spurted, poured,
White cheeks, black beard, red matted, red.
That's how it is with them:

His Majesty, her Majesty.
How blessed they were, how happy—
Now death, tears, pain, all's theirs.

CHORUS
Where is he now?

SERVANT
Inside. Shouting.
"Open the door. Show them.
The people, show them.
His father's murderer.
His mother's—I won't say it.
Banish me, drive me away,
My judgement, the curse I spoke.
I'll not stay here."
His strength has gone.
He's blind. Crushed.
They're opening the doors.
See for yourself.
A sight to turn all loathing into tears.

Music. OEDIPUS *is revealed.*

CHORUS
All human pain is here.
Why, lord, why? Such madness,
Such pouncing on disaster.
Which god bears down on you?
Feoo, feoo.
I can't bear it. Can't bear to look.
So much to ask, to say to you
And I shudder, I turn away.

OEDIPUS
Aee aee. Aee aee.
Feoo feoo.
THEEStanoss eYOH.
Where now? Where go now?
I hear my own voice, fading.
God, where are you taking me?

CHORUS
To a place
None may speak of, none may see.

OEDIPUS
Yoh.
Darkness.
It billows,
If fills, it chokes.
Oee moee.
Stabbing, pins,
Pain,
What I did to them.

CHORUS
Pain on pain, your agony,
The torment of those you loved.

OEDIPUS
Yoh.
You're here,
My friend, still my friend.
Feoo feoo.
Stayed by me.
It's dark.
I recognise your voice.

CHORUS
How could you bear it?
Your eyes, your own eyes?
What god was this?

OEDIPUS
Apollo's words, his oracle,
My hands, no one else, these hands.
Why should I see?
Ugliness. I need no eyes.

CHORUS
It's as you say.

OEDIPUS
What have I left to see,
To hear, to love?
Take me away. Please,
Take me, I'm dead,
God's cursed me, dead.

CHORUS
What you did,
What's happened here—
Why did you solve this riddle?

OEDIPUS
Damn him, damn him who found me,
Unpinned my ankles, saved me.
I should have died then, not lived
To savage those I love.

CHORUS
What you say is true.

OEDIPUS
No father-killer then,
Mother-husband.
God's enemy, their son,
The cursed ones,
Their brother, my children.
Evil outrunning evil.
All foulness, its name is Oedipus.

Music ends.

CHORUS
Even so, Majesty—
To blind yourself! Does any crime
Deserve such punishment?

OEDIPUS
Enough!
Enough wise counsel!
What I did was right.
Was I to use these eyes to look on him,
There in the Underworld, the father I killed,
Or on her, my mother? For what I did to them
I should be ripped apart.
My children, was I to smile at them,
Sown where I sowed them? What eyes have I
For Thebes, my Thebes, its towers, its temples?
Its king! I tore myself from Thebes:
I cursed myself, decreed my own exile,
Unclean, unclean,
Laios' son who fouled the gods.
Eyes, ears—
I should dam up my ears,
Seal myself, silence, darkness.
No more hurting.
Why, Kithairon, yoh?
Why shelter me, not kill me,
Why let me come to Thebes?
Corinth, Polybos I called my father,
Why didn't you see, destroy,
The festering soul, your princeling?
Crossroads, three roads,
A stand of trees, you drank his blood,
My father's blood, my own heart's blood,
I poured it,
You drank and drank, remember?
I came to Thebes, I married.
Married! Seed, blood-seeding seed,
The father, mother, wife,
The husband-son,
The children-brothers-sisters,
All one, all evil.
I did it, won't speak of it.
Foulness. In the name of God,
Hide me, kill me, drown me,
The sea, all gone, away.
Over here.
Touch me. It's all right.
You're frightened. Don't be.
My sin, *my* guilt, it's not contagious.

> *Enter* KREON, *with* SERVANTS *bringing
> two small children,* ANTIGONE *and* ISMENE.

CHORUS
His Honour's here.
He'll hear your prayers, decide what to do.
His Honour: as things now are,
He holds all power in Thebes.

OEDIPUS
Oee moee.
How can I ask him?

After all I did, I said,
What can I say to him?

KREON
Oedipus, I won't laugh at you,
Throw back in your face
What you said before.
You men: respect your fellow-citizens,
Respect the Sun above, lord of all life.
Neither he, nor the cleansing rain,
Nor Mother Earth, should see
This foulness. Take it inside.
Let those it most concerns,
Its own relatives, ourselves, take care of it.

OEDIPUS
Wait. Such kindness,
So unexpected, so undeserved.
One favour. For your own sake, Majesty, not mine.

KREON
What is it you ask so humbly?

OEDIPUS
Banish me. Now.
Where no one in Thebes will see me.

KREON
We await Apollo's orders.

OEDIPUS
It was clear enough.
The oracle. The father-killer must die.

KREON
Things are different now.
We must ask again.

OEDIPUS
About . . . this?
The gods' plaything? Ask what?

KREON
They decide, and we obey.
You know that now.

OEDIPUS
I order you, then . . . I beg you . . .
Her Majesty, inside,
Bury her, funeral rites.
Your sister, Majesty.
As for me, send me away,
Send me far from Thebes.
Kithairon, there let me live, there die.
They chose it, my father, my mother.
They wanted me dead: I'll die.
How, I don't know.
No sickness will end my life, nothing ordinary.
Something strange, terrible—I've been saved for that.
Well, let it come.

Your Honour, one more thing: the children.
Not the boys, they're grown.
They can look after each other.
My daughters. My poor little girls.
They sat beside me,
Never ate a meal
Without their father, shared all I had
Take care of them.
Let me hold them, stroke them.
Your Honour, Majesty,
They're here. It's as if I saw them.
They're crying. I hear them.
You did it. You pitied me.
You did it. My darlings.
Let me touch them, speak to them.

KREON
I know what they mean to you.

OEDIPUS
God reward you, a better fate than mine.
Darlings, where are you? Come here.
Let me hold you, your brother's hands.
They stole your father's eyes, his bright eyes,
Your father knew nothing, saw nothing,
Sowed you where he himself was sown.
I'm crying for you: look.
I can't see you. I see your future.
Bitterness, unhappiness.
On the city's feast-days, what will you do?
Shouting, dancing. You'll sit at home in tears.
When you're old enough to marry,
Who'll have you? Who'll take you
For what you are, forget your father
Who killed where he should not have killed,
Married where he should not have married,
Made children where he was made?
That's what they'll say.
You'll die unmarried, dry old maids.
Majesty, Menoikeus' son, we're dead,
Their parents. You're all they have.
Be kind to them. Don't make them
Outcasts, beggars, wanderers.
Don't make them me.
They're little girls. Your sister's children.
Be kind to them. Say yes, Majesty.
Touch my hand.
Antigone, Ismene, I won't say more.
When you're older, you'll understand.
Be happy. Be happier than me.

KREON
Enough now. Go in.

Music.

OEDIPUS
No choice.

KREON
It's time.

OEDIPUS
You know what I ask?

KREON
Ask again, as we go inside.

OEDIPUS
Send me far from Thebes.

KREON
God's choice, not mine.

OEDIPUS
Cursed by God, I go.

KREON
They'll give what you ask.

OEDIPUS
You know this?

KREON
I promise nothing.

OEDIPUS
Take me inside.

KREON
Leave the children.

OEDIPUS
No! No!

KREON
Give no more orders.
You were powerful once; no more.

CHORUS
People of Thebes, see: Oedipus.
He solved the riddle. He ruled this land.
All envied him. His power, his wealth.
Now the storms of life have swamped him.
Look at him now, and learn:
We're mortal. Count none of us happy
Till we come, untroubled, to the day we die.

Exeunt.

6 Timeless Themes in Greek Drama

Western drama is an art form that originated in Greece. It had its beginnings in the religious ceremonies of the Greeks and initially served a ritual function linking the Greeks with their gods. In the hands of the great Greek dramatists, drama gradually became less concerned with the activities of the gods, emphasizing instead human personality and universal human themes.

Sophocles
Antigone
Conflict Between Individual Conscience and the State's Laws

In *Antigone,* the dramatist Sophocles expresses the Greeks' high esteem for humanity and its potential. He also deals with a theme that recurs in Western thought over the centuries: the conflict between individual morality and the requirements of the state, between personal conscience and the state's laws. Creon, king of Thebes, forbids the burial of Polyneikes, Antigone's brother, because he rebelled against the state. The body, decrees Creon, shall remain unburied, food for dogs and vultures, despite the fact that Antigone is his niece and betrothed to his son. Antigone believes that a higher law compels her to bury her brother, even though this means certain death for her and for her sister Ismene, if the latter helps Antigone.

SCENE II

CREON (*to* ANTIGONE)
You there. You, looking at the ground. Tell me.
Do you admit this or deny it? Which?

ANTIGONE
Yes, I admit it. I do not deny it.

CREON (*to* GUARD)
Go. You are free. The charge is dropped.

                              Exit GUARD
                    Now you,
Answer this question. Make your answer brief.
You knew there was a law forbidding this?

ANTIGONE
Of course I knew it. Why not? It was public.

CREON
And you have dared to disobey the law?

ANTIGONE
Yes. For this law was not proclaimed by Zeus,
Or by the gods who rule the world below.
I do not think your edicts have such power
That they can override the laws of heaven,
Unwritten and unfailing, laws whose life
Belongs not to today or yesterday
But to time everlasting; and no man
Knows the first moment that they had their being.
If I transgressed these laws because I feared
The arrogance of man, how to the gods
Could I make satisfaction? Well I know,
Being a mortal, that I have to die,
Even without your proclamations. Yet
If I must die before my time is come,
That is a blessing. Because to one who lives,
As I live, in the midst of sorrows, death
Is of necessity desirable.
For me, to face death is a trifling pain
That does not trouble me. But to have left
The body of my brother, my own brother,

Lying unburied would be bitter grief.
And if these acts of mine seem foolish to you,
Perhaps a fool accuses me of folly.

CHORUS
The violent daughter of a violent father,
She cannot bend before a storm of evils.

CREON (*to* ANTIGONE)
Stubborn? Self-willed? People like that, I tell you,
Are the first to come to grief. The hardest iron,
Baked in the fire, most quickly flies to pieces.
An unruly horse is taught obedience
By a touch of the curb. How can you be so proud?
You, a mere slave? (*to* CHORUS) She was well schooled
      already
In insolence, when she defied the law.
And now look at her! Boasting, insolent,
Exulting in what she did. And if she triumphs
And goes unpunished, I am no man—she is.
If she were more than niece, if she were closer
Than anyone who worships at my altar,
She would not even then escape her doom,
A dreadful death. Nor would her sister. Yes,
Her sister had a share in burying him.
(*to* ATTENDANT) Go bring her here. I have just seen her,
      raving,
Beside herself. Even before they act,
Traitors who plot their treason in the dark
Betray themselves like that. Detestable!
(*to* ANTIGONE) But hateful also is an evil-doer
Who, caught red-handed, glorifies the crime.

ANTIGONE
Now you have caught me, will you do more than kill
me?

CREON
No, only that. With that I am satisfied.

ANTIGONE
Then why do you delay? You have said nothing
I do not hate. I pray you never will.
And you hate what I say. Yet how could I
Have won more splendid honor than by giving
Due burial to my brother? All men here
Would grant me their approval, if their lips
Were not sealed up in fear. But you, a king,
Blessed by good fortune in much else besides,
Can speak and act with perfect liberty.

CREON
All of these Thebans disagree with you.

ANTIGONE
No. They agree, but they control their tongues.

CREON
You feel no shame in acting without their help?

ANTIGONE
I feel no shame in honoring a brother.

CREON
Another brother died who fought against him.

ANTIGONE
Two brothers. The two sons of the same parents.

CREON
Honor to one is outrage to the other.

ANTIGONE
Eteocles will not feel himself dishonored.

CREON
What! When his rites are offered to a traitor?

ANTIGONE
It was his brother, not his slave, who died.

CREON
One who attacked the land that he defended.

ANTIGONE
The gods still wish those rites to be performed.

CREON
Are the just pleased with the unjust as their equals?

ANTIGONE
That may be virtuous in the world below.

CREON
No. Even there a foe is never a friend.

ANTIGONE
I am not made for hatred but for love.

CREON
Then go down to the dead. If you must love,
Love them. While I yet live, no woman rules me.

CHORUS
Look there. Ismene, weeping as sisters weep,
The shadow of a cloud of grief lies deep.
On her face, darkly flushed; and in her pain
Her tears are falling like a flood of rain.
                    Enter ISMENE *and* ATTENDANTS

CREON
You viper! Lying hidden in my house,
Sucking my blood in secret, while I reared,
Unknowingly, two subverters of my throne.
Do you confess that you have taken part
In this man's burial, or deny it? Speak.

ISMENE
If she will recognize my right to say so,
I shared the action and I share the blame.

ANTIGONE
No. That would not be just. I never let you
Take any part in what you disapproved of.

ISMENE
In your calamity, I am not ashamed
To stand beside you, beaten by this tempest.

ANTIGONE
The dead are witnesses of what I did,
To love in words alone is not enough.

ISMENE
Do not reject me, Sister! Let me die
Beside you, and do honor to the dead.

ANTIGONE
No. You will neither share my death nor claim
What I have done. My death will be sufficient.

ISMENE
What happiness can I have when you are gone?

ANTIGONE
Ask Creon that. He is the one you value.

ISMENE
Do you gain anything by taunting me?

ANTIGONE
Ah, no! By taunting you, I hurt myself.

ISMENE
How can I help you? Tell me what I can do.

ANTIGONE
Protect yourself. I do not grudge your safety.

ISMENE
Antigone! Shall I not share your fate?

ANTIGONE
We both have made our choices life, and death.

ISMENE
At least I tried to stop you. I protested.

ANTIGONE
Some have approved your way; and others, mine.

ISMENE
Yet now I share your guilt. I too am ruined.

ANTIGONE
Take courage. Live your life. But I long since
Gave myself up to death to help the dead. . . .

Haemon, grief-stricken at the condemnation of his fiancée Antigone, approaches his father Creon, and tries to resolve the crisis. Creon is suspicious about Haemon's loyalty.

CREON
We soon shall know better than seers could tell us.
My son, Antigone is condemned to death.
Nothing can change my sentence. Have you learned

Her fate and come here in a storm of anger,
Or do you love me and support my acts?

HAEMON
Father, I am your son. Your greater knowledge
Will trace the pathway that I mean to follow.
My marriage cannot be of more importance
Than to be guided always by your wisdom.

CREON
Yes, Haemon, this should be the law you live by!
In all things to obey your father's will.
Men pray for children round them in their homes
Only to see them dutiful and quick
With hatred to requite their father's foe,
With honor to repay their father's friend.
But what is there to say of one whose children
Prove to be valueless? That he has fathered
Grief for himself and laughter for his foes.
Then, Haemon, do not, at the lure of pleasure,
Unseat your reason for a woman's sake.
This comfort soon grows cold in your embrace:
A wicked wife to share your bed and home.
Is there a deeper wound than to find worthless
The one you love? Turn from this girl with loathing,
As from an enemy, and let her go
To get a husband in the world below.
For I have found her openly rebellious,
Her only out of all the city. Therefore,
I will not break the oath that I have sworn.
I will have her killed. Vainly she will invoke
The bond of kindred blood the gods make sacred.
If I permit disloyalty to breed
In my own house, I nurture it in strangers.
He who is righteous with his kin is righteous
In the state also. Therefore, I cannot pardon
One who does violence to the laws or thinks
To dictate to his rulers; for whoever
May be the man appointed by the city,
That man must be obeyed in everything,
Little or great, just or unjust. And surely
He who was thus obedient would be found
As good a ruler as he was a subject;
And in a storm of spears he would stand fast
With loyal courage at his comrade's side.
But disobedience is the worst of evils.
For it is this that ruins cities; this
Makes our homes desolate; armies of allies
Through this break up in rout. But most men find
Their happiness and safety in obedience.
Therefore we must support the law, and never
Be beaten by a woman. It is better
To fall by a man's hand, if we must fall,
Than to be known as weaker than a girl.

CHORUS
We may in our old age have lost our judgment,
And yet to us you seem to have spoken wisely.

HAEMON
The gods have given men the gift of reason,
Greatest of all things that we call our own.
I have no skill, nor do I wish to have it,
To show where you have spoken wrongly. Yet
Some other's thought, beside your own, might prove
To be of value. Therefore it is my duty,
My natural duty as your son, to notice,
On your behalf, all that men say, or do,
Or find to blame. For your frown frightens them,
So that the citizen dares not say a word
That would offend you. I can hear, however,
Murmurs in darkness and laments for her.
They say: "No woman ever less deserved
Her doom, no woman ever was to die
So shamefully for deeds so glorious.
For when her brother fell in bloody battle,
She would not let his body lie unburied
To be devoured by carrion dogs or birds.
Does such a woman not deserve reward,
Reward of golden honor?" This I hear,
A rumor spread in secrecy and darkness.
Father, I prize nothing in life so highly
As your well-being. How can children have
A nobler honor than their father's fame
Or father than his son's? Then do not think
Your mood must never alter; do not feel
Your word, and yours alone, must be correct.
For if a man believes that he is right
And only he, that no one equals him
In what he says or thinks, he will be found
Empty when searched and rested. Because a man
Even if he be wise, feels no disgrace
In learning many things, in taking care
Not to be over-rigid. You have seen
Trees on the margin of a stream in winter:
Those yielding to the flood save every twig,
And those resisting perish root and branch.
So, too, the mariner who never slackens
His taut sheet overturns his craft and spends
Keel uppermost the last part of his voyage.

Let your resentment die. Let yourself change.
For I believe—if I, a younger man,
May have a sound opinion—it is best
That men by nature should be wise in all things.
But most men find they cannot reach that goal;
And when this happens, it is also good
To learn to listen to wise counselors.

CHORUS
Sir, when his words are timely, you should heed them.
And Haemon, you should profit by his words.
Each one of you has spoken reasonably.

CREON
Are men as old as I am to be taught
How to behave by men as young as he?

HAEMON
Not to do wrong. If I am young, ignore
My youth. Consider only what I do.

CREON
Have you done well in honoring the rebellious?

HAEMON
Those who do wrong should not command respect.

CREON
Then that disease has not infected her?

HAEMON
All of our city with one voice denies it.

CREON
Does Thebes give orders for the way I rule?

HAEMON
How young you are! How young in saying that!

CREON
Am I to govern by another's judgment?

HAEMON
A city that is one man's is no city.

CREON
A city is the king's. That much is sure.

HAEMON
You would rule well in a deserted country.

Aeschylus
The Persians
Hybris

The Greek struggle against the Persians was an apt subject for drama. In 499 B.C., the Ionian Greeks in Asia Minor revolted against their Persian rulers; Athens sent twenty ships to aid the Ionians. To punish the Athenians, Darius I, king of Persia, sent a force to the peninsula of Attica, where Athens is located. In 490 B.C. on the plains of Marathon, an Athenian army of about 10,000 men defeated the Persians. Ten years later, Xerxes, Darius' son and heir, organized a huge invasion force aimed at making Greece a Persian province. Realizing that their independence and freedom were at stake, many Greek cities put aside their quarrels and united against the common enemy. In 480 B.C. on the Bay of Salamis near Athens, the Athenian navy defeated the Persian armada, and the next year the Spartan army crushed the Persians at Plataea.

Herodotus (c. 484–c. 424 B.C.), often called "the father of history," took note of the strategy that lay behind the Greek victory in the battle of Salamis. He tells us that the Athenian general Themistocles (c. 527–460 B.C.) sent a slave to the Persian commander with the story that some of Athens' allies, fearing entrapment, were planning to sail out of the Bay of Salamis. As Themistocles hoped, the Persians, eager for a decisive victory, sailed into the narrow waters of the bay. Unable to deploy its more numerous ships in this cramped space, the Persian fleet was destroyed by the Greek ships.

The great Greek dramatist Aeschylus (525–456 B.C.) was an Athenian nobleman and patriot who had fought at the battle of Marathon. In his play, *The Persians,* Aeschylus glorified the Athenian victory at Salamis. In the first passage excerpted below, Aeschylus portrays Themistocles' cleverness in luring the Persians into the bay and the heroic determination of the Athenian crews. A Persian messenger who witnessed the disaster tells the queen what he saw.

MESSENGER
The one that started the whole disaster, lady, was
Some Curse or Evil Spirit which appeared from
   somewhere.
For a man, a Greek, arrived from the Athenian camp. . . .
And spoke to your son Xerxes words to this effect,
That once the darkness and the black of night should
   come,
The Greeks would not remain, but to their rowers' seats
Would leap in disarray, each man for himself,
And run away in secret flight to save their lives.
Your son, the moment that he heard, not comprehending
The treachery of the Greek, the jealousy of the gods,
Proclaimed to all his captains the following command,
That when the rays of the sun should cease to scorch the
   earth,
And darkness covered all the vault of sky,
They should order the main body of ships in three
   divisions

To guard the exit routes and straits of sounding sea,
While others were to circle round to Ajax's isle [Salamis];
That if the Greeks avoided an evil fate of death
By finding some escape in secret with their ships,
The order was posted for all his captains, "off with their
   heads."
So many were his words, and from a cheerful heart;
He did not know what was about to come from the gods.
His men, without disorder, but with obedient hearts,
Got them their suppers and each sailor in the crews
Attached his oar around its neatly fitted peg.
But when the radiance of the sun had disappeared
And night came on, each sailor, master of an oar,
Went aboard his ship, and all who managed heavy arms.
And line of ships of war called out to other line;
The captains kept at oar as each had been assigned.
And all night long the masters of the ships maintained
The sailing back and forth by all the naval host.
And night departed, and the army of the Greeks did not

In any way attempt to sail out in secret.
But when the white-horsed chariot of dawn appeared
And filled the entire earth with radiance to behold,
The first thing was a sound, a shouting from the Greeks,
A joyful song, and to it, making shrill response,
From the island rocks about there came an antiphony
Of echoes; fear stood next to each one of our men,
Tripped up in their hopes: for not as if in flight
Were the Greeks raising then a solemn paean-strain
   [hymn to the gods],
But rushing into battle with daring confidence;
A trumpet, too, blazed over everything its sound.
At once, with measured stroke of surging, sea-dipped oar,
They struck the brine and made it roar from one
   command,
And quickly all of them were visible to sight.
Their right wing first, in order just as they had been
Arranged, led off, and next the whole remaining force
Came out to the attack, and with the sight we heard
A loud voice of command: "O sons of Greeks, go on,
Bring freedom to your fatherland, bring freedom to
Your children, wives, and seats of your ancestral gods;
And your forbears' graves; now the struggle is for all."
Of course, on our side, too, a roar of Persian tongues
Went forth in answer; the moment would not brook delay.
Immediately ship struck its brazen-plated beak
On ship. The ramming was begun by a Greek ship
And it snapped off from one of the Phoenicians the whole
Curving stern, and men on both sides shot their spears.
At first the streaming Persian force withstood the shocks;
But when their crowd of ships was gathered in the straits,
And no assistance could be given one to another,
But they were being struck by their own brazen rams,
They kept on breaking all their equipage of oars,
And the ships of the Greeks, with perfect plan and order,
   came
Around them in a circle and struck, and hulls of ships
Were overturned; and the sea no longer was visible,
Filled as it was with shipwrecks and the slaughter of
   men.
The beaches, too, and the reefs around were filled with
   corpses.
Now every ship that came with the Persian armament

Was being rowed for quick escape, no order left.
And they kept striking us, deboning us, like tunnies
   [tuna]
Or a catch of fish, with broken fragments of oars, or bits
Of flotsam from the wrecks; and all this time, moaning
And wailing held control of that area of sea,
Until the eye of black night took it away.
So great a crowd of ills, not even if I took
Ten days in order to tell, could I tell the tale in full.
For be assured of this, that never in one day
Did such a huge number of men go to their deaths.

QUEEN
Aeee! A huge sea of ills has broken out
And overwhelmed the Persians and all the barbarian race.

A characteristic theme in Greek tragedy was *hubris*, overweening pride or arrogance. When individuals evinced hubris, forgetting their human fallibility and overstepping the bounds of moderation, they were inevitably punished. For Xerxes' intemperate ambition to become master of both Asia and Greece he must pay. The suffering of the Persians, says Aeschylus, should make people aware of what they can and cannot do, as the ghost of Darius, Xerxes' father, laments.

And heaps of corpses even generations hence
Will signify in silence to the eyes of men
That mortal man should not think more than mortal
   thoughts.
For hybris blossomed forth and grew a crop of ruin,
And from it gathered in a harvest full of tears.
As you look upon these deeds and recompense for them,
Remember Athens and Greece and let no man hereafter,
Despising what he has from heaven, turn lustful eyes
To others, and spill a store of great prosperity.
For Zeus is standing by, the punisher of thoughts
Too overboastful, a harsh and careful scrutineer.
In face of this, when Xerxes, who lacks good sense,
   returns,
Counsel him with reasoning and good advice,
To cease from wounding God with overboastful rashness.

Euripides

Medea

The Ordeal of Women

Women occupied a subordinate position in Greek society. A woman's chief functions were to bear male heirs for her husband and to manage his household. In Athens, respectable women were secluded in their homes; they did not go into the marketplace or eat at the same table as their husbands and guests. Nor did women have political rights; they could not vote or hold office. In order to exercise her property rights, a woman was represented by a male guardian— usually a father, husband, brother, or son.

Parents usually arranged the marriage of their daughters. A father who discovered that his daughter had been unchaste could sell her into slavery. Adultery was a crime. A husband was compelled by law to divorce his adulterous wife and could have her lover executed.

The Greek dramatist Euripides (c. 485–406 B.C.) applied a keen critical spirit to the great question of individual life versus the demands of society. His play *Medea* focuses on a strong-willed woman whose despair at being cast off by her husband leads her to exact a terrible revenge. But in the following passage, Medea might speak for the deepest feelings of any Greek woman.

It was everything to me to think well of one man,
And he, my own husband, has turned out wholly vile.
Of all things which are living and can form a judgement
We women are the most unfortunate creatures.
Firstly, with an excess of wealth it is required
For us to buy a husband and take for our bodies
A master; for not to take one is even worse.
And now the question is serious whether we take
A good or bad one; for there is no easy escape
For a woman, nor can she say no to her marriage.
She arrives among new modes of behaviour and manners,
And needs prophetic power, unless she has learnt at home,

How best to manage him who shares the bed with her.
And if we work out all this well and carefully,
And the husband lives with us and lightly bears his yoke,
Then life is enviable. If not, I'd rather die.
A man, when he's tired of the company in his home,
Goes out of the house and puts an end to his boredom
And turns to a friend or companion of his own age.
But we are forced to keep our eyes on one alone.
What they say of us is that we have a peaceful time
Living at home, while they do the fighting in war.
How wrong they are! I would very much rather stand
Three times in the front of battle than bear one child.

Aristophanes

Lysistrata

Political Satire

Aristophanes (c. 448–c. 380 B.C.), the greatest Athenian comic playwright, wrote *Lysistrata* in 412 B.C. to convey his revulsion for the Peloponnesian War that was destroying Greece. In the play, the women of Athens, led by Lysistrata, resolve to refrain from sexual relations with their husbands until the men make peace. When the women seize the Acropolis—the rocky hill in the center of Athens— the men resort to force but are doused with water. At this point a commissioner, accompanied by four constables, enters and complains about the disturbance; Koryphaios, one of the doused men, vents his anger. The ensuing dialogue between the commissioner and Lysistrata reflects some attitudes of Greek men and women toward each other.

COMMISSIONER . . . That's what women are good for: a complete disaster.

MAN I Save your breath for actual crimes, Commissioner. Look what's happened to us. Insolence, insults, insufferable effrontery, and apart from that, they've soaked us. It looks as though we pissed in our tunics.

COMMISSIONER By Poseidon, that liquid deity, you got what you deserved. It's all our own fault. We taught them all they know. We are the forgers of fornication. We sowed in them sexual license and now we reap rebellion . . . (*shrugs*) What do you expect? This is what happens. . . . (*indicates doors of Acropolis*) Take my own case.

I'm the Commissioner for Public Safety. I've got men to pay. I need the money and look what happens. The women have shut me out of the public treasury. (*taking command*) All right, men. On your feet. Take up that log over there. Form a line. Get a move on. You can get drunk later. I'll give you a hand. (*They ram the gates without success. After three tries, as they are stepping back, Lysistrata opens the door. Calonike and Myrrhine accompany her.*)

LYSISTRATA Put that thing down! I'm coming out of my own free will. What we want here is not bolts and bars and locks, but common sense.

COMMISSIONER Sense? Common sense? You . . . you . . . you. . . . Where's a policeman? Arrest her! Tie her hands behind her back.

LYSISTRATA (*who is carrying wool on a spindle or a knitting needle*) By Artemis, goddess of the hunt, if he touches me, you'll be dropping one man from your payroll. (*Lysistrata jabs him*)

COMMISSIONER What's this? Retreat? Get back in there. Grab her, the two of you.

MYRRHINE (*holding a large chamber pot*) By Artemis, goddess of the dew, if you lay a hand on her, I'll kick the shit out of you.

COMMISSIONER Shit? Disgusting. Arrest her for using obscene language.

CALONIKE (*carrying a lamp*) By Artemis, goddess of light, if you lay a finger on her, you'll need a doctor.

COMMISSIONER Apprehend that woman. Get her, NOW!

BOEOTIAN (*from the roof, with a broom*) By Artemis, goddess of witchcraft, if you go near her, I'll break your head open.

COMMISSIONER Good God, what a mess. Athens' finest disgraced! Defeated by a gaggle of girls. Close ranks, men! On your marks, get set, CHARGE!

LYSISTRATA (*holds her hands up and they stop*) Hold it! We've got four battalions of fully equipped infantry women back there.

COMMISSIONER Go inside and disarm them.

LYSISTRATA (*gives a loud whistle and women crowd the bottlenecks and the doorway with brooms, pots and pans, etc.*) Attack! Destroy them, you sifters of flour and beaters of eggs, you pressers of garlic, you dough girls, you bar maids, you market militia. Scratch them and tear them, bite and kick. Fall back, don't strip the enemy—the day is ours. (*the policemen are overpowered*)

COMMISSIONER (*in tears*) Another glorious military victory for Athens!

LYSISTRATA What did you think we were? There's not an ounce of servility in us. A woman scorned is something to be reckoned with. You underestimated the capacity of freeborn women.

COMMISSIONER Capacity? I sure as hell did. You'd cause a drought in the saloons if they let you in.

MAN I Your honor, there's no use talking to animals. I know you're a civil servant, but don't overdo it.

MAN II Didn't we tell you? They gave us a public bath, fully dressed, without any soap.

WOMAN II What did you expect, sonny? You made the first move—we made the second. Try it again and you'll get another black eye. (*flute*) We are really sweet little stay-at-homes by nature, all sweetness and light, good little virgins, perfect dolls (*they all rock to and fro coyly*). But if you stick your finger in a hornet's nest, you're going to get stung.

MEN ALL (*and drums—they beat their feet rhythmically on the ground*)

Oh Zeus, Oh Zeus.
Of all the beasts that thou has wrought,
What monster's worse than woman?
Who shall encompass with his thought
Their endless crimes? Let me tell you . . . no man!

They've seized the heights, the rock, the shrine.
But to what end I know not.
There must be *reasons* for the crime (*to audience*)
Do you know why? (*pause*) I thought not.

MAN I Scrutinize those women. Assess their rebuttals.

MAN II 'Twould be culpable negligence not to probe this affair to the bottom.

COMMISSIONER (*as if before a jury*) My first question is this, gentlemen of the . . . What possible motive could you have had in seizing the Treasury?

LYSISTRATA We wanted to keep the money. *No money, no war.*

COMMISSIONER You think that money is the cause of the war?

LYSISTRATA Money is the cause of all our problems. . . . They'll not get another penny.

COMMISSIONER Then what do you propose to do?

LYSISTRATA Control the Treasury.

COMMISSIONER Control the Treasury?

LYSISTRATA Control the Treasury. National economics and home economics—they're one and the same.

COMMISSIONER No, they're not.

LYSISTRATA Why do you say so?

COMMISSIONER The national economy is for the war effort.

LYSISTRATA Who needs the war effort?

COMMISSIONER How can we protect the city?

LYSISTRATA Leave that to us.

ALL MEN You?

ALL WOMEN Us.

COMMISSIONER God save us.

LYSISTRATA Leave that to us.

COMMISSIONER Subversive nonsense!

LYSISTRATA Why get so upset? There's no stopping us now.

COMMISSIONER It's a downright crime.

LYSISTRATA We *must* save you.

COMMISSIONER (*pouting*) What if I don't want to be saved?

LYSISTRATA All the more reason to.

COMMISSIONER Might I ask where you got these ideas of war and peace?

LYSISTRATA If you'll allow me, I'll tell you.

COMMISSIONER Out with it then, or I'll . . .

LYSISTRATA Relax and put your hands down.

COMMISSIONER I can't help myself. You make me so damned angry.

CALONIKE Watch it.

COMMISSIONER Watch it yourself, you old wind bag.

LYSISTRATA Because of our natural self-restraint, we women have tolerated you men ever since this war began. We tolerated you and kept our thoughts to ourselves. (You never let us utter a peep, anyway.) But that does not mean that we were happy with you. We knew you all too well. Very often, in the evening, at suppertime, we would listen to you talk of some enormously important decision you had made. Deep down inside all we felt was pain, but we would force a smile and ask, "How was the assembly today, dear? Did you get to talk about peace?" And my husband would answer, "None of your business. Shut up!" And I would shut up.

CALONIKE I wouldn't have.

COMMISSIONER I'd have shut your mouth for you.

LYSISTRATA But then we would find out that you had passed a more disgusting resolution, and I would ask you, "Darling, how did you manage to do something so absolutely stupid?" And my husband would glare at me and threaten to slap my face if I did not attend to the distaff side of things. And then he'd always quote Homer: "The men must see to the fighting."

COMMISSIONER Well done. Well done.

LYSISTRATA What do you mean? Not to let us advise against your idiocy was bad enough, but then again we'd actually hear you out in public saying things like, "Who can we draft? There's not a man left in the country." Someone else would say, "Quite right, not a man left. Pity." And so we women got together and decided to save Greece. There was no time to lose. Therefore, you keep quiet for a change and listen to us. For we have valuable advice to give this country. If you'll listen, we'll put you back on your feet again.

COMMISSIONER You'll do what? I'm not going to put up with this. I'm not going . . .

LYSISTRATA SILENCE!

COMMISSIONER I categorically decline to be silent for a woman. Women wear hats.

LYSISTRATA If that's what is bothering you, try one on and shut up! (*puts one on him*)

CALONIKE Here's a spindle.

MYRRHINE And a basket of wool.

CALONIKE Go on home. There's a sweetheart. Put on your girdle, wind your wool, and mind the beans don't boil over.

LYSISTRATA "THE WOMEN MUST SEE TO THE FIGHTING."

COMMISSIONER Beside the point, beside the point. Things are in a tangle. How can you set them straight?

LYSISTRATA Simple.

COMMISSIONER Explain.

LYSISTRATA Do you know anything about weaving? Say the wool gets tangled. We lift it up, like this, and work out the knots by winding it this way and that, up and down, on the spindles. That's how we'll unravel the war. We'll send our envoys this way and that, up and down, all over Greece.

COMMISSIONER Wool? Spindles? Are you out of your mind? War is a serious business.

LYSISTRATA If you had any sense, you'd learn a lesson from women's work.

COMMISSIONER Prove it.

LYSISTRATA The first thing we have to do is give the wool a good wash, get the dirt out of the fleece. We beat out the musk and pick out the hickies. Do the same for the city. Lambast the loafers and discard the dodgers. Then our spoiled wool—that's like your job-hunting sycophants—sack the spongers, decapitate the dabblers. But toss together into the wool basket the good [resident] aliens, the allies, the strangers, and begin spinning them into a ball. The colonies are loose threads; pick up the ends and gather them in. Wind them all into one, make a great bobbin of yarn, and weave, without bias or seam, a garment of government fit for the people.

COMMISSIONER It's all very well this weaving and bobbing—when you have absolutely no earthly idea what a war means.

LYSISTRATA You disgusting excuse for a man! The pain of giving birth was only our first pain. You took our boys and sent *them to their deaths in Sicily.*

COMMISSIONER Quiet! I beg you, let that memory lie still.

LYSISTRATA And now, when youth and beauty are still with us and our blood is hot, you take our husbands away, and we sleep alone. That's bad enough for us married women. But I pity the virgins growing old, alone in their beds.

COMMISSIONER Well, men grow old too, you know.

LYSISTRATA But it's not the same. A soldier's discharged, bald as a coot he may be, and . . . zap! he marries a nymphette. But a woman only has one summer, and when that has slipped by, she can spend her days and her years consulting oracles and fortune tellers, but they'll never send her a husband.

MEN ALL There's something rotten in the state of Athens. An ominous aroma of constitutional rot. My nose can smell a radical dissenter, An anarchist, tyrannous, feminist plot.

The Spartans are behind it. They must have masterminded This anarchist, tyrannous, feminist plot.

7 Socrates: The Rational Individual

Socrates (469–399 B.C.) marked a decisive turning point in Greek philosophy and in the history of Western thought. The Socratic conception of the rational individual became an essential component of the tradition of classical humanism. Socrates agreed with the Sophists that the study of physical nature was less important than the study of man. But whereas the Sophists concentrated on teaching specific skills—how to excel in debates, for example—Socrates was concerned with comprehending and improving human character. Although ethical concerns lay at the center of Socrates' thought, he never provided a list of ethical commands; in Socratic philosophy, there is nothing comparable to the Ten Commandments. What he did provide was a method—the dialectic or dialogue—of arriving at knowledge, including moral values.

For Socrates, the dialogue (the asking and answering of questions between two or more individuals) was the sole avenue to moral insights and self-knowledge. The interchange implied that a human mind was not a passive vessel into which a teacher poured knowledge. Participants in a dialogue were obliged to play an active role and to think critically about human values. The use of the dialogue implied further that relations between people should involve rational discussion through which people learn from each other and improve themselves.

When Socrates was seventy, he was accused by his enemies of corrupting the youth of Athens and of not believing in the city's gods but in other, new divinities, and he went on trial for his life.

Plato

The Apology

Knowledge of Socrates' trial comes principally from *The Apology* written by Plato, Socrates' most illustrious student. (The original meaning of *apology* was a defense or explanation.) In the first passage from *The Apology*, Socrates tells the court that the Delphic Oracle, the prophetess of Apollo at Delphi, had said that there was no one wiser than Socrates. Not considering himself wise, Socrates resolved to discover what the oracle meant, by conversing with people reputed to be wise.

I went to a man who seemed wise: thinking that there, if any-where, I should prove the answer wrong, and be able to say to the oracle, "You said that I am the wisest of men; but this man is wiser than I am." So I examined him—I need not tell you his name, he was a public man, but this was the result, Athenians. When I conversed with him, I came to see that, though many persons, and chiefly he himself, thought that he was wise, yet he was not wise. And then I tried to show him that he was not wise, though he fancied that he was; and by that I gained his hatred, and the hatred of many of the by-standers. So when I went away, I thought to myself, "I am wiser than this man: neither of us probably knows anything that is really good, but he thinks that he has knowledge, when he has it not, while I, seeing that I have no knowledge, do not think that I have." In this point, at least, I seem to be a little wiser than he is; I do not think that I know what I do not know. Next I went to another man, who seemed to be still wiser, with just the same result. And there again I gained his hatred. . . . After the public men I went to the po-ets, tragic, dithyrambic [frenzied], and others, thinking there to find myself manifestly more ignorant than they. So I took up the poems on which I thought that they had spent most pains, and asked them what they meant wishing also for instruction. I am ashamed to tell you the truth, my friends, but I must say it. In short, almost any of the bystanders would have spoken better about the works of these poets than the poets themselves. So I soon found that it is not by wis-dom that the poets create their works, but by a certain nat-ural power, and by inspiration, like soothsayers and prophets: for though such persons say many fine things, they know nothing of what they say. And the poets seemed to me to be in a like case. And at the same time I perceived that, because of their poetry, they thought that they were the wisest of men in other matters too, which they were not. So I went away again, thinking that I had the same advantage over them as over the public men.

Finally I went to the artisans: for I was conscious, in a word, that I had no knowledge at all, and I was sure that I should find that they knew many fine things. And in that I was not mistaken. They knew what I did not know, and so far they were wiser than I. But, Athenians, it seemed to me that the skilled craftsmen made the same mistake as the poets. Each of them claimed to have great wisdom in the highest matters because he was skilful in his own art; and this fault of theirs threw their real wisdom into the shade. So I asked my-self on behalf of the oracle whether I would choose to remain as I was, neither wise in their wisdom nor ignorant in their ignorance, or to have both, as they had them. And I made an-swer to myself and to the oracle that it were better for me to remain as I was.

This search, Athenians, has gained me much hatred of a very fierce and bitter kind, which has caused many false ac-cusations against me; and I am called by the name of wise. For the bystanders always think that I am wise myself in any matter wherein I convict another man of ignorance. But in truth, my friends, perhaps it is God who is wise: and by this oracle he may have meant that man's wisdom is worth little or nothing. He did not mean, I think, that Socrates is wise: he only took me as an example, and made use of my name, as though he would say to men: "He among you is wisest, who, like Socrates, is convinced that for wisdom he is verily worth-less." And therefore I still go about searching and testing every man whom I think wise, whether he be a citizen or a stranger, according to the word of the God [Apollo]; and whenever I find that he is not wise, I point that out to him in the service of the God. And I am so busy in this pursuit that I have never had leisure to take any part worth mentioning in public matters, or to look after my private affairs. I am in very great poverty by my service to the God.

And besides this, the young men who follow me about, who are the sons of wealthy persons and with much leisure, by nature delight in hearing men cross-questioned: and they often imitate me among themselves: then they try their hand at cross-questioning other people. And, I imagine, they find a great abundance of men who think that they know a great deal, when in truth they know little or nothing. And then the persons who are cross-questioned are angry with me in-stead of with themselves: and say that Socrates is an abom-inable fellow who corrupts the young. And when they are asked, Why, what does he do? what does he teach? they have nothing to say; but, not to seem at a loss, they repeat the stock charges against all philosophers, and say that he inves-tigates things in the air and under the earth, and that he teaches people to disbelieve in the gods, and "to make the worst appear the better reason." For I fancy they would not like to confess the truth, that they are shown up as mere ig-norant pretenders to knowledge. And so they have filled your ears with their fierce slanders for a long time, for they are zealous and fierce, and numerous: they are well-disciplined too, and plausible in speech. . . .

Had Socrates been willing to compromise and to stop teaching his philosophy, it is likely that he would not have received the death penalty. How-ever, for Socrates the pursuit of truth was the highest human activity; it involved the person's whole being. It transformed the individual, enabling him to live in accordance with moral values that had been arrived at through thought and that could be defended rationally.

. . . But I know well that it is evil and base to do wrong and to disobey my better, whether he be man or god. And I will never choose what I know to be evil, and fear and fly from what may possibly be a good. And so, even if you acquit me now, and do not listen to Anytus' [his prosecutor's] argu-ment that I ought never to have been brought to trial, if I was to be acquitted; and that as it is, you are bound to put me to death, because if I were to escape, all your children would forthwith be utterly corrupted by practising what Socrates teaches: if you were therefore to say to me, "Socrates, this time we will not listen to Anytus: we will let you go: but on this condition, that you cease from carrying on this search, and from philosophy: if you are found doing that again, you shall die:" I say, if you offered to let me go on these terms, I should reply:—"Athenians, I hold you in the highest regard and love; but I will obey the God rather than you: and as long as I have breath and power I will not cease from philosophy, and from exhorting you and setting forth the truth to any of you whom I meet, saying as I am wont, 'My excellent friend, you are a citizen of Athens, a city very great and very famous for wisdom and power of mind: are you not ashamed of caring so much for the making of money, and for reputation and honour? Will you not spend thought or care on wisdom and truth and the perfecting of your soul?'" And if he dispute my words, and say that he does care for these things, I shall not forthwith release him and go away: I shall question him and cross-examine him: and if I think that he has not virtue, though he says that he has, I shall reproach him for setting the least value on the most important things; and the greater value on the more worthless. This shall I do to every one whom I meet, old or young, citizen or stranger; but especially to the citizens, for they are more nearly akin to me. For know well, the God commands me so to do. And I think that nothing better has ever happened to you in your city than my service to the God. For I spend my whole life in going about persuading you all, both young and old, to give your first and chiefest care to the perfection of your souls: and not till you have done that to care for your bodies or your wealth. I tell you, that virtue does not come from wealth, but that wealth and every other good, whether public or private, which men have, come from virtue. If then I corrupt the youth by this teaching, the mischief is great; but if any man says that I teach anything else, he speaks falsely. And therefore, Athenians, I say, either listen to Anytus, or do not listen to him: either acquit me, or do not acquit me: but be sure that I shall not alter my life; no, not if I have to die for it many times.

Do not interrupt me, Athenians. Remember the request which I made to you, and listen to my words. I think that it will do you good to hear them. I have something more to say to you, at which perhaps you will cry out: but do not do that. Be sure that if you kill me, a man such as I say I am, you will harm yourselves more than you will harm me. Meletus [another prosecutor] and Anytus can do me no harm; that is impossible, for I do not think that God will allow a good man to be harmed by a bad one. They may indeed kill me, or drive me into exile, or deprive me of my civil rights; and perhaps Meletus and others think these things great evils. But I do not think so: I think that to do as he is doing, and to try to kill a man unjustly, is a much greater evil. And now, Athenians, I am not going to argue for my own sake at all, as you might think, but for yours, that you may not sin against the God and reject his gift to you, by condemning me. If you put me to death, you will hardly find another man to fill my

place. The God has sent me to attack the city, if I may use a ludicrous simile, just as if it were a great and noble horse, which was rather sluggish from its size and needed a gadfly to rouse it: and I think that I am the gadfly that the God has set upon the city: for I never cease settling on you as it were at every point, and rousing, and exhorting, and reproaching each man of you all day long. You will hardly find any one else, my friends, to fill my place: and, if you take my advice, you will spare my life. You are indignant, as drowsy persons are when they are awakened, and, of course, if you are persuaded by Anytus, you could easily kill me with a single blow, and then sleep on undisturbed for the rest of your lives. . . .

Perhaps someone will say, "Why cannot you withdraw from Athens, Socrates, and hold your peace?" It is the most difficult thing in the world to make you understand why I cannot do that. If I say that I cannot hold my peace because that would be to disobey the God, you will think that I am not in earnest and will not believe me. And if I tell you that no greater good can happen to a man than to discuss human excellence every day and the other matters about which you have heard me arguing and examining myself and others, and that an unexamined life is not worth living, then you will believe me still less. But that is so, my friends, though it is not easy to persuade you. . . .

Socrates is convicted and sentenced to death.

. . . Perhaps, my friends, you think that I have been convicted because I was wanting in the arguments by which I could have persuaded you to acquit me, if I had thought it right to do or to say anything to escape punishment. It is not so. I have been convicted because I was wanting, not in arguments, but in impudence and shamelessness—because I would not plead before you as you would have liked to hear me plead, or appeal to you with weeping and wailing, or say and do many other things which I maintain are unworthy of me, but which you have been accustomed to from other men. But when I was defending myself, I thought that I ought not to do anything unworthy of a free man because of the danger which I ran, and I have not changed my mind now. I would very much rather defend myself as I did, and die, than as you would have had me do, and live. . . .

And now I wish to prophesy to you, Athenians, who have condemned me. For I am going to die, and that is the time when men have most prophetic power. And I prophesy to you who have sentenced me to death that a far more severe punishment than you have inflicted on me will surely overtake you as soon as I am dead. You have done this thing, thinking that you will be relieved from having to give an account of your lives. But I say that the result will be very different. There will be more men who will call you to account, whom I have held back, though you did not recognize it. And they will be harsher toward you than I have been, for they will be younger, and you will be more indignant with them. For if you think that you will restrain men from reproaching you for not living as you should, by putting them to death, you are very much mistaken. That way of escape is neither possible nor honorable. It is much more honorable and much easier not to suppress others, but to make yourselves as good as you can. This is my parting prophecy to you who have condemned me.

8 Plato: The Philosopher-King

Plato (c. 429–347 B.C.), an Athenian aristocrat and disciple of Socrates, based his philosophy on Socrates' teachings. Plato was greatly affected by the deterioration of Athenian politics during and immediately after the Peloponnesian War. The rise of demagogues, the violent conflicts between oligarchs and democrats, and the execution of Socrates convinced Plato that Athenian democracy was a failure. His hostility toward democracy also stemmed from his upper-class background and temperament.

Socratic philosophy held promise of reforming the individual through the critical use of reason. Plato felt that the individual could not undergo a moral transformation while living in a wicked and corrupt society. For the individual to be able to achieve virtue, the state must be reformed.

Plato

The Republic

In *The Republic,* Plato proposed organizing government in harmony with the needs of human nature. Those people who are driven by a desire for food, possessions, and sexual gratification, Plato said, should be farmers, tradesmen, or artisans. Those who are naturally courageous and assertive should be soldiers. And the few who have the capacity for wisdom—the philosophers—should be entrusted with political power.

In the ideal state, Plato asserted, the many would be ruled by the few who have a natural endowment for leadership. These philosopher-kings, the finest product of the state's carefully designed educational program, would wield absolute power: the people would lose their right to participate in political affairs, and the state would manufacture propaganda and strictly control education in order to keep the masses obedient. In exchange, the citizens would gain leaders distinguished by their rationality, wisdom, and virtue. In the form of a dialogue between Socrates and a man called Glaucon, Plato in the following reading presented his views on the character of the philosopher.

[SOCRATES] Unless either philosophers become kings in their countries or those who are now called kings and rulers come to be sufficiently inspired with a genuine desire for wisdom; unless that is to say, political power and philosophy meet together . . . there can be no rest from troubles, my dear Glaucon, for states, nor yet, as I believe, for all mankind. . . . There is no other way of happiness either for the state or for the individual. . . .

Now . . . we must, I think, define . . . whom we mean by these lovers of wisdom who, we have dared to assert, ought to be our rulers. Once we have a clear view of their character, we shall be able to defend our position by pointing to some who are naturally fitted to combine philosophic study with political leadership, while the rest of the world should accept their guidance and let philosophy alone.

[GLAUCON] Yes, this is the moment for a definition. . . .

[S] . . . One trait of the philosophic nature we may take as already granted: a constant passion for any knowledge that will reveal to them something of that reality which endures for ever and is not always passing into and out of existence. And, we may add, their desire is to know the whole of that reality; they will not willingly renounce any part of it as relatively small and insignificant, as we said before when we compared them to the lover and to the man who covets honour.

[G] True.

[S] Is there not another trait which the nature we are seeking cannot fail to possess—truthfulness, a love of truth and a hatred for falsehood that will not tolerate untruth in any form?

[G] Yes, it is natural to expect that.

[S] It is not merely natural, but entirely necessary that an instinctive passion for any object should extend to all that is closely akin to it; and there is nothing more closely akin to wisdom than truth. So the same nature cannot love wisdom and falsehood; the genuine lover of knowledge cannot fail, from his youth up, to strive after the whole of truth.

[G] I perfectly agree.

[S] Now we surely know that when a man's desires set strongly in one direction, in every other channel they flow more feebly, like a stream diverted into another bed. So when the current has set towards knowledge and all that goes with it, desire will abandon those pleasures of which the body is the instrument and be concerned only with the pleasure which the soul enjoys independently—if, that is to say, the love of wisdom is more than a mere pretence. Accordingly, such a one will be temperate and no lover of money; for he will be the last person to care about the things for the sake of which money is eagerly sought and lavishly spent.

[G] That is true.

[S] Again, in seeking to distinguish the philosophic nature, you must not overlook the least touch of meanness. Nothing could be more contrary than pettiness to a mind constantly bent on grasping the whole of things, both divine and human.

[G] Quite true.

[S] And do you suppose that one who is so high-minded and whose thought can contemplate all time and all existence will count this life of man a matter of much concern?

[G] No, he could not.

[S] So for such a man death will have no terrors.

[G] None.

[S] A mean and cowardly nature, then, can have no part in the genuine pursuit of wisdom.

[G] I think not.

[S] And if a man is temperate and free from the love of money, meanness, pretentiousness, and cowardice, he will not be hard to deal with or dishonest. So, as another indication of the philosophic temper, you will observe whether, from youth up, he is fair-minded, gentle, and sociable.

[G] Certainly.

[S] Also you will not fail to notice whether he is quick or slow to learn. No one can be expected to take a reasonable delight in a task in which much painful effort makes little headway. And if he cannot retain what he learns, his for-

getfulness will leave no room in his head for knowledge; and so, having all his toil for nothing, he can only end by hating himself as well as his fruitless occupation. We must not, then, count a forgetful mind as competent to pursue wisdom; we must require a good memory.

[G] By all means.

[S] Further, there is in some natures a crudity and awkwardness that can only tend to a lack of measure and proportion; and there is a close affinity between proportion and truth. Hence, besides our other requirements, we shall look for a mind endowed with measure and grace, which will be instinctively drawn to see every reality in its true light.

[G] Yes.

[S] Well then, now that we have enumerated the qualities of a mind destined to take its full part in the apprehension of reality, have you any doubt about their being indispensable and all necessarily going together?

[G] None whatever.

[S] Then have you any fault to find with a pursuit which none can worthily follow who is not by nature quick to learn and to remember, magnanimous and gracious, the friend and kinsman of truth, justice, courage, temperance?

Plato said that genuine philosophers are "those whose passion it is to see the truth." For Plato, unlike the Sophists, standards of beauty, justice, and goodness exist that are universally valid—that apply to all peoples at all times. Plato held that these standards are in a higher world, the realm of Forms or Ideas. This world of Forms is known only through the mind, not the senses. For example, a sculptor observes many bodies but they all possess flaws; in his mind's eye he perceives the world of Ideas and tries to reproduce with his art the perfect human form. Plato says that the ordinary person, basing opinion on everyday experience, has an imperfect understanding of beauty, goodness, and justice, whereas the philosopher, through reason, reaches beyond sense perception to the realm of Forms and discovers truth. Such people are the natural rulers of the state; only they are capable of a correct understanding of justice; only they have the wisdom to reform the state in the best interests of all its citizens.

The distinction between a higher world of truth and a lower world of imperfection, deception, and illusion is illustrated in Plato's famous "Allegory of the Cave." Plato, through the dialogue of Socrates and Glaucon, compares those persons without a knowledge of the Forms to prisoners in a dark cave.

[S] Next, said I, here is a parable to illustrate the degrees in which our nature may be enlightened or unenlightened. Imagine the condition of men living in a sort of cavernous chamber underground, with an entrance open to the light and a long passage all down the cave. Here they have been from childhood, chained by the leg and also by the neck, so that they cannot move and can see only what is in front of them, because the chains will not let them turn their heads. At some distance higher up is the light of a fire burning behind them; and between the prisoners and the fire is a track with a parapet built along it, like the screen at a puppet-show, which hides the performers while they show their puppets over the top.

[G] I see, said he.

[S] Now behind this parapet imagine persons carrying along various artificial objects, including figures of men and animals in wood or stone or other materials, which project above the parapet. Naturally, some of these persons will be talking, others silent.

[G] It is a strange picture, he said, and a strange sort of prisoners.

[S] Like ourselves, I replied; for in the first place prisoners so confined would have seen nothing of themselves or of one another, except the shadows thrown by the fire-light on the wall of the Cave facing them, would they?

[G] Not if all their lives they had been prevented from moving their heads.

[S] And they would have seen as little of the objects carried past.

[G] Of course.

[S] Now, if they could talk to one another, would they not suppose that their words referred only to those passing shadows which they saw?

[G] Necessarily.

[S] And suppose their prison had an echo from the wall facing them? When one of the people crossing behind them spoke, they could only suppose that the sound came from the shadow passing before their eyes.

[G] No doubt.

[S] In every way, then, such prisoners would recognize as reality nothing but the shadows of those artificial objects.

[G] Inevitably. . . .

To the prisoners chained in the cave, the shadows of the artificial objects constitute reality. When a freed prisoner ascends from the cave to the sunlight, he sees a totally different world. Returning to the cave, he tries to tell the prisoners that the shadows are only poor imitations of reality, but they laugh at him, for their opinions have been shaped by the only world they know. The meaning of the parable is clear: the philosophers who ascend to the higher world of Forms possess true knowledge; everyone else possesses mere opinions, deceptive beliefs, and illusions. The philosophers have a duty to guide the ignorant.

[S] Now consider what would happen if their release from the chains and the healing of their unwisdom should come

about in this way. Suppose one of them were set free and forced suddenly to stand up, turn his head, and walk with eyes lifted to the light; all these movements would be painful, and he would be too dazzled to make out the objects whose shadows he had been used to see. What do you think he would say, if someone told him that what he had formerly seen was meaningless illusion, but now, being somewhat nearer to reality and turned towards more real objects, he was getting a truer view? Suppose further that he were shown the various objects being carried by and were made to say, in reply to questions, what each of them was. Would he not be perplexed and believe the objects now shown him to be not so real as what he formerly saw?

[G] Yes, not nearly so real.

[S] And if he were forced to look at the fire-light itself, would not his eyes ache, so that he would try to escape and turn back to the things which he could see distinctly, convinced that they really were clearer than these other objects now being shown to him?

[G] Yes.

[S] And suppose someone were to drag him away forcibly up the steep and rugged ascent and not let him go until he had hauled him out into the sunlight, would he not suffer pain and vexation at such treatment, and, when he had come out into the light, find his eyes so full of its radiance that he could not see a single one of the things that he was now told were real?

[G] Certainly he would not see them all at once.

[S] He would need, then, to grow accustomed before he could see things in that upper world. At first it would be easiest to make out shadows, and then the images of men and things reflected in water, and later on the things themselves. After that, it would be easier to watch the heavenly bodies and the sky itself by night, looking at the light of the moon and stars rather than the Sun and the Sun's light in the day-time.

[G] Yes, surely.

[S] Last of all, he would be able to look at the Sun and contemplate its nature, not as it appears when reflected in water or any alien medium, but as it is in itself in its own domain.

[G] No doubt.

[S] And now he would begin to draw the conclusion that it is the Sun that produces the seasons and the course of the year and controls everything in the visible world, and moreover is in a way the cause of all that he and his companions used to see.

[G] Clearly he would come at last to that conclusion.

[S] Then if he called to mind his fellow prisoners and what passed for wisdom in his former dwelling place, he would surely think himself happy in the change and be sorry for them. They may have had a practice of honouring and commending one another, with prizes for the man who had the keenest eye for the passing shadows and the best memory for the order in which they followed or accompanied one another, so that he could make a good guess as to which was going to come next. Would our released prisoner be likely to covet those prizes or to envy the men exalted to honour and power in the Cave? Would he not feel like Homer's Achilles, that he would far sooner "be on earth as a hired servant in the house of a landless man" or endure anything rather than go back to his old beliefs and live in the old way?

[G] Yes, he would prefer any fate to such a life.

[S] Now imagine what would happen if he went down again to take his former seat in the Cave. Coming suddenly out of the sunlight, his eyes would be filled with darkness. He might be required once more to deliver his opinion on those shadows, in competition with the prisoners who had never been released, while his eyesight was still dim and unsteady; and it might take some time to become used to the darkness. They would laugh at him and say that he had gone up only to come back with his sight ruined; it was worth no one's while even to attempt the ascent. If they could lay hands on the man who was trying to set them free and lead them up, they would kill him.

[G] Yes, they would.

[S] Every feature in this parable, my dear Glaucon, is meant to fit our earlier analysis. The prison dwelling corresponds to the region revealed to us through the sense of sight, and the fire-light within it to the power of the Sun. The ascent to see the things in the upper world you may take as standing for the upward journey of the soul into the region of the intelligible; then you will be in possession of what I surmise, since that is what you wish to be told. Heaven knows whether it is true; but this, at any rate, is how it appears to me. In the world of knowledge, the last thing to be perceived and only with great difficulty is the essential Form of Goodness. Once it is perceived, the conclusion must follow that, for all things, this is the cause of whatever is right and good; in the visible world it gives birth to light and to the lord of light, while it is itself sovereign in the intelligible world and the parent of intelligence and truth. Without having had a vision of this Form no one can act with wisdom, either in his own life or in matters of state. . . .

For Plato, the perfect state, like the well-formed soul, is one governed by reason. By contrast, in the imperfect state, as in the imperfect soul, greed, selfishness, desire, and disorder predominate. Democracy is flawed, said Plato, because most people lack the ability to deal intelligently with matters of state. In the end, the democratic state degenerates into anarchy, and the way is prepared for a tyrant. Plato viewed the tyrant as the most despicable of persons. A slave to his own passions, said Plato, the tyrant is like a lunatic who "dreams that he can lord it over all mankind and heaven besides." The character of the philosopher is the very opposite of the sick soul of the tyrant. In the following passage, Plato discusses what he regards as democracy's weaknesses.

[S] And when the poor win, the result is a democracy. They kill some of the opposite party, banish others, and grant the rest an equal share in civil rights and government, officials being usually appointed by lot.

[G] Yes, that is how a democracy comes to be established, whether by force of arms or because the other party is terrorized into giving way.

[S] Now what is the character of this new régime? Obviously the way they govern themselves will throw light on the democratic type of man.

[G] No doubt.

[S] First of all, they are free. Liberty and free speech are rife everywhere; anyone is allowed to do what he likes.

[G] Yes, so we are told.

[S] That being so, every man will arrange his own manner of life to suit his pleasure. The result will be a greater variety of individuals than under any other constitution. So it may be the finest of all, with its variegated pattern of all sorts of characters. Many people may think it the best, just as women and children might admire a mixture of colours of every shade in the pattern of a dress. At any rate if we are in search of a constitution, here is a good place to look for one. A democracy is so free that it contains a sample of every kind; and perhaps anyone who intends to found a state, as we have been doing, ought first to visit this emporium of constitutions and choose the model he likes best.

[G] He will find plenty to choose from.

[S] Here, too, you are not obliged to be in authority, however competent you may be, or to submit to authority, if you do not like it; you need not fight when your fellow citizens are at war, nor remain at peace when they do, unless you want peace; and though you may have no legal right to hold office or sit on juries, you will do so all the same if the fancy takes you. . . .

. . . When he [the democrat] is told that some pleasures should be sought and valued as arising from desires of a higher order, others chastised and enslaved because the desires are base, he will shut the gates of the citadel against the messengers of truth, shaking his head and declaring that one appetite is as good as another and all must have their equal rights. So he spends his days indulging the pleasure of the moment, now intoxicated with wine and music, and then taking to a spare diet and drinking nothing but water; one day in hard training, the next doing nothing at all, the third apparently immersed in study. Every now and then he takes a part in politics, leaping to his feet to say or do whatever comes into his head. . . . His life is subject to no order or restraint, and he has no wish to change an existence which he calls pleasant, free, and happy.

That well describes the life of one whose motto is liberty and equality. . . .

In a democratic country you will be told that liberty is its noblest possession, which makes it the only fit place for a free spirit to live in.

[G] True; that is often said.

[S] Well then, as I was saying, perhaps the insatiable desire for this good to the neglect of everything else may transform a democracy and lead to a demand for despotism. A democratic state may fall under the influence of unprincipled leaders, ready to minister to its thirst for liberty with too deep draughts of this heady wine; and then, if its rulers are not complaisant enough to give it unstinted freedom, they will be arraigned as accursed oligarchs and punished. Law-abiding citizens will be insulted as nonentities who hug their chains; and all praise and honour will be bestowed, both publicly and in private, on rulers who behave like subjects and subjects who behave like rulers. In such a state the spirit of liberty is bound to go to all lengths. . . .

. . . The parent falls into the habit of behaving like the child, and the child like the parent: the father is afraid of his sons, and they show no fear or respect for their parents, in order to assert their freedom. . . . To descend to smaller matters, the schoolmaster timidly flatters his pupils, and the pupils make light of their masters as well as of their attendants. Generally speaking, the young copy their elders, argue with them, and will not do as they are told; while the old, anxious not to be thought disagreeable tyrants, imitate the young and condescend to enter into their jokes and amusements. . . .

Putting all these items together, you can see the result: the citizens become so sensitive that they resent the slightest application of control as intolerable tyranny, and in their resolve to have no master they end by disregarding even the law, written or unwritten.

[G] Yes, I know that only too well.

[S] Such then, I should say, is the seed, so full of fair promise, from which springs despotism.

9 The Mystical Side of Plato's Thought

A champion of reason, Plato aspired to study human life and arrange it according to universally valid standards. In contrast to Sophist relativism, he maintained that objective and eternal standards do exist. Although Plato advocated the life of reason and wanted to organize society according to rational rules, his writing also reveals a religious-mystical side. At times, Plato seems like a mystic seeking to escape from this world into a higher reality, a realm that is without Earth's evil and injustice. Because Platonism is a two-world philosophy, which believes in a higher world as the source of values and in the soul's immortality, it has had an important effect on religious thought. Christian (as well as Jewish and Muslim) thinkers could harmonize Plato's stress on a higher nonmaterial reality and an immortal soul with their faith. The concept of the world of Forms is found in several of Plato's dialogues, but nowhere is it more clearly stated than in his *Phaedo*.

Plato

Phaedo

The *Phaedo* consists of a discussion between Socrates and three of his friends—Cebes, Simmias, and Crito—who visit him in prison on the day of his execution. The topic of the dialogue is the impending death of Socrates and his certainty that the soul is immortal. Socrates argues that the physical senses of the body impede the soul from gaining wisdom and truth; therefore, the philosopher should constantly prepare for death by keeping his soul as free as possible from the body. When death does come, the philosopher, the lover of wisdom, should welcome it, because death is the complete separation of the soul (or intellect) from the body. After death, the soul of the philosopher can contemplate the truth in the world of Forms, free from the restrictions of the body.

"And is it just this that is named 'death'—a release and parting of soul from body?"

"Indeed it is."

"And it's especially those who practise philosophy aright, or rather they alone, who are always eager to release it, as we say, and the occupation of philosophers is just this, isn't it—a release and parting of soul from body?"

"It seems so."

"Then wouldn't it be absurd, as I said at the start, for a man to prepare himself in his life to live as close as he can to being dead, and then to be resentful when this comes to him?"

"It would be absurd, of course."

"Truly then, Simmias, those who practise philosophy aright are cultivating dying, and for them least of all men does being dead hold any terror. Look at it like this: if they've set themselves at odds with the body at every point, and desire to possess their soul alone by itself, wouldn't it be quite illogical if they were afraid and resentful when this came about—if, that is, they didn't go gladly to the place where, on arrival, they may hope to attain what they longed for throughout life, namely wisdom—and to be rid of the company of that with which they'd set themselves at odds? Or again, many have been willing to enter Hades of their own accord, in quest of human loves, of wives and sons who have died, led by this hope, that there they would see and be united with those they desired; will anyone, then, who truly longs for wisdom, and who firmly holds this same hope, that nowhere but in Hades will he attain it in any way worth mentioning, be resentful at dying; and will he not go there gladly? One must suppose so, my friend, if he's truly a lover of wisdom; since this will be his firm belief, that nowhere else but there will he attain wisdom purely. Yet if that is so, wouldn't it, as I said just now, be quite illogical if such a man were afraid of death?"

"Yes, quite illogical!"

"Then if you see a man resentful that he is going to die, isn't this proof enough for you that he's no lover of wisdom after all, but what we may call a lover of the body? And this same man turns out, in some sense, to be a lover of riches and of prestige, either one of these or both."

"It's just as you say." . . .

Socrates reasons that there are two types of knowledge: the unchanging and invisible Forms that can only be known by the intellect and the constantly changing everyday visible objects that are known by the senses. He then points out that humans are part body and part soul. The body belongs to this visible, changing world, and it is mortal; but the soul belongs to the unchanging and invisible world of the Forms, and it is immortal. Human souls preexist and they do not die with the body.

"Yes, it certainly is true, Cebes, as I see it; and we're not deceived in making just those admissions: there really is such a thing as coming to life again, living people *are* born from the dead, and the souls of the dead exist." . . .

. . . "Then our souls did exist earlier, Simmias, before entering human form, apart from bodies; and they possessed wisdom."

"Unless maybe, Socrates, we get those pieces of knowledge at the very moment of birth; that time still remains."

"Very well, my friend; but then at what other time, may I ask, do we lose them? We aren't born with them, as we agreed just now. Do we then lose them at the very time at which we get them? Or have you any other time to suggest?"

"None at all, Socrates. I didn't realize I was talking nonsense."

"Then is our position as follows, Simmias? If the objects we're always harping on exist, a beautiful, and a good and all such Being, and if we refer all the things from our sense-perceptions to that Being, finding again what was formerly ours, and if we compare these things with that, then just as surely as those objects exist, so also must our soul exist before we are born. . . .

. . . "Consider, then, Cebes, if these are our conclusions from all that's been said: soul is most similar to what is divine, immortal, intelligible, uniform, indissoluble, unvarying, and constant in elation to itself; whereas body, in its turn, is most similar to what is human, mortal, multiform, non-intelligible, dissoluble, and never constant in relation to itself. Have we anything to say against those statements, my dear Cebes, to show that they're false?"

"We haven't."

"Well then, that being so, isn't body liable to be quickly dissolved, whereas soul must be completely indissoluble, or something close to it?" . . .

. . . "Of course."

"Can it be, then, that the soul, the invisible part, which goes to another place of that kind, noble, pure and invisible, to 'Hades' in the true sense of the word, into the presence of the good and wise God—where, God willing, my own soul too must shortly enter—can it be that this, which we've found to be a thing of such a kind and nature, should on separation from the body at once be blown apart and perish, as most men say? Far from it, my dear Cebes and Simmias; rather, the truth is far more like this: suppose it is separated in purity, while trailing nothing of the body with it, since it had no avoidable commerce with it during life, but shunned it; suppose too that it has been gathered together alone into itself, since it always cultivated this—nothing else but the right practice of philosophy, in fact, the cultivation of dying without complaint—wouldn't this be the cultivation of death?"

"It certainly would." . . .

10 Aristotle: Political and Ethical Thought

Aristotle (384–322 B.C.) was born at Stagira, a Greek city-state on the Macedonian coast. About 367 B.C., he came to Athens to study with Plato, and he remained a member of Plato's Academy for twenty years. In 342 B.C., Philip II, king of Macedonia, invited Aristotle to tutor his son Alexander, who was then fourteen years old. When Alexander succeeded Philip and set out to conquer the Persian Empire, Aristotle left Macedonia for Athens, where he opened a school of philosophy called the Lyceum, named for a nearby temple to Apollo Lyceus. Aristotle synthesized the thought of earlier philosophers, including his teacher Plato, and was the leading authority of his day in virtually every field of knowledge.

Aristotle
Politics and *Nicomachean Ethics*

Scientific thinking encompasses both rationalism and empiricism. Rationalism—pursuit of truth through thought alone, independent of experience with the natural world—was advocated by Plato. This approach points in the direction of theoretical mathematics. Like Plato, Aristotle valued reason, but unlike his teacher he also had great respect for the concrete details of nature obtained through sense experience. Aristotle demonstrated his empirical approach: observing nature and collecting, classifying, and analyzing data. Aristotle's empiricism is the foundation of such sciences as geology, botany, and biology.

When he turned to the study of politics, Aristotle also followed an empirical methodology. He undertook a series of historical studies of the constitutions of 158 Greek city-states. The most significant and complete study that has survived describes the constitution of Athens. On the basis of these extensive surveys, Aristotle proceeded to write *Politics,* his masterwork of political philosophy, excerpted in the second reading.

Like Socrates and Plato, Aristotle based his ethics on reason. People could achieve moral well-being, said Aristotle, when they avoided extremes of behavior and rationally chose the way of moderation. In his *Nicomachean Ethics,* dedicated to his son Nicomachus, Aristotle described the "proud man." This passage, excerpted in the second reading, sketches characteristics that make up the Greek ideal of excellence.

In the following selection from *Politics,* Aristotle begins by defining the nature of a state and its purpose.

POLITICS

It is clear therefore that the state cannot be defined merely as a community dwelling in the same place and preventing its members from wrong-doing and promoting the exchange of goods and services. Certainly all these must be present if there is to be a state, but even the presence of every one of them does not *ipso facto* [by that fact] make a state. The state is intended to enable all, in their households and their kinships, to live *well,* meaning by that a full and satisfying life.

He then addresses the problem of where the sovereign power of the state ought to reside.

. . . "Where ought the sovereign power of the state to reside?" With the people? With the propertied classes? With the good? With one man, the best of all the good? With one man, the tyrant? There are objections to all these. Thus suppose we say the people is the supreme authority, then if they use their numerical superiority to make a distribution of the property of the rich, is not that unjust? It has been done by a valid decision of the sovereign power, yet what can we call it save the very height of injustice? Again, if the majority, having laid their hands on everything, distribute the possessions of the few, they are obviously destroying the state. But that cannot be goodness which destroys its possessor and justice cannot be destructive of the state. So it is clear that this process, though it may be the law, cannot be just. Or, if that is just, the actions taken by a tyrant must be just; his superior power enables him to use force, just as the masses force their will on the rich. Thirdly, if it is just for the few and wealthy to rule, and if they too rob and plunder and help themselves to the goods of the many, is that just? If it is, then it is just in the former case also. The answer clearly is that all these three are bad and unjust. The fourth alternative, that the good should rule and have the supreme authority, is also not free from objection; it means that all the rest must be without official standing, debarred from holding office under the constitution. The fifth alternative, that one man, the best, should rule, is no better; by making the number of rulers fewer we leave still larger numbers without official standing. It might be objected too that it is a bad thing for any human being, subject to all possible disorders and affections of the human mind, to be the sovereign authority, which ought to be reserved for the law itself. . . .

. . . [A]t the moment it would seem that the most defensible, perhaps even the truest, answer to the question would be to say that the majority ought to be sovereign. . . . For where there are many people, each has some share of goodness and intelligence, and when these are brought together, they become as it were one multiple man with many pairs of feet and hands and many minds. So too in regard to character and powers of perception. That is why the general public is a better judge of works of music and poetry; some judge some parts, some others, but their joint pronouncement is a verdict upon the whole. . . .

Aristotle seeks to determine what is the best constitution. His conclusion reflects the premise developed in his *Ethics* that moderation, or the middle way, is the path to virtue in all things. So, Aristotle says that in forming a constitution for the state, power should reside in the hands of the middle class rather than the aristocracy or the poor.

If we were right when in our *Ethics* we stated that Virtue is a Mean and that the happy life is life free and unhindered and according to virtue, then the best life must be the middle way, [or the mean] . . . between two extremes which it is open to those at either end to attain. And the same principle must be applicable to the goodness or badness of cities and states. For the constitution of a city is really the way it lives.

In all states there are three sections of the community— the very well-off, the very badly-off, and those in between. Seeing therefore that it is agreed that moderation and a middle position are best, it is clear that in the matter of possessions to own a middling amount is best of all. This condition is most obedient to reason, and following reason is just what is difficult both for the exceedingly rich, handsome, strong, and well-born, and for the opposite, the extremely poor, the weak, and the downtrodden. The former commit deeds of violence on a large scale, the latter are delinquent and wicked in petty ways. The misdeeds of the one class are due to *hubris* [overweening pride, arrogance], the misdeeds of the other to rascality. . . . There are other drawbacks about the two extremes. Those who have a super-abundance of all that makes for success, strength, riches, friends, and so forth, neither wish to hold office nor understand the work; and this is ingrained in them from childhood on; even at school they are so full of their superiority that they have never learned to do what they are told. Those on the other hand who are greatly deficient in these qualities are too subservient. So they cannot command and can only obey in a servile régime, while the others cannot obey in any régime and can command only in a master-slave relationship. The result is a state not of free men but of slaves and masters, the one full of envy, the other of contempt. Nothing could be farther removed from friendship or from the whole idea of a shared partnership in a state. . . . The state aims to consist as far as possible of those who are like and equal, a condition found chiefly among the middle section. . . . The middle class is also the steadiest element, the least eager for change. They neither covet, like the poor, the possessions of others, nor do others covet theirs, as the poor covet those of the rich. . . .

It is clear then both that the political partnership which operates through the middle class is best, and also that those cities have every chance of being well-governed in which the middle class is large, stronger if possible than the other two together, or at any rate stronger than one of them. . . . For this reason it is a happy state of affairs when those who take part in the life of the state have a moderate but adequate amount of property. . . . Tyranny often emerges from an overenthusiastic democracy or from an oligarchy, but much more rarely from middle-class constitutions or from those very near to them.

The superiority of the middle type of constitution is clear also from the fact that it alone is free from fighting among factions. Where the middle element is large, there least of all arise faction and counter-faction among citizens. . . .

In his *Politics,* Aristotle often disagreed with Plato's ideas in his *Republic,* including his view of the status of women. Plato argued that when it came to governing and other tasks in everyday life, the basic difference between men and women was that women are not as physically as strong as men. Therefore, he declared that the best and the brightest of both sexes should fully participate in government. Aristotle, however, fell back on the more traditional Greek view that the free adult male should rule over women. In *Politics*, he emphasizes the difference between the ruler and the ruled, and argues that it is natural for the male to rule over the female, for women have a limited capacity for thought.

There are . . . three parts of household-management, one being the rule of a master, which has already been dealt with, next the rule of a father, and a third which arises out of the marriage relationship. This is included because rule is exercised over wife and children—over both of them as free persons, but in other respects differently: over a wife, rule is as by a statesman; over children, as by a king. For the male is more fitted to rule than the female, unless conditions are quite contrary to nature; and the elder and fully grown is more fitted than the younger and undeveloped. . . .

. . . [I]t becomes clear that both ruler and ruled must have a share in virtue, but that there are differences in virtue in each case, as there are also among those who by nature rule. An immediate indication of this is afforded by the soul, where we find natural ruler and natural subject, whose virtues we regard as different—one being that of the rational element, the other of the nonrational. It is therefore clear that the same feature will be found in the other cases too, so that most instances of ruling and being ruled are natural. For rule of free over slave, male over female, man over boy, are all different, because, while parts of the soul are present in each case, the distribution is different. Thus the deliberative faculty in the soul is not present at all in a slave; in a female it is present but ineffective, in a child present but undeveloped.

ETHICS

The following selection from *Ethics* shows how Aristotle's ethical theory rests on the principles of moderation and balance. Aristotle notes that some people become "angry at the wrong things, more than is right, and longer, and cannot be appeased until they inflict vengeance or punishment." On the other extreme, foolish and slavish people endure every insult without defending themselves. Between these extremes is the proud man, "who is angry at the right thing and with the right people, and, further, as he ought, when he ought, and as long as he ought."

Even-tempered and moderate in all things, such a man "tends to be unperturbed and not to be led by passion."

. . . In the first place, then, as has been said, the proud man is concerned with honours; yet he will also bear himself with moderation towards wealth and power and all good or evil fortune, whatever may befall him, and will be neither overjoyed by good fortune nor over-pained by evil. For not even towards honour does he bear himself as if it were a very great thing. . . .

He does not run into trifling dangers, nor is he fond of danger, because he honours few things; but he will face great dangers, and when he is in danger he is unsparing of his life, knowing that there are conditions on which life is not worth having. And he is the sort of man to confer benefits, but he is ashamed of receiving them; for the one is the mark of a superior, the other of an inferior. And he is apt to confer greater benefits in return; for thus the original benefactor besides being paid will incur a debt to him, and will be the gainer by the transaction. They seem also to remember any service they have done, but not those they have received (for he who receives a service is inferior to him who has done it, but the proud man wishes to be superior), and to hear of the former with pleasure, of the latter with displeasure. . . . It is a mark of the proud man also to ask for nothing or scarcely anything, but to give help readily, and to be dignified towards people who enjoy high position and good fortune, but unassuming towards those of the middle class; for it is a difficult and lofty thing to be superior to the former, but easy to be so to the latter, and a lofty bearing over the former is no mark of ill-breeding, but among humble people it is as vulgar as a display of strength against the weak. Again, it is characteristic of the proud man not to aim at the things commonly held in honour, or the things in which others excel; to be sluggish and to hold back except where great honour or a great work is at stake, and to be a man of few deeds, but of great and notable ones. He must also be open in his hate and in his love (for to conceal one's feelings, i.e. to care less for truth than for what people will think, is a coward's part), and must speak and act openly; for he is free of speech because he is contemptuous, and he is given to telling the truth, except when he speaks in irony to the vulgar. He must be unable to make his life revolve round another, unless it be a friend; for this is slavish, and for this reason all flatterers are servile and people lacking in self-respect are flatterers. Nor is he given to admiration; for nothing to him is great. Nor is he mindful of wrongs; for it is not the part of a proud man to have a long memory, especially for wrongs, but rather to overlook them. Nor is he a gossip; for he will speak neither about himself nor about another, since he cares not to be praised nor for others to be blamed; nor again is he given to praise; and for the same reason he is not an evil-speaker, even about his enemies, except from haughtiness. With regard to necessary or small matters he is least of all men given to lamentation or the asking of favours; for it is the part of one who takes such matters seriously to behave so with respect to them. He is one who will possess beautiful and profitless things rather than profitable and useful ones; for this is more proper to a character that suffices to itself.

Further, a slow step is thought proper to the proud man, a deep voice, and a level utterance; for the man who takes few things seriously is not likely to be hurried, nor the man who thinks nothing great to be excited, while a shrill voice and a rapid gait are the results of hurry and excitement.

Such, then, is the proud man; the man who falls short of him is unduly humble, and the man who goes beyond him is vain.

4

Hellenistic Civilization

Greek civilization, or Hellenism, passed through three distinct stages: the Hellenic Age, the Hellenistic Age, and the Greco-Roman Age. The Hellenic Age began about 800 B.C. with the early city-states, reached its height in the fifth century B.C., and endured until the death of Alexander the Great in 323 B.C. At that time, the ancient world entered the Hellenistic Age, which ended in 30 B.C., when Egypt, the last major Hellenistic state, fell to Rome. The Greco-Roman Age lasted five hundred years, encompassing the period of the Roman Empire up to the collapse of the Empire's western half in the last part of the fifth century A.D.

Although the Hellenistic Age absorbed the heritage of classical (Hellenic) Greece, its style of civilization changed. During the first phase of Hellenism, the polis had been the center of political life. The polis had given Greeks an identity, and only within the polis could Greeks live a good and civilized life. With the coming of the Hellenistic Age, this situation changed. Kingdoms and empires eclipsed the city-state in power and importance. Cities retained a large measure of autonomy in domestic affairs but had lost their freedom of action in foreign affairs. Dominated by monarchs, cities were no longer self-sufficient and independent communities as they had been in the Hellenic period.

Monarchy—the essential form of government in the Hellenistic world—was not admired by the Greeks of the Hellenic Age. They agreed with Aristotle that monarchy was suitable only for non-Greeks, who lacked the capacity to govern themselves.

As a result of Alexander the Great's conquests of the lands between Greece and India, tens of thousands of Greek soldiers, merchants, and administrators settled in eastern lands. Their encounters with the different peoples and cultures of the Near East widened the Greeks' horizon and weakened their ties to their native cities. Because of these changes, the individual had to define a relationship not to the narrow, parochial society of the polis, but to the larger world. The Greeks had to examine their place in a world more complex, foreign, and threatening than the polis. They had to fashion a conception of a community that would be more comprehensive than the city-state.

Hellenistic philosophers struggled with these problems of alienation and community. They sought to give people the inner strength to endure in a world where the polis no longer provided security. In this new situation, philosophers no longer assumed that the good life was tied to the affairs of the city. Freedom from emotional stress—not active citizenship and social responsibility—was the avenue to the good life. This pronounced tendency of people to withdraw into themselves and seek emotional comfort helped shape a cultural environment that contributed to the spread and triumph of Christianity in the Greco-Roman Age.

1 Hellenistic Culture: Universalism and Cosmopolitanism

During the Hellenistic Age, Greek civilization spread to the Near East in the wake of Alexander's conquests, and Mesopotamian, Egyptian, Persian, and Jewish traditions—particularly religious beliefs—moved westward. Thousands of Greeks settled in newly established cities throughout the ancient Near East, carrying with them Greek urban institutions and culture, laws, cults, educational methods, artistic and architectural styles, customs, and dress. The new Hellenistic cities were dominated by a Greek upper class, which recruited native non-Greeks to its ranks to the degree that they became *Hellenized,* that is, adopted the Greek language and lifestyle. Through intermarriage, education in Greek schools, and the prospect of political and economic advantage, non-Greeks came to participate in and contribute to a common Greek civilization that spread from the western Mediterranean to the Indus River.

Cultural exchange permeated all phases of cultural life. Sculpture showed the influence of many lands. Historians wrote world histories, not just local ones. Greek astronomers worked with data collected over the centuries by the Babylonians. Greeks increasingly demonstrated a fascination with Near Eastern religious cults. Philosophers helped to break down the barriers between peoples by asserting that all inhabit a single fatherland. As the philosopher Crates said, "My fatherland has no single tower, no single roof. The whole earth is my citadel, a home ready for us all to live in."

Plutarch
CULTURAL FUSION

The Greek biographer Plutarch (c. A.D. 46–120) provides a glowing account of Alexander the Great in the following passage. Plutarch saw Alexander as a philosopher in action and an apostle of universalism and human brotherhood. Many modern historians reject this assessment of Alexander's intentions, but the scope of his conquests and their significance in reducing the distinctions between Near Easterners and Greeks remain impressive.

[W]hen Alexander was civilizing Asia, Homer was commonly read, and the children of the Persians, of the Susianians, and of the Gedrosians[1] learned to chant the tragedies of Sophocles and Euripides . . . yet through Alexander Bactria[2] and the Caucasus learned to revere the gods of the Greeks. Plato wrote a book on the One Ideal Constitution, but because of its forbidding character he could not persuade anyone to adopt it; but Alexander established more than seventy cities among savage tribes, and sowed all Asia[3] with Grecian magistracies, and thus overcame its uncivilized and brutish manner of living. Although few of us read Plato's *Laws,* yet hundreds of thousands have made use of Alexander's laws, and continue to use them. Those who were vanquished by Alexander are happier than those who escaped his hand; for these had no one to put an end to the wretchedness of their existence, while the victor compelled those others to lead a happy life. . . . Thus Alexander's new subjects would not have been civilized, had they not been vanquished; Egypt

[1]The Susianians lived in and near the city of Susa, the capital of the Persian Empire; the Gedrosians lived just north of the Arabian Sea, in what is now southeastern Iran and western Pakistan.
[2]Bactria, a northeastern province of the ancient Persian Empire, was located in the area of modern Afghanistan and Central Asia.

[3]"All Asia" referred to western Asia Minor at first, then, as Alexander's conquests spread further, the term was broadened to include the other territory to the east, extending to what is now India and Central Asia.

would not have its Alexandria, nor Mesopotamia its Seleuceia, nor Sogdiana its Prophthasia, nor India its Bucephalia,[1] nor the Caucasus a Greek city hard by; for by the founding of cities in these places savagery was extinguished and the worse element, gaining familiarity with the better, changed under its influence. If, then, philosophers take the greatest pride in civilizing and rendering adaptable the intractable and untutored elements in human character, and if Alexander has been shown to have changed the savage natures of countless tribes, it is with good reason that he should be regarded as a very great philosopher.

Moreover, the much-admired *Republic* of Zeno, the founder of the Stoic sect, may be summed up in this one main principle: that all the inhabitants of this world of ours should not live differentiated by their respective rules of justice into separate cities and communities, but that we should consider men to be of one community and one polity, and that we should have a common life and an order common to us all, even as a herd that feeds together and shares the pasturage of a common field. This Zeno wrote, giving shape to a dream or, as it were, shadowy picture of a well-ordered and philosophic commonwealth; but it was Alexander who gave effect to the idea. For Alexander did not follow Aristotle's advice to treat the Greeks as if he were their leader, and other peoples as if he were their master; to have regard for the Greeks as for friends and kindred, but to conduct himself toward other peoples as though they were plants or animals; for to do so

would have been to cumber his leadership with numerous battles and banishments and festering seditions. But, as he believed that he came as a heaven-sent governor to all, and as a mediator for the whole world, those whom he could not persuade to unite with him, he conquered by force of arms, and he brought together into one body all men everywhere, uniting and mixing in one great loving-cup, as it were, men's lives, their characters, their marriages, their very habits of life. He bade them all consider as their fatherland the whole inhabited earth, as their stronghold and protection his camp, as akin to them all good men, and as foreigners only the wicked; they should not distinguish between Grecian and foreigner by Grecian cloak and targe [shield], or scimitar [curved sword] and jacket; but the distinguishing mark of the Grecian should be seen in virtue, and that of the foreigner in iniquity; clothing and food, marriage and manner of life they should regard as common to all, being blended into one by ties of blood and children. . . .

. . . For he did not overrun Asia like a robber nor was he minded to tear and rend it, as if it were booty and plunder bestowed by unexpected good fortune, after the manner in which Hannibal later descended upon Italy. . . . But Alexander desired to render all upon earth subject to one law of reason and one form of government and to reveal all men as one people, and to this purpose he made himself conform. But if the deity that sent down Alexander's soul into this world of ours had not recalled him quickly, one law would govern all mankind, and they all would look toward one rule of justice as though toward a common source of light. But as it is, that part of the world which has not looked upon Alexander has remained without sunlight.

---

[1]Seleuceia (named for one of Alexander's generals) was near modern Baghdad. Prophthasia, a city founded by Alexander, was in Sogdiana, north of modern Afghanistan. Bucephalia, on a northern branch of the Indus River, was named for Alexander's horse Bucephalus.

2 Greek Culture and the Jews in the Hellenistic Age

Like other Near Eastern people, the Jews—both in Judea and the Diaspora (Jews who lived outside Palestine)—came under the influence of Hellenism. As Greek settlements sprang up in Judea, Jews had increasing contact with Greek soldiers, artisans, and merchants. Some Jewish scholars came to admire the rich Greek philosophical tradition. The Hebrew Scriptures were translated into Greek for use by Greek-speaking Jews, Greek words entered the Hebrew language, and newly constructed synagogues employed Hellenistic architectural styles. Radical Hellenizers, mainly prosperous aristocrats, adopted Greek games, dress, entertainment, and eating habits; these efforts to assimilate pagan ways were resisted by simple folk and the devout who clung tenaciously to Mosaic law. Thus Greek influences both enriched Hebrew culture and threatened its integrity.

First Book of Maccabees
JEWISH RESISTANCE TO FORCED HELLENIZATION

The clash of Greek and Hebrew cultures came to a head when the Seleucid king Antiochus IV (174–163 B.C.) decided to impose Hellenization upon the Jews of Judea. (His predecessor, Antiochus III, had seized Palestine from Ptolemaic Egypt.) In 167 B.C. he desecrated the Temple in Jerusalem by erecting an altar to Zeus in the Temple court and offering pigs, unclean animals in Jewish law, as a sacrifice. He forbade ritual circumcision, the sign of the covenant between Jews and their god, Yahweh. In the following selection from the first book of the Maccabees, an anonymous Jewish historian, writing shortly after 134 B.C., describes the causes of the great rebellion against forced Hellenization. The text reveals that some Jews were already so Hellenized that they supported the policies of the Seleucid king.

The outrage of loyalist Jews against forced Hellenization was epitomized by Mattathias, whose battle cry was "Let everybody who is zealous for the Law and stands by the covenant come out after me." Led by one of Mattathias's sons, Judah the Maccabeus (the "hammerer"), the Jews successfully fought the Syrians, venting their anger also against the Hellenized Jews who sided with Antiochus. In 140 B.C., the Jews, under Judah's brother Simon, regained their independence.

THE PERSECUTION

1 [41]Then the king wrote to his whole kingdom that all should be one people, [42]and that each should give up his customs. [43]All the Gentiles accepted the command of the king. Many even from Israel gladly adopted his religion; they sacrificed to idols and profaned the sabbath. [44]And the king sent letters by messengers to Jerusalem and the cities of Judah; he directed them to follow customs strange to the land, [45]to forbid burnt offerings and sacrifices and drink offerings in the sanctuary, to profane sabbaths and feasts, [46]to defile the sanctuary and the priests, [47]to build altars and sacred precincts and shrines for idols, to sacrifice swine and unclean animals, [48]and to leave their sons uncircumcised. They were to make themselves abominable by everything unclean and profane, [49]so that they should forget the [Mosaic] law and change all the ordinances. [50]"And whoever does not obey the command of the king shall die."

[51]In such words he wrote to his whole kingdom. And he appointed inspectors over all the people and commanded the cities of Judah to offer sacrifice, city by city. [52]Many of the people, every one who forsook the law, joined them, and they did evil in the land; [53]they drove Israel into hiding in every place of refuge they had.

[54]Now on the fifteenth day of Chislev [in 167 B.C.] they erected a desolating sacrilege upon the altar of burnt offering. They also built altars in the surrounding cities of Judah, [55]and burned incense at the doors of the houses and in the streets. [56]The books of the law which they found they tore to pieces and burned with fire. [57]Where the book of the covenant was found in the possession of any one, or if any one adhered to the law, the decree of the king condemned him to death. [58]They kept using violence against Israel, against those found month after month in the cities. [59]And on the twenty-fifth day of the month they offered sacrifice on the altar which was upon the altar of burnt offering. [60]According to the decree, they put to death the women who had their children circumcised, [61]and their families and those who circumcised them; and they hung the infants from their mothers' necks.

[62]But many in Israel stood firm and were resolved in their hearts not to eat unclean food. [63]They chose to die rather than to be defiled by food or to profane the holy covenant; and they did die. [64]And very great wrath came upon Israel.

Philo of Alexandria

APPRECIATION OF GREEK CULTURE AND SYNTHESIS OF REASON AND REVELATION

Living in the cosmopolitan world of Alexandria dominated by Greek thought and culture, Alexandrian Jews felt compelled to demonstrate that their faith was not incompatible with reason, that there was no insurmountable gulf separating Mosaic religion from Greek philosophy. The leading figure in this effort to explain and justify the Hebrew Scriptures in terms of Greek philosophy—to prove that Mosaic law, revealed by God, was compatible with truth discovered by natural reason—was Philo of Alexandria (c. 20 B.C.–50 A.D.). Scion of a wealthy, aristocratic Jewish family, Philo was intimately familiar with the Greek cultural tradition and greatly admired Plato. He believed that Plato's view of God, as presented in the *Timaeus,* was compatible with Hebrew Scripture. In that work Plato had posited an eternal God who had existed prior to his creation of the world and continued to exist as an incorporeal and transcendent being.

On several points Philo disagreed with Greek philosophy. For example, holding that only God was eternal, he could not accept the Platonic view of the eternity of Ideas or Forms. Nor could he accept the position of Greek philosophy that the laws of nature were inexorable, for this precluded divine miracles. In these and other instances, Philo skillfully used the tools of Greek logic to harmonize differing viewpoints. His blending of Platonism with Scripture would be continued by Christian thinkers who admired Philo's achievement.

In the following selections, Philo expresses his admiration for Greek culture.

There was a time when I had leisure for philosophy and for the contemplation of the universe and its contents, when I made its spirit my own in all its beauty and loveliness and true blessedness, when my constant companions were divine themes and verities, wherein I rejoiced with a joy that never cloyed or sated. I had no base or abject thoughts nor grovelled in search of reputation or of wealth or bodily comforts, but seemed always to be borne aloft into the heights with a soul possessed by some God-sent inspiration, a fellow-traveller with the sun and moon and the whole heaven and universe. Ah then I gazed down from the upper air, and straining the mind's eye beheld, as from some commanding peak, the multitudinous world-wide spectacles of earthly things, and blessed my lot in that I had escaped by main force from the plagues of mortal life. But, as it proved, my steps were dogged by the deadliest of mischiefs, the hater of the good, envy, which suddenly set upon me and ceased not to pull me down with violence till it had plunged me in the ocean of civil cares, in which I am swept away, unable even to raise my head above the water. Yet amid my groans I hold my own, for, planted in my soul from my earliest days I keep the yearning for culture which ever has pity and compassion for me, lifts me up and relieves my pain. To this I owe it that sometimes I raise my head and with the soul's eyes—dimly indeed because the mist of extraneous affairs has clouded their clear vision—I yet make shift to look around me in my desire to inhale a breath of life pure and unmixed with evil. And if unexpectedly I obtain a spell of fine weather and a calm from civil turmoils, I get me wings and ride the waves and almost tread the lower air, wafted by the breezes of knowledge which often urges me to come to spend my days with her, a truant as it were from merciless masters in the shape not only of men but of affairs, which pour in upon me like a torrent from different sides. Yet it is well for me to give thanks to God even for this, that though submerged I am not sucked down into the depths, but can also open the soul's eyes, which in my despair of comforting hope I thought had now lost their sight, and am irradiated by the light of wisdom, and am not given over to lifelong darkness. So behold me daring, not only to read the sacred messages of Moses, but also in my love of knowledge to peer into each of them and unfold and reveal what is not known to the multitude.

. . . For instance when first I was incited by the goads of philosophy to desire her I consorted in early youth with one of her handmaids, Grammar, and all that I begat by her, writing, reading and study of the writings of the poets, I dedicated to her mistress. And again I kept company with another, namely Geometry, and was charmed with her beauty, for she shewed symmetry and proportion in every part. Yet I took none of her children for my private use, but brought them as a gift to the lawful wife. Again my ardour moved me to keep company with a third; rich in rhythm, harmony and melody was she, and her name was Music, and from her I begat diatonics, chromatics and enharmonics, conjunct and disjunct melodies, conforming with the consonance of the fourth, fifth or octave intervals. And again of none of these did I make a secret hoard, wishing to see the lawful wife a lady of wealth with a host of servants ministering to her.

Philo sought to demonstrate the truth of Judaism to a non-Jewish culture. In the passage below, he employs the categories of Greek philosophy to provide proof for God's existence and his creation of the universe.

Doubtless hard to unriddle and hard to apprehend is the Father and Ruler of all, but that is no reason why we should shrink from searching for Him. But in such searching two principal questions arise which demand the consideration of the genuine philosopher. One is whether the Deity exists, a question necessitated by those who practise atheism, the worst form of wickedness, the other is what the Deity is in essence. Now to answer the first question does not need much labour, but the second is not only difficult but perhaps impossible to solve. Still, both must be examined. We see then that any piece of work always involves the knowledge of a workman. Who can look upon statues or painting without thinking at once of a sculptor or painter? Who can see clothes or ships or houses without getting the idea of a weaver and a shipwright and a housebuilder? And when one enters a well-ordered city in which the arrangements for civil life are very admirably managed, what else will he suppose but that this city is directed by good rulers? So then he who comes to the truly Great City, this world, and beholds hills and plains teeming with animals and plants, the rivers, spring-fed or winter torrents, streaming along, the seas with their expanses, the air with its happily tempered phases, the yearly seasons passing into each other, and then the sun and moon ruling the day and night, and the other heavenly bodies fixed or planetary and the whole firmament revolving in rhythmic order, must he not naturally or rather necessarily gain the conception of the Maker and Father and Ruler also? For none of the works of human art is self-made, and the highest art and knowledge is shewn in this universe, so that surely it has been wrought by one of excellent knowledge and absolute perfection. In this way we have gained the conception of the existence of God.

3 Hellenistic Philosophy: Epicureanism

Hellenistic philosophy marks a second stage in the evolution of Greek thought. In the Hellenic Age, philosophers dealt primarily with the individual's relationship to the city-state. In the Hellenistic Age, philosophers were concerned with defining the individual's relationship to a wider, often competitive and hostile community that consisted of a plurality of peoples and a variety of cultures. In particular, the later philosophers sought to help people become ethically self-sufficient so that they could attain peace of mind in such an environment. Among the most significant schools of philosophy that emerged during the Hellenistic Age were Stoicism and Epicureanism.

Epicurus
SELF-SUFFICIENCY

Epicureanism was named for its founder, Epicurus (341–270 B.C.), who established a school at Athens in 307 or 306 B.C. To achieve peace of mind, taught Epicurus, one should refrain from worrying about death or pleasing the gods, avoid intense involvements in public affairs, cultivate friendships, and pursue pleasure prudently. The following excerpts from Epicurus's works reveal his prescription for achieving emotional well-being. The passages have been grouped according to particular subjects.

THE GODS

. . . We must grasp this point, that the principal disturbance in the minds of men arises because they think that these celestial bodies are blessed and immortal, and yet have wills and actions and motives inconsistent with these attributes; and because they are always expecting or imagining some everlasting misery [inflicted on them by the gods], such as is depicted in legends, or even fear the loss of feeling in death . . . and, again, because they are brought to this pass not by reasoned opinion, but rather by some irrational presentiment . . . and, by learning the true causes of celestial phenomena and all other occurrences that come to pass from time to time, we shall free ourselves from all which produces the utmost fear in other men.

It is vain to ask of the gods what a man is capable of supplying for himself.

DEATH

. . . So death, the most terrifying of ills, is nothing to us, since so long as we exist, death is not with us; but when death comes, then we do not exist. It does not then concern either the living or the dead, since for the former it is not, and the latter are no more.

But the many at one moment shun death as the greatest of evils, at another yearn for it as a respite from the evils in life. But the wise man neither seeks to escape life nor fears the cessation of life, for neither does life offend him nor does the absence of life seem to be any evil. And just as with food he does not seek simply the larger share and nothing else, but rather the most pleasant, so he seeks to enjoy not the longest period of time, but the most pleasant.

REASON AND PHILOSOPHY

Let no one when young delay to study philosophy, nor when he is old grow weary of his study. For no one can come too early or too late to secure the health of his soul. And the man who says that the age for philosophy has either not yet come or has gone by is like the man who says that the age for happiness is not yet come to him, or has passed away. Wherefore both when young and old a man must study philosophy, that as he grows old he may be young in blessings through the grateful recollection of what has been and that in youth he may be old as well, since he will know no fear of what is to come. We must then meditate on the things that make our happiness, seeing that when that is with us we have all, but when it is absent we do all to win it.

A man cannot dispel his fear about the most important matters if he does not know what is the nature of the universe but suspects the truth of some mythical story. So that without natural science it is not possible to attain our pleasures unalloyed.

We must not pretend to study philosophy, but study it in reality: for it is not the appearance of health that we need, but real health.

LIVING WELL

When, therefore, we maintain that pleasure is the end, we do not mean the pleasures of profligates and those that consist in sensuality, as is supposed by some who are either ignorant or disagree with us or do not understand, but freedom from pain in the body and from trouble in the mind. For it is not continuous drinkings and revellings, nor the satisfaction of lusts, nor the enjoyment of fish and other luxuries of the wealthy table, which produce a pleasant life, but sober reasoning, searching out the motives for all choice and avoidance, and banishing mere opinions, to which are due the greatest disturbance of the spirit.

Of all this the beginning and the greatest good is prudence. Wherefore prudence is a more precious thing even than philosophy; for from prudence are sprung all the other virtues, and it teaches us that it is not possible to live pleasantly without living prudently and honourably and justly. . . .

—————

Of all the things which wisdom acquires to produce the blessedness of the complete life, far the greatest is the possession of friendship.

—————

We must release ourselves from the prison of affairs and politics.

—————

A free life cannot acquire many possessions, because this is not easy to do without servility to mobs or monarchs. . . .

—————

The noble soul occupies itself with wisdom and friendship. . . .

—————

The first measure of security is to watch over one's youth and to guard against what makes havoc of all by means of pestering desires.

4   Hellenistic Literature: Romance and Epic

In several ways Hellenistic literature gave expression to the new world that emerged after Alexander the Great's conquests. Unlike their Hellenic predecessors, who flourished in the vibrant world of the independent city-state, Hellenistic poets and dramatists dwelled in cities that were dominated by monarchies. As a result, their interest gravitated away from politics to everyday concerns and ordinary people. They wrote about common workers, lovers, children, pets, nature, and so on. There is a close parallel between the subject matter of literature, which focused on the particulars of the human condition, and the visual arts, which also depicted daily events and common people, including fishermen, drunken women, hunchbacks, infants, and a boy with a deer. Also like the visual arts, Hellenistic literature evidenced a sophisticated realism, giving careful attention to detail. Finally, literature reflected the broader frontiers of the age: Some of the themes selected by Greek writers showed the impact of Near Eastern cultures, and some of the writers of the period were not Greek by birth.

Longus
Daphnis and Chloe
A Hellenistic Romance

As historical fiction, the Hellenistic romance was the precursor of the modern romance novel. It was introduced during the first century B.C. and reached its height in the second and third centuries A.D. The plot generally revolves around an admirable heroine who, separated from her gallant lover either because of natural disasters or human maliciousness, eventually reunites with him.

The best known of the later Hellenistic romances is *Daphnis and Chloe,* written by Longus in the third century A.D. Daphnis and Chloe are orphans in Lesbos who were raised by shepherds; they meet, fall in love, and eventually marry. Their romance focuses on their emotional development as lovers—they move from immature, infatuated children to complete sexual partners. "Love made something serious flare up" when Daphnis sets a trap for a she-wolf. Daphnis and a goat fall into the pit of the trap, and Chloe and the cowherd, Dorcon, arrive to help them.

In the following passage from *Daphnis and Chloe,* Longus recounts how Chloe first became enamored of Daphnis' beauty and how this led to her all-consuming love for him.

So Daphnis waited in tears for someone to pull him out—if anyone was ever going to. But Chloe, who had seen the whole thing, came running to the pit and finding that Daphnis was alive called a cowherd in a neighbouring field to come and help. When he arrived he started looking for a long rope for Daphnis to hold on to, so as to be pulled out; and there was no rope to be found. But Chloe untied her breastband and gave the cowherd that to let down. So they stood on the edge of the pit and pulled, while Daphnis clung to the breastband with both hands and came up with it. . . .

Having made sure that both the sheep and the goats were grazing properly, they sat down against the trunk of an oak and looked to see if Daphnis had got blood on any part of his body as a result of his fall. There was no sign of a wound and no trace of blood, but his hair and the rest of his body were plastered with loose earth and mud. . . .

So he went off with Chloe to the sanctuary of the Nymphs,[1] where he gave her his shirt and knapsack to look after, while he stood in front of the spring and started washing his hair and his whole body. His hair was black and thick, and his body was slightly sunburnt—it looked as though it was darkened by the shadow of his hair. It seemed to Chloe, as she watched him, that Daphnis was beautiful; and as he had never seemed beautiful to her before, she thought that this beauty must be the result of washing. Moreover, when she washed his back, she found that the flesh was soft and yielding; so she secretly touched her own body several times to see if it was any softer. Then, as the sun was setting, they drove their flocks home, and nothing out of the ordinary had happened to Chloe except that she had set her heart on seeing Daphnis washing again.

When they got to the pasture next day, Daphnis sat down under the usual oak and began to play his pipe. At the same time he kept an eye on the goats, which were lying down and apparently listening to the music. Chloe sat beside him and kept watch over her flock of sheep; but most of the time she was looking at Daphnis. While he was piping he again seemed to her beautiful, and this time she thought that the beauty was caused by the music; so when he had finished she picked up the pipe herself, in the hope that she too might become beautiful. She also persuaded him to have another wash; and while he was washing she looked at him, and after looking at him she touched him. And again she went away full of admiration, and this admiration was the beginning of love.

She did not know what was wrong with her, for she was only a young girl who had been brought up in the country and had never even heard the word "love" used by anyone else. But she felt sick at heart, and she could not control her eyes, and she was always talking about Daphnis. She took no interest in food, she could not sleep at night, she paid no attention to her flock. One moment she would be laughing, the next she would be crying. Now she would be lying down, now she would be jumping up again. Her face would grow pale, and then grow fiery red. In fact cows that have been stung by gadflies behave less oddly than she did.

One day when she was alone she found herself talking like this: "There's something wrong with me these days, but I don't know what it is. I'm in pain, and yet I've not been injured. I feel sad, and yet none of my sheep have got lost. I'm burning hot, and yet here I am sitting in the shade. How often I've been scratched by brambles and not cried! How often I've been stung by bees and not screamed! But this thing that's pricking my heart hurts more than anything like that. Daphnis *is* beautiful, but so are the flowers. His pipe does sound beautiful, but so do the nightingales—and I don't worry about them. If only I *were* his pipe, so that he'd breathe into me! If only I were a goat, so that I could have him looking after me! You wicked water, you made Daphnis beautiful but when I tried washing it made no difference. Oh, Nymphs, I'm dying—and even you do nothing to save the girl who was nursed in your cave. Who will put garlands on you when I'm gone? Who will rear the poor lambs? Who will look after my chattering locust? I had a lot of trouble catching her, so that she could talk me to sleep in front of the cave—and now I can't sleep because of Daphnis, and she chatters away for nothing."

That was how she suffered and that was how she talked, as she tried to find a name for love. . . .

Longus subsequently recounts a "beauty-contest" between Daphnis and Dorcon, during which Chloe serves as judge. The prize for the victor is "the privilege of kissing Chloe." Daphnis wins the contest, due to his compliment for Chloe, and she rushes to kiss him. He then suffers the pangs of love for Chloe.

Chloe waited no longer but, partly because she was pleased by the compliment and partly because she had been wanting to kiss Daphnis for a long time, she jumped up and kissed him. It was an artless and inexperienced sort of kiss, but one which was quite capable of setting a heart on fire. So Dorcon ran off in dismay, and began to look for some other

---

[1]Nymphs are beautiful maiden-deities, generally associated with Zeus.

method of satisfying his love. But Daphnis reacted as if he had been stung rather than kissed. He suddenly looked almost indignant and shivered several times and tried to control his pounding heart; he wanted to look at Chloe, but when he did so he blushed all over. Then for the first time he saw with wonder that her hair was as golden as fire, that her eyes were as big as the eyes of an ox, and that her complexion was really even whiter than the milk of the goats. It was as if he had just got eyes for the first time, and had been blind all his life before.

So he stopped eating any food except for a mere taste, and if he had to drink he did no more than moisten his lips. Before, he had been more talkative than a locust; now he was taciturn. Before, he had been more active than a goat: now he sat idle. His flock was forgotten; even his Pan-pipe[2] was thrown aside. His face was paler than grass at midsummer. The only person that he would talk to was Chloe; and if ever he was apart from her and alone, he would rave away to himself like this: 'Whatever is Chloe's kiss doing to me? Her lips are softer than roses and her mouth is sweeter than honey, but her kiss hurts more than the sting of a bee. I've often kissed kids, and I've often kissed newborn puppies and the calf that Dorcon gave her, but this kiss is something quite new. My breath's coming in gasps, my heart's jumping up and down, my soul's melting away—but all the same I want to kiss her again. Oh, what an unlucky victory! Oh, what a strange disease—I don't even know what to call it. Had Chloe drunk poison just before she kissed me? If so, how did she manage not to be killed? Hear how the nightingales are singing—and my pipe is silent. Look how the kids are frisking about—and I'm sitting still. Look how the flowers are blooming—and I'm not making any garlands. Yes, the violets and the hyacinths are in flower, but Daphnis is withering away. Is Dorcon going to seem better-looking than I am after all?'

That was how the worthy Daphnis suffered, and that was how he talked; for it was his first experience of love, and the language of love. . . .

Their love passes through stages: kissing, embracing, and dreaming about being naked together. Finally, Daphnis yearns to make love to Chloe, but recognizes that he does not know how. He subsequently receives lessons in lovemaking from an "experienced woman" named Lycaenion.

Lycaenion began to educate Daphnis as follows. She told him to sit down beside her, just as he was, and start kissing her in a quite ordinary way. Then while still kissing her, he was to take her in his arms and lie down on the ground. So Daphnis sat down, and started kissing her, and after a while lay down; and when she felt him get big and ready for action, she raised him up from where he lay on his side, slipped her body under his,

and deftly guided him into the passage that he had been trying so long to find. After that she made no special efforts; for Nature herself taught Daphnis all that remained to be done.

Daphnis immediately decides to put his new knowledge into practice with Chloe, but Lycaenion cautions him to be wary, because she is "an experienced woman" and Chloe is a virgin, and so love-making for her will be painful. Consequently, Daphnis decides to postpone his pleasure until after he marries Chloe. The couple's plans to marry are, however, thwarted, first by Chloe's foster parents, Dryas and Nape (who believe that Daphnis is not good enough for her), and then by Daphnis' foster parents, Lamon and Myrtale (who feel likewise about Chloe). Ultimately, Daphnis and Chloe are reunited with their real, well-to-do parents—Dionysophanes and Cleariste (Daphnis) and Megalces and Rhode (Chloe)—and a joyous pastoral wedding is planned.

Dionysophanes cried out even more loudly than Megacles had done, and jumping up he led in Chloe, very beautifully dressed, and said:

"Here's the baby that you exposed! By the mercy of providence a ewe nursed this girl of yours, just as a she-goat nursed my Daphnis. Take your tokens and your daughter—and when you've done so, give her back to me as a bride for Daphnis. We exposed them both—we've found them both! Both of them were looked after by Pan, and the Nymphs, and Love!"

Megacles applauded this proposal, and sent for Rhode, his wife, and clasped Chloe to his bosom. Then they all stayed there for the night; for Daphnis swore that he would not let anyone take Chloe away from him—not even her own father.

Next day, by common consent they drove back into the country; for Daphnis and Chloe were very anxious to do so, as they could not bear living in town. It was their idea too that their wedding should be a pastoral affair. So they went to Lamon's cottage, where they introduced Dryas to Megacles and presented Nape to Rhode. Then they started making preparations for the wedding-feast. And so in the presence of the Nymphs her father gave Chloe away, and along with many other things presented the tokens as thank-offerings, and gave Dryas what he needed to make up a total of ten thousand drachmas.

And there in front of the cave, as the weather was fine, Dionysophanes had couches of green leaves heaped up, and after inviting all the villagers to lie on them he entertained them lavishly. Lamon and Myrtale were there, and Dryas and Nape, and Dorcon's relations, and Philetas and his sons, and Chromis and Lycaenion. Not even Lampis was missing, for he had been judged worthy of forgiveness.

As was only to be expected with guests like these, everything that took place was of an agricultural and rustic nature. One man sang the kind of songs that reapers sing, another cracked the sort of jokes that are heard round the wine-press.

---

[2]Pan is the ancient Greek god of shepherds and forests, with the legs, ears, and horns of a goat; and the torso of man, who plays the pipes.

Philetas played his pipe; Lampis played a flute; Dryas and Lamon danced; Chloe and Daphnis kissed one another. Even the goats were there, grazing close by as if they too were taking part in the feast. The visitors from town did not find this altogether pleasant; but Daphnis called to some of the goats by name, and fed them with green leaves, and seized them by the horns and kissed them.

And it was not only then that they behaved like this, for as long as they lived they spent most of their time in pastoral pursuits, worshipping the Nymphs and Pan and Love as their gods, possessing a great many flocks of sheep and goats, and thinking that fruit and milk made a most delicious diet. Moreover, when they had a baby boy, they put him out to nurse with a she-goat; and when a little daughter was born to them next, they made her suck away at the teat of a ewe. And they called him Philopoimen, or Lover-of-flocks, and her Agelaia, or Lover-of-herds. Thus they and this way of life grew old together.

They also decorated the cave and set up images in it, and consecrated an altar to Love the Shepherd, and gave Pan a temple to live in instead of the pine, calling him Pan the Warrior.

But it was only later that they did these things and invented these names. Now, when night fell, all the guests escorted them to the bridal chamber, some playing Pan-pipes, some playing flutes, and some holding up great torches. When they were near the door, the peasants began to sing in harsh grating voices as if they were breaking the soil with hoes instead of singing a wedding-song. But Daphnis and Chloe lay down naked together, and began to embrace and kiss one another; and for all the sleep they got that night they might as well have been owls. For Daphnis did some of the things that Lycaenion had taught him; and then for the first time Chloe realized that what had taken place on the edge of the wood had been nothing but childish play.

Apollonius of Rhodes
Argonautica
A Homeric-Style Epic

Callimachus (c. 305–240 B.C.), an Alexandrian scholar-poet, felt that no one could duplicate the great epic poems of Homer or the plays of the fifth-century B.C. dramatists. He urged poets to write short, finely crafted poems instead of composing on a grand scale.

One of Callimachus's students was probably Apollonius of Rhodes (third–second century B.C.), who took issue with his mentor when he wrote the *Argonautica.* This Homeric-style epic (in four books) tells the story of Jason, who sailed with his warriors, the Argonauts, on the ship *Argo* to recover the Golden Fleece. Jason is the son of Aeson, king of Iolcus, whose throne had been usurped by his half brother, Pelias. An oracle warns Pelias that a descendant of Aeson, wearing only one sandal, will kill him. Returning to Ioclus to claim his father's throne, a now mature Jason loses a sandal helping an old woman, really the goddess Hera in disguise, across a river. When he arrives at his uncle's palace, Pelias agrees to return the throne, if Jason would first recover the Golden Fleece which is guarded by a dragon in the Black Sea port of Colchis.

Jason and the Argonauts have many adventures before arriving at Colchis, where King Aeetes agrees to return the fleece if Jason would submit to a trial to test his courage and strength. The king orders Jason to yoke to a plough a pair of bulls that "blow flame from their mouths." Meanwhile, Medea, Aeetes' daughter, has fallen in love with Jason. In the passages excerpted below, Apollonius brilliantly captures both the physical and psychological dimensions of love.

Eros, meanwhile, went unseen through the gray mist,
distracting as the gadfly that attacks the heifers
and that the cowherds call the breese. Quickly beneath
the lintel in the entrance he strung his bow and took
from his quiver an arrow, not shot before, to bring much
     pain.
With quick feet he slipped unseen across the threshold
and glanced sharply around. He crept, crouched down,
past Aeson's son, and fitted his notched arrow end
to the middle of the string, stretched it with both hands,
and shot Medea. She was struck utterly speechless.
But he himself darted away from the high-roofed hall
and laughed aloud, but the shaft burned in the girl's heart,
deep down, like a flame, and she kept glancing at Jason
with sparkling eyes, and her breath came in panting gasps
in her distress. She forgot everything else, and her soul
melted in sweet anguish. As when a toiling woman
piles dry sticks around a piece of burning wood
that she may make a fire beneath her roof by night
if she has waked very early, the flame from the small brand
grows miraculously and consumes all the kindling—
so coiled beneath Medea's heart there burned in secret
destructive love. The color of her tender cheeks
turned now to pale, now to red, she was so distraught.

Medea suffers when she learns of the ordeal her father is imposing on Jason.

                    She pondered in her soul
all the many concerns that the loves arouse in one.
Before her eyes everything was vivid still—
how he looked, what clothes he wore, how he spoke,
how he sat on his chair, and how he moved to the door.
In her excitement she thought that there could be no other
such man. In her ears there rang continuously his voice
and the honey-sweet words that he spoke. She feared for him
     lest the bulls
or even Aeetes himself destroy him. She grieved for him
as though he were already dead, and a delicate tear
trickled down her cheek in her very terrible pity and grief.
Weeping softly, she lifted her voice and cried aloud,
"Why does this agony take me, unhappy that I am?
Whether he perish, the best of all heroes or worst,
let him go. I hope that he will escape unharmed—yes,
may this happen, revered goddess, daughter of Perses,
may he make the voyage home, escaping doom, but if
it be his fate to be worsted by oxen, may he know
this first, that I do not rejoice in his disaster."
So then the girl's mind was racked by anxiety. . . .

She cannot sleep.

                    But sweet sleep did not
capture Medea. In longing for Jason, her many cares

kept her awake. She feared the mighty strength of the bulls
by which he was destined to die by an unfitting doom in the
     field
of Ares. For pity a tear flowed from her eye. Always
within her agony bored, smoldering through the flesh
and her delicate nerves and deep beneath the nape of her neck
where pain enters most piercingly when the unwearied
loves plant in the heart their shifts of suffering.
And quickly did her heart leap within her breast
as when in a house a sunbeam quivers when it darts
from water just poured in a cauldron or pail perhaps; now here,
now there, on the quick eddy it flickers and bounces along.
So did the young girl's heart quiver within her breast.

Medea awaits a meeting with Jason.

Nor did Medea's heart turn to other thoughts,
though she sang and danced. But no song that she sang, no
     game that she played,
pleased her for very long, but she would stop, distraught,
nor did she keep her eyes steadily upon
the throng of her serving maids, but she would peer at the
     paths
far-off, turning her face aside. Often her heart
broke within her breast when she thought that she heard the
     fall
of a footstep or the sound of the wind passing by. But soon,
even as she yearned for him, he appeared to her
striding high into view, like Sirius from Ocean,
which rises lovely and conspicuous to see
but brings unspeakable disaster to flocks. So Jason
came to her, beautiful to see, but he,
when he appeared, provoked lovesick suffering.
Her heart fell from her breast, her eyes were misted over,
and a hot blush covered her cheeks. She had the strength
to lift her knees neither forward nor back, but her feet beneath
were fixed fast. All her serving maids meanwhile
had drawn aside from them. So they two stood
opposite one another, speechless and silent, like
oaks or tall pines which, rooted side by side,
are silent for the want of wind, but then again
stirred by the breath of a breeze murmur ceaselessly—
so they were about to speak, stirred by the breath of Eros.

Lovingly, she hands him a magic drug that will give him the strength of a god when he battles the bulls.

He spoke, flattering her. She cast her eyes askance
and smiled as sweetly as nectar. Her soul melted within.
Elated by his praise, she gazed up at him,
face to face, and did not know what word to say
first, she was so eager to tell him everything
at once. Ungrudgingly she took from her fragrant sash
the drug, and he at once accepted it with joy.

And now she would have drawn all the soul from her breast
and put it into his hands, delighting in his desire,
so did love flash forth from Jason's blond hair,
a sweet flame, and he captured the sparkle of her eyes.
Her heart warmed within and melted away, as the dew
melts around the roses, warmed by the rays of dawn.
And now both would fix their eyes upon the ground,
bashfully, and now again would cast glances
at one another, smiling with all the light of desire
beneath their radiant brows.

Roman Civilization

The city-state was the foundation of Greek society in the Hellenic Age; in the Hellenistic Age, Greek cities became subordinate to larger political units, ruled by autocratic monarchs. Hellenistic philosophers conceived of a still broader political arrangement: a world-state in which people of different nationalities were bound together by the ties of common citizenship and law that applied to all. It was Rome's great achievement to construct such a world-state.

Roman history falls into two broad periods—the Republic and the Empire. The Roman Republic began in 509 B.C. with the overthrow of the Etruscan monarchy and lasted until 27 B.C., when Octavian (Augustus) became in effect the first Roman emperor, ending almost five hundred years of republican self-government. For the next five hundred years, Rome would be governed by emperors.

In 264 B.C., when the Roman Republic had established dominion over the Italian peninsula, there were four other great powers in the Mediterranean world. Carthage controlled North Africa, Corsica, Sardinia, and parts of Spain and Sicily. The other powers—Macedonia, Egypt, and Syria—were the three Hellenistic kingdoms carved out of the empire of Alexander the Great. By 146 B.C., Rome had emerged victorious over the other powers, and by 30 B.C. they were all Roman provinces.

The Roman Republic, which had conquered a vast empire, was not destroyed by foreign armies but by internal weaknesses. In the century after 133 B.C., the Senate, which had governed Rome well during its march to empire, degenerated into a self-seeking oligarchy; it failed to resolve critical domestic problems and fought to preserve its own power and prestige. When Rome had been threatened by foreign enemies, all classes united in a spirit of patriotism. This social harmony broke down when the threat from outside diminished, and the Republic was torn by internal dissension and civil war.

In the chaotic years following Julius Caesar's assassination in 44 B.C., Octavian (Augustus) emerged victorious over his rivals, becoming the unchallenged ruler of Rome. Although eager for personal power, Augustus was by no means a self-seeking tyrant; he was a creative statesman who prevented the renewal of civil war that had plagued the Republic and introduced needed reforms in Italy and the provinces. His long reign, from 27 B.C. to A.D. 14, marks the beginning of the *Pax Romana,* the Roman Peace, which endured until A.D. 180.

The period of the Pax Romana was one of the finest in the ancient world. Revolts against Roman rule were few, and Roman legions ably defended the Empire's borders. The Mediterranean world had never enjoyed so many years of peace, effective government, and economic well-being. Stretching from Britain to the Arabian Desert and from the Danube River to the sands of the Sahara, the Roman Empire united some seventy million people. In many ways the Roman Empire was the fulfillment of the universalism and cosmopolitanism of the Hellenistic Age. The same law bound together Italians, Spaniards, North Africans, Greeks, Syrians, and other peoples. Although dissatisfaction was sometimes violently expressed and separatist tendencies persisted, notably in Judea and Gaul, people from diverse backgrounds viewed themselves as Romans even though they had never set foot in the capital city.

In the seventy years following Augustus' reign, political life was sometimes marred by conspiracies and assassinations, particularly after an emperor's death left the throne vacant. Marcus Cocceius Nerva, who reigned from A.D. 96 to 98, introduced a practice that led to orderly succession and gave Rome four exceptionally competent emperors. He adopted as his son and designated as his heir Trajan (Marcus Ulpius Traianus), a man of proven ability. From the accession of Nerva to the death of Marcus Aurelius Antoninus in A.D. 180, the Roman Empire was ruled by the "Five Good Emperors." Marcus Aurelius abandoned the use of adoption and allowed his son Commodus (Lucius Aelius Aurelius, A.D. 180–192) to succeed to the throne. An extravagant despot, Commodus was murdered in A.D. 192.

During the third century the Roman Empire suffered hard times, and the ordered civilization of the Pax Romana was destroyed. The Empire was plunged into anarchy as generals vied for the throne. Taking advantage of the weakened border defenses, the barbarians (Germanic tribesmen) crossed the Danube frontier and pillaged Roman cities. Both civil war and barbarian attacks greatly disrupted the Roman economy, which even during good times suffered from basic weaknesses.

Two later emperors—Diocletian (G. Aurelius Valerius Diocletianus, A.D. 285–305) and Constantine (Flavius Valerius Constantinus, A.D. 306–337)—tried to keep the Empire from dissolution by tightening control over the citizenry. Although heavy taxes, requisitioning of goods, and forced labor provided some stability, these measures also turned many citizens against the oppressive state. At the end of the fourth and the opening of the fifth century, several barbarian tribes poured into the Empire in great numbers. In succeeding decades Germanic tribes overran Roman provinces and set up kingdoms on lands that had been Roman. The Roman Empire in the west fell; the eastern provinces, however, survived as the Byzantine Empire.

The history of the Roman Empire influenced Western civilization in many ways. From Latin, the language of Rome, came the Romance languages: French, Italian, Spanish, Portuguese, and Romanian. Roman law became the basis of the legal codes of most modern European states. Rome preserved Greek culture, the foundation of Western learning and aesthetics, and spread it to other lands. And Christianity, the religion of the West, was born in the Roman Empire.

1 The Spread of Greek Philosophy to Rome

One of the chief consequences of Roman expansion was growing contact with Greek culture. During the third century B.C., Greek civilization started to exercise an increasing and fruitful influence on the Roman mind. Greek teachers, both slave and free, came to Rome and introduced Romans to Hellenic cultural achievements. As they conquered the eastern Mediterranean, Roman generals began to ship libraries and works of art from Greek cities to Rome. Roman sculpture and painting imitated Greek prototypes. In time, Romans acquired from Greece knowledge of scientific thought, medicine, and geography. Roman writers and orators used Greek history, poetry, and oratory as models. Roman philosophers borrowed the ideas of Greek philosophical schools and adapted them to Roman culture.

Lucretius
DENUNCIATION OF RELIGION

The writings of the Greek philosopher Epicurus (see page 91) soon won admirers in Rome. Lucretius (c. 96–c. 55 B.C.), the leading Roman Epicurean philosopher, lived in a time of civil war, which was fostered by two generals, Marius and Sulla. Distraught by the seemingly endless strife, Lucretius yearned for philosophical tranquillity. Like Epicurus, he believed that religion prompted people to perform evil deeds and caused them to experience terrible anxiety about death and eternal punishment. Like his mentor, Lucretius advanced a materialistic conception of nature, one that left no room for the activity of gods—mechanical laws, not the gods, governed all physical happenings. To dispel the fear of punishment after death, Lucretius marshaled arguments to prove that the soul perishes with the body. He proposed that the simple life, devoid of political involvement and excessive passion, was the highest good. Epicurus' disparagement of politics and public service and rejection of the goals of power and glory ran counter to the accepted Roman ideal of virtue. On the other hand, his praise of the quiet life amid a community of friends and his advice on how to deal with life's misfortunes with serenity had great appeal to first-century Romans who were disgusted with civil strife.

In the following selection from *On the Nature of Things*, Lucretius expresses his hostility to religion and his admiration for Epicurus, "the first to stand firm in defiance" of the fables about the gods.

When before our eyes man's life lay groveling, prostrate,
Crushed to the dust under the burden of Religion
(Which thrust its head from heaven, its horrible face
Glowering over mankind born to die),
One man, a Greek [Epicurus], was the first mortal who dared
Oppose his eyes, the first to stand firm in defiance.
Not the fables of gods, nor lightning, nor the menacing
Rumble of heaven could daunt him, but all the more
They whetted his keen mind with longing to be
First to smash open the tight-barred gates of Nature.
His vigor of mind prevailed, and he strode far
Beyond the fiery battlements of the world,
Raiding the fields of the unmeasured All.
Our victor returns with knowledge of what can arise,
What cannot, what law grants each thing its own
Deep-driven boundary stone and finite scope.
Religion now lies trampled beneath our feet,
And we are made gods by the victory.

> In Greek mythology, Agamemnon was compelled to sacrifice his daughter Iphigenia. A seer had declared that the goddess Artemis demanded the sacrifice. For Lucretius, this event illustrates how religion "gives birth to evil and blasphemous deeds."

You hear these things, and I fear you'll think yourself
On the road to evil, learning the fundamentals
Of blasphemy. Not so! Too often Religion
Herself gives birth to evil and blasphemous deeds.

At Aulis, for instance: the pride of the Greek people,
The chosen peers, defiled Diana's[1] altar
With the shameful blood of the virgin Iphigenia.
As soon as they tressed her hair with the ritual fillet [headband],
The tassels spilling neatly upon each cheek,
And she sensed her grieving father beside the altar
With the acolytes nearby, hiding the knife,
And countrymen weeping to look upon her—mute
With fear, she fell to her knees, she groped for the earth.
Poor girl, what good did it do her then, that she
Was the first to give the king the name of "father"?
Up to the altar the men escorted her, trembling:
Not so that when her solemn rites were finished
She might be cheered in the ringing wedding-hymn,
But filthily, at the marrying age, unblemished
Victim, she fell by her father's slaughter-stroke. . . .

> Lucretius attempts to explain why people came to believe in powerful gods.

How the idea of gods spread to all nations,
Stocking their cities with altars and making men tremble
To undertake the solemn rites, which flourish
With all our luxury and magnificence
(Even now sowing in us the seeds of horror,
Urging us on to rear across the world

---

[1] Diana was the Roman goddess of nature and protector of women.

New shrines to the gods to crowd on festival days),
Is not hard to explain in a few words.
In those days mortal men saw while awake
The excellent countenances of the gods,
Or rather in dreams they gasped at their vast size.
Men lent sensation to these giant forms
For they moved their limbs, it seemed, and spoke proud
    words
As arrogant as their beauty and great strength.
Eternal life they gave them, for their faces
And their physiques persisted ever-present,
And they thought that beings endowed with such great
    power
Could never be put to rout by any force.
They thought the gods preeminently blest,
For the fear of death could hardly trouble them;
Also because in dreams they saw them do
Miraculous things, and many, without an effort.
Then too they saw the systems of the sky
Turn in sure order, and the changing seasons,
But could not understand why this occurred.
Their refuge, then: assign to the gods all things,
Have them steer all things with a single nod.
In the heavens they placed the holy haunts of the gods
For through the heavens wheeled the night and the moon,
The moon and the day, the night and night's stark signs,
And night-roaming torches of heaven and gliding flames,
Clouds, sun, storms, snow, high winds and hail and light-
    ning
And the sudden growl and great and menacing rumble.

Unhappy human race—to grant such feats
To gods, and then to add vindictiveness!
What wailing did they bring forth for themselves,
What wounds for us, what tears for our descendants!
It's no piety to be seen at every altar,
To cover your head and turn to the stone idol,
Or to flatten yourself on the ground and lift your palms
To the shrines, or to spray altars with the blood

Of cattle—so much!—or to string vow on vow.
To observe all things with a mind at peace
Is piety. For when we look up to the heavenly
Shrines of this great world, the stars that glitter, the sky
Studded, when we think of the journeying sun and moon,
Then in hearts heavy-laden with other cares
That Trouble is roused to boot, and rears its head—
That the limitless power of gods, the power that wheels
The stars and planets, may be aimed at us.
Then ignorance assails the mind in doubt
About the universe's origin,
About the end, how long the walls of the world
Can suffer the straining of such stir and motion,
Or whether, granted everlasting health
By the gods, they can in endless course disdain
The turning age and the vast strength of time.
And worse, whose soul does not contract in fear
Of the gods, whose limbs don't crawl with terror when
The scorched earth under the terrible lightning bolt
Quakes, and a grumbling rolls through the great sky?
Don't people and nations tremble, and arrogant kings
Cringe, stricken into shock by fear of the gods,
Lest for some foul deed done or proud word said
The heavy time has come to pay the price?
When a high hard gale across the plains of the sea
Rakes a commander and his fleet along
With all his mighty elephants and legions,
Won't he beseech the "Peace of the Gods" in terror
And pray for peaceful breezes and fair winds?
In vain, for the whirlpool's got him anyway
And borne him down unto the shoals of Death.
So thoroughly is human grandeur crushed
By a hidden force; the glorious rods and axes,
Those splendid mockeries, are trampled under.
Well, when the whole earth staggers underfoot
And cities are battered and fall, or threaten to fall,
What wonder if self-loathing seizes men
And they grant wondrous power over all affairs
To gods, to steer and rule the universe?

2 Roman Stoicism

Stoicism, the leading school of thought in the Hellenistic world, appealed to Roman thinkers. Founded by Zeno of Citium (335–267 B.C.), who established an
academy in Athens, Stoicism taught that universal principles, or natural law, un-
derlay the universe. Natural laws applied to all people and were grasped
through reason, which was common to all human beings. Stoicism gave expression to the universalism of the Hellenistic Age; it held that all people—Greek
and barbarian, free and slave, rich and poor—were essentially equal, for they all
had the capacity to reason and were all governed by the same universal laws.
Living according to the law of reason that pervades the cosmos provides the

individual with the inner fortitude to deal with life's misfortunes, said the Stoics; it is the path to virtue. In the tradition of Socrates, the Stoics regarded people as morally self-sufficient, capable of regulating their own lives. The Romans valued the Stoic emphasis on self-discipline and the molding of character according to worthy standards. The Stoic doctrine of natural law that applied to all peoples harmonized with the requirements of Rome's multinational Empire.

Cicero

ADVOCATE OF STOICISM

Marcus Tullius Cicero (106–43 B.C.), a leading Roman statesman, was also a distinguished orator, an unsurpassed Latin stylist, and a student of Greek philosophy. His letters, more than eight hundred of which have survived, provide modern historians with valuable insights into late republican politics. His orations before the Senate and law courts have been models of eloquence and rhetorical technique for students of Latin and later European languages.

Like many other Romans, Cicero was influenced by Stoicism. Cicero adopted the Stoic belief that natural law governs the universe and applies to all and that all belong to a common humanity. The gift of reason, which is common to all people, enables us to comprehend this natural law and to order our lives in accordance with its principles, which are unchangeable and eternal. Natural law as understood by right reason commands people to do what is right and deters them from doing what is wrong. Thus there is a unity of knowledge and virtue. For Cicero, the laws of the state should accord with the natural law underlying the universe. Adherence to such rationally formulated laws creates a moral bond among citizens and the peoples of all nations and states. In the following passage from his philosophic treatise, *The Laws,* Cicero explored the implications of the Stoic concept of natural law.

. . . Now let us investigate the origins of Justice.

Well then, the most learned men have determined to begin with Law, and it would seem that they are right, if, according to their definition, Law is the highest reason, implanted in Nature, which commands what ought to be done and forbids the opposite. This reason, when firmly fixed and fully developed in the human mind, is Law. And so they believe that Law is intelligence whose natural function it is to command right conduct and forbid wrongdoing. They think that this quality has derived its name in Greek from the idea of granting to every man his own, and in our language I believe it has been named from the idea of choosing. For as they have attributed the idea of fairness to the word law, so we have given it that of selection, though both ideas properly belong to Law. Now if this is correct, as I think it to be in general, then the origin of Justice is to be found in Law, for Law is a natural force; it is the mind and reason of the intelligent man, the standard by which Justice and Injustice are measured. But since our whole discussion has to do with the reasoning of the populace, it will sometimes be necessary to speak in the popular manner, and give the name of law to that which in written form decrees whatever it wishes, either by command or prohibition. For such is the crowd's definition of law. But in determining what Justice is, let us begin with that supreme Law which had its origin ages before any written law existed or any State had been established.

. . . I shall seek the root of Justice in Nature, under whose guidance our whole discussion must be conducted.

. . . [T]hat animal which we call man, endowed with foresight and quick intelligence, complex, keen, possessing memory, full of reason and prudence, has been given a certain distinguished status by the supreme God who created him; for he is the only one among so many different kinds and varieties of living beings who has a share in reason and thought, while all the rest are deprived of it. But what is more divine, I will not say in man only, but in all heaven and earth, than reason? And reason, when it is full grown and perfected, is rightly called wisdom. Therefore, since there is nothing better than reason, and since it exists both in man and God, the first common possession of man and God is reason. But those who have reason in common must also have right reason in common. And since right reason is Law, we must believe that men have Law also in common with the gods. Further, those who share Law must also share Justice; and those who share these are to be regarded as members of the same commonwealth. If indeed they obey the same authorities and powers, this is true in a far greater degree; but as a matter of fact they do obey this celestial system, the divine mind, and the God of transcendent power. Hence we must now conceive of this whole universe as one commonwealth of which both gods and men are members.

Moreover, virtue exists in man and God alike, but in no other creature besides; virtue, however, is nothing else than Nature perfected and developed to its highest point; therefore there is a likeness between man and God. As this is true, what relationship could be closer or clearer than this one? For this reason, Nature has lavishly yielded such a wealth of things adapted to man's convenience and use that what she produces seems intended as a gift to us, and not brought forth by chance; and this is true, not only of what the fertile earth bountifully bestows in the form of grain and fruit, but also of the animals; for it is clear that some of them have been created to be man's slaves, some to supply him with their products, and others to serve as his food. Moreover innumerable arts have been discovered through the teachings of Nature; for it is by a skilful imitation of her that reason has acquired the necessities of life. . . .

. . . [O]ut of all the material of the philosophers' discussions, surely there comes nothing more valuable than the full realization that we are born for Justice, and that right is based, not upon men's opinions, but upon Nature. This fact will immediately be plain if you once get a clear conception of man's fellowship and union with his fellow-men. For no single thing is so like another, so exactly its counterpart, as all of us are to one another. Nay, if bad habits and false beliefs did not twist the weaker minds and turn them in whatever direction they are inclined, no one would be so like his own self as all men would be like all others. And so, however we may define man, a single definition will apply to all. This is a sufficient proof that there is no difference in kind between man and man; for if there were, one definition could not be applicable to all men; and indeed reason, which alone raises us above the level of the beasts and enables us to draw inferences, to prove and disprove, to discuss and solve problems, and to come to conclusions, is certainly common to us all, and, though varying in what it learns, at least in the capacity to learn it is invariable. For the same things are invariably perceived by the senses, and those things which stimulate the senses, stimulate them in the same way in all men; and those rudimentary beginnings of intelligence to which I have referred, which are imprinted on our minds, are imprinted on all minds alike; and speech, the mind's interpreter, though differing in the choice of words, agrees in the sentiments expressed. In fact, there is no human being of any race who, if he finds a guide, cannot attain to virtue.

Seneca

The Moral Epistles

Lucius Annaeus Seneca (4 B.C.–A.D. 65) was born at Corduba (Cordova), Spain, into a highly educated family. His father was a distinguished rhetorician, politician, and historian. Sent to school in Rome, Seneca studied rhetoric and philosophy, particularly Stoicism. From A.D. 54 to 62, he was a key advisor to the emperor Nero (A.D. 54–68). In A.D. 65, the notoriously unstable emperor accused Seneca of participating in a conspiracy against him and compelled him to commit suicide.

In everything he wrote, Seneca sought the rational order inherent within the universe. His one hundred and twenty-four Epistles reveal the Stoic quest for virtue, and his twelve Moral Dialogues expound the Stoic ideals of virtue, duty, and honor. The sentiments expressed in the following moral essays, written in the form of epistles (letters) to his friend Lucilius, a prominent Roman civil servant, reveal Seneca's Stoic humanitarianism.

ON GLADIATORS

But nothing is more harmful to a good disposition than to while the time away at some public show. I return from such entertainments more greedy, more dissipated, nay, even more cruel and inhuman. By chance I fell in with a public show at midday, expecting some sport, buffoonery [clownish amusement], or other relaxation, now that the spectators had seen their fill of human gore. All the bloody deeds of the morning were mere mercy: for now, all trifling apart, they commit downright murder. The combatants have nothing with which to shield the body; they are exposed to every stroke of their antagonist; and every stroke is a wound. And this some prefer to their fighting well armored! There is no helmet or shield to repel the blow; no defense, no art—for these are but so many balks and delays of death. In the morning men are exposed to lions and bears; at noon gladiators who fight to the death are ordered out against one another, and the conqueror is detained for another slaughter. Death alone puts an end to this business. "Kill, burn, scourge," is all they cry. "Why is he so afraid of the sword's point? Why is he so timorous to kill? Why does he not die more manfully?" They are urged on with floggings if they refuse to fight and are obliged to give and take wounds with an open breast. They are called upon to cut one another's throats.

ON SLAVERY

It by no means displeases me, Lucilius, to hear from those who confer with you, that you live on friendly terms with your slaves. This attests to your good sense and education. Are they slaves? No, they are men; they are comrades; they are humble friends. Nay, rather fellow-servants, if you reflect on the equal power of Fortune over both you and them. I therefore laugh at those who think it scandalous for a gentleman to permit, at times, his servant to sit down with him at supper. Why should he not? It is only proud custom that has ordained that a master dine surrounded by at least a dozen slaves and stuff himself, while the poor servants are not allowed to open their lips, even to speak. The slightest murmur is restrained by a rod; nor are mere accidents excused, such as a cough, a sneeze, or a hiccup. Silence interrupted by a word is sure to be punished severely. Thus the slaves must stand, perhaps the whole night, without taking a bit of food or drink or speaking a word. Whence it often happens that such as are not allowed to speak before their masters will speak disrespectfully of them behind their backs. In contrast, those slaves who have been allowed not only to speak before their masters, but sometimes with them, whose mouths were not sewed up, have been ready to incur the most imminent danger, even to the sacrificing of their lives, for their master's safety. Slaves are not naturally our enemies, but we make them such.

I pass by the more cruel and inhuman actions, wherein we treat slaves not as men but as beasts of burden. . . .

Were you to consider, that he whom you call your slave, is sprung from the same origin, enjoys the same climate, breathes the same air, and is subject to the same condition of life and death as yourself, you will think it possible to see him as a free-born person, as he is free to see you as a slave. After the fall of Marius,[1] how many people born of the most splendid parentage and not unjustly expecting a senatorial office for their exploits in war, did fortune cut down? She made one a shepherd, another a caretaker of a country cottage. Can you now despise the man whose fortune is such, into which, while you despise it, you may fall?

I will not discuss at length the treatment of slaves towards whom we behave cruelly and arrogantly. But this is the essence of what I would prescribe: treat your inferiors as you would have a superior treat you. As often as you think of the power that you have over a slave, reflect on the power that your master has over you. But you say, "I have no master." Be it so. The world goes well with you at present; it may not do so always. You may one day be a slave yourself. Do you know at what time Hecuba[2] became a slave, or Croesus,[3] or the mother of Darius,[4] or Plato, or Diogenes?[5] Live therefore courteously with your slave; talk with him, dine with him.

---

[1]Gaius Marius (c. 155–86 B.C.) was a famous Roman general.

[2]In the *Iliad,* Hecuba, the wife of Priam, king of Troy, was enslaved by the Greeks after their conquest of Troy.

[3]Croesus, king of Lydia in Asia Minor from 560 to 546 B.C., was famous for his wealth, but died in slavery after losing his kingdom in battle.

[4]Darius III of Persia (336–330 B.C.) was defeated by Alexander the Great, who also captured Darius' mother, wives, and children.

[5]Diogenes (c. 412–323 B.C.), a famous Greek philosopher of the Cynic school, was captured by pirates and put up for sale in Crete. He is reported to have said, "Sell me to that man; he needs a master." He was bought by a wealthy Greek, who restored his freedom.

Marcus Aurelius
Meditations

Emperor Marcus Aurelius Antoninus (A.D. 161–180) was the last of the great Roman Stoics and the last of the so-called Five Good Emperors. His death brought an end to the Pax Romana. A gentle and peace-loving man, Marcus Aurelius was not spared violence and personal misfortune during his reign. Troops returning from Syria brought back a plague, which spread throughout the Empire. Marcus hurried to the east to quell an uprising by the commander of the forces in Asia, who declared himself emperor. Although the mutiny quickly died out, Marcus Aurelius' wife perished on the journey. Four of his five sons died young, and his fifth son, Commodus, who succeeded to the throne, was a tyrant.

For the last fourteen years of his life, Marcus Aurelius had to deal with tribesmen from north of the Danube who broke through the defenses and plundered what is now the Balkan peninsula. Marcus took personal command of the hard-pressed legions on the frontier. During this period he wrote the *Meditations,* twelve books containing his reflections on duty, human dignity, the self-sufficiency of reason, and other themes traditionally discussed by Stoic thinkers. Written in Greek, this deeply personal expression of Stoic philosophy has been called "the highest ethical product of the ancient mind." Excerpts from the *Meditations* follow.

BOOK TWO

Begin each day by telling yourself: Today I shall be meeting with interference, ingratitude, insolence, disloyalty, ill-will, and selfishness—all of them due to the offenders' ignorance of what is good or evil. But for my part I have long perceived the nature of good and its nobility, the nature of evil and its meanness, and also the nature of the [evildoer] himself, who is my brother (not in the physical sense, but as a fellow-creature similarly endowed with reason and a share of the divine); therefore none of those things can injure me, for nobody can implicate me in what is degrading. Neither can I be angry with my brother or fall foul of him; for he and I were born to work together, like a man's two hands, feet, or eyelids, or like the upper and lower rows of his teeth. To obstruct each other is against Nature's law—and what is irritation or aversion but a form of obstruction?

A little flesh, a little breath, and a Reason to rule all—that is myself. . . . As one already on the threshold of death, think nothing of the first—of its viscid [thick] blood, its bones, its web of nerves and veins and arteries. The breath, too; what is that? A whiff of wind; and not even the same wind, but every moment puffed out and drawn in anew. But the third, the Reason, the master—on this you must concentrate. Now that your hairs are grey, let it play the part of a slave no more, twitching puppetwise at every pull of self-interest; and cease to fume at destiny by ever grumbling at today or lamenting over tomorrow. . . .

Hour by hour resolve firmly, like a Roman and a man, to do what comes to hand with correct and natural dignity, and with humanity, independence, and justice. Allow your mind freedom from all other considerations. This you can do, if you will approach each action as though it were your last, dismissing the wayward thought, the emotional recoil from the commands of reason, the desire to create an impression, the admiration of self, the discontent with your lot. See how little a man needs to master, for his days to flow on in quietness and piety: he has but to observe these few counsels, and the gods will ask nothing more.

BOOK THREE

If mortal life can offer you anything better than justice and truth, self-control and courage—that is, peace of mind in the evident conformity of your actions to the laws of reason, and peace of mind under the visitations of a destiny you cannot control—if, I say, you can discern any higher ideal, why, turn to it with your whole soul, and rejoice in the prize you have found. . . .

Never value the advantages derived from anything involving breach of faith, loss of self-respect, hatred, suspicion, or execration of others, insincerity, or the desire for something which has to be veiled and curtained. One whose chief regard is for his own mind, and for the divinity within him and the service of its goodness, will strike no poses, utter no complaints, and crave neither for solitude nor yet for a crowd. . . . No other care has he in life but to keep his mind from straying into paths incompatible with those of an intelligent and social being. . . .

BOOK FOUR

Men seek for seclusion in the wilderness, by the seashore, or in the mountains—a dream you have cherished only too fondly yourself. But such fancies are wholly unworthy of a philosopher, since at any moment you choose you can retire within yourself. Nowhere can man find a quieter or more untroubled retreat than in his own soul; above all, he who possesses resources in himself, which he need only contemplate to secure immediate ease of mind—the ease that is but another word for a well-ordered spirit. Avail yourself often, then, of this retirement, and so continually renew yourself. Make your rules of life brief, yet so as to embrace the fundamentals; recurrence to them will then suffice to remove all vexation, and send you back without fretting to the duties to which you must return. . . .

If the power of thought is universal among mankind, so likewise is the possession of reason, making us rational creatures. It follows, therefore, that this reason speaks no less universally to us all with its "thou shalt" or "thou shalt not." So then there is a world-law; which in turn means that we are all fellow-citizens and share a common citizenship, and that the world is a single city. Is there any other common citizenship that can be claimed by all humanity? And it is from this world-polity that mind, reason, and law themselves derive. If not, whence else? As the earthy portion of me has its origin from earth, the watery from a different element, my breath from one source and my hot and fiery parts from another of their own elsewhere (for nothing comes from nothing, or can return to nothing), so too there must be an origin for the mind. . . .

BOOK FIVE

At day's first light have in readiness, against disinclination to leave your bed, the thought that "I am rising for the work of man." Must I grumble at setting out to do what I was born for, and for the sake of which I have been brought into the world? Is this the purpose of my creation, to lie here under the blankets and keep myself warm? "Ah, but it is a great deal more pleasant!" Was it for pleasure, then, that you were born, and not for work, not for effort? Look at the plants, the sparrows, ants, spiders, bees, all busy at their own tasks, each doing his part towards a coherent world-order; and will you refuse man's share of the work, instead of being prompt to carry out Nature's bidding? "Yes, but one must have some repose as well." Granted; but repose has its limits set by nature, in the same way as food and drink have; and you overstep these limits, you go beyond the point of sufficiency; while on the other hand, when action is in question, you stop short of what you could well achieve.

3 Catullus: Republican Rome's Greatest Poet

Gaius Valerius Catullus (c. 84– c. 54 B.C.) is generally regarded as the greatest lyric poet of the Roman Republic, even though he died early at the age of around thirty. He was a native of northern Italy and his father, a friend of Julius Caesar, provided him with a gentleman's education. In his early twenties, Catullus came to Rome and fell in love with Clodia, the wife of the governor of Cisalpine Gaul. For the older Clodia, Catullus was a refreshing diversion from her many other lovers, and he nicknamed her "Lesbia" after Sappho of Lesbos (see page 38). Clodia, however, eventually jilted Catullus in favor of his friend Caelius.

Catullus

LYRIC POEMS

There is a love/hate theme in much of Catullus' poetry which reveals the torment he experiences, as a result of Clodia's numerous affairs and his struggles to break free of passion's grip. The following poem is one of the most tender, simple, and most famous of Catullus' lyrics. It is about Clodia's lament related to the death of her pet sparrow.

Mourn, ye Graces[1] and Loves, and all you whom the Graces love. My lady's sparrow is dead, the sparrow my lady's pet, whom she loved more than her very eyes; for honey-sweet he was, and knew his mistress as well as a girl knows her own mother. Nor would he stir from her lap, but hopping now here, now there, would still chirp to his mistress alone. Now he goes along the dark road, thither whence they say no one returns. But curse upon you, cursed shades of Orcus,[2] which devour all pretty things! Such a pretty sparrow you have taken away. Ah, cruel! Ah, poor little bird! All because of you my lady's darling eyes are heavy and red with weeping.

The following poem details the degree to which Catullus is enamored of Clodia/Lesbia, who makes him feel like a god when he looks at her.

He seems to me to be equal to a god, he, if it may be seems to surpass the very gods, who sitting opposite you again

and again gazes at you and hears you sweetly laughing. Such a thing takes away all my senses, alas! for whenever I see you, Lesbia, at once no sound of voice remains within my mouth, but my tongue falters, a subtle flame steals down through my limbs, my ears ring with inward humming, my eyes are shrouded in twofold night.

Idleness, Catullus, does you harm, you riot in your idleness and wanton too much. Idleness ere now has ruined both kings and wealthy cities.

Tormented by Clodia's many lovers, Catullus struggles to break away from the "insane desire" that draws him to her.

I look no more for her to be my lover
As I love her. That thing I could never be.
Nor pray I for her purity—that's over.
Only this much I pray, that I be free.
Free from insane desire I myself, and guarded
In peace at last. O heaven, grant that yet
The faith by which I've lived may be rewarded.
Let me forget.

[1]The Graces are three sister goddesses who are attendants of Aphrodite (Venus). Aglaia personifies splendor or radiance, Euphrosyne personifies joy, and Thalia personifies flowering or blooming.
[2]Orcus (meaning death) was the Roman underworld, as well as a misconstrued reference to Pluto, the god of the underworld.

4 The Golden Age of Latin Poetry

Cultural historians employ the term *Golden Age* to describe Latin literature during the Ciceronian and Augustan periods. Whereas Latin prose reached its apex with Cicero in the late Republic, the reign of Augustus was distinguished by the greatest poetry ever composed in Latin. The literary activity of the *Silver Age*— the period from the death of Augustus in A.D. 14 to about A.D. 150—saw a decline in the quality of Latin prose and poetry. In comparison to the preceding period, the literature of the Silver Age was characterized by a new type of rhetoric intended more to impress than to persuade and enlighten. Hence it often appeared affected, pompous, and superficial.

Virgil
The Aeneid

Publius Vergilius Maro or Virgil (70–19 B.C.), the first important poet of the Augustan Age, was born of humble stock and educated in rhetoric and literature, as well as philosophy, particularly Epicureanism. He admired Augustus, his patron, for ending the civil wars and bringing order to the Roman world. Augustus urged Virgil to compose a grand opus that would glorify Rome's imperial achievement. Virgil began his task in 29 B.C., but it took him ten years to produce the *Aeneid,* which became a masterpiece in world literature, and made Virgil the "Homer of the Romans."

The *Aeneid* is a long poem that recounts the tale of Aeneas and the founding of Rome. In the *Iliad,* Homer dealt with the conflict between the early Greeks and the Trojans. Roman legend held that a Trojan remnant led by Prince Aeneas, son of Venus (the goddess of love), and a mortal father, Anchises, escaped the sacking of Troy. The first six books of the *Aeneid* describe the wanderings of Aeneas and demonstrated the influence of Homer's *Odyssey;* the last six books detail wars in Italy and show the *Iliad*'s imprint.

In Book Six, Aeneas and the Trojans arrive at Cumae, an ancient city in Campania, near present-day Naples, Italy. There, Aeneas consults with the Sybil, prophetess and priestess of Apollo, about how to descend into the underworld. In the following passage, the Sibyl interrupts Aeneas' prayers to tell him about the difficulty of the journey he is about to undertake. She tells him that to gain admittance to the underworld, he must acquire a golden bough, but before embarking on such a mission, he must first bury the body of his friend.

Breaking in, the Sibyl said:

"Offspring
Of gods by blood, Trojan Anchises' son,
The way downward is easy from Avernus.[1]
Black Dis's[2] door stands open night and day.
But to retrace your steps to heaven's air,
There is the trouble, there is the toil. A few
Whom a benign Jupiter[3] has loved or whom
Fiery heroism has borne to heaven,
Sons of gods, could do it. All midway
Are forests, then Cocytus,[4] thick and black,
Winds through the gloom. But if you feel such love,
And such desire to cross the Stygian[5] water
Twice, to view the night of Tartarus[6] twice—
If this mad effort's to your liking, then
Consider what you must accomplish first.
A tree's deep shade conceals a bough whose leaves
And pliant twigs are all of gold, a thing
Sacred to Juno[7] of the lower world.
The whole grove shelters it, and thickest shade
In dusky valleys shuts it in. And yet
No one may enter hidden depths
Below the earth unless he picks this bough,

The tree's fruit, with its foliage of gold.
Proserpina[8] decreed this bough, as due her,
Should be given into her own fair hands
When torn away. In place of it a second
Grows up without fail, all gold as well,
Flowering with metallic leaves again.
So lift your eyes and search, and once you find it
Pull away the bough. It will come willingly,
Easily, if you are called by fate.
If not, with all your strength you cannot conquer it,

Cannot lop it off with a sword's edge.
A further thing is this: your friend's dead body—
Ah, but you *don't* know!—lies out there unburied,
Polluting all your fleet with death
While you are lingering, waiting on my counsel
Here at my door. First give the man his rest,
Entomb him; lead black beasts to sacrifice;
Begin with these amends. Then in due course
You'll see the Stygian forest rise before you,
Regions not for the living." . . .

Before descending further, Aeneas and the Sibyl make sacrifices to the gods and goddesses of the underworld. Sibyl banishes the "unblest" before allowing Aeneas to go deeper into the cave mouth. Once he is inside the Underworld, Aeneas encounters Cares, Disease, Dread, Hunger, and Discord, as well as a plethora of hellish monsters. He finally looks upon "the souls of the unburied."

The cavern was profound, wide-mouthed, and huge,
Rough underfoot, defended by dark pool
And gloomy forest. Overhead, flying things

---

[1]*Avernus* is the site of an extinct volcano in southern Italy where a lake formed.

[2]*Dis* refers to the Underworld itself but it can also mean the Roman god of the Underworld, commonly identified as Pluto.

[3]*Jupiter* is the chief Roman god who commands the sky, light, and weather.

[4]*Cocytus* (wailing) is a river in the Underworld that flows into the Acheron River.

[5]*Stygian* water is a reference to the Styx River in the Underworld.

[6]*Tartarus* is the lowest region of the Underworld where wicked people are punished.

[7]*Juno* is the wife of Jupiter who is jealous of her husband's many affairs with both goddesses and mortal women.

[8]*Proserpina* is the wife of Pluto, god of the Underworld.

Could never safely take their way, such deathly
Exhalations rose from the black gorge
Into the dome of heaven. The priestess here
Placed four black bullocks, wet their brows with wine,
Plucked bristles from between the horns and laid them
As her first offerings on the holy fire,
Caging aloud to Hecatë[9] supreme
In heaven and Erebus.[10] Others drew knives
Across beneath and caught warm blood in bowls.
Aeneas by the sword's edge offered up
To Night, the mother of the Eumenidës,[11]
And her great sister, Earth, a black-fleeced lamb,
A sterile cow to thee, Proserpina.
Then for the Stygian king he lit at night
New altars where he placed over the flames
Entire carcasses of bulls, and poured
Rich oil on blazing viscera. Only see:
Just at the light's edge, just before sunrise,
Earth rumbled underfoot, forested ridges
Broke into movement, and far howls of dogs
Were heard across the twilight as the goddess
Nearer and nearer came.

        "Away, away,"
The Sibyl cried, "all those unblest, away!
Depart from all the grove! But you, Aeneas,
Enter the path here, and unsheathe your sword.
There's need of gall and resolution now."

She flung herself wildly into the cave-mouth,
Leading, and he strode boldly at her heels.
Gods who rule the ghosts; all silent shades;
And Chaos[12] and infernal Fiery Stream,
And regions of wide night without a sound,
May it be right to tell what I have heard,
May it be right, and fitting, by your will,
That I describe the deep world sunk in darkness
Under the earth.

      Now dim to one another
In desolate night they walked on through the gloom,
Through Dis's homes all void, and empty realms,
As one goes through a wood by a faint moon's
Treacherous light, when Jupiter veils the sky
And black night blots the colors of the world.

Before the entrance, in the jaws of Orcus,[13]
Grief and avenging Cares have made their beds,
And pale Diseases and sad Age are there,
And Dread, and Hunger that sways men to crime,
And sordid Want—in shapes to affright the eyes—
And Death and Toil and Death's own brother, Sleep,
And the mind's evil joys; on the door sill
Death-bringing War, and iron cubicles
Of the Eumenidës, and raving Discord,
Viperish hair bound up in gory bands.
In the courtyard a shadowy giant elm
Spreads ancient boughs, her ancient arms where dreams,
False dreams, the old tale goes, beneath each leaf
Cling and are numberless. There, too,
About the doorway forms of monsters crowd—
Centaurs,[14] twiformed Scyllas,[15] hundred-armed
Briareus,[16] and the Lernaean hydra[17]
Hissing horribly, and the Chimaera[18]
Breathing dangerous flames, and Gorgons,[19] Harpies,[20]

Huge Geryon,[21] triple-bodied ghost.
Here, swept by sudden fear, drawing his sword,
Aeneas stood on guard with naked edge
Against them as they came. If his companion,
Knowing the truth, had not admonished him
How faint these lives were—empty images
Hovering bodiless—he had attacked
And cut his way through phantoms, empty air.

The path goes on from that place to the waves
Of Tartarus's Acheron.[22] Thick with mud,
A whirlpool out of a vast abyss
Boils up and belches all the silt it carries
Into Cocytus. Here the ferryman,
A figure of fright, keeper of waters and streams,
Is Charon,[23] foul and terrible, his beard
Grown wild and hoar, his staring eyes all flame,

---

[9]*Hecatë* is a divinity in the Underworld.

[10]*Erebus* is the lower region of the Underworld—a place of shadows and mystery

[11]*Eumenidës* are the Furies, who came to be known as "The Benevolent Ones," relating to the kind way they treated Orestes after he sought refuge in Athens, following the murder of his mother.

[12]*Chaos* was, prior to creation, a vast darkness from which everything else was created.

[13]*Orcus* represents Death and was often confused with Pluto. His name is also associated with the Underworld, the place to which he carried people away by force.

[14]*Centaurs* are mythical creatures with the body and legs of a horse and the head, arms, and torso of a man.

[15]*Sycllas* was a sea nymph who became a sea monster.

[16]*Briareus* is one of three mythical giants, called Hecatonchires, with fifty heads and 100 arms who assisted the gods in their battle with the Titans.

[17]*Lernaean hydra* is a nine-headed monster.

[18]*Chimaera* is a three-headed monster, with the front quarters of a lion, the hind quarters of a goat, and the tail of a serpent that breathes fire.

[19]*Gorgon* is one of three sister monsters with snakes for hair, who turned anyone who looked at them into stone.

[20]*Harpies* are monsters that have the body of a bird and the head of a woman.

[21]*Geryon* is a monster who has a large herd of red cattle.

[22]*Acheron* (woe) is a river in the Underworld.

[23]*Charon* is the Ferryman on the Styx River.

His sordid cloak hung from a shoulder knot.
Alone he poles his craft and trims the sails
And in his rusty hull ferries the dead,
Old now—but old age in the gods is green.

Here a whole crowd came streaming to the banks,
Mothers and men, the forms with all life spent
Of heroes great in valor, boys and girls
Unmarried, and young sons laid on the pyre
Before their parents' eyes—as many souls
As leaves that yield their hold on boughs and fall
Through forests in the early frost of autumn,
Or as migrating birds from the open sea
That darken heaven when the cold season comes
And drives them overseas to sunlit lands.
There all stood begging to be first across
And reached out longing hands to the far shore.

But the grim boatman now took these aboard,
Now those, waving the rest back from the strand.
In wonder at this and touched by the commotion,
Aeneas said:
              "Tell me, Sister, what this means,
The crowd at the stream. Where are the souls bound?
How are they tested, so that these turn back,
While those take oars to cross the dead-black water?"

Briefly the ancient priestess answered him:

"Cocytus is the dear pool that you see,
The swamp of Styx[24] beyond, infernal power
By which the gods take oath and fear to break it.
All in the nearby crowd you notice here
Are pauper souls, the souls of the unburied.
Charon's the boatman. Those the water bears
Are souls of buried men. He may not take them
Shore to dread shore on the hoarse currents there
Until their bones rest in the grave, or till
They flutter and roam this side a hundred years;
They may have passage then, and may return,
To cross the deeps they long for." . . .

Aeneas finally encounters the sad ghost of his father
Anchises—the goal of his mission. Anchises points
out to his son those souls destined for reincarnation
in another body.

            "Tell us, happy souls,
And you, great seer, what region holds Anchises,
Where is his resting place? For him we came
By ferry across the rivers of Erebus."
And the great soul answered briefly:
                        "None of us
Has one fixed home. We walk in shady groves

And bed on riverbanks and occupy
Green meadows fresh with streams. But if your hearts
Are set on it, first cross this ridge; and soon
I shall point out an easy path."
                        So saying,
He walked ahead and showed them from the height
The sweep of shining plain. Then down they went
And left the hilltops.
              Now Aeneas' father
Anchises, deep in the lush green of a valley,
Had given all his mind to a survey
Of souls, till then confined there, who were bound
For daylight in the upper world. By chance
His own were those he scanned now, all his own
Descendants, with their futures and their fates,
Their characters and acts. But when he saw
Aeneas advancing toward him on the grass,
He stretched out both his hands in eagerness
As tears wetted his cheeks. He said in welcome:

"Have you at last come, has that loyalty
Your father counted on conquered the journey?
Am I to see your face, my son, and hear
Our voices in communion as before?
I thought so, surely; counting the months I thought
The time would come. My longing has not tricked me.
I greet you now, how many lands behind you,
How many seas, what blows and dangers, son!
How much I feared the land of Libya
Might do you harm."
              Aeneas said;
                        "Your ghost,
Your sad ghost, father, often before my mind,
Impelled me to the threshold of this place.
My ships ride anchored in the Tuscan sea.
But let me have your hand, let me embrace you,
Do not draw back."
                  At this his tears brimmed over
And down his cheeks. And there he tried three times
To throw his arms around his father's neck,
Three times the shade untouched slipped through his hands
Weightless as wind and fugitive as dream.
Aeneas now saw at the valley's end
A grove standing apart, with stems and boughs
Of woodland rustling, and the stream of Lethe[25]
Running past those peaceful glades. Around it
Souls of a thousand nations filled the air,
As bees in meadows at the height of summer
Hover and home on flowers and thickly swarm
On snow-white lilies, and the countryside
Is loud with humming. At the sudden vision
Shivering, at a loss, Aeneas asked
What river flowed there and what men were those
In such a throng along the riverside.

---

[24]*Styx* (hateful) is the nine-looped river surrounding the Underworld.

[25]*Lethe* is the river of forgetfulness.

His father Anchises told him:

                        "Souls for whom
A second body is in store: their drink
Is water of Lethe, and it frees from care
In long forgetfulness. For all this time
I have so much desired to show you these
And tell you of them face to face—to take
The roster of my children's children here,
So you may feel with me more happiness
At finding Italy."

                  "Must we imagine,
Father, there are souls that go from here
Aloft to upper heaven, and once more
Return to bodies' dead weight? The poor souls,
How can they crave our daylight so?"

                             "My son,
I'll tell you, not to leave you mystified,"
Anchises said, and took each point in order: . . .

Later, Anchises describes the illustrious future that will be Rome's. Then, as Aeneas watches a procession of figures from the great Roman past, Augustus appears "beautifully formed" and "in shining armor." Anchises then relates to Aeneas the burdens a ruler must bear as he carries the weight of his people's concerns, knowing he can only correct a limited number of problems before his finite time on earth comes to an end. Anchises also weeps because he knows that the Augustan Golden Age will never again be repeated in the history of Rome. The intensely patriotic Virgil thus ascribed to Rome a divine mission to bring peace and civilized life to the world, and he praised Augustus as a divinely appointed ruler who had fulfilled Rome's mission.

. . . Turn your two eyes
This way and see this people, your own Romans.
Here is Caesar, and all the line of Julius
   [founder of the Julian family],
All who shall one day pass under the dome
Of the great sky: this is the man, this one,
Of whom so often you have heard the promise,
Caesar Augustus, son of the deified [Julius Caesar],
Who shall bring once again an Age of Gold
To Latium,[26] to the land where Saturn [Roman god] reigned
In early times. He will extend his power
Beyond the Garamants[27] and Indians,
Over far territories north and south

Others will cast more tenderly in bronze
Their breathing figures, I can well believe,
And bring more lifelike portraits out of marble;
Argue more eloquently, use the pointer
To trace the paths of heaven accurately
And accurately foretell the rising stars.
Roman, remember by your strength to rule
Earth's peoples—for your arts are to be these:
To pacify, to impose the rule of law,
To spare the conquered, battle down the proud.

         "See there, how Marcellus[28] comes
With spoils of the commander that he killed:
How the man towers over everyone.
Cavalry leader, he'll sustain the realm
Of Rome in hours of tumult, bringing to heel
The Carthaginians and rebellious Gaul,
And for the third time in our history
He'll dedicate an enemy general's arms
To Father Romulus."[29]

               But here Aeneas
Broke in, seeing at Marcellus' side
A young man beautifully formed and tall
In shining armor, but with clouded brow
And downcast eyes:

           "And who is that one, Father,
Walking beside the captain as he comes:
A son, or grandchild from the same great stock?
The others murmur, all astir. How strong
His presence is! But night like a black cloud
About his head whirls down in awful gloom."
His father Anchises answered, and the tears
Welled up as be began:

              "Oh, do not ask
About this huge grief of your people, son.
Fate will give earth only a glimpse of him,
Not let the boy live on. Lords of the sky,
You thought the majesty of Rome too great
If it had kept these gifts. How many groans
Will be sent up from that great Field of Mars[30]
To Mars' proud city, and what sad rites you'll see,
Tiber, as you flow past the new-built tomb.
Never will any boy of Ilian race
Exalt his Latin forefathers with promise
Equal to his; never will Romulus' land
Take pride like this in any of her sons.

---

[26]*Latium* was the ancient country in which stood the towns of Lavinium and Alba longa; Rome was established in that region and became its most significant city.

[27]*Garamants* (Garamantes) were a warlike nomadic people living in the northwestern Sahara.

[28]*Marcellus* was the son of Octavia, Augustus' sister, who was adopted by Augustus, but who died at the age of nineteen. Virgil reputedly attended the funeral.

[29]*Romulus*, along with his twin brother, Remus, are considered to be the legendary founders of Rome. They were suckled by a she-wolf and raised by a shepherd. Romulus also served as Rome's first king.

[30]*Mars* was the father of Romulus and the Roman god of war.

Weep for his faithful heart, his old-world honor,
His sword arm never beaten down! No enemy
Could have come through a clash with him unhurt,
Whether this soldier went on foot or rode,
Digging his spurs into a lathered mount.
Child of our mourning, if only in some way
You could break through your bitter fate. For you
Will be Marcellus. Let me scatter lilies,
All I can hold, and scarlet flowers as well,
To heap these for my grandson's shade at least,
Frail gifts and ritual of no avail."

So raptly, everywhere, father and son
Wandered the airy plain and viewed it all.
After Anchises had conducted him
To every region and had fired his love
Of glory in the years to come, he spoke
Of wars that he must fight, of Laurenitines,

And of Latinus' city, then of how
He might avoid or bear each toil to come.

There are two gates of Sleep, one said to be
Of horn, whereby the true shades pass with ease,
The other all white ivory agleam
Without a flaw, and yet false dreams are sent
Through this one by the ghosts to the upper world.
Anchises now, his last instructions given,
Took son and Sibyl there and let them go
By the Ivory Gate.
                            Aeneas made his way
Straight to the ships to see his crews again,
Then sailed directly to Caieta's[31] port.
Bow anchors out, the sterns rest on the beach.

---

[31]*Caieta* is the place where Aeneas' nurse was buried.

Horace

Epodes

A major poet during the Augustan Golden Age—Quintus Horatius Flaccus better known as Horace (65–8 B.C.)—was the son of a freed slave and a friend of Virgil. Horace broadened his education in Athens by studying literature and Stoic and Epicurean philosophy, and his writings often reflect Greek ideals. Horace enjoyed the luxury of country estates, banquets, fine clothes, and courtesans, along with the simple pleasures of mountain streams and clear skies, but he was also capable of tirades against social situations that he found to be repulsive.

In his early poems, called *Epodes* (c. 30 B.C.), Horace made the transition from satirist to lyric poet. His *Epodes* are indictments of the aristocrats for their licentious behavior and political stupidity, which often leads to the horrors of war. In *Epode 12,* Horace exhibits a personal animosity toward lecherous old women he has seen during the course of his life.

What do you want with me, woman? An elephant's more
    your type.
    Why do you send me gifts, and why these
letters? I'm not a muscular boy, and my nose isn't stuffed.
    I have one sharp sense; I can scent a
polyp or a stinking goat lurking in hairy armpits
    more keenly than hounds a sow in hiding.
What a sweat and what a rank smell rise all over her
    flabby flesh, when a penis is primed,
and she fumbles to ease her insatiable frenzy, and then her
    makeup runs, her complexion of moist
chalk and crocodile dung, and then as she reaches the peak of
    her
    spasm, she tears at the mattress and sheets.

And she attacks me for being squeamish with bitter words:
    "You are not so limp with Inachia;
three times a night for Inachia, always soft for one
    tumble with me. May Lesbia[1] die in
torment, the bawd who procured me a sluggish bull like you,
    after I'd had Amyntas of Coos,[2]
O the sinews of his inflexible rod were firmer than
    a young tree deeprooted in a hill.

---

[1]Lesbia is a reference to Sappho of Lesbos, the famous female Greek lyric poet (see page 38).

[2]Amyntas of Coos is a specific reference to someone Horace knew in Asia Minor.

Woolly fleeces were dipped again and again in Tyrian[3]
 purple, and for whom? You, no one else,
so there'd be no guest your own age whose mistress
 seemed to think more of him than yours.
O, I am so unhappy: you avoid me, as a lamb fears
 savage wolves, and deer the lions."

In 23 B.C. Horace began to write his most famous lyric poems about Roman society the *Carmina*, better known as his *Odes*. In this collection of eighty-eight poems he assumed many voices, including satire, and patterned the meters after Greek poets such as Sappho. Unquestionably a civilized man, Horace sought to rise above the Roman masses whose crassness, materialism, and pleasure-seeking he found to be repugnant. His odes touched upon many themes—the pleasures of good wine, the beauty of nature, the benefit of moderation, the molding of character, and the beauty of friendship.

Horace urged his fellow Romans to think about how they lived their lives and warned them of the wastefulness of luxury. "Why do we try for so much so hard with such little time?" he asked.

The money increases, followed by worry and
greed for still more. I have been right to be fearful
of raising my head into everyone's notice . . .

The more a man will deny to himself, so much
the more is given by the gods: stripping myself,
I seek the camp that knows no greed, a deserter
 longing to leave the wealthy side,

a more glorious master of things I reject
than if I were said to have buried in my barns
harvest from the plowed fields . . .
 and had no good of all my goods.

A brook with clear water, a few wooded acres,
and confidence in my crops: a happier life
than fertile Africa's glittering governor
 was given—not that he knows it.

He also instructed the Romans to reap today's harvest, not putting trust in tomorrow, by reminding them of the dangers of civil war and class conflict:

Is there a field not fertile with Latin blood,
that will not speak with its graves of unholy
 battles, and of the crash of the West
 in ruins, as the Parthians[4] listened?

Is there a gorge or a river not touched by war
and its sorrows? Is there a sea that has not
 been discolored by slaughtered Romans?
 Is there a shore that has not seen our blood?

Horace could also be lighthearted, such as when he wrote about the magically intoxicating powers of wine.

 . . . manhood was often aglow with strong wine.
You [wine] apply to a mind that is dull most times
the pleasure of your rack[5]; you unlock the thoughts
 and secret plans of a clever man
 by the power of joy-giving Bacchus;[6]

you restore the hopes of minds that are troubled,
and bring power and courage to the poor man:
 after you, not a shiver for crowned
 heads and their anger, nor for soldiers' swords.

Bacchus, and Venus, if she will be so kind,
and the Graces who like to stay together,
 and burning lamps will prolong your life
 till Phoebus' return drives the stars away.

---

[3]Tyrian purple, better known as Royal purple, was a color used during the Roman Empire; it was named for the city of Tyre, in ancient Phoenicia, where it was first made.

[4]Parthia was an ancient kingdom, located to the southeast of the Caspian Sea.

[5]A rack is an instrument of torture that stretches its victim in opposite directions.

[6]Bacchus is the Roman god of wine and intoxication.

Ovid

The Art of Love

The greatest of the Latin elegists during the Golden Age was Publius Ovidius Naso or Ovid (43 B.C.–A.D. 17). Unlike Horace and Virgil, Ovid did not experience the civil wars during his adult years. Consequently, he was less inclined to praise the Augustan peace. He was married three times and supposedly had a mistress, Corinna, to whom he wrote *Amores* (love letters). As a result of his marriages and affairs, Ovid's poetry reveals a preference for romance and humor and a fondness for love and sensual themes.

Ovid is best remembered for his advice to lovers contained in his most famous work—*Ars Amatoria* (Art of Love). Written when Ovid was fifty years old, the poem concerns itself with the art of seduction and is divided into three books. Book I deals with how to attract a woman who is the object of a man's desire.

Few indeed
Will turn you down—and (willing or not) a male proposition
    Is something they all enjoy. Draw a blank,
Rejection brings no danger. But why should you be rejected
    When new thrills delight, when what's not ours
Has more allure than what is? The harvest's always richer
    In another man's fields, the herd
Of our neighbour has fuller udders.
                            But first you must
        get acquainted
        With your quarry's maid—she can help
In the early stages. Make sure she enjoys the full confidence
    Of her mistress: make sure you can trust
Her with your secret liaison. Corrupt her with promises,
    Corrupt her with prayers. If
She's willing, you'll get what you want. She'll await the propitious
    Time (like a doctor) when her mistress is in
A receptive, seducible mood, when she's bursting out all over
    With cheerfulness, like a wheat-crop in rich soil.
When hearts are rejoicing, and have no sorrow to constrict them,
    They're wide open. Venus[1] can steal
In by persuasive guile. Grim Troy long faced her besiegers,
    But a light-hearted change of mood
Fell for that troop-gravid horse.
                            Another time to try her
    Is when she's been miffed by a rival. Make it your job
To ensure she gets her revenge. Prime her maid to egg her on while
    Combing her hair each morning, put an oar in
To boost Ma'am's plain sailing, sigh to herself, and murmur:
    "What a pity it is you can't just pay him out
With a tit-for-tat, then talk about *you* in persuasive
    Language, swear you're dying of mad
Passion. But lose no time, don't let the wind subside or
    The sails drop slack. Fury, like brittle ice,
Melts with delay. . . .

This selection from Book II tells a man how he can retain a woman once he has acquired her.

                            Don't give your mistress costly
Presents: let them be small, but chosen with skill

And discretion. At harvest-time, when fields are full, boughs heavy,
    Send round a basket of fruit—
Say it came from your country estate (though you really bought it
    At some smart city shop). Give her grapes,
Or the chestnuts to which Amaryllis[2] was so devoted—
    No, not chestnuts, she's off them these days:
Much too cheap. Why not try a poulterer's hoop of thrushes
    By way of remembrance? (It's shameful to use such gifts
In the hope of a death, to bribe the elderly or barren:
    I've no time for those who give presents a bad name.)
Would you be well advised to send her love-poems?
    Poetry, I fear, is held in small esteem.
Girls praise a poem, but go for expensive presents.
    Any illiterate oaf can catch their eye
Provided he's rich. Today is truly the Golden
    Age: gold buys honours, gold
Procures love. If Homer dropped by—with all the Muses,[3]
    But empty-handed—he'd be shown the door.
There *are* a few cultured girls (not many, it's true), and others
    Who'd like to be cultured, but aren't;
Flatter any of these with poems: a bravura declamation
    Even of trash—this will suffice to win
Their approval. Clever or stupid, they'll take a poem fashioned
    In the small hours, for *them* as a cute little gift.

Make your mistress ask as a favour for what you intended,
    All along, to do yourself
In the way of self-interest. You've promised manumission
    To one slave? See that he begs it, first, from her.
You plan to spare another his flogging, or the chain-gang?
    Then put her in your debt for a "change of heart"
That never existed. The benefit's yours, give her the credit,
    Waste not want not, while she
Plays the Lady Bountiful. You're anxious to keep your mistress?
    Convince her she's knocked you all of a heap
With her stunning looks. If it's purple she's wearing, praise purple;
    When she's in a silk dress, say silk
Suits her best of all; if her mantle's gold-embroidered

---

[1]Venus (Greek, Aphrodite) was the Roman goddess of love.

[2]Amaryllis in classical poetry—the general name for a shepherdess.
[3]Muses were the nine daughters of Zeus and Mnemosyne, each of whom presided over a different science or art.

Say she's dearer than gold to you; if tweeds
Take her fancy, back tweeds. She's in her slip? She inflames you
  (Tell her) with passion—but ask, at the same time,
Very, shyly, "Aren't you cold?" Compliment the way she's parted
  Or curled her hair, Admire
Her singing voice, her gestures as she dances,
  Cry "Encore!" when she stops. You can even praise
Her performance in bed, her talent for love-making—
  Spell out what turned you on.
Though she may show fiercer in action than any Medusa,
  Her lover will always describe her as kind
And gentle. But take care not to give yourself away while
  Making such tongue-in-cheek compliments, don't allow
Your expression to ruin the message. Art's most effective
  When concealed. Detection discredits you for good. . . .

Take care not to criticize girls for their shortcomings: many
  Have found it advantageous to pretend
Such things didn't exist. Andromeda's[4] dusky complexion
  Left wing-footed Perseus[5] silent. Although
Everyone else thought Andromache[6] too large a woman,
  To Hector[7] alone she looked
Just the right size. Habit breeds tolerance: a long-established
  Love will condone much, whereas
At first it's all-sensitive. While a new graft's growing
  In the green cortex, a light
Breeze can detach it; but soon time-strengthened, the tree will
  Outface all winds, hold firm,
Bear adopted fruit. Time heals each physical blemish,
  The erstwhile flaw will fade:
Young nostrils cannot abide the stink of tanning leather,
  But age inures them to it, after a while
They don't even notice the smell. Labels minimize feelings—
  She's blacker than pitch? Try "brunette".
If she squints, compare her to Venus. She croaks? She's Minerva![8]
  A living skeleton? "Svelte" is the word. Call her "trim"
When she's minuscule, or "plumpish" when she's a Fat
  Lady—
  Use proximate virtues to camouflage each fault.

Don't ask her age, don't inquire under just which consul
  She was born—leave that kind of chore
To the Censor's[9] office, especially if she's past her girlish
  Prime, and already plucking those first

White hairs. Such ladies, in this (or even a higher) age-group
  Are good value, a field worth sowing, ready to bear.
Besides, they possess a wider range of knowledge
  And experience, the sole source
Of true skill: they make up for their years with sophistication,
  Camouflaging their age through art; they know
A thousand postures—name yours—for making love in,
  More ways than any pillow-book could reveal,
They need no stimuli to warm up their passions—
  Men and women should share the same
Pleasures. I hate it unless both lovers reach a climax:
  That's why I don't much go for boys.
I can't stand a woman who puts out because she has to,
  Who lies there dry as a bone
With her mind on her knitting. Pleasure by way of duty
  Holds no charms for me, I don't want
Any dutiful martyrs. I love the sights that betray their rapture,
  That beg me to go slow, to keep it up
Just a little longer. It's great when my mistress comes, eyes swooning,
  Then collapses, can't take any more
For a long while. Such joys attend you in your thirties:
  Nature does not bestow them on green youth.
For the hasty, new-bottled wine; for me, a vintage
  Laid down long years before.

Book III is reserved for Ovid's advice to women, such as this selection that details how a woman can best hide her physical flaws and charm her love, but he warns that as a women she should do everything without appearing to be artificial.

But don't let your lover find all those jars and bottles
  On your dressing-table: the best
Make-up remains unobtrusive. A face so thickly plastered
  With pancake it runs down your sweaty neck
Is bound to create repulsion. And that goo from unwashed fleeces—
  Athenian maybe, but my dear, the *smell!*—
That's used for face-cream: avoid it. When you have company
  Don't dab stuff on your pimples, don't start cleaning your teeth:
The result may be attractive but the *process* is sickening—
  Much that is vile in the doing gives pleasure when done.
A statue—signed, let's say, by that industrious sculptor
  Myron[10]—began as a mere lump
Of deadweight marble; the gold for your ring must first be
  Worked and shaped, your woollen dress was made
From greasy yarn; that splendid representation of Venus
  Posed naked, wringing out her seawet hair,

---

[4]Andromeda, wife of Perseus, whom he rescued from a sea serpent.

[5]Perseus, a son of Zeus, who killed the Gorgon Medusa.

[6]Andromache, Trojan wife of Hector, who was captured by the Greeks during the fall of Troy.

[7]According to Homer's *Iliad*, Hector was the Trojan prince who was killed by the Greek war hero Achilles.

[8]Minerva was the Roman goddess of wisdom.

[9]A censor was one of two men in ancient Rome charged with watching over public morality and behavior, and who was responsible for taking the public census.

[10]Myron was a Greek sculptor who lived during the fifth century B.C.; his most famous work is the *Discus Thrower.*

Was a rough and uncut stone once. So leave us to imagine
  You're asleep while you're at your toilet: only emerge
When the public picture's complete. I don't want to know how
  That complexion's built up. Shut your door,
Don't reveal the half-finished process. Most of your actions
  Would offend if you didn't conceal them: there's a lot
Men are better not knowing. Look closely at those splendid
  Gold statues adorning the theatre—thin gilded foil
On a wooden frame! That's why the public can't come near
  them
  Till they're finished—and that's why you
Should keep men out while you're making up. Still, I don't
  forbid you
  To let them watch you comb your rippling hair
Out down your back—but mind you don't lose your temper
  As you tear at those tangled knots! . . .
A flawless face is a rarity: mask each blemish,
  Hide your physical faults—as far as you can.
Sit, if you're short, lest standing you seem to be sitting;
  Stretch out that pint-sized form,
Recline on a couch (but discourage rude measurement by
  spreading
  A wrap or blanket across your legs).
The over-lean girl should wear more amply textured
  Dresses, a robe that's draped
Loose from her shoulders. Puce [purplish brown] stripes off-
  set a pallid
  Complexion, while Nilotic [Egyptian or from the Nile re-
  gion of Egypt] linen transforms
The swarthy. Got ugly feet? Just keep them hidden
  In smart white bootees. Scrawny calves? Don't raise
Your skirt above the ankle. Protruding collar-bones? Mask
  them with pads.
  Is your trouble a flat bust?
Wear a good bra. If you have rough nails, coarse fingers,
  Don't gesture too much while you talk.
Bad breath? You should never converse on an empty stomach
  And keep your mouth well back from your lover's face!

If your teeth are decayed, or horsy, or protruding,
  A guffaw can cost you dear. Believe it or not,
Girls even learn how to laugh: in their quest for decorum
  This is one more skill they must acquire.
Don't open the mouth too wide, control those dimples, keep
  your
  Teeth concealed behind your lips,
Don't split your sides with endless hilarity, but rather
  Laugh in a restrained, a ladylike way—
Some women distort their features with lop-sided guffaws,
  some
  Get so cross-eyed with mirth
You'd swear they were weeping. Others utter a harsh unlovely
  Braying noise, like a she-ass hitched to the mill.
Where does art not enter ? Girls learn to make even tears at-
  tractive,
  To cry when and how they please.
Indeed, some mispronounce words with deliberate affectation,
  Bring them lispingly off the tongue:
Charm lurks in such errors of consciously faulty diction—
  What grace of speech they had they soon unlearn.
These hints are useful, so pay them proper attention—
  And mind you learn to walk in a feminine way!
No mean part of elegance derives from gait and carriage:
  These can attract or repel
Admiring strangers. One girl sways her hips artfully, catches
  The breeze with her flowing mantle, points her feet
In short dainty steps; another—like some red-cheeked peas-
  ant housewife—
  Clumps and waddles along, with hearty strides.
Moderation's best, as so often: don't play the country bump-
  kin,
  But equally, don't lay your affectations on
Too thick. No harm, though, in baring your left-hand shoulder
  And upper arm: for those
With a milk-white skin this works wonders—just let me see it,
  And I'm mad to press kisses on the naked flesh!

5 A Satirical Attack on Roman Vices

Juvenal (Decimus Junius Juvenalis, c. A.D. 60–c. 131), Rome's greatest satirical poet, found much fault with the Rome of his day. He attacked the haughtiness of the wealthy, the barbaric tastes of commoners, and the failures of parents. Holding that human beings were irremediably corrupt, he had no illusions about reforming human nature. He had no confidence in Roman moralists who believed that human beings could acquire inner moral strength, nor did he hope that calling attention to the evils afflicting Roman society could remedy them.

Juvenal
The Satires

In the following passage from his *Satires,* Juvenal focuses on the underside of life in Rome: crowded, noisy, and unsafe streets; bullies itching to fight; criminals who steal and murder; and the suffering poor.

. . . A man's word
Is believed just to the extent of the
  wealth in his coffers stored.
Though he swear on all the altars from
  here to Samothrace,[1]
A poor man isn't believed. . . .

Anyway, a poor man's the butt of jokes if
  his cloak has a rip
Or is dirty, if his toga is slightly soiled, if
  a strip
Of leather is split in his shoes and gapes,
  if coarse thread shows
New stitches patching not one but many
  holes. Of the woes
Of unhappy poverty, none is more
  difficult to bear
Than that it heaps men with ridicule.
  Says an usher, "How dare
You sit there? Get out of the rows
  reserved for knights to share. . . ."

. . . What poor man ever inherits
A fortune or gets appointed as clerk to a
  magistrate?
Long ago the penniless Romans ought to
  have staged a great
Mass walkout. It's no easy job for a man
  to advance
When his talents are balked by his
  impoverished circumstance,
But in Rome it's harder than
  elsewhere. . . .
Here most of the sick die off because
  they get no sleep
(But the sickness is brought on by the
  undigested heap
Of sour food in their burning stomachs),
  for what rented flat
Allows you to sleep? Only rich men in
  this city have that.
There lies the root of the illness—carts
  rumbling in narrow streets

And cursing drivers stalled in a traffic
  jam—it defeats
All hope of rest. . . .

. . . Though we hurry, we merely crawl;
We're blocked by a surging mass ahead,
  a pushing wall
Of people behind. A man jabs me,
  elbowing through, one socks
A chair pole against me, one cracks my
  skull with a beam, one knocks
A wine cask against my ear. My legs are
  caked with splashing
Mud, from all sides the weight of
  enormous feet comes smashing
On mine, and a soldier stamps his
  hobnails through to my sole. . . .

. . . a piece of a pot
Falls down on my head, how often a
  broken vessel is shot
From the upper windows, with what a
  force it strikes and dints
The cobblestones! . . .

The besotted bully, denied his chance in
  the shabby bars
Of killing somebody, suffers torments,
  itching to fight.
Like Achilles[2] bemoaning his friend, he
  tosses about all night,
Now flat on his face, now on his back—
  there's no way at all
He can rest, for some men can't sleep till
  after a bloody brawl.
But however rash and hot with youth
  and flushed with wine,
He avoids the noble whose crimson cloak
  and long double line
Of guards with brass lamps and torches
  show they're too much to handle.
But for me, whom the moon escorts, or
  the feeble light of a candle
Whose wick I husband and trim—he
  has no respect for me.

---

[1]Samothrace, an island in the northern Aegean Sea, is best known today as the place where the famous statue of the Winged Victory (Nike) was found.

[2]Achilles, the Greeks' most formidable warrior in Homer's *Iliad,* was torn by grief when his best friend Patroclus was killed by the Trojans.

Now hear how the pitiful fight begins—
    if a fight it be,

When he delivers the punches and I am
    beaten to pulp.
He blocks my way and tells me to stop. I
    stop, with a gulp—
What else can you do when a madman
    stronger than you attacks? . . .

This is the poor man's freedom: having
    been soundly mauled
And cut to pieces by fists, he begs and
    prays, half dead,
To be allowed to go home with a few
    teeth still in his head.

But these aren't your only terrors. For
    you can never restrain
The criminal element. Lock up your
    house, put bolt and chain
On your shop, but when all's quiet,
    someone will rob you or he'll
Be a cutthroat perhaps and do you in
    quickly with cold steel. . . .

Juvenal also gives us an unflattering picture of
women and marriage.

You once had your wits about you,
    Postumus; but now you think
Of taking a wife? What Fury, what
    serpents, are driving you mad?

Can you let a termagant [shrewish woman]
    boss you when rope is so easily had
And so many windows open on dizzy
    leaps and the height
Of the Aemilian bridge so handy?
    If none of these modes of flight
Is to your taste, don't you think it
    might be better to take
Some boy as bedmate, who'd never
    quarrel all night, or make
You promise gifts as you twine, or
    complain if you resist
His pleas and sleep, instead of panting,
    and leave him unkissed? . . .

And who is so deeply in love he never
    shrinks at all
From the very woman he praises to the
    skies—what's more,
Hates her at least sixteen hours out
    of the twenty-four? . . .

If you don't intend to love the woman
    you embrace

And marry in legal form, there seems
    no reason for you
To marry, no reason why you should
    waste the supper and new
Wedding cakes that must be given to
    well-stuffed guests who leave
When the party's over, or waste the
    gift of the bridal eve,
The rich tray gleaming with coins
    engraved with victories
In Dacia and Germany. If you simply
    must appease
Yourself with a wife and are devoted
    to one, incline
Your head, submit your neck to the
    marriage yoke. You'll find
No woman who spares the man who loves
    her. Though she glow
With passion, she loves to torment
    and plunder her lover. So,
The more he's good and desirable as
    a husband, the less
Beneficial by far will be his wife.
    You'll never address
A gift if she says no, never sell
    things if she objects,
Never buy anything unless she consents.
    And she will select
Your friends for you and turn your now
    aged friend from the door. . . .

You'll have to despair of knowing
    any peace at home
If your mother-in-law's alive. She
    teaches your wife to delight
In stripping you of wealth. . . .

There's hardly a case in court that
    a woman's fuss didn't start.

The bed where a wife lies never is free
    of complaints and a host
Of quarrels back and forth. There'll
    be little sleep in that bed.
There she assails her husband, worse
    than a tigress is said
To be at the loss of her cubs. Aware
    of her own secret deeds,
She pretends to grieve, denounces
    the boys he's known, and weeps
At some feigned mistress, always with
    floods of tears at hand
Ever ready at their station, waiting
    for her command
On how they should flow. You think,
    poor worm, it's love they show. . . .

6

Early Christianity

Christianity, the core religion of Western civilization, emerged during the first century of the Roman Empire. The first Christians were followers of Jesus Christ, a Jew, who, in the tradition of the Hebrew prophets, called for a moral reformation of the individual. Jesus' life, teachings, crucifixion, and the belief that he had risen from the dead convinced his followers that Jesus had shown humanity the way to salvation. Dedicated disciples spread this message throughout the Mediterranean world.

Surviving persecution and gaining in numbers, Christians influenced all classes from slave to aristocrat, and Christianity had become the state religion of Rome by the end of the fourth century. The reasons for the spread and triumph of Christianity are diverse. The poor and oppressed of the Roman world were drawn to Jesus' message of love and compassion, his concern for humanity; the promise of eternal life had an immense attraction to people who were burdened with misfortune and fearful of death. Jesus' call for a moral transformation of the individual addressed itself to the inner conscience of men and women of all social classes.

The Judeo-Christian and Greco-Roman (classical humanist) traditions constitute the foundations of Western civilization. Nevertheless, they represent two contrasting views of the world. For classical humanists, the ultimate aim of life was the achievement of excellence in this world, the maximum cultivation of human talent; early Christians subordinated this world to a higher reality. For Christians, the principal purpose of life was the attainment of salvation—entrance into a heavenly kingdom after death.

In the Greco-Roman tradition, reason was autonomous, that is, the intellect depended on its own powers and neither required nor accepted guidance from a supernatural authority. For example, Socrates held that ethical standards were arrived at through rational thought alone; they were not divine commandments revealed to human beings by a heavenly lawmaker. Conservative Christian churchmen, believing that Greek intellectualism posed a threat to Christian teachings, wanted nothing to do with Greek philosophy. But other Christians, recognizing the value of Greek philosophy, sought to integrate Greek learning into the Christian framework. Greek philosophy, they said, could help Christians clarify, organize, and explain their teachings. Those who advocated studying and utilizing Greek philosophy prevailed; thus Christianity preserved rational thought, the priceless achievement of the Greek mind. In the process, however, philosophy lost its autonomy, for early Christian thinkers insisted that to reason properly, one must first believe in God and his revelation, with the Bible as the ultimate authority. Without these prior conditions, the Christians argued, reason would lead to error. Thus, for early Christian thinkers, unlike their Greek predecessors, reason was not autonomous: it was subject to divine authority as interpreted by the church.

In the late Roman Empire, when Roman institutions were breaking down and classical values were being discarded, Christianity was a dynamic movement. Surviving the barbarian invasions, the Christian church gave form and direction to the European culture that emerged in the Middle Ages.

1 The Teachings of Jesus

During the reign (A.D. 14–37) of the Emperor Tiberius, the Roman governor in Judea, Pontius Pilate, executed an obscure Jewish religious teacher, Jesus of Nazareth, on charges of sedition. While performing healings and exorcisms, Jesus expounded a message of hope and salvation for sinners who repented. To the Jews who were attracted to Jesus' person and teachings, Jesus appeared to be a new prophet or even the long-awaited Messiah, the divinely promised leader who would restore Israel to freedom and usher in a new age.

Jesus made enemies among those powerful Jewish leaders who believed that the popular preacher was undermining their authority and weakening respect for the requirements of Jewish law. The Romans viewed Jesus as a political agitator who might lead the Jews in a revolt against Roman rule. Some Jewish leaders denounced Jesus to the Roman authorities, who executed him.

According to Christian teaching, Jesus was resurrected from the dead three days later, thus assuring his followers that he was the Son of God. With this assurance, his loyal followers continued to preach his teachings, forming small congregations of those faithful to his mission and words. They soon spread out as missionaries to Jewish and Gentile communities throughout the Roman Empire. These followers of Jesus, the Messiah, or in Greek, *Christos* (the Anointed One), were the founders of the Christian Church.

Like Socrates, Jesus himself never wrote a book; all we know of his life and teachings are the recollections of his disciples, passed down orally until put in written form some thirty to seventy years after his death. These primary sources include the gospels ("good news") attributed to Matthew, Mark, Luke, and John; the letters of the Apostle Paul and others; the Acts of the Apostles, a historical account of their missionary work; and the book of Revelation, a prophetic portrayal of the coming messianic kingdom of Jesus and God's destruction of the powers of evil. These works, written several decades after Jesus' death and collected together definitively in the fourth century, comprise the New Testament, the Christian sacred scriptures. They reflect the ways in which the early Christians remembered Jesus' teachings and the meaning of his life and ministry.

The Gospel According to Matthew
SIGNS OF THE END OF THE WORLD

Jesus speaks to his followers about the signs of the end of the world in the twenty-fourth chapter of the Gospel According to Matthew, an attenuated version of which can also be found in Mark, chapter 13, and Luke, chapter twenty-one. The theme of this passage has its origins in the Hebrew Scriptures, in the Book of Daniel which was the first apocalypse. The English word apocalypse comes from the Greek noun *apokelypsis*. Although the word is often used to refer to catastrophic events, its basic meaning is "a revelation," a divine revelation concerning things to come. The word apocalypse is also part of the title of the final book of the New Testament, the Revelation to John, which firmly established the Christian apocalyptic tradition. Christians later appropriated the Book of Daniel as their own, linking it with the Revelation to John. But the genesis of the Christian apocalyptic tradition is found in Matthew, chapter twenty-four. Along with Daniel and Revelation, this passage in Matthew has informed Christian teaching about the end of the world and the Last Judgment, that time when Jesus is supposed to come again to judge humankind. The Christian apocalyptic tradition found a powerful advocate in the fifth century in Augustine of Hippo (see page 128), and it has been an influential aspect of Christian theology ever since. Because of the following passage, many Christians, throughout the centuries, have anxiously awaited the return of Jesus.

THE END AND THE SECOND COMING

Introduction

24 Jesus left the Temple, and as he was going away his disciples came up to draw his attention to the Temple buildings. He said to them in reply. "You see all these? In truth I tell you, not a single stone here will be left on another: everything will be pulled down." And while he was sitting on the Mount of Olives the disciples came and asked him when they were by themselves. "Tell us, when is this going to happen, and what sign will there be of your coming and of the end of the world?"

The beginning of sorrows

And Jesus answered them. "Take care that no one deceives you, because many will come using my name and saying, 'I am the Christ,' and they will deceive many. You will hear of wars and rumours of wars; see that you are not alarmed, for this is something that must happen, but the end will not be yet. For nation will fight against nation, and kingdom against kingdom. There will be famines and earthquakes in various places. All this is only the beginning of the birthpangs.

"Then you will be handed over to be tortured and put to death; and you will be hated by all nations on account of my name. And then many will fall away; people will betray one another and hate one another. Many false prophets will arise; they will deceive many, and with the increase of lawlessness, love in most people will grow cold; but anyone who stands firm to the end will be saved.

"This good news of the kingdom will be proclaimed to the whole world as evidence to the nations. And then the end will come.

Jesus refers to the prophecy of the desolation of the temple in Daniel 11:31, which is to occur just prior to the end of the world. Then, in verse twenty-one, Jesus speaks of the time of tribulation, which is also alluded to in Daniel 12:1.

The great tribulation of Jerusalem

"So when you see *the appalling abomination,* of which the prophet Daniel spoke, set up in the holy place (let the reader understand), then those in Judaea must escape to the mountains; if anyone is on the housetop, he must not come down to collect his belongings from the house; if anyone is in the fields, he must not turn back to fetch his cloak. Alas for those with child, or with babies at the breast, when those days come! Pray that you will not have to make your escape in winter or on a Sabbath. For then there will be *great distress, unparalleled since the world* began, and such as will never be again. And if that time had not been shortened, no human being would have survived; but shortened that time shall be, for the sake of those who are chosen.

"If anyone says to you then, 'Look, here is the Christ,' or 'Over here,' do not believe it; for false Christs and false prophets will arise and provide great signs and portents, enough to deceive even the elect, if that were possible. Look! I have given you warning.

The coming of the Son of man

"If, then, they say to you. 'Look, he is in the desert,' do not go there; 'Look, he is in some hiding place,' do not believe it; because the coming of the Son of man will be like lightning striking in the east and flashing far into the west. Wherever the corpse is, that is where the vultures will gather.

When Jesus predicts that immediately following the time of tribulation, the Son of man will appear in the clouds, he again refers back to the prophet Daniel who wrote about "one like a son of man" to whom would be given "an everlasting dominion" over all peoples and nations (Daniel 7:13–14). The author of the Revelation to John specifically applies these passages to Jesus: "Behold, he is coming with the clouds, and every eye will see him . . ." (Revelation 1:7). Although Jesus says that all of this will happen before this generation will pass away, he also declares that no one knows the day or hour when the Son of man will appear.

The universal significance of this coming

"Immediately after this distress of those days the sun will be darkened, the moon will not give its light, the stars will fall from the sky and the powers of the heavens will be shaken. And then the sign of the Son of man will appear in heaven; then, too, all the peoples of the earth will beat their breasts; and they will see the Son of man coming on the clouds of heaven with power and great glory. And he will send his angels with a loud trumpet to gather his elect from the four winds, from one end of heaven to the other.

The time of this coming

"Take the fig tree as a parable: as soon as its twigs grow supple and its leaves come out, you know that summer is near. So with you when you see all these things: know that he is near, right at the gates. In truth I tell you, before this generation has passed away, all these things will have taken place. Sky and earth will pass away, but my words will never pass away. But as for that day and hour, nobody knows it, neither the angels of heaven, nor the Son, no one but the Father alone.

Be on the alert

"As it was in Noah's day, so will it be when the Son of man comes. For in those days before the Flood people were eating, drinking, taking wives, taking husbands, right up to the day Noah went into the ark, and they suspected nothing till the Flood came and swept them all away. This is what it will be like when the Son of man comes. Then of two men in the fields, one is taken, one left; of two women grinding at the mill, one is taken, one left.

"So stay awake, because you do not know the day when your master is coming. You may be quite sure of this, that if the householder had known at what time of the night the burglar would come, he would have stayed awake and would not have allowed anyone to break through the wall of his house. Therefore, you too must stand ready because the Son of man is coming at an hour you do not expect.

Parable of the conscientious steward

"Who, then, is the wise and trustworthy servant whom the master placed over his household to give them their food at the proper time? Blessed that servant if his master's arrival finds him doing exactly that. In truth I tell you, he will put him in charge of everything he owns. But if the servant is dishonest and says to himself, 'My master is taking his time,' and sets about beating his fellow-servants and eating and drinking with drunkards, his master will come on a day he does not expect and at an hour he does not know. The master will cut him off and send him to the same fate as the hypocrites, where there will be weeping and grinding of teeth."

2   Jesus the Logos

The idea of the *Logos* was an established concept by the time of Jesus. The word Logos was first used to refer to divine reason around 600 B.C. by the philosopher Heraclitus. In later times, the Stoics taught that there was a principle of order in the universe, an impersonal God that they called by various names, including Logos or Divine Reason. Moreover, since the Logos was implanted in every human soul, humans shared reason with God and could understand the principle of order that pervaded the universe. Around the time of Jesus, the Jewish philosopher Philo (20 B.C.–A.D. 45) of Alexandria attempted to integrate Hebrew religious thought with Greek philosophy by utilizing the concept of the Logos. Philo transformed the idea of the Logos from the impersonal God of the Stoics into a divine being who was the mediator between God and humans. About a century later, the author of the Gospel According to John, a Hellenized Jew, utilized the concept of the Logos in the introduction to his gospel.

The Gospel According to John
CREATION FROM "THE WORD"

The primary meaning of the Greek term *logos* is "word," and that is the way it is translated in the first fourteen verses of the first chapter of the Gospel According to John. John, however, uses the term somewhat like Philo, asserting that the Logos was God, that he preexisted from eternity, and that he was active in the creation. Then John introduces John the Baptist who baptized Jesus and bore witness to him (cf. Matthew 3:1–17, Mark 1:1–11, and Luke 3:1–23). Finally, John announces that Jesus was the incarnation of the Logos, that he was the Son of God in the flesh sent from God the Father and that those who believe in him will also become children of God.

PROLOGUE

In the beginning was the Word:
the Word was with God.
and the Word was God.
He was with God in the beginning.
Through him all things came into being,
not one thing came into being except through him.
What has come into being in him was life,
life that was the light of men;
and light shines in darkness,
and darkness could not overpower it.
A man came, sent by God.
His name was John.
He came as a witness,
to bear witness to the light,
so that everyone might believe through him.
He was not the light,
he was to bear witness to the light.

The Word was the real light
that gives light to everyone;
he was coming into the world.
He was in the world
that had come into being through him,
and the world did not recognise him.
He came to his own
and his own people did not accept him.
But to those who did accept him
he gave power to become children of God,
to those who believed in his name
who were born not from human stock
or human desire
or human will
but from God himself.
The Word became flesh,
he lived among us,
and we saw his glory,
the glory that he has from the Father as only Son of the Father,
full of grace and truth.

3 The Apostle Paul

After the execution of Jesus by the Roman authorities in Judea around A.D. 30, his disciples, believing that he had risen from the dead, sought a clearer understanding of his life and teachings. They became convinced that Jesus' mission, calling people to repent of their sins so as to receive God's forgiveness and to conduct their lives according to a high code of ethics, must be carried on. They proceeded to spread the gospel, the "good news," to their fellow Jews and eventually to other peoples throughout the Roman world.

The disciples of Jesus were soon joined in this mission by a man known to us as the Apostle Paul, the first great theologian of the new Christian Church. Paul started his life as a pious Jew named Saul. He was born in Tarsus, a Greek city in Asia Minor. A Roman citizen as well as a Pharisee, Paul studied the Hebrew Scriptures in Judea and joined in the early persecution of Jesus' followers. But, through a visionary experience, Paul was converted to the belief that Jesus was indeed the Messiah spoken of in the Scriptures. Paul was convinced that he was called to be the Apostle to the Gentiles (non-Jews) and that Christianity was a religion for all people, not only for Jews. He traveled widely throughout Syria, Asia Minor, and Greece, converting both Jews and Gentiles. He kept in touch with the new Christian communities by visits and letters. In his letters, several of which are included in the New Testament, Paul interpreted Christianity and began to build a Christian theology. He died around A.D. 65.

PAUL'S FIRST LETTER TO THE CORINTHIANS: THE RESURRECTION OF JESUS

Paul was the first to write about the importance of the death and resurrection of Jesus. He taught that Jesus was crucified to redeem humankind and that his resurrection sealed that redemption. Moreover, Jesus' resurrection assured the future resurrection of the body for Christians. This was possible because Jesus not only was the Messiah but also he was the Son of God. In his first letter to the Christians of Corinth, the great commercial center of Roman Greece, Paul declares that the resurrection of Jesus is the crucial doctrine of Christianity.

The fact of the resurrection

15 I want to make quite clear to you, brothers, what the message of the gospel that I preached to you is; you accepted it and took your stand on it, and you are saved by it, if you keep to the message I preached to you; otherwise your coming to believe was in vain. The tradition I handed on to you in the first place, a tradition which I had myself received, was that Christ died for our sins, in accordance with the scriptures, and that he was buried; and that on the third day, he was raised to life, in accordance with the scriptures; and that he appeared to Cephas; and later to the Twelve; and next he appeared to more than five hundred of the brothers at the same time, most of whom are still with us, though some have fallen asleep; then he appeared to James, and then to all the apostles. Last of all he appeared to me too, as though I was a child born abnormally.

For I am the least of the apostles and am not really fit to be called an apostle, because I had been persecuting the Church of God; but what I am now, I am through the grace of God, and the grace which was given to me has not been wasted. Indeed, I have worked harder than all the others—not I, but the grace of God which is with me. Anyway, whether it was they or I, this is what we preach and what you believed.

Now if Christ is proclaimed as raised from the dead, how can some of you be saying that there is no resurrection of the dead? If there is no resurrection of the dead, then Christ cannot have been raised either and if Christ has not been raised, then our preaching is without substance, and so is your faith. What is more, we have proved to be false witnesses to God, for testifying against God that he raised Christ to life when he did not raise him—if it is true that the dead are not raised. For, if the dead are not raised, neither is Christ; and if Christ has not been raised, your faith is pointless and you have not, after all, been released from your sins. In addition, those who have fallen asleep in Christ are utterly lost. If our hope in Christ has been for this life only, we are of all people the most pitiable.

In fact, however, Christ has been raised from the dead, as the first-fruits of all who have fallen asleep. As it was by one man that death came, so through one man has come the resurrection of the dead. Just as all die in Adam, so in Christ all will be brought to life; but all of them in their proper order: Christ the first-fruits, and next, at his coming, those who belong to him. After that will come the end, when he will hand over the kingdom to God the Father, having abolished every principality, every ruling force and power. For he is to be king *until he has made* his enemies his footstool, and the last of the enemies to be done away with is death, for *he has put all things under his feet.*

PAUL'S LETTER TO THE ROMANS: OBEDIENCE TO GOVERNMENT

The basic theme of Paul's letter to the Romans is that sinners are justified (made righteous) through the grace of God, by faith in Jesus, not by keeping the Jewish law. In the thirteenth chapter, excerpted below, he advises the Romans to obey all governmental authorities. This passage was used by Christian monarchs throughout the centuries to elicit submission to their rule.

Submission to civil authority

13 Everyone is to obey the governing authorities, because there is no authority except from God and so whatever authorities exist have been appointed by God. So anyone who disobeys an authority is rebelling against God's ordinance; and rebels must expect to receive the condemnation they deserve. Magistrates bring fear not to those who do good, but to those who do evil. So if you want to live with no fear of authority, live honestly and you will have its approval, it is there to serve God for you and for your good. But if you do what is wrong, then you may well be afraid; because it is not for nothing that the symbol of authority is the sword: it is there to serve God, too, as his avenger, to bring retribution to wrongdoers. You must be obedient, therefore, not only because of this retribution, but also for conscience's sake. And this is why you should pay taxes, too, because the authorities are all serving God as his agents, even while they are busily occupied with that particular task. Pay to each one what is due to each: taxes to the one to whom tax is due, tolls to the one to whom tolls are due, respect to the one to whom respect is due, honour to the one to whom honour is due.

4 Christianity and Greco-Roman Learning

Should the cultural inheritance of the Greco-Roman world be retained or discarded? This was a formidable problem for early Christian thinkers. Those who urged abandoning Greco-Roman learning argued that such knowledge would corrupt the morality of the young and would lead Christians to doubt Scripture. On the other hand, several Christian intellectuals, particularly those educated in the Greco-Roman classics, defended the study of pagan works. Their view ultimately prevailed.

Christians preserved the intellectual tradition of Greece. However, philosophy underwent a crucial change: philosophic thought among Christians had to be directed in accordance with the requirements of their faith. The intellect was not fully autonomous; it could not question or challenge Christian teachings but had to accept the church's dictums regarding God's existence, the creation of the universe, the mission of Jesus, and the purpose of life and death.

Tertullian
WHAT HAS JERUSALEM TO DO WITH ATHENS?

A native of Carthage, Tertullian (Quintus Septimus Florens Tertullianus, c. A.D. 160–c. 240) became a Christian about A.D. 190 and thereafter was a defender of Christian morals against both pagans and less rigorous Christians. He emphasized the sacredness of life and the Christian abhorrence of violence. His *Prescriptions Against Heretics* reveals hostility toward Greco-Roman learning, an attitude shared by some other early Christian thinkers.

. . . Worldly wisdom culminates in philosophy with its rash interpretation of God's nature and purpose. It is philosophy that supplies the heresies[1] with their equipment. . . . The idea of a mortal soul was picked up from the Epicureans,[2] and the denial of the restitution of the flesh was taken from the common tradition of the philosophical schools. . . . Heretics and philosophers [ponder] the same themes and are caught up in the same discussions. What is the origin of evil and why? The origin of man, and how? . . . A plague on Aristotle, who taught them dialectic [logical argumentation], the art which destroys as much as it builds, which changes its opinions like a coat, forces its conjectures, is stubborn in argument, works hard at being contentious and is a burden even to itself. For it reconsiders every point to make sure it never finishes a discussion.

From philosophy come those fables and . . . fruitless questionings, those "words that creep like as doth a canker." To hold us back from such things, the Apostle [Paul] testifies expressly in his letter to the Colossians [Colossians 2:8] that

we should beware of philosophy. "Take heed lest any man [beguile] you through philosophy or vain deceit, after the tradition of men," against the providence of the Holy Ghost. He had been at Athens where he had come to grips with the human wisdom which attacks and perverts truth, being itself divided up into its own swarm of heresies by the variety of its mutually antagonistic sects. What has Jerusalem to do with Athens, the Church with [Plato's] Academy, the Christian with the heretic? Our principles come from the Porch of Solomon,[3] who had himself taught that the Lord is to be sought in simplicity of heart. I have no use for a Stoic or a Platonic or a dialectic Christianity. After Jesus Christ we have no need of speculation, after the Gospel no need of research. When we come to believe, we have no desire to believe anything else; for we begin by believing that there is nothing else which we have to believe.

---

[3]The Stoic philosophers took their name from the Greek word *stoa*, covered walk, the place where Zeno, their founder, used to teach. *Porch of Solomon* is used to designate the teachings of King Solomon, who built the great Temple in Jerusalem. Tertullian makes it clear he follows Solomon's wisdom.

---

[1]A heresy is any belief that differs from official or standard doctrine.
[2]Chapter 4, page 88.

Clement of Alexandria
IN DEFENSE OF GREEK LEARNING

In the following passage, Clement of Alexandria (c. A.D. 150–c. 220) expresses his admiration for Greek learning. A Greek Christian theologian, Clement combined Christianity with Platonism.

The Greeks should not be condemned by those who have merely glanced at their writings, for comprehension of these works requires careful investigation. Philosophy is not the originator of false practices and base deeds as some have calumniated it; nor does it beguile us and lead us away from faith.

Rather philosophy is a clear image of truth, a divine gift to the Greeks. Before the advent of the Lord, philosophy helped the Greeks to attain righteousness, and it is now conducive to piety; it supplies a preparatory teaching for those who will later embrace the faith. God is the cause of all good things: some given primarily in the form of the Old and the New Testament; others are the consequence of philosophy. Perchance too philosophy was given to the Greeks primarily till the Lord should call the Greeks to serve him. Thus philosophy acted as a schoolmaster to the Greeks, preparing them for Christ, as the laws of the Jews prepared them for Christ.

The way of truth is one. But into it, as into a perennial river, streams flow from all sides. We assert that philosophy, which is characterized by investigation into the form and nature of things, is the truth of which the Lord Himself said, "I am the truth." Thus Greek preparatory culture, including philosophy itself, is shown to have come down from God to men.

Some do not wish to touch either philosophy or logic or to learn natural science. They demand bare faith alone, as if they wished, without bestowing any care on the vine, straightway to gather clusters from the first. I call him truly learned who brings everything to bear on the truth; so that from geometry, music, grammar, and philosophy itself, he culls what is useful and guards the faith against assault. And he who brings everything to bear on a right life, learning from Greeks and non-Greeks, this man is an experienced searcher after truth. And how necessary it is for him who desires to be partaker of the power of God to treat of intellectual subjects by philosophising.

According to some, Greek philosophy apprehended the truth accidentally, dimly, partially. Others will have it that Greek philosophy was instituted by the devil. Several hold that certain powers descending from heaven inspired the whole of philosophy. But if Greek philosophy does not comprehend the whole of truth and does not encompass God's commandments, yet it prepares the way for God's teachings; training in some way or other, molding character, and fitting him who believes in Providence for the reception of truth.

5 Christianity and Society

Although the principal concern of Jesus' followers was the attainment of salvation, Christians still had to deal with the world and its ways. In the process of doing so, they developed attitudes and customs that have had an enduring influence on Western culture.

Clement of Alexandria
Christ the Educator

In *Christ the Educator,* excerpted below, Clement of Alexandria describes behavior that a Christian should avoid.

Generally speaking, riches that are not under complete control are the citadel of evil. If the ordinary people look on them covetously, they will never enter the kingdom of heaven, because they are letting themselves become contaminated by the things of this world and are living above themselves in self-indulgence. Those concerned for their salvation should take this as their first principle, that, although the whole of creation is ours to use, the universe is made for the sake of self-sufficiency, which anyone can acquire by a few things. They who rejoice in the holdings in their storehouses are foolish in their greed. . . .

But, as it is, love of money is proved to be the citadel of evil, and, as the Apostle says, "the root of all evil." "Some in their eagerness to get rich have strayed from the faith, and have involved themselves in many troubles."[*] Poverty of heart is the true wealth,[†] and the true nobility is not that founded on riches, but that which comes from a contempt for it. It is disgraceful to boast about one's possessions; not to be concerned about them any longer very clearly proves the just man. Anyone who wishes can buy such things from the market; but wisdom is bought, not with any earthly coin, nor in any market, but is acquired in heaven, at a good price: the incorruptible Word, the gold of kings.

In the feasts of reason that we have, let the wild celebrations of the holiday season have no part, or the senseless

---

[*]Cf. 1 Tim. 6.10
[†]Cf. Matt. 5.3.

night-long parties that delight in wine-drinking. The wild celebration ends up as a drunken stupor, with everyone freely confiding the troubles of his love affairs. But love affairs and drunkenness are both contrary to reason, and therefore do not belong to our sort of celebrations. And as for all-night drinking parties, they go hand-in-hand with the holiday celebration and, in their wine-drinking, promote drunkenness and promiscuity. They are brazen celebrations that work deeds of shame. The exciting rhythm of flutes and harps, choruses and dances, Egyptian castanets and other entertainments get out of control and become indecent and burlesque, especially when they are re-enforced by cymbals and drums and accompanied by the noise of all these instruments of deception. . . .

Leave the pipe to the shepherd, the flute to the men who are in fear of gods and are intent on their idol-worshiping. Such musical instruments must be excluded from our wineless feasts, for they are more suited for beasts and for the class of men that is least capable of reason than for men. . . . In general, we must completely eliminate every such base sight or sound—in a word, everything immodest. . . . Truly, the devious spells of syncopated tunes and of the plaintive rhythm of Carian music* corrupt morals by their sensual and affected style, and insidiously inflame the passions. . . . [L]et no passionate love songs be permitted [at meals]; let our songs be hymns to God. . . .

We ourselves must steer completely clear of all indecent talk, and those who resort to it we must silence by a sharp look, or by turning our face away, or by what is called a grunt of disgust, or by some pointed remark. "For the things that come out of the mouth," Scripture says, "defile a man"† and reveal him as uncouth, barbaric, undisciplined, and unrestrained, and as completely without self-possession, decorum, or modesty.

Now, what are these protecting mufflers for the ears? And what the directions He gives for eyes so prone to stumble? The precaution of cultivating the friendship of good people, and of turning deaf ear to those who would lead us away from the truth. "Evil associations corrupt good manners," the [Athenian poet Menander] says. But a quotation from the Apostle is more to the point: "Hate what is evil, hold to what is good."‡ He who associates with the holy will become holy.

It is imperative, then, that we neither listen to nor look at nor talk about obscene things. And it is even more imperative that we keep free of every immodest action, exposing or laying bare any parts of our body improperly, or looking at its private parts. . . .

It is no less urgent that we keep ourselves pure in our choice of words, avoiding those which should be alien to the ears of one who believes in Christ. That is why, I believe, the Educator has forbidden us to utter the least thing that is un-

becoming, to keep us far from immorality. He is ever skillful in cutting to the very roots of sin, commanding: "Thou shalt not lust,"§ to safeguard the other command: "Thou shalt not commit adultery."‖ Adultery is only the fruit of lust, and lust is its evil root. . . .

It remains for us now to consider the restriction of sexual intercourse to those who are joined in wedlock. Begetting children is the goal of those who wed. . . . We have received the command: "Be fruitful,"# and we must obey. In this role man becomes like God, but he cooperates, in his human way, in the birth of another man. . . .

We should consider boys as our sons, and the wives of other men as our daughters. We must keep a firm control over the pleasures of the stomach, and an absolutely uncompromising control over the organs beneath the stomach. . . . First of all, it is decidedly wrong ever to touch youths [young boys] in any sexual way as though they were girls. . . . The Word . . . commands emphatically, through Moses: "Thou shalt not lie with mankind as with womankind, for it is an abomination."**

. . . Pleasure sought for its own sake, even within the marriage bonds, is a sin and contrary both to law and to reason. Moses cautioned them, then, to keep away from their pregnant wives until they be delivered. . . .

Wantonness has many names and is of many kinds. When it centers about sexual pleasure in a disoriented way, it is called lewdness, something vulgar and common and very impure, and, as its name suggests, preoccupied with coition. As this vice increases, a great swarm of diseases flows from it: gourmandizing, drunkenness, lust, and particularly dissipation and every sort of craze for pleasure in which lust plays the tyrant. A thousand-and-one like vices join the company and aid in effecting a thoroughly dissolute character. . . .

Yet, marriage in itself merits esteem and the highest approval, for the Lord wished men to "be fruitful and multiply." He did not tell them, however, to act like libertines, nor did He intend them to surrender themselves to pleasure as though born only to indulge in sexual relations. Let the Educator put us to shame with the word of Ezechiel: "Put away your fornications."†† Why, even unreasoning beasts know enough not to mate at certain times. To indulge in intercourse without intending children is to outrage nature, whom we should take as our instructor. . . .

. . . [W]omen who resort to some sort of deadly abortion drug kill not only the embryo but, along with it, all human kindness. . . .

Impure passion makes a man resemble a boar or pig, and, according to Scripture, fornication with a kept prostitute is seeking death. . . .

---

*Carian melodies were a sort of funeral dirge.
†Matt. 15.18.
‡Rom. 12.9.

§Cf. Matt. 5.27, 28.
‖*Ibid.*: Exod. 20.14; Deut. 5.18.
#Cf. Gen. 1.28.
**Lev. 18.22.
††Ezech. 43.9

Saint Benedict of Nursia
The Christian Way of Life
WHAT ARE THE INSTRUMENTS OF GOOD WORKS?

In the following selection from his monastic book of rules, Saint Benedict of Nursia advises his monks on the attitudes and conduct necessary to live a virtuous Christian life.

In the first place, to love the Lord God with the whole heart, whole soul, whole strength, then his neighbor as himself.

Then not to kill, not to commit adultery, not to steal, not to covet, not to bear false witness, to honor all men, and what anyone would not have done to him, let him not do to another. To deny himself, that he may follow Christ, to chasten the body, to renounce luxuries, to love fasting. To relieve the poor, to clothe the naked, to visit the sick, to bury the dead, to help in tribulation, to console the afflicted.

To make himself a stranger to the affairs of the world, to prefer nothing before the love of Christ, not to give way to anger, not to bear any grudge, not to harbour deceit in the heart, not to forsake charity. Not to swear, lest haply he perjure himself, to utter truth from his heart and his mouth. Not to return evil for evil, not to do injuries, but rather to bear them patiently, to love his enemies, not to curse again those who curse him, but rather to bless them, to endure persecution for righteousness' sake. Not to be proud, not given to wine, not gluttonous, not addicted to sleep, not slothful, not given to murmur, not a slanderer. To commit his hope to God; when he sees anything good in himself to attribute it to God, and not to himself, but let him always know that which is evil is his own doing, and impute it to himself. To fear the day of judgment, to dread hell, to desire eternal life with all spiritual longing, to have the expectation of death every day before his eyes. To watch over his actions at all times, to know certainly that in all places the eye of God is upon him; those evil thoughts which come into his heart to dash to pieces on Christ, and to make them known to his spiritual senior. To keep his lips from evil and wicked discourse, not to be fond of much talking, not to speak vain words or such as provoke laughter, not to love much or violent laughter. To give willing attention to the sacred readings, to pray frequently every day, to confess his past sins to God, in prayer, with tears and groanings; from thence forward to reform as to those sins.

Not to fulfill the desires of the flesh, to hate his own will, in all things to obey the commands of the abbot, even though he himself (which God forbid) should do otherwise, remembering our Lord's commands: "What they say, do; but what they do, do ye not." Not to desire to be called a saint before he is one, but first to be one that he may be truly called one; every day to fulfill the commands of God in his deeds, to love chastity, to hate no one, not to have jealousy or envy, not to love contention, to avoid self-conceit; to reverence seniors, to love juniors, to pray for enemies in the love of Christ, to be reconciled with his adversary, before the going down of the sun, and never to despair of the mercy of God. . . .

The Apostle Paul
THE SUBMISSIVE ROLE OF WOMEN

Passages in the New Testament concerning the role of women in Christian society have greatly affected the Western view of the relationship between the sexes. Paul's letter to the Ephesians and his first letter to Timothy contain passages emphasizing the traditional, submissive role of women in the Christian Church.

Although conservative theologians accept the Pauline authorship of these letters, liberal scholars date Ephesians about A.D. 95, thirty years after Paul's death, and 1 Timothy about A.D. 130. If the later dates are correct, the following passages reflect the attitude of the developing Christian Church rather than Paul's own opinion. Nonetheless, these passages, and others like them, have had an enormous influence on Christian attitudes toward women.

EPHESIANS 6

The morals of the home

Be subject to one another out of reverence for Christ. Wives should be subject to their husbands as to the Lord, since, as Christ is head of the Church and saves the whole body, so is a husband the head of his wife; and as the Church is subject to Christ, so should wives be to their husbands, in everything. Husbands should love their wives, just as Christ loved the Church and sacrificed himself for her to make her holy by washing her in cleansing water with a form of words, so that when he took the Church to himself she would be glorious, with no speck or wrinkle or anything like that, but holy and faultless. In the same way, husbands must love their wives as they love their own bodies; for a man to love his wife is for him to love himself. A man never hates his own body, but he feeds it and looks after it; and that is the way Christ treats the Church, because we are parts of his Body. *This is why a man leaves his father and mother and becomes attached to his wife, and the two become one flesh.* This mystery has great significance, but

I am applying it to Christ and the Church. To sum up: you also, each one of you, must love his wife as he loves himself; and let every wife respect her husband.

TIMOTHY 2

Women in the assembly

Similarly, women are to wear suitable clothes and to be dressed quietly and modestly, without braided hair or gold and jewellery or expensive clothes; their adornment is to do the good works that are proper for women who claim to be religious. During instruction, a woman should be quiet and respectful. I give no permission for a woman to teach or to have authority over a man. A woman ought to be quiet, because Adam was formed first and Eve afterwards, and it was not Adam who was led astray but the woman who was led astray and fell into sin. Nevertheless, she will be saved by child-bearing, provided she lives a sensible life and is constant in faith and love and holiness.

Augustine of Hippo
WOMEN, SEX, AND MARRIAGE

Augustine (Aurelius Augustinus, A.D. 354–430), bishop of Hippo (now Souk-Ahras in modern Algeria), was one of the great intellects of the early Christian Church. He is best known as a theologian, but his ideas about women, sex, and marriage had a crucial influence on Western attitudes about these subjects during medieval and modern times. Augustine's belief that women ought to be subject to their husbands is evident in a passage from his *Confessions* where he describes the relationship that his mother Monica had with his father Patricius.

When she reached a marriageable age, she was given to a husband whom she served as lord. . . . She also endured his infidelities, never quarreling with her husband about them. . . . Though he had an excellent, friendly disposition, he also had a terrible temper. She learned not to oppose, either with actions or words, an angry husband. . . . Many wives, whose husbands were more gentle than hers, carried marks of blows on their dishonored faces, and talking among themselves they would complain about the behavior of their husbands. But my

mother, speaking in jest but with serious intent, would blame their tongues, saying to them that they had heard the marriage contract read and they were bound to regard it as an instrument by which they were made servants; accordingly, they should bear in mind their agreement and they ought not to oppose their lords. They, knowing that she endured such a wild husband, were amazed that it had never been rumored, nor was there any clear sign, that Patricius had beaten his wife or that there had been any domestic strife between them, even for one day. When they asked her in confidence why this was so, she taught them her rule which I have mentioned above. Those who followed it, thanked her for it; those who did not follow it, were still molested and subjected.

For Augustine, there is a hierarchy of piety when it comes to the sexual life of the Christian. The highest moral stance is virginity, but failing that, marriage without sex is better than marriage with sex. Thus, the ideal marriage is a "spiritual" marriage with complete sexual abstinence. But because such a condition is beyond most people, sexual intercourse and procreation in marriage is good and guiltless if there is no sexual pleasure involved. Augustine's view of women and marriage was based in his firm belief that any sexual pleasure is sinful and evil, whether in or out of marriage. He believed that before the fall of Adam and Eve, when God originally instituted marriage, sex and procreation could have occurred without lust. But lust resulted from their disobedience, and because of lust, their original sin is passed on from parents to children. In the following selection, Augustine contrasts the good of marriage with the evil lust that is responsible for sin being passed from parents to children.

It is then manifest that that [lust] must not be laid to the account of marriage, in spite of which, even if it had not come into being, marriage would have existed. The good of marriage is not taken away by the evil, although the evil is by marriage turned to a good use. Such, however, is the present condition of mortal men, that the connubial intercourse and lust are simultaneous in action; and on this account it happens, that as the lust is blamed, so also the nuptial commerce, however lawful and honourable, is thought to be reprehensible by those persons who either are unwilling or unable to draw the distinction between them. . . .

The evil, however, at which even marriage blushes for shame is not the fault of marriage, but of the lust of the flesh. Yet because without this evil it is impossible to effect the good purpose of marriage, even the procreation of children, whenever this process is approached, secrecy is sought, witnesses are removed, and even the presence of the very children which happen to be born of the process is avoided as soon as they reach the age of observation. Thus it comes to pass that marriage is permitted to effect all that is lawful in its state, only it must not forget to conceal all that is improper. Hence it follows that infants, although incapable of sinning, are yet not born without the contagion of sin,—not, indeed, because of what is lawful in matrimony, but of its improper element: for from the lawful a natural creature is born; from the improper, sin. Of the natural creature so born, God is the Maker, who created man, and who united male and female under the law of the nuptial union; but of the sin the origin lies in the subtlety of the devil who deceives, and in the will of the man who yields to the deception.

In the following selection, Augustine blames the wife for the evil lust associated with sexual intercourse, thus further revealing his attitude about women and marriage.

Therefore, if I were to ask any good Christian who has a wife, and even though he may still be having children by her, whether he would like to have his wife in that kingdom; mindful in my case of the promises of God, and of that life where this incorruptible shall put on incorruption, and this mortal shall put on immortality; [though] at present hesitating from the greatness, or at least from a certain degree of love, he would reply with execration that he is strongly averse to it. Were I to ask him again, whether he would like his wife to live with him there, after the resurrection, when she had undergone that angelic change which is promised to the saints, he would reply that he desires this as strongly as he dislikes the other. Thus a good Christian is found in one and the same woman to love the creature of God, whom he desires to be transformed and renewed; but to hate the corruptible and mortal conjugal connection and sexual intercourse: *i.e.* to love in her what is characteristic of a human being, to hate what belongs to her as a wife.

Finally, in a treatise on the subject of marriage, Augustine concludes that it is better not to marry, but those who cannot restrain themselves should follow the advice of the Apostle Paul in 1 Corinthians 7:9.

[I]t is a good to marry, since it is a good to beget children, to be the mother of a family; but it is better not to marry, since it is better for human society itself not to have need of marriage. For, such is the present state of the human race that not only some who do not check themselves are taken up with marriage, but many are wanton and given over to illicit intercourse. Since the good Creator draws good out of their evils, there is no lack of numerous progeny and an abundance of generation whence holy friendships might be sought out.

In this regard it is gathered that in the earliest times of the human race, especially to propagate the people of God, through whom the Prince and Saviour of all peoples might both be prophesied and be born, the saints were obliged to make use of this good of marriage, to be sought not for its own sake but as necessary for something else. But now, since the opportunity for spiritual relationship abounds on all sides and for all peoples for entering into a holy and pure association, even they who wish to contract marriage only to have children are to be admonished that they practice the greater good of continence.

And so it seems to me that at this time only those who do not restrain themselves ought to be married in accord with this saying of the same Apostle: "But if they do not have self-control, let them marry, for it is better to marry than to burn."

6 The Christian World-View

Building on the life and teachings of Jesus as reported in the Gospels and apostolic letters collected in the New Testament, the early Christian thinkers formulated a comprehensive world-view. The Christian view stressed the sinful nature of human beings—their almost unlimited capacity for evildoing. The church taught that only through the gift of God's grace could individuals overcome the consequences of sin and obtain salvation. Christian leaders drew a sharp distinction between a spiritual realm (called the City of God by Saint Augustine) and the secular world (the City of Man), where Christians had to live out their earthly, material existence. Christians were urged to live in the world, but not to live by its values. Rather, they were to imitate the ways of Jesus in thought, word, and deed, as interpreted by the authorities of the church.

The task of living a Christian life in a secular world was not easy. Not the least of the problems was how Christians could relate to the political power structure of earthly societies. The task of finding a Christian basis for relations between church and state has been a continuous process since early Christian times. It has had wide repercussions in creating a distinctive Christian view of the legitimate powers of the state.

Augustine of Hippo
The City of God

Augustine of Hippo was one of the great theologians of the early Christian church. He formulated a view of life and of the individual that became definitive for Western Christians until it was partially superseded by the writings of Thomas Aquinas in the thirteenth century. Although Augustine admired the achievements of Socrates and Plato, he could not accept their central premise: that in the search for truth the individual relied on reason alone.

The sacking of Rome by the Visigoths in A.D. 410 shocked the entire Roman world. Pagans blamed the catastrophe on the Christians; by abandoning the old gods, said pagans, Christians had brought down the wrath of heaven on Rome. In reply to these charges, Saint Augustine wrote the *City of God,* setting forth the Christian view of the world and humanity.

The theme of the first group of passages from Augustine's *City of God* is a crucial element in the Christian outlook: that when human beings turn away from God to follow their own desires as Adam and Eve did, they fall into evil and become afflicted with many miseries, which can only be relieved through God's grace.

I have already said, in previous Books, that God had two purposes in deriving all men from one man. His first purpose was to give unity to the human race by the likeness of nature. His second purpose was to bind mankind by the bond of peace, through blood relationship, into one harmonious whole. I have said further that no member of this race would ever have died had not the first two [Adam and Eve]—one created from nothing and the second from the first—merited this death by disobedience. The sin which they committed was so great that it impaired all human nature—in this sense, that the nature has been transmitted to posterity with a propensity to sin and a necessity to die. . . .

When a man lives "according to man" and not "according to God" he is like the Devil. . . .

When man lives according to himself, that is to say, according to human ways and not according to God's will, then surely he lives according to falsehood. Man himself, of course, is not a lie, since God who is his Author and Creator could not be the Author and Creator of a lie. Rather, man has been so constituted in truth that he was meant to live not according to himself but to Him who made him—that is, he was meant to do the will of God rather than his own. It is a lie not to live as a man was created to live.

Man indeed desires happiness even when he does so live as to make happiness impossible. . . . The happiness of man can come not from himself but only from God, and that to live according to oneself is to sin, and to sin is to lose God. . . .

Moreover, our first parents [Adam and Eve] only fell openly into the sin of disobedience because, secretly, they had begun to be guilty. Actually, their bad deed could not have been done had not bad will preceded it; what is more, the root of their bad will was nothing else than pride. For, "pride is the beginning of all sin." And what is pride but an appetite for inordinate exaltation? Now, exaltation is inordinate when the soul cuts itself off from the very Source [God] to which it should keep close and somehow makes itself and becomes an end to itself. This takes place when the soul becomes inordinately pleased with itself, and such self-pleasing occurs when the soul falls away from the unchangeable Good which ought to please the soul far more than the soul can please itself. Now, this falling away is the soul's own doing, for, if the will had merely remained firm in the love of that higher immutable Good which lighted its mind into knowledge and warmed its will into love, it would not have turned away in search of satisfaction in itself and, by so doing, have lost that light and warmth. And thus Eve would not have believed that the serpent's lie was true, nor would Adam have preferred the will of his wife to the will of God. . . .

This life of ours—if a life so full of such great ills can properly be called a life—bears witness to the fact that, from its very start, the race of mortal men has been a race condemned. Think, first, of that dreadful abyss of ignorance from which all error flows and so engulfs the sons of Adam in a darksome pool that no one can escape without the toll of toils and tears and fears. Then, take our very love for all those things that prove so vain and poisonous and breed so many heartaches, troubles, griefs, and fears; such insane joys in discord, strife, and war; such wrath and plots of enemies, deceivers, sycophants; such fraud and theft and robbery; such perfidy and pride, envy and ambition, homicide and murder, cruelty and savagery, lawlessness and lust; all the shameless passions of the impure—fornication and adultery, incest and unnatural sins, rape and countless other uncleannesses too nasty to be mentioned; the sins against religion—sacrilege and heresy, blasphemy and perjury; the iniquities against our neighbors—calumnies and cheating, lies and false witness, violence to persons and property; the injustices of the courts and the innumerable other miseries and maladies that fill the world, yet escape attention.

It is true that it is wicked men who do such things, but the source of all such sins is that radical canker [sinfulness] in the mind and will that is innate in every son of Adam. . . .

Yet, for all this blight of ignorance and folly, fallen man has not been left without some ministries of Providence, nor has God, in His anger, shut up His mercies. There are still within the reach of man himself, if only he will pay the price of toil and trouble, the twin resources of law and education. With the one, he can make war on human passion; with the other, he can keep the light of learning lit even in the darkness of our native ignorance. . . .

From this all but hell of unhappiness here on earth, nothing can save us but the grace of Jesus Christ, who is our Saviour, Lord and God. In fact, the very meaning of the name, Jesus, is Saviour, and when we say "save" we mean, especially, that He saves us from passing from the misery of this mortal life to a still more miserable condition, which is not so much a life as death. . . .

Augustine saw a conflict between the earthly city, visible, temporal, and corrupt, and the City of God, invisible, eternal, and perfect. Those Christians favored with God's grace lived in this earthly city as strangers and pilgrims passing through on their journey to their true homeland, the heavenly kingdom. The fate of the earthly city was of no ultimate concern to these Christians. For Augustine, this earthly world represented the forces of evil that would finally be destroyed at the end of time, when Christ would come again.

What we see, then, is that two societies have issued from two kinds of love. Worldly society has flowered from a selfish love which dared to despise even God, whereas the communion of saints is rooted in a love of God that is ready to trample on self. In a word, this latter relies on the Lord, whereas the other boasts that it can get along by itself. The city of man seeks the praise of men, whereas the height of glory for the other is to hear God in the witness of conscience. The one lifts up its head in its own boasting; the other says to God: "Thou art my glory, thou liftest up my head."

In the city of the world both the rulers themselves and the people they dominate are dominated by the lust for domination; whereas in the City of God all citizens serve one another in charity, whether they serve by the responsibilities of office or by the duties of obedience. The one city loves its leaders as symbols of its own strength; the other says to its God: "I love thee, O Lord, my strength." Hence, even the wise men in the city of man live according to man, and their only goal has been the goods of their bodies or of the mind or of both; though some of them have reached a knowledge of God, "they did not glorify him as God or give thanks but became vain in their reasonings, and their senseless minds have been darkened. For while professing to be wise" (that is to say, while glorying in their own wisdom, under the domination of pride), "they have become fools, and they have changed the glory of the incorruptible God for an image made like to corruptible man and to birds and four-footed beasts and creeping things" (meaning that they either led their people, or imitated them, in adoring idols shaped like these things), "and they worshiped and served the creature rather than the Creator who is blessed forever." In the City of God, on the contrary, there is no merely human wisdom, but there is a piety which worships the true God as He should be worshiped and has as its goal that reward of all holiness whether in the society of saints on earth or in that of angels of heaven, which is "that God may be all in all." . . .

Augustine says that history reveals the intermingling of the City of God and the City of Man in time and space, and the incessant combat between the partisans of these two cities. This struggle will continue until time itself is annulled by God when Christ returns—and the saints are separated from sinners at the Last Judgment. Then the saints will join Jesus and be with him for eternity, and the sinners will be separated from God and confined to hell, also for eternity.

. . . In the eternal City of God, each and all of the citizens are personally immortal with an immortality which the holy angels never lost and which even human beings can come to share. This is to be achieved by the supreme omnipotence of the Creator, the Founder of the City. . . .

Who can measure the happiness of heaven, where no evil at all can touch us, no good will be out of reach; where life is to be one long laud extolling God, who will be all in all; where there will be no weariness to call for rest, no need to call for toil, no place for any energy but praise. . . .

. . . There will be such poise, such grace, such beauty as become a place where nothing unbecoming can be found. Wherever the spirit wills, there, in a flash, will the body be. Nor will the spirit ever will anything unbecoming either to itself or to the body.

In heaven, all glory will be true glory, since no one could ever err in praising too little or too much. True honor will never be denied where due, never be given where undeserved, and, since none but the worthy are permitted there, no one will unworthily [pursue] glory. Perfect peace will reign, since nothing in ourselves or in any others could disturb this peace.

CHAPTER

7

The Early Middle Ages

The establishment of Germanic kingdoms in the fifth and sixth centuries A.D. Roman lands marked the end of the ancient world and the start of the Middle Ages, a period that spanned a thousand years. During the Middle Ages the center of Western civilization shifted northward from the lands bordering the Mediterranean Sea to parts of Europe that Greco-Roman civilization had barely penetrated.

The Early Middle Ages (500–1050) marked an age of transition. The humanist culture that characterized the Greco-Roman past had disintegrated, and a new civilization was emerging in Latin Christendom, which covered western and central Europe. Medieval civilization consisted of a blending of the remnants of Greco-Roman culture with Germanic customs and Christian principles. The central element was Christianity; the Christian view of a transcendent God and the quest for salvation pervaded the medieval outlook, and the church was the dominant institution.

During the Early Middle Ages, Latin Christendom was a pioneer society struggling to overcome invasions, a breakdown of central authority, a decline in trade and town life, and a deterioration of highly refined culture. The Latin Christian church, centered in Rome and headed by the pope, progressively gave form and unity to the new civilization. Christian clergy preserved some of the learning of the ancient world, which they incorporated into the Christian outlook. Dedicated missionaries converted various Germanic, Celtic, and Slavic peoples to Latin Christianity. From Italy to the North Sea and from Ireland to Poland, an emerging Christian tradition was providing unity to people with differing cultural traditions.

The center of emerging medieval civilization was the kingdom of the Franks, located in Gaul (France) and western Germany. Migrating westward from their homeland in the valley of the Rhine River, the Germanic Franks conquered Roman Gaul in the fifth and sixth centuries. Charlemagne (768–814), the greatest of the Frankish rulers, added large areas of Germany and Italy to his kingdom. On Christmas Day in the year 800, Pope Leo III crowned Charlemagne emperor of the Romans, a sign that the memory of Imperial Rome still persisted. Without Roman law, a professional civil service, and great cities serving as centers of trade, however, Charlemagne's empire was only a pale shadow of the Roman Empire. Rather, the crowning of a German king as emperor of the Romans by the pope signified something new: the intermingling of Germanic, Christian, and Roman elements that came to characterize medieval Latin Christendom.

Charlemagne's empire rested more on the strength of the emperor's personality than it did on viable institutions. Charlemagne's heirs were unable to hold the empire together; power passed gradually into the hands of large landholders, who exercised governmental authority in their own regions. Also contributing to this decline in centralized authority were devastating raids by Muslims from Spain, North Africa, and Mediterranean islands; Northmen from Scandinavia; and Magyars from western Asia. Europe had entered an age of feudalism, in which public authority was dispersed among lords and held as if it were private inheritable property.

Feudalism rested on an economic base known as manorialism. Although family farms owned by free peasants still existed, the essential agricultural arrangement in medieval society was the village community (manor), headed by a lord or his steward and farmed by serfs, who were bound to the land. A lord controlled at least one manorial village; great lords might possess scores. Much land was held by various clerical institutions; the church's manors were similar to those run by nonclerics.

Feudalism was an improvised response to the challenge posed by ineffectual central authority, and it provided some order and law during a period of breakdown. Medieval feudal practices were not uniform but differed from region to region. In later centuries, when kings reasserted their authority and fashioned strong central governments, the power of lords declined.

Latin Christendom (western and central Europe) was only one of three new civilizations based on religion that emerged after the decline of the Roman Empire; Byzantium and Islam were the other two. During the Early Middle Ages both of these eastern civilizations were far more advanced than Latin Christendom. And yet it was Latin Christendom, not Byzantine or Islamic civilizations, that eventually produced the modern world.

1 The Byzantine Cultural Achievement

During the Early Middle Ages, when learning was in retreat in Latin Christendom, Byzantine civilization preserved the intellectual tradition of ancient Greece. Although the Roman Empire in the West fell to the German tribes, the eastern provinces of the Empire survived. They did so because they were richer, more urbanized, and more populous and because the main thrust of the Germanic and Hunnish invaders had been directed at the western regions. In the eastern parts, Byzantine civilization took shape. Its religion was Christianity, its culture Greek, and its machinery of administration Roman. Contacts with Byzantine learning during the High Middle Ages stimulated learning in the Latin West.

Theophylact Simocattes
THE VALUE OF REASON AND HISTORY

In the following selection Theophylact Simocattes, a seventh-century Byzantine historian, shows respect for the tradition of reason that was inherited from the classical world and familiarity with Homer, the wellspring of Greek literature. Like Thucydides, he values history, considering it a far better avenue to knowledge than the myths and fables created or embellished by poets.

Man is adorned not only by the endowments of nature but also by the fruits of his own efforts. For reason, which he possesses, is an admirable and divine trait by which he renders to God his adoration and homage. Through reason he enters into knowledge of himself and does not remain ignorant of the ordering of his creation. Accordingly, through reason men come together with each other and, turning away from external considerations, they direct their thoughts toward the mystery of their own nature.

Reason has given many good things to men and is an excellent helpmate of nature. The things which nature has withheld from man, reason provides in the most effective manner, embellishing those things which are seen, adding spice to those that are tasted, roughening or softening things to the touch, composing poetry and music for the ear, soothing the soul by lessening discord, and bringing sounds into concord. Is not reason also the most persuasive master of the crafts?—reason which has made a well-woven tunic from wool, which from wood has constructed carts for farmers, oars for sailors, and small wicker shields for soldiers as protection against the dangers of the battlefield.

Most important of all, reason provides the hearer with that pleasure which reflects the greatest amount of experience, the study of history, which is the instructor of the spirit. Nothing can be more seductive than history for the minds of those who desire to learn. It is sufficient to cite an example from Homer to demonstrate this: Soon after he had been thrown on the beach by violent waves of the sea, the son of Laertes, Odysseus, almost naked and with his body emaciated from the mishap of the shipwreck, was graciously received at the court of Alcinous. There he was clothed in a bright robe and given a place at the table of the king. Although only just arrived, he was granted permission to speak and an opportunity to relate his adventures. His recital pleased the Phocaeans so much that the banquet seemed to have changed into a theater. Indeed, they lent him an attention altogether remarkable, nor did they feel during his long narration any tedium, although he described the many misfortunes he had suffered. For listening brings an overwhelming desire (to hear more) and thus easily accepts a strange tale.

It is for this reason that in learning the poets are considered most estimable, for they realize that the spirits of men are fond of stories, always yearning to acquire knowledge and thirsty for strange narrations. Thus the poets create myths for men and clothe their phrases with adornments, fleshing out the fables with method, and embellishing their nonsense with meter as if with enchanted spells. This artifice has succeeded so well that poets are considered to be theologians, intimately associated with the gods. It is believed that through the poets' mouths the gods reveal their own personal affairs and also whether a felicitous or a calamitous event will happen to men in their lifetime.

This being so, one may term history the common teacher of all men: it shows which course to follow and which to avoid as profitless. The most competent generals are those who have been instructed by history, for history reveals how to draw up troops and by what means to outmaneuver the enemy through ambush. History renders these generals more prudent because they know about the misfortunes of others, and it directs them through observation of the mistakes of others. Similarly, it has shown that men become happier through good conduct, pushing men to higher peaks of virtue through gradual advances. For the old man history is his support and staff, while for the young, it is the fairest and wisest instructor, applying (the fruit of) great experience to new situations and thus anticipating somewhat the lessons of time. I now dedicate my own zeal and efforts to history, although I know that I am undertaking a greater task than I am able to fulfill effectively, since I lack elegance of expression, profundity of thought, purity of syntax, and skill in composition. If any parts of my work should prove pleasing in any way, let this be ascribed rather to the result of chance than to my own skill.

Procopius
THE BUILDING OF SAINT SOPHIA

In his work dealing with the construction of the church of Saint Sophia, the Byzantine historian Procopius of Caesarea (c. 499–565) illumined a different aspect of the Byzantine cultural achievement, its artistic genius. Procopius discussed the construction of this magnificent edifice, the baffling technical problems it posed, and their resolution. Built in A.D. 360, the church was the most awesome architectural achievement of the reign of the emperor Justinian, and it became a landmark of imperial glory. Justinian spared nothing to build Saint Sophia, employing the talents of mathematicians who had studied ancient treatises on vaulting and curved surfaces and bringing to bear the greatest technical and artistic skills of Byzantine civilization, to achieve a result of unparalleled beauty. The following is Procopius' description of the construction of Saint Sophia.

[T]he Emperor, disregarding all questions of expense, eagerly pressed on to begin the work of construction, and began to gather all the artisans from the whole world. And Anthemius of Tralles, the most learned man in the skilled craft which is known as the art of building, not only of all his contemporaries, but also when compared with those who had lived long before him, ministered to the Emperor's enthusiasm, duly regulating the tasks of the various artisans, and preparing in advance designs of the future construction; and associated with him was another master-builder, Isidorus by name, a Milesian by birth, a man who was intelligent and worthy to assist the Emperor Justinian. Indeed this also was an indication of the honour in which God held the Emperor, that He had already provided the men who would be most serviceable to him in the tasks which were waiting to be carried out. And one might with good reason marvel at the discernment of the Emperor himself, in that out of the whole world he was able to select the men who were most suitable for the most important of his enterprises.

So the church has become a spectacle of marvellous beauty, overwhelming to those who see it, but to those who know it by hearsay altogether incredible. For it soars to a height to match the sky, and as if surging up from amongst the other buildings it stands on high and looks down upon the remainder of the city, adorning it, because it is a part of it, but glorying in its own beauty, because, though a part of the city and dominating it, it at the same time towers above it to such a height that the whole city is viewed from there as from a watch-tower. Both its breadth and its length have been so carefully proportioned, that it may not improperly be said to be exceedingly long and at the same time unusually broad. And it exults in an indescribable beauty. For it proudly reveals its mass and the harmony of its proportions, having neither any excess nor deficiency, since it is both more pretentious than the buildings to which we are accustomed, and considerably more noble than those which are merely huge, and it abounds exceedingly in sunlight and in the reflection of the sun's rays from the marble. Indeed one might say that its interior is not illuminated from without by the sun, but that the radiance comes into being within it, such an abundance of light bathes this shrine. And the face itself of the church (which would be the part which faces the rising sun, that portion of the building in which they perform the mysteries in worship of God) was constructed in the following manner. . . .

reason of the seeming insecurity of its composition, altogether terrifying." The result, according to Procopius, is a triumph of technique, of art, of soul. It is an ethereal structure that seems to float, diverting the spectator from the building's innumerable unsettling details to an all-encompassing spiritual vision in which the mind is lifted upward to God. The exaltation it inspires, he says, is a tribute to the proximity of God and the genius of Justinian.

. . . And upon this circle rests the huge spherical dome which makes the structure exceptionally beautiful. Yet it seems not to rest upon solid masonry, but to cover the space with its golden dome suspended from Heaven. All these details, fitted together with incredible skill in mid-air and floating off from each other and resting only on the parts next to them, produce a single and most extraordinary harmony in the work, and yet do not permit the spectator to linger much over the study of any one of them, but each detail attracts the eye and draws it on irresistibly to itself. So the vision constantly shifts suddenly, for the beholder is utterly unable to select which particular detail he should admire more than all the others. But even so, though they turn their attention to every side and look with contracted brows upon every detail, observers are still unable to understand the skilful craftsmanship, but they always depart from there overwhelmed by the bewildering sight. So much, then, for this.

It was by many skilful devices that the Emperor Justinian and the master-builder Anthemius and Isidorus secured the stability of the church, hanging, as it does, in mid-air. Some of these it is both hopeless for me to understand in their entirety, and impossible to explain in words. . . .

The whole ceiling is overlaid with pure gold, which adds glory to the beauty, yet the light reflected from the stones prevails, shining out in rivalry with the gold. And there are two stoa-like colonnades,[1] one on each side, not separated in any way from the structure of the church itself, but actually making the effect of its width greater, and reaching along its whole length, to the very end, while in height they are less than the interior of the building. And they too have vaulted ceilings and decorations of gold. One of these two colonnaded stoas has been assigned to men worshippers, while the other is reserved for women engaged in the same exercise. But they have nothing to distinguish them, nor do they differ from one another in any way, but their very equality serves to beautify the church, and their similarity to adorn it. But who could fittingly describe the galleries of the women's side, or enumerate the many colonnades and the colonnaded

---

Procopius describes in detail the construction and design of the church, which consists of a basically rectangular unit with four great arches, topped by a windowed circular structure, upon which a massive dome was placed, "marvelous in its grace, but by

---

[1]In ancient Greek architecture, a stoa was a covered walk, usually having columns on one side and a wall on the other.

aisles by means of which the church is surrounded? Or who could recount the beauty of the columns and the stones with which the church is adorned? One might imagine that he had come upon a meadow with its flowers in full bloom. For he would surely marvel at the purple of some, the green tint of others, and at those on which the crimson glows and those from which the white flashes, and again at those which Nature, like some painter, varies with the most contrasting colours. And whenever anyone enters this church to pray, he understands at once that it is not by any human power or skill, but by the influence of God, that this work has been so finely turned. And so his mind is lifted up toward God and exalted, feeling that He cannot be far away, but must especially love to dwell in this place which He has chosen. And this does not happen only to one who sees the church for the first time, but the same experience comes to him on each successive occasion, as though the sight were new each time. Of this spectacle no one has ever had a surfeit, but when present in the church men rejoice in what they see, and when they leave it they take proud delight in conversing about it. Furthermore, concerning the treasures of this church—the vessels of gold and silver and the works in precious stones, which the Emperor Justinian has dedicated here—it is impossible to give a precise account of them all. But I shall allow my readers to form a judgment by a single example. That part of the shrine which is especially sacred, where only priests may enter, which they call the Inner Sanctuary, is embellished with forty thousand pounds' weight of silver.

So the church of Constantinople (which men are accustomed to call the Great Church), speaking concisely and merely running over the details with the finger-tips, as it were, and mentioning with a fleeting word only the most notable features, was constructed in such a manner by the Emperor Justinian. But it was not with money alone that the Emperor built it, but also with labour of the mind and with the other powers of the soul.

2 Islam

The vital new religion of Islam emerged in the seventh century among the Arabs of Arabia. Its founder was Muhammad (c. 570–632), a prosperous merchant in Mecca, a trading city near the Red Sea. When Muhammad was about forty, he believed that he was visited by the angel Gabriel, who ordered him to "recite in the name of the Lord!" Transformed by this vision, Muhammad was convinced that he had been chosen to serve as a prophet.

Although most desert Arabs worshiped tribal gods, in the towns and trading centers many Arabs were familiar with Judaism and Christianity, and some had accepted the idea of one God. Rejecting the many deities of the tribal religions, Muhammad offered the Arabs a new monotheistic faith, Islam, which means "surrender to Allah" (God).

Muhammad
The Koran

Islamic standards of morality and rules governing daily life are set by the Koran, the book that Muslims believe contains the words of Allah as revealed to Muhammad. Muslims see their religion as the completion and perfection of Judaism and Christianity. They regard the ancient Hebrew prophets as sent from God and value their messages about compassion and the oneness of humanity. Muslims also regard Jesus as a great prophet but do not consider him divine. They see Muhammad as the last and greatest of the prophets and believe that he was entirely human, not divine. Muslims worship only Allah, the creator and ruler of heaven and earth, a single, all-powerful God who is merciful, compassionate, and just. Following are excerpts from the Koran.

GOD

God: there is no god but Him, the Living, the Eternal One. Neither slumber nor sleep overtakes Him. His is what the heavens and the earth contain. Who can intercede with Him except by His permission? He knows what is before and behind men. They can grasp only that part of His knowledge which He wills. His throne is as vast as the heavens and the earth, and the preservation of both does not weary Him. He is the Exalted, the Immense One. (2:255–257)

In the Name of God, the Compassionate, the Merciful
It is the Merciful who has taught the Koran.

He created man and taught him articulate speech. The sun and the moon pursue their ordered course. The plants and the trees bow down in adoration.

He raised the heaven on high and set the balance of all things, that you might not transgress that balance. Give just weight and full measure.

He laid the earth for His creatures, with all its fruits and blossom-bearing palm, chaff-covered grain and scented herbs. Which of your Lord's blessings would you deny?

He created man from potter's clay, and the jinn [spirits] from smokeless fire. Which of your Lord's blessings would you deny? (55:1–18)

All that is in the heavens and the earth gives glory to God. He is the Mighty, the Wise One.

It is He that has sovereignty over the heavens and the earth. He ordains life and death, and has power over all things.

He is the First and the Last, the Visible and the Unseen. He has knowledge of all things.

It was He who created the heavens and the earth in six days, and then mounted the throne. He knows all that goes into the earth and all that emerges from it, all that comes down from heaven and all that ascends to it. He is with you wherever you are. God is cognizant of all your actions.

He has sovereignty over the heavens and the earth. To God shall all things return. He causes the night to pass into the day, and causes the day to pass into the night. He has knowledge of the inmost thoughts of men. (57:1–7)

RIGHTEOUSNESS AND MERCY

Righteousness does not consist in whether you face towards the East or the West. The righteous man is he who believes in God and the Last Day, in the angels and the Book and the prophets; who, though he loves it dearly, gives away his wealth to kinsfolk, to orphans, to the destitute, to the traveller in need and to beggars, and for the redemption of captives; who attends to his prayers and renders the alms levy; who is true to his promises and steadfast in trial and adver-

sity and in times of war. Such are the true believers; such are the God-fearing. (2:176–178)

Serve God and associate none with Him. Show kindness to parents and kindred, to orphans and to the destitute, to near and distant neighbours, to those that keep company with you, to the traveller in need, and to the slaves you own. God does not love arrogant and boastful men, who are themselves niggardly and enjoin others to be niggardly; who conceal the riches which God of His bounty has bestowed upon them (We have prepared a shameful punishment for the unbelievers); and who spend their wealth for the sake of ostentation, believing neither in God nor in the Last Day. He that chooses Satan for his friend, an evil friend has he. (4:36–39)

CHRISTIANITY

And remember the angels' words to Mary. They said:* "God has chosen you. He has made you pure and exalted you above womankind. Mary, be obedient to your Lord; bow down and worship with the worshippers."

This is an account of a divine secret. We reveal it to you.† You were not present when they cast lots to see which of them should have charge of Mary; nor were you present when they argued about her.

The angels said to Mary: "God bids you rejoice in a word from Him. His name is the Messiah, Jesus the son of Mary. He shall be noble in this world and in the hereafter, and shall be one of those who are favoured. He shall preach to men in his cradle and in the prime of manhood, and shall lead a righteous life."

"Lord" she said, "how can I bear a child when no man has touched me?"

He replied: "Even thus. God creates whom He will. When He decrees a thing He need only say: 'Be,' and it is. He will instruct him in the Scriptures and in wisdom, in the Torah and in the Gospel, and send him forth as an apostle to the Israelites. He will say: 'I bring you a sign from your Lord. From clay I will make for you the likeness of a bird. I shall breathe into it and, by God's leave, it shall become a living bird. By God's leave I shall heal the blind man and the leper, and raise the dead to life. I shall tell you what to eat and what to store up in your houses. Surely that will be a sign for you, if you are true believers. I come to confirm the Torah which preceded me and to make lawful to you some of the things you are forbidden. I bring you a sign from your Lord: therefore fear God and obey me. God is my Lord and your Lord: therefore serve Him. That is a straight path.'" (3:42–51)

People of the Book,‡ do not transgress the bounds of your religion. Speak nothing but the truth about God. The

---

*Cf. Luke i, 26–38
†Muhammad.
‡Christians.

Messiah, Jesus the son of Mary, was no more than God's apostle and His Word which He cast to Mary: a spirit from Him. So believe in God and His apostles and do not say: "Three." Forbear, and it shall be better for you. God is but one God. God forbid that He should have a son! His is all that the heavens and the earth contain. God is the all-sufficient protector. The Messiah does not disdain to be a servant of God, nor do the angels who are nearest to Him. Those who through arrogance disdain His service shall all be brought before Him. (4:171–172)

HEAVEN AND HELL
THAT WHICH IS COMING

In the Name of God, the Compassionate, the Merciful

When that which is coming comes—and no soul shall then deny its coming—some shall be abased and others exalted.

When the earth shakes and quivers, and the mountains crumble away and scatter abroad into fine dust, you shall be divided into three multitudes: those on the right (blessed shall be those on the right); those on the left (damned shall be those on the left); and those to the fore (foremost shall be those). Such are they that shall be brought near to their Lord in the gardens of delight: a whole multitude from the men of old, but only a few from the latter generations.

They shall recline on jewelled couches face to face, and there shall wait on them immortal youths with bowls and ewers and a cup of purest wine (that will neither pain their heads nor take away their reason); with fruits of their own choice and flesh of fowls that they relish. And theirs shall be the dark-eyed houris [beautiful virgins], chaste as hidden pearls: a guerdon [reward] for their deeds.

There they shall hear no idle talk, no sinful speech, but only the greeting, "Peace! Peace!"

Those on the right hand—happy shall be those on the right hand! They shall recline on couches raised on high in the shade of thornless sidrs and clusters of talh;* amidst gushing waters and abundant fruits, unforbidden, neverending.

We created the houris and made them virgins, loving companions for those on the right hand: a multitude from the men of old, and a multitude from the latter generations.

As for those on the left hand (wretched shall be those on the left hand!) they shall dwell amidst scorching winds and seething water: in the shade of pitch-black smoke, neither cool nor refreshing. For they have lived in comfort and persisted in the heinous sin,† saying: "When we are once dead and turned to dust and bones, shall we be raised to life? And our forefathers, too?"

Say: "Those of old, and those of the present age, shall be brought together on an appointed day. As for you sinners who deny the truth, you shall eat the fruit of the Zaqqūm tree and fill your bellies with it. You shall drink scalding water: yet you shall drink it as the thirsty camel drinks."

Such shall be their fare on the Day of Reckoning. (56:1–56)

WOMEN

Men have authority over women because God has made the one superior to the other, and because they spend their wealth to maintain them. Good women are obedient. They guard their unseen parts because God has guarded them. As for those from whom you fear disobedience, admonish them and send them to beds apart and beat them. Then if they obey you, take no further action against them. Surely God is high, supreme.

If you fear a breach between a man and his wife, appoint an arbiter from his people and another from hers. If they wish to be reconciled God will bring them together again. Surely God is all-knowing and wise. (4:34–35)

---

*Probably the banana fruit.
†Idolatry.

---

3 Islam and the Greek Learning

In the eighth and ninth centuries, Muslim civilization, which creatively integrated Arabic, Byzantine, Persian, and Indian cultural traditions, entered its golden age. Muslim science, philosophy, and mathematics, based largely on the achievements of the ancient Greeks, made brilliant contributions to the sum of knowledge at a time when Latin Christendom had lost much of Greco-Roman thought and culture. The Muslims had acquired Greek learning from the older Persian and Byzantine civilizations, which had kept alive the Greek inheritance. By translating Greek works into Arabic and commenting on them, Muslim scholars performed the great historical task of preserving the philosophical and scientific heritage of ancient Greece. Along with this heritage, the original contributions of Muslim scholars and scientists were also passed on to Christian Europe.

Avicenna
LOVE OF LEARNING

The most eminent Muslim thinker, Ibn-Sina, known to the West as Avicenna (980–1037), was a poet, doctor, scientist, and philosopher who wrote on every field of knowledge. His philosophical works, which relied heavily on Aristotle, had an important influence on medieval Christian thinkers. In his autobiography, excerpted below, Avicenna describes his love for learning and his debt to ancient Greece.

[In] Bukhara [in present-day Uzbekistan] I was put under teachers of the Koran and of letters. By the time I was ten I had mastered the Koran and a great deal of literature, so that I was marvelled at for my aptitude. . . . Then there came to Bukhara a man called Abū ʿAbd Allāh al-Nātilī who claimed to be a philosopher; my father invited him to stay in our house, hoping that I would learn from him also. Before his advent I had already occupied myself with Muslim jurisprudence, attending Ismāʿīl the Ascetic; so I was an excellent enquirer, having become familiar with the methods of postulation and the techniques of rebuttal according to the usages of the canon lawyers. I now commenced reading the *Isagoge* (of Porphyry)[1] with al-Nātilī: when he mentioned to me the definition of *genus* as a term applied to a number of things of different species in answer to the question "What is it?" I set about verifying this definition in a manner such as he had never heard. He marvelled at me exceedingly, and warned my father that I should not engage in any other occupation but learning; whatever problem he stated to me, I showed a better mental conception of it than he. So I continued until I had read all the straightforward parts of Logic with him; as for the subtler points, he had no acquaintance with them.

From then onward I took to reading texts by myself; I studied the commentaries, until I had completely mastered the science of Logic. Similarly with Euclid[2] I read the first five or six figures with him, and thereafter undertook on my own account to solve the entire remainder of the book. Next I moved on to the *Almagest* (of Ptolemy);[3] when I had finished the prolegomena [introductory essay] and reached the geometrical figures, al-Nātilī told me to go on reading and to solve the problems by myself; I should merely revise what I read with him, so that he might indicate to me what was right and what was wrong. The truth is that he did not really teach this book; I began to solve the work, and many were the complicated figures of which he had no knowledge until I presented them to him, and made him understand them. Then al-Nātilī took leave of me, setting out for Gurganj.

I now occupied myself with mastering the various texts and commentaries on natural science and metaphysics, until all the gates of knowledge were open to me. Next I desired to study medicine, and proceeded to read all the books that have been written on this subject. Medicine is not a difficult science, and naturally I excelled in it in a very short time, so that qualified physicians began to read medicine with me. I also undertook to treat the sick, and methods of treatment derived from practical experience revealed themselves to me such as baffle description. At the same time I continued between whiles to study and dispute on law, being now sixteen years of age.

The next eighteen months I devoted entirely to reading; I studied Logic once again, and all the parts of philosophy. During all this time I did not sleep one night through, nor devoted my attention to any other matter by day. I prepared a set of files; with each proof I examined, I set down the syllogistic premises and put them in order in the files, then I examined what deductions might be drawn from them. I observed methodically the conditions of the premises, and proceeded until the truth of each particular problem was confirmed for me. Whenever I found myself perplexed by a problem, or could not find the middle term in any syllogism, I would repair to the mosque and pray, adoring the All-Creator, until my puzzle was resolved and my difficulty made easy. At night I would return home, set the lamp before me, and busy myself with reading and writing; whenever sleep overcame me or I was conscious of some weakness, I turned aside to drink a glass of wine until my strength returned to

---

[1]Porphyry (A.D. 233–c. 305) wrote a history of philosophy and edited the lectures of Plotinus, the Neoplatonist. The *Isagoge* was Porphyry's introduction to the categories of Aristotle.

[2]Euclid was an Alexandrian mathematician who lived around 300 B.C. He creatively synthesized earlier developments in geometry.

[3]Ptolemy was a mathematician, geographer, and astronomer who worked at Alexandria in the second century A.D. His *Almagest,* a Greek-Arabic term meaning "the greatest" summed up antiquity's knowledge of astronomy and became the authoritative text during the Middle Ages.

me; then I went back to my reading. If ever the least slumber overtook me, I would dream of the precise problem which I was considering as I fell asleep; in that way many problems revealed themselves to me while sleeping. So I continued until I had made myself master of all the sciences; I now comprehended them to the limits of human possibility. All that I learned during that time is exactly as I know it now; I have added nothing more to my knowledge to this day.

I was now a master of Logic, natural sciences and mathematics. I therefore returned to metaphysics; I read the *Metaphysica* (of Aristotle), but did not understand its contents and was baffled by the author's intention; I read it over forty times, until I had the text by heart. Even then I did not understand it or what the author meant, and I despaired within myself, saying, "This is a book which there is no way of understanding." But one day at noon I chanced to be in the booksellers' quarter, and a broker was there with a volume in his hand which he was calling for sale. He offered it to me, but I returned it to him impatiently, believing that there was no use in this particular science. However he said to me, "Buy this book from me: it is cheap, and I will sell it to you for four dirhams. The owner is in need of the money." So I bought it, and found that it was a book by Abū Naṣr al-Fārābī *On the Objects of the Metaphysica.* I returned home and

hastened to read it; and at once the objects of that book became clear to me, for I had it all by heart. I rejoiced at this, and upon the next day distributed much in alms to the poor in gratitude to Almighty God.

Now the Sultan of Bukhara at that time was Nūḥ ibn Manṣūr, and it happened that he fell sick of a malady which baffled all the physicians. My name was famous among them because of the breadth of my reading; they therefore mentioned me in his presence, and begged him to summon me. I attended the sick-room, and collaborated with them in treating the royal patient. So I came to be enrolled in his service. One day I asked his leave to enter their library, to examine the contents and read the books on medicine; he granted my request, and I entered a mansion with many chambers, each chamber having chests of books piled one upon another. In one apartment were books on language and poetry, in another law, and so on; each apartment was set aside for books on a single science. I glanced through the catalogue of the works of the ancient Greeks, and asked for those which I required; and I saw books whose very names are as yet unknown to many—works which I had never seen before and have not seen since. I read these books, taking notes of their contents; I came to realize the place each man occupied in his particular science.

4 Islamic Literature

The colorful court of the fifth Abbasid caliph Harun ar-Rashid (r. 786–809) serves as the historical backdrop for many of the tales in the collection known as the *Thousand and One Arabian Nights.* It was composed between the eighth and sixteenth centuries by various authors and is one of the most famous and popular works of fiction in world literature. Drawing on earlier oral traditions, the tales blend familiar anecdotes with Persian and Indian fairy tales and Arabic legends and romances, as well as Egyptian tales of love. The stories excite the imagination, for they are filled with adventure, heroism, amorous encounters, magic, and the sights and flavor of the East.

Thousand and One Arabian Nights

Each individual tale exists within a larger framework story, which takes place in the islands off India and China. Shahryar accedes to the empire of his father, while his younger brother, Shah Zaman, becomes "King of Samarkand in Barbarian land." At his brother's court, Shah Zaman witnesses Shahryar's wife committing adultery and other illicit acts, and he tells his brother of his wife's betrayal. Shahryar, vowing revenge, commands that his wife be put to death along with all of her attendants and their companions. He then swears an oath—to marry a maiden every night, to violate her virginity, and to slay her the next morning. Eventually, there are virtually no virgins left in the realm, except for the two daughters of Shahryar's Chief Wazir, the elder of whom is Scheherazade.

Trusting in her own intelligence and wit, Scheherazade asks to marry King Shahryar, because she believes she can offer herself as a ransom for other women. Her father objects, but Scheherazade remains intransigent and prepares for her night with Shahryar by concocting a plan with her sister, Dunyazade. After Scheherazade is ravished by Shahryar, she signals for Dunyazade, who then begs Shahryar to allow Scheherazade to tell her a story. The trick, however, is that Scheherazade never finishes the tale, thereby prolonging her life.

The following tale deals with a *jinni* (better known by its Anglicized name "genie"). In Islamic folklore, jinn (the plural of jinni) are mythical demons or spirits (some good, many evil) who are considered to be lower than the angels. Since they were created from a smokeless fire, they can conceivably assume any form. King Sulayman (Solomon) confined many of them using magic, but the rest of them were destined to wander in solitary, obscure places around the world. In a multitude of ways, jinn are very much like human beings, including their need to eat, to reproduce, and to die. Jinn also savor punishing human beings for their errors, but they can be controlled by those who possess the correct knowledge of their behavior. Of special importance is the value the fisherman of this tale places on the role of Allah (God) in his life.

THE FISHERMAN AND THE JINNI

It is Related, O auspicious King, that there was once a fisherman, very old and poor, who was married and had three children.

He used to cast his net four times a day, never more often. Now once, when he had gone to the shore at noon, he set down his basket and, casting his net, waited for it to sink to the bottom. When it had done so he twitched the cords and found it so heavy that he could not pull it in. So, bringing the ends to shore, he made them fast to a wooden stake. Then he undressed and, diving into the sea, laboured till he had hauled the net ashore. Dressing himself again in high good humour he examined the net and found that it contained a dead ass. Disgusted at this sight, he exclaimed: "Be it as Allah wills!" and added: "Yet it is a strange gift that Allah has seen good to send me." Then he recited this verse:

Blind diver in the dark
Of night and loss,
Luck delights not in energy;
Cease, and be still.

After he had freed the net and squeezed the water out of it, he waded into the sea and cast it again, invoking the name of Allah. When the net had sunk to the bottom, he again tried to pull it ashore but this time it was even heavier and harder to shift. Thinking that he had caught some great fish, he fastened the ends to the stake and, undressing again, dived in and carried the net to shore. This time he found a great earthen jar full of mud and sand. In his disappointment at this sight, he proclaimed these verses:

I said I wished that fortune would die or fly away,
Who lets a man be virtuous and then keeps back his
  pay.
I left my house to look for luck
(A search I now abandon);

She dropped the wise men in the muck
  For all the fools to stand on,
And, having fixed this state of things,
She either died or sprouted wings.

Then he threw away the jar and cleaned his net, asking pardon from Allah the while for his lack of submission to the divine will. And finally, coming down to the sea, he cast for the third time and waited for the net to sink. When he hauled in this time, the net was full of broken pots and pieces of glass. Seeing this, he recited the stanza of a certain poet.

Be not astonished that the golden wind
Blow the world forward, leaving you behind.
There are no dinars[1] in a rose-wood pen
For any but a merchant's hand to find.

Then lifting his face to the sky, he cried: "Allah, Allah! Thou knowest that I cast my net but four times in the day; and see! I have already cast it thrice." After this, he once more cast his net into the sea, again invoking the name of Allah, and waited for it to sink. This time, in spite of all his efforts, he could not move the net an inch, so hard was it held against the rocks below the water. Again he undressed crying: "Be it as Allah wills!" and diving for the fourth time, began to work the net until he had freed it and brought it to shore. This time he found in it a great jar of yellow copper, heavy and unhurt, its mouth stopped with lead and sealed with the seal of the lord Sulayman, son of David. Seeing this, the fisherman was delighted and said: "Here is something that I can sell at the market of the coppersmiths. It must be worth at least ten dinars of gold." Then, after trying to shake the jar and finding it too heavy he continued: "First I had better open the jar and hide whatever it contains in my basket; then I shall be able to sell the thing itself to the coppersmiths." So he took his knife and began to work the lead until he had removed it.

----
[1]The Islamic dinar is 4.3 grams of gold.

Then he turned the jar over and shook it, but nothing came out except a cloud of smoke which rose to the blue sky and also spread along the earth. Finally the smoke, to the utter amazement of the fisherman, came clear of the vase and shaking and thickening, turned to an *Ifrit*[2] whose head reached to the clouds while his feet were on the ground. The head of this Ifrit was like a dome, his hands like pitchforks, his legs like the masts of a ship, and his mouth like a cave in which the teeth had the appearance of great stones. His nostrils were like jugs, his eyes like torches, and his hair was dusty and matted. At the appearance of this being the fisherman was so frightened that his muscles quivered, his teeth chattered together, and he stood with burning mouth, and eyes that could not see the light.

When the Jinni, in his turn, saw the fisherman, he cried: "There is no other God but Allah, and Sulayman is Allah's prophet!" Then, speaking directly to the fisherman, he said: "O great Sulayman, O thou prophet of Allah, slay me not. Never again will I be disobedient or mutiny against thy just decrees." Then said the fisherman: "Darest thou, O blasphemous giant, to call Sulayman the prophet of Allah? Sulayman has been dead for eighteen hundred years and we have come to the end of the world's time. What tale is this? How did you come to be in this jar?" At these words the Jinni altered his tone and said: "There is no other God but Allah. I bring good news, O fisherman!" "What news is that?" asked the poor man. And the Jinni answered: "News of your death, instant and most horrible." "Let Allah be far from rewarding you for such news, prince of the Afarit! Why do you wish my death and how have I deserved it? I delivered you out of your jar, breaking your long imprisonment in the sea." But the Ifrit only answered: "Consider and choose the manner of death you would prefer and the way that I shall kill you." "But what is my fault? What is my fault?" repeated the wretched fisherman. "Listen to my story and you shall know," said the Ifrit. "Speak then, and make your tale a short one," said the fisherman, "for my soul is ready to run out of my feet for very fear." So the Ifrit began:

Know that I am Sakhr El-Jinni, one of the rebel Afarit who mutinied against Sulayman, son of David. There was a time when Sulayman sent his wazir Assef, son of Barkhia, against me, who overpowered me in spite of all my strength and led me into the presence of Sulayman. You may believe that at that moment I humbled myself very low. Sulayman, seeing me, prayed to Allah and conjured me both to take that faith and to promise him obedience. When I refused, he had

---

[2]Ifrit (plural Afarit) is a diabolic, evil spirit.

this jar brought before him and imprisoned me within it. Then he sealed it with lead and impressed thereon the Most High Name. Lastly, certain faithful Jinn took me upon their shoulders at his order and cast me into the middle of the sea. I stayed in the water for a hundred years and kept on saying: "I shall give eternal riches to him who sets me free!" But the hundred years passed and no one set me free. So, when I was entering on the second hundred years, I swore: "To him who sets me free will I both show and give all the treasures upon earth!" But no one freed me, and four hundred years passed away, and I said: "To him who frees me I will give the three wishes of his heart!" But still no one set me free. So I flew into a heat of passion in my jar and swore: "Now I will kill the man who frees me, my only gift being the choice of the death!" And it is you, O fisherman, who have set me free; therefore I let you choose the death you die.

Hearing the Ifrit speak in this way, the fisherman could not help exclaiming: "O Allah, the bad luck of it! It *would* have been left for me to do this freeing! Spare me, O Jinni, and Allah will spare you; kill me, and be very sure that He will raise up one to slay you also." Then said the Ifrit: "I shall kill you because you freed me. There is no help for it." On this the fisherman exclaimed: "Prince of the Afarit, indeed! Is this how you repay good with evil? The proverb does not lie which says:

If you would know the taste of bitterness
Seek sorrow out and comfort her distress;
You need not feed a jackal cub to see
Just how ungrateful gratitude can be."

But the Ifrit said: "You have used words enough. Prepare to meet your end." Then the fisherman reasoned with himself in this way: "Though I am a man and he is a Jinni, yet Allah has given me my share of brains. I think I see a trick, a stroke of subtlety, which may undo him yet." Then aloud to the Ifrit he said: "You are determined that I should die?" And when the other said: "No doubt of that!" the fisherman solemnly addressed him thus: "I conjure you by the Most High Name graved on the seal of Sulayman to answer me one question truthfully!" And when the Ifrit, dashed by hearing the Most High Name, promised that he would answer truthfully, the fisherman asked: "How could this jar which, as it is, scarcely could hold a foot or hand of yours, have ever held the whole of you?" "Can it be that you doubt this thing?" asked the Ifrit. And the other answered: "Never would I believe it unless I saw you with my own eyes entering the jar!"

But at this point Shahrazade saw the coming of morning and fell silent.

5 The Transmission of Learning

Greco-Roman humanism, in retreat since the Late Roman Empire, continued its decline in the centuries immediately following Rome's demise. The old Roman schools closed, and Roman law faded into disuse. Europeans' knowledge of the Greek language was almost totally lost, and aside from clerics, few people could read and write Latin. Many literary works of classical antiquity were either lost or unread. European culture was much poorer than the high civilizations of Byzantium, Islam, and ancient Rome.

During this period of cultural poverty, the few persons who were learned generally did not engage in original thought but salvaged and transmitted remnants of classical civilization. These individuals retained respect for the inheritance of Greece and Rome while remaining devoted to Chrisitanity. In a rudimentary way, they were struggling to create a Christian culture that combined the intellectual tradition of Greece and Rome with the religious teachings of the Christian Church.

Cassiodorus

THE MONK AS SCRIBE

One such scholar seeking to transmit ancient learning was Cassiodorus (c. 490–575), who served three Ostrogothic kings in Italy. Cassiodorus wrote theological treatises and the twelve-volume *History of the Goths,* but his principal achievement was collecting Greek and Latin manuscripts. Like other Christian scholars before and after him, Cassiodorus maintained that the study of secular literature was an aid to understanding sacred writings. He retired to a monastery where he fostered the monastic practice of copying Christian and pagan manuscripts. Without this effort of monks, many important secular and Christian writings might have perished.

In the following reading from his Introduction to *Divine and Human Readings,* Cassiodorus gave his views on the importance of the monastic scribe's vocation. Cassiodorus believed that through his pen the scribe preaches the word of God and is inspired by his text to know God more fully.

ON SCRIBES AND THE REMEMBERING OF CORRECT SPELLING

1. I admit that among those of your tasks which require physical effort that of the scribe,[1] if he writes correctly, appeals most to me; and it appeals, perhaps not without reason, for by reading the Divine Scriptures he wholesomely instructs his own mind and by copying the precepts of the Lord he spreads them far and wide. Happy his design, praiseworthy his zeal, to preach to men with the hand alone, to unleash tongues with the fingers, to give salvation silently to mortals, and to fight against the illicit temptations of the devil with pen and ink. Every word of the Lord written by the scribe is a wound inflicted on Satan. And so, though seated in one spot, with the dissemination of his work he travels through different provinces. The product of his toil is read in holy places; people hear the means by which they may turn themselves away from base desire and serve the Lord with heart undefiled. Though absent, he labors at his task. I cannot deny that he may receive a renovation of life from these many blessings, if only he accomplishes things of this sort, not with a vain show of ambition, but with upright zeal. Man multiplies the

---

[1]Scribes were persons trained to copy by hand the texts of books, or to take dictation.

heavenly words, and in a certain metaphorical sense, if one may so express himself, that which the virtue of the Holy Trinity utters is written by a trinity of fingers. O sight glorious to those who contemplate it carefully! With gliding pen the heavenly words are copied so that the devil's craft, by means of which he caused the head of the Lord to be struck during His passion, may be destroyed. They deserve praise too for seeming in some way to imitate the action of the Lord, who, though it was expressed figuratively, wrote His law with the use of His all-powerful finger. Much indeed is there to be said about such a distinguished art, but it is enough to mention the fact that those men are called scribes (*librarii*) who serve zealously the just scales (*libra*) of the Lord.

2. But lest in performing this great service copyists introduce faulty words with letters changed or lest an untutored corrector fail to know how to correct mistakes, let them read the works of ancient authors on orthography [spelling]. . . .

. . . I have collected as many of these works as possible with eager curiosity. . . . [If you] read [them] with unremitting zeal, they will completely free you from the fog of ignorance, so that what was previously unknown may become for the most part very well known.

3. In addition to these things we have provided workers skilled in bookbinding, in order that a handsome external form may clothe the beauty of sacred letters; in some measure, perhaps, we imitate the example in the parable of the Lord,* who amid the glory of the heavenly banquet has clothed in wedding garments those whom He judges worthy of being invited to the table. And for the binders, in fitting manner, unless I err, we have represented various styles of binding in a single codex,[2] that he who so desires may choose for himself the type of cover he prefers.

4. We have also prepared cleverly constructed lamps which preserve their illuminating flames and feed their own fire and without human attendance abundantly maintain a very full clearness of most copious light; and the fat oil in them does not fail, although it is burned continually with a bright flame.

5. Nor have we by any means allowed you to be unacquainted with the hour meters which have been discovered to be very useful to the human race. I have provided a sundial for you for bright days and a water clock which points out the hour continually both day and night, since on some days the bright sun is frequently absent, and rain water passes in marvellous fashion into the ground, because the fiery force of the sun, regulated from above, fails. And so the art of man has brought into harmony elements which are naturally separated; the hour meters are so reliable that you consider an act of either as having been arranged by messengers. These instruments, then, have been provided in order that the soldiers of Christ,[3] warned by most definite signs, may be summoned to the carrying out of their divine task as if by sounding trumpets.

---

*Matthew 22:11.

[2]A codex consists of the rectangular sheets on which scribes have written, bound together on one side, like a modern book. Invented in the late first century A.D., the codex gradually replaced scrolls as the predominant way to store written texts.

[3]"Soldiers of Christ" is a metaphor to describe monks in their vocation.

Boethius
The Consolation of Philosophy

Boethius (480–c. 525), a descendant of a noble family, was an important figure in the intellectual life of this transitional period. He was the last Latin-speaking scholar of the Roman world to have mastered the Greek language and to have an intimate knowledge of Greek philosophy. He translated some of Aristotle's treatises on logic into Latin and wrote commentaries on Aristotle, Cicero, and Porphyry, a Neoplatonist philosopher. Boethius served the Ostrogoth Theodoric I, who ruled Italy. A sudden turn of fortune deprived him of power and prestige when Theodoric ordered him executed for allegedly participating in a plot against the throne. While in prison awaiting execution, Boethius wrote *The Consolation of Philosohy* in which he sought comfort from Lady Philosophy.

In Book 1 of *The Consolation of Philosophy.* Boethius despairs of his recent change in fortune when Lady Philosophy, the personification of highest capabilities of human reason, appears. He tells her that he had become a public servant because of Plato's judgment that wise men ought to be rulers. Despite his innocence he has been condemned to death. How is it possible, he wonders, that the wicked should prevail over virtue; how can God permit such injustice? Lady Philosophy begins by reminding him that the world is governed by divine reason. Then she tells him that there are two basic causes for his sickness—he no longer understands that God rules the world, and he has forgotten his own human identity, that is, he no longer knows that he possesses an immortal soul. Book 2 features a discussion about the fickle nature of the goddess Fortune, who no longer favors Boethius. Lady Philosophy reminds Boethius of the bountiful blessings that Fortune had previously bestowed on him. Then, in the tradition of Plato and the Stoics, she tells him that Fortune can never take away the happiness that resides within a person. Happiness is the highest good of a rational person. She goes on to inform him that Fortune will have no power over him after this life is over, when his mind, the higher aspect of the soul, will continue to live, free from the prison of this world. Finally, she reminds him that even a tyrant cannot control a free mind.

"So why, mortal men, do you pursue happiness outside yourselves, when it lies within?" Error and ignorance derange you. I shall briefly outline for you the hinge on which the greatest happiness turns. Is there anything more precious to you than yourself? Nothing, you will reply. Well then, as long as you are in command of yourself, you will possess what you would never wish to lose, and what Fortune can never withdraw from you. So that you may acknowledge that true happiness cannot reside in this realm of chance, you must grasp this argument: If happiness is the highest good of a rational nature, and if what can be taken from you in any way cannot be the highest (for what cannot be taken away ranks higher than what can), it is obvious that the fluidity of Fortune cannot hope to win happiness. . . .

"Now you are that same person who I know held the rooted conviction, instilled by numerous proofs, that the minds of men are in no wise mortal, and since it is obvious that the happiness which chance brings ends with the body's death, there can be no doubt, assuming that such happiness can confer well-being, that when death signals the end the whole human race is plunged into misery. Yet we know that many have come to enjoy such well-being not only in death, but even in pain and torture. So how can that happiness whose cessation does not make us wretched induce well-being in us by its presence? . . . How can a person exercise rights over any other, except over his body and that which ranks below his body, namely his fortune? You can exercise no dominion whatever, can you, over a free mind? Or disturb from its natural serenity a mind at one with itself through the steadying influence of reason? When the tyrant thought that by a torture he would force a free man to betray his associates in the conspiracy against him, the free man bit through his tongue, and threw it in the face of the storming tyrant. In this way that sage made a virtue out of the tortures which the tyrant believed were instruments of cruelty. . . ."

The theme of Book 3 is the essence of true happiness and how to achieve it. Lady Philosophy points out that there are five false paths to happiness: the ambition for wealth, high position, power, fame, and physical pleasures. Then, in the form of a Platonic dialogue in the following passage, she points Boethius to the true Good, which resides in God, who is true happiness. Humans can attain goodness and happiness by becoming as godlike as possible.

CHAPTER 10

"So now that you have seen what is the shape of the imperfect good, and also that of the perfect good, I think that I must now show you the region in which the perfection of happiness is set.

"Any consideration of this must, I think, first investigate whether any good of this kind, as defined by you a little earlier, can exist in this world. We shall thus ensure that we are not beguiled by some vacuous mental image which is remote from the true reality lying before us. Now it cannot be denied that the perfect good exists, and that it is, so to say, the source of all goods, for everything said to be imperfect is so described because it is less than perfect. The logical conclusion is that if in any class of objects something imperfect appears, that class must also contain something perfect; for if such perfection is removed, one cannot even imagine how that which is called imperfect has come into existence. The universe does not take its rise from things which were curtailed or incomplete; rather, it issues from things which are intact and fully developed, and it disintegrates into this parlous and sterile world of ours. Now if, as we demonstrated a little earlier, there is what we may call imperfect happiness in a good that is brittle, there can be no doubt of the existence of some unalloyed and perfect happiness."

"That conclusion," I said, "is as solid and as true as it can possibly be."

"Now as for the abode of that happiness," she went on, "ponder it in this way. The belief which human minds share demonstrates that God, the source of all things, is good; for since nothing better than God can be imagined, who can doubt that if something has no better, it is good? Reason in fact establishes that God's goodness is such as to demonstrate further that perfect good resides within him. Were this not the case, he could not be the source of all things, for there would be something more preeminent, which would be in possession of perfect good, and would be seen to take precedence ahead of him, since all perfect things clearly take precedence over things less complete. So to prevent the argument advancing into infinity, we must allow that the highest God is totally full of the highest and perfect good. Now we have established that the perfect good is true happiness, so true happiness must reside in the highest God."

"I grant that," I said. "No possible counter-argument can be raised against it."

"But we have already conceded that the highest good is happiness."

"Indeed we have," I replied.

"And so," she said, "we must acknowledge that God is happiness itself."

"I cannot refute your earlier assertions", I said, "and I do see that this rider necessarily follows."

"Now consider," she added, "whether the same conclusion is also reached even more demonstrably from this: there cannot be two highest goods which differ from each other. Indeed, it is clear that if two goods differ, the one is not the other, and accordingly neither can possibly be perfect, since each lacks the other. Now clearly if something is not perfect, it is not the highest. So it is totally impossible for highest goods to differ from each other. But we have concluded that both happiness and God are the highest good, so the highest divinity must itself be the highest happiness."

"No possible conclusion", I said, "could be truer in fact, surer in logic, or worthier of God."

"But we have shown that God and true happiness are one and the same."

"We have indeed," I said.

"Therefore we can safely conclude that God's substance too lies in the good itself, and nowhere else. . . ."

Book 4 addresses a second theme: Why is there so much evil and suffering in the world? Why is vice so dominant while virtue struggles to survive? In response, Lady Philosophy maintains that evil does not prevail. Evil people will never escape punishment; they are weak. Good people become divine by attaining the good, and they are powerful. Boethius then brings up another, closely related issue—the seemingly irrational operation of chance in the world that appears to be antithetical to the governance of Providence. Lady Philosophy explains that Fate operates in this world according to the plan of Providence, divine reason. This leads into the topic of Book 5, where Boethius wonders whether there is such a thing as chance. Lady Philosophy answers that chance cannot exist because Providence rules the universe. Boethius then asks the inevitable question: How can humans have free will if all is governed by divine Providence?

CHAPTER 3

At this I said: "I fear that I am further disconcerted by a still more difficult doubt."

"What is it?" she asked. "Mind you, I can guess what is worrying you."

"There seems to be a considerable contradiction and inconsistency", I said, "between God's foreknowing all things and the existence of any free will. If God foresees all things and cannot be in any way mistaken, then what Providence has foreseen will happen must inevitably come to pass. So if God has prior knowledge from eternity not only of men's actions but also of their plans and wishes, there will be no freedom of will; for the only action and any sort of intention which can possibly exist in the future will be foreknown by divine Providence, which cannot be misled. If such actions and aspirations can be forcibly diverted in some direction other than was foreseen, certain foreknowledge of the future will no longer exist, but instead there will be vacillating opinion; and I regard it is sacrilege to believe this of God.

"I do not subscribe to the argument by which some believe that they can disentangle this knotty problem. What they suggest is that Providence's foreknowledge of a future event is not the cause of its happening, but that it is the other way round. Since something is about to happen, this cannot be hidden from divine Providence, and in this sense, they claim, the element of necessity is reversed Their argument is that things foreseen do not therefore happen by necessity, but that things which will happen are necessarily foreseen. The assumption here is that we are toiling over the problem of which is the cause of which: is foreknowledge the cause of the necessity of future events, or is the necessity of future events the cause of Providence? In fact, however, we are struggling to show that whatever the sequence of causes, the outcome of things foreknown is necessary, even if such foreknowledge does not appear to impose an inevitable outcome upon future events. . . ."

If God foresees everything and if what God foresees must happen, how can humans be free to choose what they wish to choose? Indeed, if what God knows will happen must happen, then God must be responsible for everything that happens; he must even be responsible for evil. In that case, rewarding the good and punishing evil would be meaningless.

"Once this is admitted, the extent of the decline in human fortunes becomes evident. Rewards or punishments offered to good or wicked men are pointless, for they have not been won by any free, and voluntary impulse of their minds. What is now considered utterly just—punishments for the wicked and rewards for the good—will be seen to be the greatest injustice imaginable, because they have been impelled to commit good or evil not by their own will, but, by the unchanging necessity of what will be. So neither vices nor virtues will exist at all; instead all the deserts of people are mingled and undifferentiated in the melting pot. Moreover—and nothing more heinous than this can be imag-

ined—since the entire ordering of human affairs derives from Providence, and no discretion is granted to our human intentions, our vices as well are to be ascribed to the author of all things good. . . ."

Lady Philosophy's answer concludes the *Consolation*. Human reason is not able to know the way that God knows. Limited human reason sees all things as past, present, and future, but the infinite divine intelligence sees all things as eternally present. In his eternal present, God sees things that will happen in what humans consider to be the future. Nonetheless, humans have a free will. An event is necessary because of God's knowledge of it, but things happen as a result of the free will of humans. Moreover, every time humans change their minds, Providence has already anticipated these future actions. The human will is free. Therefore, humans must act virtuously, because God will punish the evil actions that he has foreseen in his perfect knowledge.

6 The Carolingian Renaissance

The Early Middle Ages witnessed a marked decline in learning and the arts. Patronage of both the liberal and the visual arts by the old Roman aristocracy was not widely copied by the Germanic ruling class that replaced the Romans. Support for learning and the arts shifted from secular to ecclesiastical patrons. Monasteries became the new centers for intellectual and artistic activities, and Christian themes and values almost entirely displaced the worldly values of Greco-Roman culture.

Under the patronage of Charlemagne (742–814), the great Frankish emperor, a conscious revival of classical Greek and Roman learning and the visual arts occurred. Charlemagne realized that his great empire could not be effectively governed without a cadre of literate clergy and administrators. To educate the leaders of the Frankish empire, Charlemagne sponsored a number of reforms designed to improve the educational institutions and the quality of literacy and learning in his realm. At court, he completely reformed the school conducted for the children of his family and his courtiers and recruited the best scholars in western Europe to staff it. Among these scholars was the English deacon Alcuin of York (735–804), who became his chief advisor on educational and religious affairs. They aimed at restoring classical learning to serve the needs of the new Christian culture.

Einhard

CHARLEMAGNE'S APPRECIATION OF LEARNING

The revival of classical learning and the visual arts under Charlemagne is called the Carolingian Renaissance, a cultural awakening that helped shape medieval civilization. One of Charlemagne's most significant decisions was ordering the making of copies of old manuscripts dating back to Roman times. Much of today's knowledge of Roman learning and literature comes from surviving Carolingian copies of older Latin texts that no longer exist. In the first reading, Charlemagne's biographer Einhard describes western Europe's greatest royal patron of the liberal arts since the fall of the western Roman Empire.

Charles [Charlemagne] had the gift of ready and fluent speech, and could express whatever he had to say with the utmost clearness. He was not satisfied with command of his native language merely, but gave attention to the study of foreign ones, and in particular was such a master of Latin that he could speak it as well as his native tongue; but he could understand Greek better than he could speak it. He was so eloquent, indeed, that he might have passed for a teacher of eloquence. He most zealously cultivated the liberal arts, held those who taught them in great esteem, and conferred great honors upon them. He took lessons in grammar of the deacon Peter of Pisa,[1] at that time an aged man. Another deacon, Albin of Britain, surnamed Alcuin, a man of Saxon extraction, who was the greatest scholar of the day, was his teacher in other branches of learning. The King spent much time and labor with him studying rhetoric, dialectics, and especially astronomy; he learned to reckon, and used to investigate the motions of the heavenly bodies most curiously, with an intelligent scrutiny. He also tried to write, and used to keep tablets and blanks in bed under his pillow, that at leisure hours he might accustom his hand to form the letters; however, as he did not begin his efforts in due season, but late in life, they met with ill success.

He cherished with the greatest fervor and devotion the principles of the Christian religion, which had been instilled into him from infancy. Hence it was that he built the beautiful basilica[2] at Aix-la-Chapelle,[3] which he adorned with gold and silver and lamps, and with rails and doors of solid brass. He had the columns and marbles for this structure brought from Rome and Ravenna,[4] for he could not find such as were suitable elsewhere. He was a constant worshipper at this church as long as his health permitted, going morning and evening, even after nightfall, besides attending mass; and he took care that all the services there conducted should be administered with the utmost possible propriety, very often warning the sextons not to let any improper or unclean thing be brought into the building or remain in it. He provided it with a great number of sacred vessels of gold and silver and with such a quantity of clerical robes that not even the door-keepers who fill the humblest office in the church were obliged to wear their everyday clothes when in the exercise of their duties. He was at great pains to improve the church reading and psalmody [singing], for he was well skilled in both, although he neither read in public nor sang, except in a low tone and with others.

He was very forward in succoring the poor, and in that gratuitous generosity which the Greeks call alms, so much so that he not only made a point of giving in his own country and his own kingdom, but when he discovered that there were Christians living in poverty in Syria, Egypt, and Africa, at Jerusalem, Alexandria, and Carthage, he had compassion on their wants, and used to send money over the seas to them. . . .

---

[1]Peter of Pisa, a famous grammarian (in Latin, the international language of the Middle Ages), was brought from Italy to teach at the school in Charlemagne's palace. He encouraged interest in pre-Christian classical writing, which influenced the court poets of that era.

[2]A basilica is usually a rectangular-shaped church, whose main chamber is divided by columns into a central nave and side aisles. There was usually a semicircular apse at the narrow end facing the east, which was the visual focal point and the location of the main altar.

[3]Aix-la-Chapelle, now Aachen, was Charlemagne's capital. It was located in what is now western Germany, near the Netherlands-Belgium frontier.

[4]Ravenna, in northeastern Italy, was the final capital of the western Roman Empire, in the fifth century; in the sixth and seventh centuries it was the capital of the Byzantine governors of Italy. Ravenna is famous for its magnificent sixth-century churches and mosaic art.

Charlemagne

AN INJUNCTION TO MONASTERIES TO CULTIVATE LETTERS

In a letter to the Abbot Baugulf of Fulda (in Germany), Charlemagne announced his decision to use monasteries as schools for training future clergymen in grammar, writing, and rhetoric.

Charles, by the grace of God, King of the Franks and Lombards and Patrician of the Romans, to Abbot Baugulf and to all the congregation, also to the faithful committed to you, we have directed a loving greeting by our ambassadors in the name of omnipotent God.

Be it known, therefore, to your devotion pleasing to God, that we, together with our faithful, have considered it to be useful that the bishoprics and monasteries entrusted by the favor of Christ to our control, in addition to the [rule] of monastic life and the intercourse of holy religion, . . . also ought to be zealous in [the cultivation of letters], teaching those who by the gift of God are able to learn, according to the capacity of each individual, so that just as the observance of the rule imparts order and grace to honesty of morals, so also zeal in teaching and learning may do the same for sentences, so that those who desire to please God by living rightly should not neglect to please him also by speaking correctly. For it is written: "Either from thy words thou shalt be justified or from thy words thou shalt be condemned."*

For although correct conduct may be better than knowledge, nevertheless knowledge precedes conduct. Therefore, each one ought to study what he desires to accomplish, so that . . . the mind may know more fully what ought to be done, as the tongue hastens in the praises of omnipotent God without the hindrances of errors. For since errors should be shunned by all men, . . . the more they ought to be avoided as far as possible by those who are chosen for this very purpose alone, so that they ought to be the especial servants of truth. For when in the years . . . [past], letters were often written to us from several monasteries in which it was stated that the brethren who dwelt there offered up in our behalf sacred and pious prayers, we have recognized in most of these letters both correct thoughts and uncouth expressions; because what pious devotion dictated faithfully to the mind, the tongue, uneducated on account of the neglect of study, was not able to express in the letter without error. . . . We began to fear lest perchance, as the skill in writing was less, so also the wisdom for understanding the Holy Scriptures might be much less than it rightly ought to be. And we all know well that, although errors of speech are dangerous, far more dangerous are errors of the understanding. Therefore, we exhort you not only not to neglect the study of letters, but also with most humble mind, pleasing to God, to study earnestly in order that you may be able more easily and more correctly to penetrate the mysteries of the divine Scriptures. Since, moreover, images . . . and similar figures are found in the sacred pages, no one doubts that each one in reading these will understand the spiritual sense more quickly if previously he shall have been fully instructed in the mastery of letters. Such men truly are to be chosen for this work as have both the will and the ability to learn and a desire to instruct others. And may this be done with a zeal as great as the earnestness with which we command it.

*Matthew, xii. 37.

7 Anglo-Saxon Mythology

Although an expression of Anglo-Saxon mythology, *Beowulf* does contain a few incontrovertible historical facts. General references are made to Germanic Anglo-Saxons' settlement of England in the sixth century and their encounters with the Danes in the 830s, and a specific incident refers to the death of Beowulf's liege lord, Heygelac of the Geats, a historical figure who was killed in battle about 521. The only surviving manuscript is the Christianized version from the late tenth or early eleventh century.

Beowulf

As the poem opens, the reader is introduced to *Evil* in the guise of the monster, Grendel, who each evening terrorizes the court of Hrothgar, the Danish king, by devouring a number of his warriors. *Good* is presented in the form of Beowulf, a prince of the Geats,[1] who seeks to gain a name for himself by slaying Grendel. During his first encounter with Grendel at Hrothgar's court, Beowulf tears the monster's arm off at the shoulder. Later that night, Beowulf confronts Grendel's mother who seeks vengeance upon Hrothgar's court by carrying off his chief advisor. Beowulf becomes a hero in the eyes of the Danes when he follows Grendel's mother to a haunted lake and slays her with a magical sword under the water. The Danes give Beowulf treasure and lands as a reward for helping them rid their territory of the race of evil monsters. The long, first part of the poem concludes with Beowulf returning to the Geats, telling his uncle, King Hygelac, of his deeds, and honoring his liege lord by giving him his reward.

The second section of the poem, excerpted below, opens with Beowulf ascending the throne of the Geats after his uncle and his cousin are killed on the battlefield. He rules the kingdom peacefully for fifty years, "until a certain one, a dragon, began to rule in the dark nights." Knowing that if he is successful in slaying the dragon he will gain the dragon's treasure, Beowulf, even though he is an old man, challenges the dragon to single combat. During the dragon's first attack, Beowulf is engulfed in flames and his terrified men betray him by fleeing.

Then he addressed each dear companion
one final time, those fighters in their helmets,
resolute and high-born: "I would rather not
use a weapon if I knew another way
to grapple with the dragon and make good my boast
as I did against Grendel in days gone by.
But I shall be meeting molten venom
in the fire he breathes, so I go forth
in mail-shirt and shield. I won't shift a foot
when I meet the cave-guard: what occurs on the wall
between the two of us will turn out as fate,
overseer of men, decides. I am resolved.
I scorn further words against this sky-borne foe.

"Men at arms, remain here on the barrow [a mound of earth],
safe in your armour, to see which one of us
is better in the end at bearing wounds
in a deadly fray. This fight is not yours,
nor is it up to any man except me
to measure his strength against the monster
or to prove his worth. I shall win the gold
by my courage, or else mortal combat,
doom of battle, will bear your lord away."

Then he drew himself up beside his shield.
The fabled warrior in his warshirt and helmet
trusted in his own strength entirely
and went under the crag. No coward path.
Hard by the rock-face that hale veteran,
a good man who had gone repeatedly
into combat and danger and come through,
saw a stone arch and a gushing stream
that burst from the barrow, blazing and wafting
a deadly heat. It would be hard to survive
unscathed near the hoard, to hold firm
against the dragon in those flaming depths.

Then he gave a shout. The lord of the Geats
unburdened his breast and broke out
in a storm of anger. Under grey stone
his voice challenged and resounded clearly.
Hate was ignited. The hoard-guard recognized
a human voice, the time was over
for peace and parleying. Pouring forth
in a hot battle-fume, the breath of the monster
burst from the rock. There was a rumble under ground.
Down there in the barrow, Beowulf the warrior
lifted his shield: the outlandish thing

---

[1]The poet presents the Geats as a tribe situated in the southeastern part of Sweden.

writhed and convulsed and vehemently
turned on the king, whose keen-edged sword,
an heirloom inherited by ancient right,
was already in his hand. Roused to a fury,
each antagonist struck terror in the other.
Unyielding, the lord of his people loomed
by his tall shield, sure of his ground,
while the serpent looped and unleashed itself.
Swaddled in flames, it came gliding and flexing
and racing towards its fate. Yet his shield defended
the renowned leader's life and limb
for a shorter time than he meant it to:
that final day was the first time
when Beowulf fought and fate denied him
glory in battle. So the king of the Geats
raised his hand and struck hard
at the enamelled scales, but scarcely cut through:
the blade flashed and slashed yet the blow
was far less powerful than the hard-pressed king
had need of at that moment. The mound-keeper
went into a spasm and spouted deadly flames:
when he felt the stroke, battle-fire
billowed and spewed. Beowulf was foiled
of a glorious victory. The glittering sword,
infallible before that day,
failed when he unsheathed it, as it never should have.
For the son of Ecgtheow, it was no easy thing
to have to give ground like that and go
unwillingly to inhabit another home
in a place beyond; so every man must yield
the leasehold of his days.

                It was not long
until the fierce contenders clashed again.
The hoard-guard took heart, inhaled and swelled up
and got a new wind; he who had once ruled
was furled in fire and had to face the worst.
No help or backing was to be had then
from his high-born comrades; that hand-picked troop
broke ranks and ran for their lives
to the safety of the wood. But within one heart
sorrow welled up: in a man of worth
the claims of kinship cannot be denied. . . .

When the dragon attacks a second time, Beowulf
stabs it in the neck and breaks his magical sword. It
is Beowulf, however, who is mortally wounded in the
third attack when the dragon bites him in the neck.
Finally, Beowulf's loyal retainer Wiglaf, his only defender, attempts to avenge his lord's mortal wound
by driving his sword into the dragon's stomach, but
it is Beowulf who wields the fatal blow.

           "As God is my witness,
I would rather my body were robed in the same

burning blaze as my gold-giver's body
than go back home bearing arms.
That is unthinkable, unless we have first
slain the foe and defended the life
of the prince of the Weather-Geats. I well know
the things he has done for us deserve better.
Should he alone be left exposed
to fall in battle? We must bond together,
shield and helmet, mail-shirt and sword."
Then he waded the dangerous reek and went
under arms to his lord, saying only:
"Go on, dear Beowulf, do everything
you said you would when you were still young
and vowed you would never let your name and fame
be dimmed while you lived. Your deeds are famous,
so stay resolute, my lord, defend your life now
with the whole of your strength. I shall stand by you."

After those words, a wildness rose
in the dragon again and drove it to attack,
heaving up fire, hunting for enemies,
the humans it loathed. Flames lapped the shield,
charred it to the boss, and the body armour
on the young warrior was useless to him.
But Wiglaf did well under the wide rim
Beowulf shared with him once his own had shattered
in sparks and ashes.

                Inspired again
by the thought of glory, the war-king threw
his whole strength behind a sword-stroke
and connected with the skull. And Naegling snapped.
Beowulf's ancient iron-grey sword
let him down in the fight. It was never his fortune
to be helped in combat by the cutting edge
of weapons made of iron. When he wielded a sword,
no matter how blooded and hard-edged the blade
his hand was too strong, the stroke he dealt
(I have heard) would ruin it. He could reap no advantage.

Then the bane of that people, the fire-breathing dragon,
was mad to attack for a third time.
When a chance came, he caught the hero
in a rush of flame and clamped sharp fangs
into his neck. Beowulf's body
ran wet with his life-blood: it came welling out.

Next thing, they say, the noble son of Weohstan
saw the king in danger at his side
and displayed his inborn bravery and strength.

He left the head alone, but his fighting hand
was burned when he came to his kinsman's aid.
He lunged at the enemy lower down
so that his decorated sword sank into its belly
and the flames grew weaker.

Once again the king
gathered his strength and drew a stabbing knife
he carried on his belt, sharpened for battle.
He stuck it deep into the dragon's flank.
Beowulf dealt it a deadly wound.
They had killed the enemy, courage quelled his life;
that pair of kinsmen, partners in nobility,
had destroyed the foe. So every man should act,
be at hand when needed; but now, for the king,
this would be the last of his many labours
and triumphs in the world.

Then the wound
dealt by the ground-burner earlier began
to scald and swell; Beowulf discovered
deadly poison suppurating inside him,
surges of nausea, and so, in his wisdom,
the prince realized his state and struggled
towards a seat on the rampart. He steadied his gaze
on those gigantic stones, saw how the earthwork
was braced with arches built over columns.
And now that thane unequalled for goodness
with his own hands washed his lord's wounds,
swabbed the weary prince with water,
bathed him clean, unbuckled his helmet.
Beowulf spoke: in spite of his wounds,
mortal wounds, he still spoke
for he well knew his days in the world

had been lived out to the end: his allotted time
was drawing to a close, death was very near.

"Now is the time when I would have wanted
to bestow this armour on my own son,
had it been my fortune to have fathered an heir
and live on in his flesh. For fifty years
I ruled this nation. No king
of any neighbouring clan would dare
face me with troops, none had the power
to intimidate me. I took what came,
cared for and stood by things in my keeping,
never fomented quarrels, never
swore to a lie. All this consoles me,
doomed as I am and sickening for death;
because of my right ways, the Ruler of mankind
need never blame me when the breath leaves my body
for murder of kinsmen. Go now quickly,
dearest Wiglaf, under the grey stone
where the dragon is laid out, lost to his treasure;
hurry to feast your eyes on the hoard.
Away you go: I want to examine
that ancient gold, gaze my fill
on those garnered jewels; my going will be easier
for having seen the treasure, a less troubled letting-go
of the life and lordship I have long maintained."

8 An Early Medieval Drama

During the Middle Ages, a few nuns distinguished themselves as writers, including Hroswitha (c. 935–c. 1001) of Gandersheim, in Saxony, Germany. She was the first Saxon poet, the first known Christian dramatist, and the first female historian in Germany. Writing in Latin, she composed eight narrative poems drawn from legends; two epic historical works, one of which celebrated the foundation of her own convent; and six plays. In all of her dramas, Hroswitha skillfully casts the Virgin Mary as the ideal for all subsequent heroines, so that her heroines acquire their boldness from their adherence to their vow of chastity. She thus further augments the elevation of Mary as the replacement for Eve. Whereas Eve's happiness issued from marriage, Hroswitha's heroines obtain their joy from maidenhood. Therefore, Hroswitha's heroines defy the stereotypical image of women, drawn primarily from Paul and Augustine, that women are purveyors of sin. With her emphasis on the moral ideal of chastity, she is a precursor of the morality plays that came into existence more than one and a half centuries after her death.

Hroswitha
Abraham

The following scenes come from Hroswitha's fourth drama, *Abraham.* They concern conversion to Christianity of the harlot Mary, niece of the holy hermit Abraham, who adopts her as his daughter after the death of her parents. The drama represents the struggle between the pleasures of the flesh and of the joys of the spirit, a higher calling. In the following passage from Scene II, Abraham seeks the assistance of Brother Ephrem to help him to educate Mary into the ways of becoming a nun.

ABRAHAM Mary, my child by adoption, whom I love as my own soul! Listen to my advice as to a father's, and to Brother Ephrem's as that of a very wise man. Strive to imitate the chastity of the holy Virgin whose name you bear.

EPHREM Child, would it not be a shame if you, who through the mystery of your name are called to mount to the stars where Mary the mother of God reigns, chose instead the low pleasures of the earth?

MARY I know nothing about the mystery of my name, so how can I tell what you mean?

EPHREM Mary, my child, means "star of the sea"—that star which rules the world and all the peoples in the world.

MARY Why is it called the star of the sea?

EPHREM Because it never sets, but shines always in the heavens to show mariners their right course.

MARY And how can such a poor thing as I am—made out of slime, as my uncle says—shine like my name?

EPHREM By keeping your body unspotted, and your mind pure and holy.

MARY It would be too great an honour for any human being to become like the stars.

EPHREM If you choose you can be as the angels of God, and when at last you cast off the burden of this mortal body they will be near you. With them you will pass through the air, and walk on the sky. With them you will sweep round the zodiac, and never slacken your steps until the Virgin's Son takes you in His arms in His mother's dazzling bridal room!

MARY Who but an ass would think little of such happiness! So I choose to despise the things of earth, and deny myself now that I may enjoy it!

EPHREM Out of the mouths of babes and sucklings! A childish heart, but a mature mind!

ABRAHAM God be thanked for it!

EPHREM Amen to that.

ABRAHAM But though by God's grace she has been given the light, at her tender age she must be taught how to use it.

EPHREM You are right.

ABRAHAM I will build her a little cell with a narrow entrance near my hermitage. I can visit her there often, and through the window instruct her in the psalter and other pages of the divine law.

EPHREM That is a good plan.

MARY I put myself under your direction, Father Ephrem.

EPHREM My daughter! May the Heavenly Bridegroom to Whom you have given yourself in the tender bud of your youth shield you from the wiles of the devil!

In this passage from Scene VI, Abraham finds a melancholic Mary, after she has run away and become a prostitute in an "inn" that is actually a brothel. She has returned to "the vanities of the world," after having lost her virginity in a "false love"—a man who pretended to be a monk. Abraham plays the part of a paying customer seeking to contract with Mary for her sexual services. To highlight the scene, Hroswitha portrays Abraham as a foolish old man—a typical Roman comedic technique.

SCENE VI

INN-KEEPER Mary, come here! Come along now and show off your charms to this young innocent!

MARY I am coming.

ABRAHAM Oh, mind, be constant! Tears, do not fall! Must I look on her whom I brought up in the desert, decked out with a harlot's face? Yes, I must hide what is in my heart. I must strive not to weep, and smile though my heart is breaking.

INN-KEEPER Luck comes your way, Mary! Not only do young gallants of your own age flock to your arms, but even the wise and venerable!

MARY It is all one to me. It is my business to love those who love me.

ABRAHAM Come nearer, Mary, and give me a kiss.

MARY I will give you more than a kiss. I will take your head in my arms and stroke your neck.

ABRAHAM Yes, like that!

MARY What does this mean? What is this lovely fragrance. So clean, so sweet. It reminds me of the time when I was good.

ABRAHAM On with the mask! Chatter, make lewd jests like an idle boy! She must not recognize me, or for very shame she may fly from me.

MARY Wretch that I am! To what have I fallen! In what pit am I sunk!

ABRAHAM You forget where you are! Do men come here to see you cry!

INN-KEEPER What's the matter, Lady Mary? Why are you in the dumps? You have lived here two years, and never before have I seen a tear, never heard a sigh or a word of complaint.

MARY Oh, that I had died three years ago before I came to this!

ABRAHAM I came here to make love to you, not to weep with you over your sins.

MARY A little thing moved me, and I spoke foolishly. It is nothing. Come, let us eat and drink and be merry, for, as you say, this is not the place to think of one's sins.

ABRAHAM I have eaten and drunk enough, thanks to your good table, Sir. Now by your leave I will go to bed. My tired limbs need a rest.

INN-KEEPER As you please.

MARY Get up my lord. I will take you to bed.

ABRAHAM I hope so. I would not go at all unless you came with me.

In Scene VII, at the brothel, Abraham reveals his true person. Mary subsequently repents of her evil ways, but she doubts that God can forgive her sins, that is, until Abraham convinces her otherwise.

SCENE VII

MARY Look! How do you like this room? A handsome bed, isn't it? Those trappings cost a lot of money. Sit down and I will take off your shoes. You seem tired.

ABRAHAM First bolt the door. Someone may come in.

MARY Have no fear. I have seen to that.

ABRAHAM The time has come for me to show my shaven head, and make myself known! Oh, my daughter! Oh, Mary, you who are part of my soul! Look at me. Do you not know me? Do you not know the old man who cherished you with a father's love, and wedded you to the Son of the King of Heaven?

MARY God, what shall I do! It is my father and master Abraham!

ABRAHAM What has come to you, daughter?

MARY Oh, misery!

ABRAHAM Who deceived you? Who led you astray?

MARY Who deceived our first parents?

ABRAHAM Have you forgotten that once you lived like an angel on earth!

MARY All that is over.

ABRAHAM What has become of your virginal modesty? Your beautiful purity?

MARY Lost. Gone!

ABRAHAM Oh, Mary, think what you have thrown away! Think what a reward you had earned by your fasting, and prayers, and vigils. What can they avail you now! You have hurled yourself from heavenly heights into the depths of hell!

MARY Oh God, I know it!

ABRAHAM Could you not trust me? Why did you desert me? Why did you not tell me of your fall? Then dear brother Ephrem and I could have done a worthy penance.

MARY Once I had committed that sin, and was defiled, how could I dare come near you who are so holy?

ABRAHAM Oh, Mary, has anyone ever lived on earth without sin except the Virgin's Son?

MARY No one, I know.

ABRAHAM It is human to sin, but it is devilish to remain in sin. Who can be justly condemned? Not those who fall suddenly, but those who refuse to rise quickly.

MARY Wretched, miserable creature that I am!

ABRAHAM Why have you thrown yourself down there? Why do you lie on the ground without moving or speaking? Get up, Mary! Get up, my child, and listen to me!

MARY No! no! I am afraid. I cannot bear your reproaches.

ABRAHAM Remember how I love you, and you will not be afraid.

MARY It is useless. I cannot.

ABRAHAM What but love for you could have made me leave the desert and relax the strict observance of our rule? What but love could have made me, a true hermit, come into the city and mix with the lascivious crowd? It is for your sake that these lips have learned to utter light, foolish words, so that I might not be known! Oh, Mary, why do you turn away your face from me and gaze upon the ground? Why do you scorn to answer and tell me what is in your mind.

MARY It is the thought of my sins which crushes me. I dare not look at you; I am not fit to speak to you.

ABRAHAM My little one, have no fear. Oh, do not despair! Rise from this abyss of desperation and grapple God to your soul!

MARY No, no! My sins are too great. They weigh me down.

ABRAHAM The mercy of heaven is greater than you or your sins. Let your sadness be dispersed by its glorious beams. Oh, Mary, do not let apathy prevent your seizing the moment for repentance. It matters not how wickedness has flourished. Divine grace can flourish still more abundantly!

MARY If there were the smallest hope of forgiveness, surely I should not shrink from doing penance.

ABRAHAM Have you no pity for me? I have sought you out with so much pain and weariness! Oh shake off this despair which we are taught is the most terrible of all sins. Despair of God's mercy—for that alone there is no forgiveness. Sin can no more embitter His sweet mercy than a spark from a flint can set the ocean on fire.

MARY I know that God's mercy is great, but when I think how greatly I have sinned, I cannot believe any penance can make amends.

ABRAHAM I will take your sins on me. Only come back and take up your life again as if you had never left it.

MARY I do not want to oppose you. What you tell me to do I will do with all my heart.

ABRAHAM My daughter lives again! I have found my lost lamb and she is dearer to me than ever.

MARY I have a few possessions here—a little gold and some clothes. What ought I to do with them?

ABRAHAM What came to you through sin, with sin must be left behind.

MARY Could it not be given to the poor, or sold for an offering at the holy altar?

ABRAHAM The price of sin is not an acceptable offering to God.

MARY Then I will not trouble any more about my possessions.

ABRAHAM Look! The dawn! It is growing light. Let us go.

MARY You go first, dearest father, like the good shepherd leading the lost lamb that has been found. The lamb will follow in your steps.

ABRAHAM Not so! I am going on foot, but you—you shall have a horse so that the stony road shall not hurt your delicate feet.

MARY Oh, let me never forget this tenderness! Let me try all my life to thank you! I was not worth pity, yet you have shown me no harshness; you have led me to repent not by threats but by gentleness and love.

ABRAHAM I ask only one thing, Mary. Be faithful to God for the rest of your life.

MARY With all my strength I will persevere, and though my flesh may fail, my spirit never will.

ABRAHAM You must serve God with as much energy as you have served the world.

MARY If His will is made perfect in me it will be because of your merits.

ABRAHAM Come, let us hasten on our way.

MARY Yes, let us set out at once. I would not stay here another moment.

The High Middle Ages: The Flowering of Medieval Civilization

The High Middle Ages (1050–1300) were an era of growth and vitality in Latin Christendom. Improvements in technology and cultivation of new lands led to an increase in agricultural production; the growing food supply, in turn, reduced the number of deaths from starvation and malnutrition, and better cultivation methods freed more people to engage in nonagricultural pursuits, particularly commerce.

During the Early Middle Ages, Italian towns had maintained a weak link with the Byzantine lands in the eastern Mediterranean. In the eleventh century, the Italians gained ascendancy over Muslim fleets in the Mediterranean and rapidly expanded their trade with the Byzantine Empire and North Africa. The growing population provided a market for silk, sugar, spices, dyes, and other Eastern goods. Other mercantile avenues opened up between Scandinavia and the Atlantic coast; between northern France, Flanders, and England; and along the rivers between the Baltic Sea in the north and the Black Sea and Constantinople in the southeast.

The revival of trade and the improved production of food led to the rebirth of towns in the eleventh century. During the Early Middle Ages, urban life had largely disappeared in Latin Christendom except in Italy, and even Italian towns had declined since Roman times both in population and as centers of trade and culture. During the twelfth century, towns throughout Latin Christendom became active centers of commerce and intellectual life. The rebirth of town life made possible the rise of a new social class: the middle class, consisting of merchants and artisans. These townspeople differed significantly from the clergy, the nobles, and the serfs—the other social strata in medieval society. The world of the townspeople was the marketplace rather than the church, the castle, or the manorial village. These merchants and artisans resisted efforts by lords to impose obligations upon them, as their livelihood required freedom from such constraints. The middle class became a dynamic force for change.

The High Middle Ages were also characterized by political and religious vitality. Strong kings extended their authority over more and more territory, often at the expense of feudal lords; in the process, they laid the foundation of the modern European state system. By the eleventh century the autonomy of the church—its freedom to select its own leaders and to fulfill its moral responsibilities—was threatened by kings and lords who appointed bishops and abbots to ecclesiastical offices. In effect, the churches and monasteries were at the mercy of temporal rulers, who distributed church positions as patronage, awarding them to their families, vassals, and loyal servants. These political appointees often lacked the spiritual character to maintain high standards of discipline among the priests or monks they supervised. Many clergy resented the subordination of the church to the economic and political interests of kings and lords. They held that for the church to fulfill its spiritual mission, it must be free from lay control. As head of the church, charged with the mission of saving souls, popes refused to accept a subordinate position to temporal rulers.

Economic, political, and religious vitality was complemented by a cultural and intellectual awakening. The twelfth and thirteenth centuries marked the high point of medieval civilization. The Christian outlook, with its otherworldly emphasis, shaped and inspired this awakening. Christian scholars rediscovered the writings of ancient Greek thinkers, which they tried to harmonize with Christian teachings. In the process, they constructed an impressive philosophical system that integrated Greek rationalism into the Christian world-view. The study of Roman law was revived, and some of its elements were incorporated into church law. A varied literature expressed both secular and religious themes, and a distinctive form of architecture, the Gothic, conveyed the overriding Christian concern with things spiritual.

1 The Medieval Church

Christianity was the integrating principle and the church the dominant institution of the Middle Ages. The church tried with great determination to make society follow divine standards, that is, it tried to shape all institutions and cultural expressions according to a comprehensive Christian outlook. As head of the church, the pope claimed authority over bishops and temporal rulers, lords and kings, who wanted to dominate churches in their territories.

Pope Gregory VII
Rules of the Pope

Like no other pope before him, Gregory VII (1073–1085) asserted the primacy of the papacy over temporal rulers. Drawn up during his pontificate, the *Dictatus Papae* (Rules of the Pope), excerpted below, represented claims and ambitions that inspired many popes and theologians throughout the Middle Ages.

1. That the Roman church was established by God alone.

2. That the Roman pontiff [bishop] alone is rightly called universal.

3. That he alone has the power to depose and reinstate bishops.

4. That his legate [emissary], even if he be of lower ecclesiastical rank, presides over bishops in council, and has the power to give sentence of deposition against them.

5. That the pope has the power to depose those who are absent (*i.e.,* without giving them a hearing).

6. That, among other things, we ought not to remain in the same house with those whom he has excommunicated.

7. That he alone has the right, according to the necessity of the occasion, to make new laws, to create new bishoprics, to make a monastery of a chapter of canons,[1] and *vice versa,*

and either to divide a rich bishopric or to unite several poor ones.

8. That he alone may use the imperial insignia.

9. That all princes shall kiss the foot of the pope alone.

10. That his name alone is to be recited in the churches.

11. That the name applied to him belongs to him alone.

12. That he has the power to depose emperors.

13. That he has the right to transfer bishops from one see to another when it becomes necessary.

14. That he has the right to ordain as a cleric anyone from any part of the church whatsoever.

15. That anyone ordained by him may rule (as bishop) over another church, but cannot serve (as priest) in it, and that such a cleric may not receive a higher rank from any other bishop.

16. That no general synod may be called without his order.

---

[1] A chapter of canons is a corporate ecclesiastical body composed of priests who administer cathedrals or monastic communities.

17. That no action of a synod and no book shall be regarded as canonical [official] without his authority.

18. That his decree can be annulled by no one, and that he can annul the decrees of anyone.

19. That he can be judged by no one.

20. That no one shall dare to condemn a person who has appealed to the apostolic seat.

21. That the important cases of any church whatsoever shall be referred to the Roman church (that is, to the pope).

22. That the Roman church has never erred and will never err to all eternity, according to the testimony of the holy scriptures.

23. That the Roman pontiff who has been canonically ordained is made holy by the merits of St. Peter, according to the testimony of St. Ennodius, bishop of Pavia, which is confirmed by many of the holy fathers, as is shown by the decrees of the blessed pope Symmachus [498–513].

24. That by his command or permission subjects may accuse their rulers.

25. That he can depose and reinstate bishops without the calling of a synod.

26. That no one can be regarded as catholic who does not agree with the Roman church.

27. That he has the power to absolve subjects from their oath of fidelity to wicked rulers.

Emperor Frederick II
HERETICS: ENEMIES OF GOD AND HUMANITY

Like many groups held together by common ideology, the medieval church wanted to protect its doctrines from novel, dissident, or erroneous interpretations. To ensure orthodoxy and competency, therefore, all preachers were licensed by the bishop; unlicensed preaching, especially by unschooled laymen, was forbidden. In the western church, heresy had not been a serious problem in the post-Roman period. But in the twelfth century, two heretical movements attracted significant numbers of supporters among both the clergy and laity and cut across frontiers and social classes. The first group was the Waldensians, or Poor Men of Lyons, founded about 1173 by Peter Waldo (d. 1217), a rich merchant of Lyons, France, who gave away his wealth to the poor and began to preach in villages in southeastern France. Neither a priest nor a theologian, Waldo had the Bible translated from Latin into the common language of the people and preached the gospel message without the consent of church authorities.

The second major heretical movement was that of the Cathari, more commonly called the Albigensians. The Albigensian heresy apparently entered western Europe from the Balkans, where similar religious ideas could be traced back to non-Christian sects of the early Roman Empire. The Albigensians were not Christians in any orthodox sense: they rejected the Old Testament and claimed the God of Israel to be the Evil One, who created the material world in which souls were trapped, separating them from the Good God. Although the Albigensians accepted the New Testament with their own emendations, they rejected the Christian doctrine of Jesus as both God and Man; they believed that Jesus was a disembodied spirit, and that all flesh was evil, marriage was evil, and the begetting of children was evil. Rejecting the medieval church, they constituted an alternative religion in the midst of Christian southern France and Italy.

The new religious movements threatened to undermine the existing religious, social, and political order. Pope Gregory IX in 1231 decided to create special courts of inquisition to seek out the dissenters, or heretics. Those who repented could be sent to prison for life; those who remained unrepentant were excommunicated from the church and turned over to the secular authorities, who executed them. The property of the guilty was confiscated and divided equally among the local bishop, the inquisitors, and the local civil ruler. The ordinary procedural standards of European penal law were abandoned in the courts of inquisition. The inquiry was secret, witnesses were not identified to the accused, guilt was presumed, legal counsel was denied, and torture was applied to verify statements given under oath.

The papal inquisitors were not permitted to function everywhere. The rulers of the northern and eastern European kingdoms forbade them entry, as did England, Portugal, and Castile. In the next reading, from the first section of the Constitutions of Melfi, promulgated for the kingdom of Sicily by the Emperor Frederick II (1220–1250) in 1231, the typical attitude of medieval Christians toward heretics (or those who gave them aid or comfort) and the savage penalties imposed are graphically depicted. Ironically, in 1245, Frederick II himself was accused of heresy and deposed by Pope Innocent IV (1243–1254), leading to a war between the emperor and the papacy.

Heretics try to tear the seamless robe of our God. As slaves to the vice of a word that means division [sect], they strive to introduce division into the unity of the indivisible faith and to separate the flock from the care of Peter [the Pope], the shepherd to whom the Good Shepherd [Christ] entrusted it. Inside they are violent wolves, but they pretend the tameness of sheep until they can get inside the sheepfold of the Lord. They are the most evil angels. They are sons of depravity from the father of wickedness and the author of evil, who are resolved to deceive simple souls. They are snakes who deceive doves. They are serpents who seem to creep in secretly and, under the sweetness of honey, spew out poison. While they pretend to administer the food of life, they strike from their tails. They mix up a potion of death as a certain very deadly poison.

. . . Indeed, these miserable Patarines [Patarenes, one group of heretics], who do not possess the holy faith of the Eternal Trinity,[1] offend at the same time three persons under one cover of wickedness: God, their neighbors, and themselves. They offend God because they do not know the faith of God, and they do not know his son. They deceive their neighbors insofar as they administer the delights of heretical wickedness to them under the guise of spiritual nourishment. They rage against themselves even more cruelly insofar as, besides risking their souls, these sectaries, lavish of life and improvident with death, also expose their bodies to the enticements of cruel death which they could avoid by true knowledge and the steadfastness of true faith. What is even worse, the survivors are not frightened by the example. We cannot contain our emotions against such men so hostile to God, to themselves, and to mankind. Therefore, we draw the sword of righteous vengeance against them, and we pursue them more urgently insofar as they are known to practice the crimes of their superstition within the Roman Church herself, which is considered the head of all the other churches, to the more evident injury of the Christian faith. . . . Because we consider this so repulsive, we have decided in the first place that the crime of heresy and these condemned sects should be numbered among the public crimes as it was promulgated in the ancient laws. . . . In order to expose the wickedness of those who, because they do not follow God, walk in darkness, even if no one reports it, we desire that the perpetrators of these crimes should be investigated diligently and should be sought after by our officials like other criminals. We order that those who become known by an inquisition [trial], even if they are touched by the evidence of a slight suspicion, should be examined by ecclesiastics and prelates. If they should be found by them to deviate from the Catholic faith in the least wise, and if, after they have been admonished by them in a pastoral way, they should be unwilling to relinquish the insidious darkness of the Devil and to recognize the God of Light, but they persist in the constancy of conceived error, we order by the promulgation of our present law that these Patarines should be condemned to suffer the death for which they strive. Committed to the judgment of the flames, they should be burned alive in the sight of the people. We do not grieve that in this we satisfy their desire, from which they obtain punishment alone and no other fruit of their error. No one should presume to intervene with us in behalf of such persons. But if anyone does, we shall turn against him the deserved stings of our indignation. . . .

. . . We order that the shelterers, believers, accomplices of Patarines, and those who support them in any way at all, who give no heed to fear for themselves so that they can protect others from punishment, should be sent into perpetual exile and all their goods confiscated.

---

[1]The central Christian doctrine that teaches that there are three divine persons in one God: Father, Son, and Holy Spirit, who are coequal, coeternal, and consubstantial.

2 Medieval Contributions to the Tradition of Liberty

In several ways the Middle Ages contributed to the development of liberty in the Western world. Townsmen organized themselves into revolutionary associations called communes to demand freedom from the domination of feudal lords. They successfully won personal liberties, the end of feudal labor services and arbitrary tax levies, and a system of municipal self-government. Another development crucial to the tradition of liberty was the resistance of lords to kings who attempted to interfere with the lords' customary rights. These actions helped to establish the tradition that kings were not above the law and could not rule arbitrarily or absolutely. There is a direct link between modern parliaments and medieval representative institutions, particularly in the case of the English Parliament.

Medieval theologians made a significant contribution to the growth of liberty. They held that a monarch's powers were limited by God's laws and by what was for the common good of Christian people. Some argued that a monarch who ignored or violated the laws and liberties of the people or the church became a tyrant and forfeited his right to be ruler. Such rulers could be, and some in fact were, deposed.

John of Salisbury
Policraticus
A Defense of Tyrannicide

One prelate who opposed the rule of tyrants was an Englishman, John of Salisbury (c.1115–1180), who became bishop of Chartres, France, in 1176. He composed a statesman's handbook, *Policraticus,* explicitly defending the assassination of tyrants. Paraphrasing the Roman statesman Cicero, John held that it was right, lawful, and just to slay a tyrant.

. . . A tyrant, then, as the philosophers have described him, is one who oppresses the people by the rulership based upon force, while he who rules in accordance with the laws is a prince. Law is the gift of God, the model of equity, a standard of justice, a likeness of the divine will, the guardian of well-being, a bond of union and solidarity between peoples, a rule defining duties, a barrier against the vices and the destroyer thereof, a punishment of violence and all wrong-doing. The law is assailed by force or by fraud, and, as it were, either wrecked by the fury of the lion or undermined by the wiles of the serpent. In whatever way this comes to pass, it is plain that it is the grace of God which is being assailed and that it is God himself who in a sense is challenged to battle. The prince fights for the laws and the liberty of the people; the tyrant thinks nothing done unless he brings the laws to nought and reduces the people to slavery. Hence the prince is a kind of likeness of divinity; and the tyrant, on the contrary, a likeness of the boldness of the Adversary [the devil], even of the wickedness of Lucifer. . . . The prince, as the likeness of the Deity, is to be loved, worshipped and cherished; the tyrant, the likeness of wickedness, is generally to be even killed. The origin of tyranny is iniquity, and springing from a poisonous root, it is a tree which grows and sprouts into a baleful pestilent growth, and to which the axe must by all means be laid.

3 Synthesis of Reason and Christian Faith: Proofs of God's Existence

Medieval learning commenced during the eleventh century in monastic and cathedral schools. The twelfth century witnessed a revived interest in classical learning and the founding of universities. During this time, a new system of critical analysis, called scholasticism, was applied to traditional theology. Scholastic thinkers assumed that some teaching of Christianity, which they accepted as true by faith, could also be demonstrated to be true by reason. They sought to explain and clarify theological doctrines by subjecting them to logical analysis. One belief that they thought could be proven using reason was the existence of God.

Anselm of Canterbury
Proslogion

For most of the Middle Ages, religious thought was dominated by the influence of Augustine (d. 430), the greatest of the Latin church fathers (see page 133). Augustine placed little value on the study of nature; for him, the City of Man (the world) was a sinful place from which people tried to escape in order to enter the City of God (heaven). Regarding God as the source of knowing, he held that reason by itself was an inadequate guide to knowledge: without faith in revealed truth, there could be no understanding.

Anselm of Canterbury (1033–1109), who is often called "the father of scholasticism," was an Augustinian who held that faith was the key to understanding. Born in Burgundy, he was consecrated Archbishop of Canterbury in England in 1093. Prior to that, when Anselm was the abbot of the monastery in Bec, in Normandy, he wrote *Proslogion,* his ontological proof of God's existence. "Ontological" means that his proof is a meditation on the rational basis of faith, based only on mental concepts, not on any experience or evidence from nature. The following passage contains his basic three-part argument: God is the greatest conceivable being; existence in reality is greater than existence in thought; therefore, God must exist in reality, not merely in thought.

CHAPTER II
THAT GOD TRULY EXISTS

Well then, Lord, You who give understanding to faith, grant me that I may understand, as much as You see fit, that You exist as we believe You to exist, and that You are what we believe You to be. Now we believe that You are something than which nothing greater can be thought. Or can it be that a thing of such a nature does not exist, since 'the Fool has said in his heart, there is no God' [Ps. xiii. 1, lii. 1]? But surely, when this same Fool hears what I am speaking about, namely, 'something-than-which-nothing-greater-can-be-thought', he understands what he hears, and what he understands is in his mind, even if he does not understand that it actually exists. For it is one thing for an object to exist in the mind, and another thing to understand that an object actually exists. Thus, when a painter plans beforehand what he is going to execute, he has [the picture] in his mind, but he does not yet think that it actually exists because he has not yet executed it. However, when he has actually painted it, then he both has it in his mind and understands that it exists because he has now made it. Even the Fool, then, is forced to agree that something-than-which-nothing-greater-can-be-thought exists in the mind, since he understands this when he hears it, and whatever is understood is in the mind. And surely that-than-which-a-greater-cannot-be-thought cannot exist in the mind alone. For if it exists solely in the mind even, it can be thought to exist in reality also, which is greater.

If then that-than-which-a-greater-cannot be-thought exists in the mind alone, this same that-than-which-a-greater-*cannot*-be-thought is that-than-which-a-greater-*can*-be-thought. But this is obviously impossible. Therefore there is absolutely no doubt that something-than-which-a-greater-cannot-be-thought exists both in the mind and in reality.

CHAPTER III
THAT GOD CANNOT BE THOUGHT NOT TO EXIST

And certainly this being so truly exists that it cannot be even thought not to exist. For something can be thought to exist that cannot be thought not to exist, and this is greater than that which can be thought not to exist. Hence, if that-than-which-a-greater-cannot-be-thought can be thought not to exist, then that-than-which-a-greater-cannot-be-thought is not the same as that-than-which-a-greater-cannot-be-thought, which is absurd. Something-than-which-a-greater-cannot-be-thought exists so truly then, that it cannot be even thought not to exist.

And You, Lord our God, are this being. You exist so truly, Lord my God, that You cannot even be thought not to exist. And this is as it should be, for if some intelligence could think of something better than You, the creature would be above its creator and would judge its creator—and that is completely absurd. In fact, everything else there is, except You alone, can be thought of as not existing. You alone, then, of all things most truly exist and therefore of all things possess existence to the highest degree; for anything else does not exist as truly, and so possesses existence to a lesser degree. Why then did 'the Fool say in his heart, there is no God.' [Ps. xiii. 1, lii. 1] when it is so evident to any rational mind that You of all things exist to the highest degree? Why indeed, unless because he was stupid and a fool?

Thomas Aquinas
Summa Theologica

An alternative approach to that of Augustine and Anselm was provided by Thomas Aquinas (1225–1274), a friar of the Order of Preachers (Dominicans), who taught theology in Paris and later in Italy. Along with Augustine and Anselm, Aquinas believed that God was the source of all truth, that human nature was corrupted by the imprint of the original sin of Adam and Eve, and that God revealed himself through the Bible and in the person of Jesus Christ. But, in contrast to Augustine and Anselm, Aquinas expressed great confidence in the power of reason to investigate the natural world.

Aquinas held that as both faith and reason came from God, they were not in opposition to each other; properly understood, they supported each other. Because reason was no enemy of faith, it should not be feared. In addition to showing renewed respect for reason, Aquinas—influenced by Aristotelian empiricism (the acquisition of knowledge of nature through experience)—valued knowledge of the natural world. He saw the natural and supernatural worlds not as irreconcilable and hostile to each other, but as a continuous ascending hierarchy of divinely created orders of being moving progressively toward the Supreme Being. In constructing a synthesis of Christianity and Aristotelianism, Aquinas gave renewed importance to the natural world, human reason, and the creative human spirit. Nevertheless, by holding that reason was subordinate to faith, he remained a typically medieval thinker.

In his most ambitious work, the *Summa Theologica,* Aquinas specifically rejects Anselm's ontological argument. Nonetheless, Aquinas argues that God's existence, even though it is a matter of faith, can be proven by natural reason, drawing on experience and evidence from nature. In the following selection, Aquinas argues for God's existence, building his argument on the categories of Aristotelian philosophy.

WHETHER GOD EXISTS?

The existence of God can be proved in five ways.

The first and more manifest way is the argument from motion. It is certain, and evident to our senses, that in the world some things are in motion. Now whatever is moved is moved by another, for nothing can be moved except it is in potentiality to that towards which it is moved; whereas a thing moves inasmuch as it is in act. For motion is nothing else than the reduction of something from potentiality to actuality. But nothing can be reduced from potentiality to actuality, except by something in a state of actuality. Thus that which is actually hot, as fire, makes wood, which is potentially hot, to be actually hot, and thereby moves and changes it. Now it is not possible that the same thing should be at once in actuality and potentiality in the same respect, but only in different respects. For what is actually hot cannot simultaneously be potentially hot; but it is simultaneously potentially cold. It is therefore impossible that in the same respect and in the same way a thing should be both mover and moved, *i.e.,* that it should move itself. Therefore, whatever is moved must be moved by another. If that by which it is moved be itself moved, then this also must needs be moved by another, and that by another again. But this cannot go on to infinity, because then there would be no first mover, and, consequently, no other mover, seeing that subsequent movers move only inasmuch as they are moved by the first mover; as the staff moves only because it is moved by the hand. Therefore it is necessary to arrive at a first mover, moved by no other; and this everyone understands to be God.

The second way is from the nature of efficient cause. In the world of sensible things we find there is an order of efficient causes. There is no case known (neither is it, indeed, possible) in which a thing is found to be the efficient cause of itself; for so it would be prior to itself, which is impossible. Now in efficient causes it is not possible to go on to infinity, because in all efficient causes following in order, the first is the cause of the intermediate cause, and the intermediate is the cause of the ultimate cause, whether the intermediate cause be several, or one only. Now to take away the cause is to take away the effect. Therefore, if there be no first cause among efficient causes, there will be no ultimate, nor any intermediate, cause. But if in efficient causes it is possible to go on to infinity, there will be no first efficient cause, neither will there be an ultimate effect, nor any intermediate efficient causes; all of which is plainly false. Therefore it is necessary to admit a first efficient cause, to which everyone gives the name of God.

The third way is taken from possibility and necessity, and runs thus. We find in nature things that are possible to be and not to be, since they are found to be generated, and to be corrupted, and consequently, it is possible for them to be and not to be. But it is impossible for these always to exist, for that which can not-be at some time is not. Therefore, if everything can not-be, then at one time there was nothing in existence. Now if this were true, even now there would be nothing in existence, because that which does not exist begins to exist only through something already existing. Therefore, if at one time nothing was in existence, it would have been impossible for anything to have begun to exist; and thus even now nothing would be in existence—which is absurd. Therefore, not all beings are merely possible, but there must exist something the existence of which is necessary. But every necessary thing either has its necessity caused by another, or not. Now it is impossible to go on to infinity in necessary things which have their necessity caused by another, as has been already proved in regard to efficient causes. Therefore we cannot but admit the existence of some being having of itself its own necessity, and not receiving it from another, but rather causing in others their necessity. This all men speak of as God.

The fourth way is taken from the graduation to be found in things. Among beings there are some more and some less good, true, noble, and the like. But *more* and *less* are predicated of different things according as they resemble in their different ways something which is the maximum, as a thing is said to be hotter according as it more nearly resembles that which is hottest; so that there is something which is truest, something best, something noblest, and, consequently, something which is most being, for those things that are greatest in truth are greatest in being. . . . Now the maximum in any genus is the cause of all in that genus, as fire, which is the maximum of heat, is the cause of all hot things. . . . Therefore there must also be something which is to all beings the cause of their being, goodness, and every other perfection; and this we call God.

The fifth way is taken from the governance of the world. We see that things which lack knowledge, such as natural bodies, act for an end, and this is evident from their acting always, or nearly always, in the same way, so as to obtain the best result. Hence it is plain that they achieve their end, not fortuitously, but designedly. Now whatever lacks knowledge cannot move towards an end, unless it be directed by some being endowed with knowledge and intelligence; as the arrow is directed by the archer. Therefore some intelligent being exists by whom all natural things are directed to their end; and this being we call God.

4 A Visionary Author and Composer

As an abbess, diplomat, writer, mystic, and composer, Hildegard of Bingen (1098–1179) was one of the most significant women during the Middle Ages. Hildegard communicated with kings, bishops, popes, and abbots, and she wrote treatises on medicine and natural history. She received a rudimentary religious education from Jutta von Sponheim (d. 1136), the abbess at the convent of Disibodenberg. After Jutta's death, Hildegard served as the abbess for twelve years, before her visions commanded her to found a new abbey at Rupertsberg, near Bingen, in 1150. Fifteen years later, she bought an unoccupied monastery in Eibingen, on the banks of the Rhine River and restored it.

Hildegard of Bingen
Symphony of the Harmony of Celestial Revelations
Mary, the Antithesis of Eve

As a composer, Hildegard created numerous innovative approaches to plainchant (a single line of melody), which is evident in her cycle of seventy lyrical poems entitled, *Symphony of the Harmony of Celestial Revelations* (Symphonia harmoniae caelestium revelationum). Hildegard believed that music was the vehicle for recovering the initial delight and splendor of the Garden of Eden. Furthermore, she asserted that before the Fall, Adam had a beautiful voice and joined with the angels in revering God. Following the Fall, music and musical instruments were devised as a means of doing a good work and the supreme way of praising God. The Latin texts of these lyrics deal with the heavenly hierarchy, including the Virgin Mary, whom Hildegard viewed as the antithesis of Eve.

8. RESPONSORY[1] FOR THE VIRGIN MARY!

Death heard your steps and fled,
troubled. The house of life
lay in ruins. But you—
you built it new.
Stiff-necked Eve,
swollen with her own
importance,
courted the serpent. But you
crushed him completely
when you conceived the Son of heaven
whom the Spirit of God inspired.
Tender one, hail!
Hail mother of love!
You bore for the world
a child sent from heaven
whom the Spirit of God inspired.

Glorify the Father,
the Spirit and the Son
whom the Spirit of God inspired.

---

[1]A responsory is an anthem sung after a liturgical reading from the Scriptures.

14. ANTIPHON[2] FOR THE VIRGIN

Banished Eve and Adam blushing
   watched as their children fell,
     helplessly rushing
       toward hell.

     Mary!
    you plead for all:
  lift up your voice and carry
our souls above on the wings of your call.

---

17. HYMN TO THE VIRGIN

In the pupil of chastity's eye
I beheld you
untouched.
Generous maid! Know that it's God
who broods over you.

For heaven flooded you like
unbodied speech
and you gave it a tongue.

Glistening
lily: before all worlds
you lured the supernal one.

How he reveled
in your charms! how your beauty
warmed to his caresses
till you gave your breast to his child.

And your womb held joy when heaven's
harmonies rang from you,
a maiden with child by God,
for in God your chastity blazed.

Yes your flesh held joy like the grass
when the dew falls, when heaven
freshens its green: O mother
of gladness, verdure of spring.

Ecclesia,[3] flush with rapture! Sing
for Mary's sake, sing
for the maiden, sing
for God's mother. Sing!

---

20. SEQUENCE[4] FOR THE VIRGIN

A royal scepter and a crown
of purple, a fortress
strong as mail! O fortress
of maidenhood, scepter
all verdant:

The way you bloomed would have startled
the grandsire of us all,
for the life father Adam
stripped from his sons (praise
to you!) slid from your loins.

You never sprang from the dew,
my blossom, nor from the rain—
that was no wind that swept
over you—for God's
radiance opened you
on a regal bough. On the morn

of the universe he saw you
blossoming, and he made you
a golden matrix, O maid
beyond praise, for his word.
Strong rib of Adam! Out of you
God sculpted woman: the mirror
of all his charms, the caress
of his whole creation. So voices

chime in heaven and the whole
earth marvels at Mary,
beloved beyond measure.

Cry, cry aloud! A serpent
hissed and a sea of grief
seeped through his forked
words into woman. The mother

of us all miscarried.
With ignorant hands she
plucked at her womb and bore
woe without bounds.

But the sunrise from your thighs
burnt the whole of her guilt away.
More than all that Eve lost
is the blessing you won.

Mary, savior,
mother of light:
may the limbs of your son be the chords of the song
the angels chant above.

---

[2]The term antiphon comes from the Greek word *antiphonia,* which means "counter sound." In medieval music, it referred to free melodies sung in the same mode that alternated between a chorus of men and a chorus of women.

[3]Ecclesia refers to a church or a congregation.

---

[4]A sequence is a hymn sung after the Gradual in the Mass and before the Gospel reading.

5 A Forbidden Love

As a young teacher of theology at the Cathedral School of Notre Dame, Peter Abelard (1079–1142) acquired a reputation for brilliance and combativeness. He tutored Héloise who lived with her uncle and guardian, Fulbert, a canon at Notre Dame. Héloise later had his child and entered a nunnery, and Abelard, on orders from Fulbert, was castrated and sought temporary refuge in a monastery. Héloise ultimately put their past behind her and learned to love Abelard as a brother in Christ, and when he died in 1142, Héloise sought a written absolution of their sins from the church, which she hung over Abelard's tomb. When she died twenty-two years later, Héloise was buried at his side. This affair, detailed in the letters the two exchanged, has become one of the great tragic romances in Western literature.

Abelard and Héloise
Letters

In the following selection from a letter Abelard wrote to an unnamed friend, he details his "calamities," including his fascination with Héloise's mind, his lust for her, and his unbounded confidence that he could lure her into his bed.

CHAPTER VI
HOW HAVING FALLEN IN LOVE WITH HELOISE HE WAS THEREBY WOUNDED AS WELL IN BODY AS IN MIND

Now there was in this city of Paris a certain young maiden by the name of *Heloise,* the niece of a certain Canon who was called *Fulbert,* who, so great was his love for her, was all the more diligent in his zeal to instruct her, so far as was in his power, in the knowledge of letters. Who, while in face she was not inferior to other women, in the abundance of her learning was supreme. For inasmuch as this advantage, namely literary knowledge, is rare in women, so much the more did it commend the girl and had won her the greatest renown throughout the realm. Seeing in her, therefore, all those things which are wont to attract lovers, I thought it suitable to join her with myself in love, and believed that I could effect this most easily. For such renown had I then, and so excelled in grace of youth and form, that I feared no refusal from whatever woman I might deem worthy of my love. All the more easily did I believe that this girl would consent to me in that I knew her both to possess and to delight in the knowledge of letters; even in absence it would be possible for us to reach one another's presence by written intermediaries, and to express many things more boldly in writing than in speech, and so ever to indulge in pleasing discussions.

So, being wholly inflamed with love for this girl, I sought an opportunity whereby I might make her familiar with me in intimate and daily conversation, and so the more easily lead her to consent. With which object in view, I came to terms with the aforesaid uncle of the girl, certain of his friends intervening, that he should take me into his house, which was hard by our school, at whatever price he might ask. Putting forward this pretext, that the management of our household gravely hindered my studies, and that the expense of it was too great a burden on me. Now he was avaricious, and most solicitous with regard to his niece that she should ever progress in the study of letters. For which two reasons I easily secured his consent and obtained what I desired, he being all agape for my money, and believing that his niece would gain something from my teaching. Whereupon earnestly beseeching me, he acceded to my wishes farther than I might presume to hope and served the purpose of my love: committing her wholly to my mastership, that as often as I returned from my school, whether by day or by night, I might devote my leisure to her instruction, and, if I found her idle, vehemently chastise her. In which matter, while marvelling greatly at his simplicity, I was no less stupefied within myself than if he had entrusted a tender lamb to a ravening wolf. For in giving her to me, not only to be taught but to be vehemently chastised, what else was he doing than giving every licence to my desires and providing an opportunity whereby, even if I did not wish, if I could not move her by blandishments I might the more easily bend her by threats and blows. But there were two things which kept him most of all from base suspicions, namely his love for his niece and the fame of my continence in the past.

What more need I say? First in one house we are united, then in one mind. So, under the pretext of discipline, we abandoned ourselves utterly to love, and those secret retreats which love demands, the study of our texts afforded us. And so, our books lying open before us, more words of love rose to our lips than of literature, kisses were more frequent than speech. Oftener went our hands to each other's bosom than to the pages; love turned our eyes more frequently to itself than it directed them to the study of the texts. That we might be the less suspected, blows were given at times, by love, not by anger, affection, not indignation, which surpassed all ointments in their sweetness. What more shall I say? No stage of love was emitted by us in our cupidity, and, if love could elaborate anything new, that we took in addition. The less experienced we were in these joys, the more ardently we persisted in them and the less satiety did they bring us. And the more this pleasure occupied me the less leisure could I find for my philosophy and to attend to my school. Most tedious was it for me to go to the school or to stay there; laborious likewise when I was keeping nightly vigils of love and daily of study. Which also so negligently and tepidly I now performed that I produced nothing from my mind but everything from memory; nor was I anything now save a reciter of things learned in the past, and if I found time to compose a few verses, they were amorous, and not secret hymns of philosophy. Of which songs the greater part are to this day, as thou knowest, repeated and sung in many parts, principally by those to whom a like manner of life appeals.

What was the sorrow, what the complaints, what the lamentations of my scholars when they became aware of this preoccupation, nay perturbation of my mind, it is not easy even to imagine. For few could fail to perceive a thing so manifest, and none, I believe, did fail save he to whose shame it principally reflected, namely the girl's uncle himself. Who indeed, when divers persons had at divers times suggested this to him, had been unable to believe it, both, as I have said above, on account of his unbounded affection for his niece and on account also of the well known continence of my previous life. For not readily do we suspect baseness in those whom we most love. Nor into vehement love can the base taint of suspicion find a way. Whence cometh the saying of Saint *Jerome* in his Epistle to *Sabinian* (the eight-and-fortieth): "We are always the last to learn of the evils of our own house, and remain ignorant of the vices of our children and wives when they are a song among the neighbours. But what one is the last to know one does at any rate come to know in time, and what all have learned it is not easy to keep hidden from one." And thus, several months having elapsed, it befell us also. Oh, what was the uncle's grief at this discovery!

What was the grief of the lovers themselves at their parting! What blushing and confusion for me! With what contrition for the girl's affliction was I afflicted! What floods of sorrow had she to bear at my shame! Neither complained of what had befallen himself, but each the other's misfortune. But this separation of our bodies was the greatest possible coupling of our minds, the denial of its satisfaction inflamed our love still further, the shame we had undergone made us more shameless, and the less we felt our shame the more expedient our action appeared. And so there occurred in us what the poets relate of Mars and Venus when they were taken. Not long after this, the girl found that she had conceived, and with the greatest exultation wrote to me on the matter at once, consulting me as to what I should decide to do; and so on a certain night, her uncle being absent, as we had planned together I took her by stealth from her uncle's house and carried her to my own country without delay. Where, in my sister's house, she stayed until such time as she was delivered of a man child whom she named *Astrolabe*.

Her uncle, however, after her flight, being almost driven mad, with what grief he boiled, with what shame he was overwhelmed no one who had not beheld him could imagine. How he should act towards me, what snares he should lay for me he knew not. If he were to kill me, or to injure my body in any way, he feared greatly lest his beloved niece might be made to pay the penalty in my country. To seize my person and coerce me anywhere against my will was of no avail, seeing that I was constantly on my guard in this respect, because I had no doubt that he would speedily assault me if it were worth his while or if he dared. At length I, in some compassion for his exceeding anxiety and vehemently accusing myself of the fraud which my love had committed, as though of the basest treachery, went to supplicate the man, promising him also such further amends as he himself should prescribe. Nor, I asserted, did it appear remarkable to any who had experienced the force of love and retained a memory of the ruin to which even the greatest men, from the very beginning of the human race, had been brought down by women. And, that I might conciliate him beyond all that he could hope, I offered him the satisfaction of joining her whom I had corrupted to myself in marriage, provided that this were done in secret lest I incurred any detriment to my reputation. He assented, and with his own word and kiss, as well as with those of his household, sealed the concord that I had required of him, the more easily to betray me.

In Héloise's response to Abelard's letter, she continues to express her love for Abelard, and chastises him for not writing to her as he did before she entered the nunnery.

And the greater the cause of grief, the greater the remedies of comfort to be applied. Not, however, by another, but by thee thyself, that thou who art alone in the cause of my grief may be alone in the grace of my comfort. For it is thou alone that canst make me sad, canst make me joyful or canst comfort me. And it is thou alone that owest me this great debt, and for this reason above all that I have at once performed all things that you didst order, till that when I could not offend thee in anything I had the strength to lose myself at thy behest. And what is more, and strange it is to relate, to such madness did my love turn that what alone it sought it cast from itself without hope of recovery when, straightway obeying thy command, I changed both my habit and my heart, that I might show thee to be the one possessor both of my body and of my mind. Nothing have I ever (God wot) required of thee save thyself, desiring thee purely, not what was thine. Not for the pledge of matrimony, nor for any dowry did I look, nor my own passions or wishes but thine (as thou thyself knowest) was I zealous to gratify.

And if the name of wife appears more sacred and more valid, sweeter to me is ever the word friend, or, if thou be not ashamed, concubine or whore. To wit that the more I humbled myself before thee the fuller grace I might obtain from thee, and so also damage less the fame of thine excellence. And thou thyself wert not wholly unmindful of that kindness in the letter of which I have spoken, written to thy friend for his comfort. Wherein thou hast not disdained to set forth sundry reasons by which I tried to dissuade thee from our marriage, from an ill-starred bed; but were silent as to many, in which I preferred love to wedlock, freedom to a bond. . . .

Give thy attention, I beseech thee, to what I demand; and thou wilt see this to be a small matter and most easy for thee. While I am cheated of thy presence, at least by written words, whereof thou hast an abundance, present to me the sweetness of thine image. In vain may I expect thee to be liberal in things if I must endure thee niggardly in words. Until now I believed that I deserved more from thee when I had done all things for thee, persevering still in obedience to thee. Who indeed as a girl was allured to the asperity of monastic conversation not by religious devotion but by thy command alone. Wherein if I deserve nought from thee, thou mayest judge my labour to have been vain. No reward for this may I expect from God, for the love of Whom it is well known that I did not anything. When thou hastenedst to God, I followed thee in the habit, nay preceded thee. For as though mindful of the wife of *Lot,* who looked back from behind him, thou deliveredst me first to the sacred garments and monastic profession before thou gavest thyself to God. And for that in this one thing thou shouldst have had little

trust in me I vehemently grieved and was ashamed. For I (God wot) would without hesitation precede or follow thee to the Vulcanian fires according to thy word. For not with me was my heart, but with thee. But now, more than ever, if it be not with thee, it is nowhere. For without thee it cannot anywhere exist. But so act that it may be well with thee, I beseech thee. And well with thee will it be if it find thee propitious, if thou give love for love, little for much, words for deeds. Would that thy love, beloved, had less trust in me, that it might be more anxious! But the more confident I have made thee in the past, the more neglectful now I find thee. Remember, I beseech thee, what I have done, and pay heed to what thou owest me. While with thee I enjoyed carnal pleasures, many were uncertain whether I did so from love or from desire. But now the end shews in what spirit I began. I have forbidden myself all pleasures that I might obey thy will. I have reserved nothing for myself, save this, to be now entirely thine. Consider therefore how great is thine injustice, if to me who deserve more thou payest less, nay nothing at all, especially when it is a small thing that is demanded of thee, and right easy for thee to perform.

And so in His Name to whom thou hast offered thyself, before God I beseech thee that in whatsoever way thou canst thou restore to me thy presence, to wit by writing me some word of comfort. To this end alone that, thus refreshed, I may give myself with more alacrity to the service of God. When in time past thou soughtest me out for temporal pleasures, thou visitedst me with endless letters, and by frequent songs didst set thy *Heloise* on the lips of all men. With me every public place, each house resounded. How more rightly shouldst thou excite me now towards God, whom thou excitedst then to desire. Consider, I beseech thee, what thou owest me, pay heed to what I demand; and my long letter with a brief ending I conclude. Farewell, my all. . . .

[T]hou knowest thyself to be bound to me by a debt so much greater in that thou art tied to me more closely by the pact of the nuptial sacrament; and that thou art the more beholden to me in that I ever, as is known to all, embraced thee with an unbounded love. Thou knowest, dearest, all men know what I have lost in thee, and in how wretched a case that supreme and notorious betrayal took me myself also from me with thee, and that my grief is immeasurably greater from the manner in which I lost thee than from the loss of thee.

6 Medieval Universities

The twelfth century witnessed a revival of classical learning and cultural creativity. Gothic cathedrals, an enduring testament to the creativeness of the religious spirit, were erected throughout Europe. Roman authors were again read and their style imitated. Latin translations of Greek philosophical and scientific texts stimulated scholars; the reintroduction of the study of Roman law began to influence political theory and institutions. These were some of the major changes that would leave a permanent mark on subsequent Western culture.

A significant achievement of this age was the emergence of universities. Arising spontaneously among teachers of the liberal arts and students of the higher studies of law, theology, and medicine, the universities gave more formal and lasting institutional structure to the more-advanced levels of schooling. The medieval universities were largely dedicated to educating young men for careers as lawyers, judges, teachers, diplomats, and administrators of both church and state. The educational foundation for such professional careers was the study of the liberal arts.

John of Salisbury
ON THE LIBERAL ARTS

The standard curriculum of medieval schools was based on intensive study of the seven liberal arts divided into two programs: the *trivium,* consisting of Latin grammar, rhetoric, and dialectic (or logic), and the *quadrivium,* consisting of arithmetic, geometry, astronomy, and music. The brilliant, twelfth-century scholar and churchman John of Salisbury (see page 161) wrote the *Metalogicon,* a defense of the liberal arts curriculum, which was under attack from conservative theologians.

WHY SOME ARTS ARE CALLED "LIBERAL"

While there are many sorts of arts, the first to proffer their services to the natural abilities of those who philosophize are the liberal arts. All of the latter are included in the courses of the Trivium and Quadrivium. The liberal arts are said to have become so efficacious among our ancestors, who studied them diligently, that they enabled them to comprehend everything they read, elevated their understanding to all things, and empowered them to cut through the knots of all problems possible of solution. Those to whom the system of the Trivium has disclosed the significance of all words, or the rules of the Quadrivium have unveiled the secrets of all nature, do not need the help of a teacher in order to understand the meaning of books and to find the solutions of questions. They (the branches of learning included in the Trivium and

Quadrivium) are called "arts" because they . . . strengthen minds to apprehend the ways of wisdom. . . . They are called "liberal," either because the ancients took care to have their children instructed in them; or because their object is to effect man's liberation, so that, freed from cares, he may devote himself to wisdom. More often than not, they liberate us from cares incompatible with wisdom. They often even free us from worry about (material) necessities, so that the mind may have still greater liberty to apply itself to philosophy.

Among all the liberal arts, the first is logic, and specifically that part of logic which gives initial instruction about words. . . . [T]he word "logic" has a broad meaning, and is not restricted exclusively to the science of argumentative reasoning. (It includes) Grammar (which) is "the science of speaking and writing correctly—the starting point of all liberal studies." Grammar is the cradle of all philosophy, and in a manner of speaking, the first nurse of the whole study of letters. It takes all of us as tender babes, newly born from nature's bosom. It nurses us in our infancy, and guides our every forward step in philosophy. With motherly care, it fosters and protects the philosopher from the start to the finish (of his pursuits). It is called "grammar" from the basic elements of writing and speaking. *Grama* means a letter or line. . . .

STUDENT LETTERS

The relationship between fathers and their sons enrolled at universities has not changed all that much since the Middle Ages, as the letters that follow demonstrate.

FATHERS TO SONS

I

I have recently discovered that you live dissolutely and slothfully, preferring license to restraint and play to work and strumming a guitar while the others are at their studies, whence it happens that you have read but one volume of law while your more industrious companions have read several. Wherefore I have decided to exhort you herewith to repent utterly of your dissolute and careless ways, that you may no longer be called a waster and your shame may be turned to good repute.

II

I have learned—not from your master, although he ought not to hide such things from me, but from a certain trustworthy source—that you do not study in your room or act in the schools as a good student should, but play and wander about, disobedient to your master and indulging in sport and in certain other dishonorable practices which I do not now care to explain by letter.

SONS TO FATHERS

I

"Well-beloved father, I have not a penny, nor can I get any save through you, for all things at the University are so dear: nor can I study in my Code or my Digest, for they are all tattered. Moreover, I owe ten crowns in dues to the Provost, and can find no man to lend them to me; I send you word of greetings and of money.

The Student hath need of many things if he will profit here; his father and his kin must needs supply him freely, that he be not compelled to pawn his books, but have ready money in his purse, with gowns and furs and decent clothing, or he will be damned for a beggar; wherefore, that men may not take me for a beast, I send you word of greetings and of money.

Wines are dear, and hostels, and other good things; I owe in every street, and am hard bested to free myself from such snares. Dear father, deign to help me! I fear to be excommunicated; already have I been cited, and there is not even a dry bone in my larder. If I find not the money before this feast of Easter, the church door will be shut in my face: wherefore grant my supplication, for I send you word of greetings and of money.

L'ENVOY

Well-beloved father, to ease my debts contracted at the tavern, at the baker's, with the doctor and the bedells [a minor college official], and to pay my subscriptions to the laundress and the barber, I send you word of greetings and of money."

II

Sing unto the Lord a new song, praise him with stringed instruments and organs, rejoice upon the high-sounding cymbals, for your son has held a glorious disputation, which was attended by a great number of teachers and scholars. He answered all questions without a mistake, and no one could get the better of him or prevail against his arguments. Moreover he celebrated a famous banquet, at which both rich and poor were honoured as never before, and he has duly begun to give lectures which are already so popular that others' classrooms are deserted and his own are filled.

A Wandering Scholar
"IN THE TAVERN LET ME DIE"

During the Middle Ages, errant students and idle clerks roamed the highways as free spirits, searching for adventure or at least for diversion. Some had given up their studies for lack of funds; others were restless or unable to secure the position they desired. These vagabonds sometimes amused themselves by composing poetry that ridiculed clerics and sang the praises of wine, gambling, and women. The following poem was written in Latin by a poet known as the "Archpoeta," who lived in the twelfth century.

Down the highway broad I walk,
Like a youth in mind,
Implicate myself in vice,
Virtue stays behind,
Avid for the world's delight
More than for salvation,
Dead in soul, I care but for
Body's exultation.

Prelate, you most circumspect,
Grace I would entreat,
It's a good death that I die,
Such a death is sweet,
O, my heart is wounded sore
When a lass comes near it,
If there's one I cannot touch,
Her I rape in spirit.

't is most difficult indeed
Overcoming Nature,
Keeping pure our mind and thought
Near a girlish creature.
Young like me, one can't observe
Rules that are unfeeling,
Can't ignore such shapes and curves
Tempting and appealing.

Who when into fire is pushed
Is by fire not scorched?
Whoso in Pavia[1] stayed
Has not been debauched,
Where Dame Venus with a sign
Gives young men a shake-up,
Snares them with her luring eyes,
With her tempting makeup?

Secondly I've been accused
That I yield to gambling,
Yet when gambling strips me bare,

Then I can't go rambling,
For outside I quake with cold
While my heart glows white,
In this state far better song,
Finer verse I write.

Thirdly to the tavern I
Must refer in turn,
This I've spurned not in the past
Nor will ever spurn,
Till the holy angels come
With a chant supernal,
Singing masses for the dead—
Requiem eternal.

In the tavern let me die,
That's my resolution,
Bring me wine for lips so dry
At life's dissolution.
Joyfully the angel's choir
Then will sing my glory:
"Sit deus propicius
Huic potatori."*

Through the cup new light bursts up
In my spirit's flare,
Nectar stimulates my heart
Etherward to fare.
Wine that in the tavern flows
Has a richer flavor
Than the watered stuff our lord's
Steward likes to savor.

Special gifts on every man
Mother Nature lavished;
I can never write a verse
When by hunger ravished,
If I'm famished, one small boy
Bests me in a trice,

---

[1]Pavia, a city in northern Italy, drew many students in the Middle Ages.

*May God be well-disposed to this toper [drunkard].

Thirst and hunger I detest
Like my own demise.

Special gifts for every man
Nature will produce,
I, when I compose my verse,
Vintage wine must use,
All the best the cellar's casks
Hold of these libations.
Such a wine calls forth from me
Copious conversations.

My verse has the quality
Of the wine I sip,
I can not do much until
Food has passed my lip,
What I write when starved and parched
Is of lowest class,
When I'm tight, with verse I make
Ovid I surpass.[2]

As a poet ne'er can I
Be appreciated
Till my stomach has been well
Filled with food and sated,
When god Bacchus[3] gains my brain's
Lofty citadel,
Phoebus[4] rushes in to voice
Many a miracle.

See, my own depravity
I have now confessed,
Disapproval of my sins
Have my friends expressed.
Not a single one of these
His own sins confesses,
Though he also likes the dice,
Likes the world's excesses.

---

[2]Roman poet (43 B.C.–A.D. 17), author of the *Metamorphoses,* who was considered a master of metrical form.

[3]Bacchus is an alternative name for Dionysus, the Greek god of wine and ecstasy.

[4]Phoebus is another name for the Greek god Apollo, who represented male beauty and moral excellence.

7 Jewish Learning

Toward the end of the eleventh century, small communities of Jews were living in many of the larger towns of Christian Europe. Most of these Jews were descended from Jewish inhabitants of the Roman Empire. Under the protection of the Roman law or of individual Germanic kings, they had managed to survive amid a sometimes hostile Christian population. But religious fanaticism unleashed by the call for the First Crusade gravely undermined Christian-Jewish relations. Bands of Crusaders began systematically to attack and massacre the Jewish inhabitants of Rhineland towns. Thousands were killed—many because they refused to become converts to Christianity; their houses were looted and burned. Efforts by the bishops and civil authorities to protect their Jewish subjects were largely ineffective. Anti-Semitism became endemic in Latin Christendom: outbreaks of violence toward the Jews persisted and bizarre myths about them emerged. Jews were seen as agents of Satan conspiring to destroy Christendom and as sorcerers employing black magic against Christians. Perhaps the most absurd (and dangerous) charge against the Jewish people was the accusation of ritual murder—that the Jews, requiring Christian blood for the Passover service, sacrificed a Christian child. Despite the vehement denials of Jews and the protests of some enlightened Christian leaders, hundreds of such libelous accusations were made, resulting in the torture, trials, murder, and expulsion of many Jews. Allegations of ritual murder and accompanying trials persisted into the twentieth century, to the consternation and anger of enlightened people who regarded the charge as so much nonsense, a lingering medieval fabrication and superstition.

Maimonides
On Education and Charity

Medieval Jews, despite frequent persecution, carried on a rich cultural and intellectual life based on their ancestral religion. The foremost Jewish scholar of the Middle Ages was Moses ben Maimon, also called by the Greek name Maimonides (1135–1204), who was born in Córdoba, Spain, then under Muslim rule. After his family emigrated from Spain, Maimonides went to Egypt, where he became physician to the sultan. During his lifetime, Maimonides achieved fame as a philosopher, theologian, mathematician, and physician; he was recognized as the leading Jewish sage of his day, and his writings were respected by Christian and Muslim thinkers as well. Like Christian scholastics and Muslim philosophers, Maimonides tried to harmonize faith with reason, to reconcile the Hebrew Scriptures and the Talmud (Jewish biblical commentary) with Greek philosophy. In his writings on ethical themes, Maimonides demonstrated piety, wisdom, and humanity. In the following passages, he discusses education and charity.

EDUCATION

Every man in Israel [every Jew] is obliged to study the Torah,[1] whether he be poor or rich, whether he be physically healthy or ailing, whether he be in full vigor of youth or of great age and weakened vitality; even if he be dependent upon alms for his livelihood, or going around from door to door begging his daily bread, yea, even he who has a wife and children to support is obliged to have an appointed time for the study of the Torah, both during the day and at night, for it is said: "But thou shalt meditate therein day and night." (Joshua, i.8)

Some of the great scholars in Israel were hewers of wood, some of them drawers of water, and some of them blind: nevertheless they engaged themselves in the study of the Torah by day and by night. Moreover, they are included among those who translated the tradition as it was transmitted from mouth of man to mouth of man, even from the mouth of Moses our Master [the biblical Moses].

Until what age in life is one obliged to study the Torah? Even until the day of one's demise; for it is said: "And lest they depart from thy heart all the days of thy life" (Deut. 4.9). Forsooth, as long as one will not occupy himself with study he forgets what he did study.

One is obligated to divide his time of study by three; one third for the study of Holy Writ, one third for the study of the Oral Torah [the interpretations of the Torah], and one third for thinking and reflecting so that he may understand the end of a thing from its beginning, and deduct one matter from another, and compare one matter to another. . . .

When a master gave a lesson which the disciples did not understand, he should not get angry at them and be moody, but go over it again and repeat it even many times, until they will understand the depth of the treatise. Likewise, a disciple shall not say, I understood, and he did not understand; but he should repeat and ask even many times. If the master angers at him and becomes moody, he may say to him: "Master, it is Torah, and I need instruction, but my mind is short of understanding!"

A disciple shall not feel ashamed before his fellows who mastered the subject the first or the second time, whereas he did not grasp it until after hearing it many times, for if he will be ashamed of such a thing, he will find himself coming in and going out of the . . . [school] without any instructions at all. The sages, therefore, said: "he who is bashful cannot be instructed and he who is in an angry mood cannot instruct." . . .

Even as a man is under command to honor his father and fear him, so is he obliged to honor his master, but fear him yet more than his father; his father brought him to life upon this world but his master who taught him wisdom, brings him to life in the world to come. . . .

Care for the poor is ingrained in the Jewish tradition. Rabbis gave the highest value to assistance, given in secret, that helps a poor person to become self-supporting. Maimonides drew upon this rabbinical tradition in his discussion of charity.

CHARITY

The law of the Torah commanded us to practise *tsedakah*,[2] support the needy and help them financially. The command in connection with this duty occurs in various expressions; e.g., "Thou shalt surely open thy hand unto him" (Deut. xv. 8), "Thou shalt uphold him; as a stranger and a settler shall he

---

[1] The Torah refers to the first five books of the Hebrew Scriptures, which the Jews believed were written by Moses. In time, *Torah* also acquired a broader meaning that encompassed the entire Hebrew Scriptures and the various commentaries.

[2] The term *tsedakah* is derived from *tsédek* (righteousness); it denotes showing kindness to others.

live with thee" (Lev. xxv. 35). The intention in these passages is identical, viz., that we should console the poor man and support him to the extent of sufficiency. . . .

There are eight degrees in alms-giving, one higher than the other: Supreme above all is to give assistance to a co-religionist who has fallen on evil times by presenting him with a gift or loan, or entering into a partnership with him, or procuring him work, thereby helping him to become self-supporting.

Inferior to this is giving charity to the poor in such a way that the giver and recipient are unknown to each other. This is, indeed, the performance of a commandment from disinterested motives; and it is exemplified by the Institution of the Chamber of the Silent which existed in the Temple,[3] where the righteous secretly deposited their alms and the respectable poor were secretly assisted.*

---

[3]The Temple to which Maimonides refers was the Temple in Jerusalem, destroyed by the Romans in A.D. 70.

*This system of charity was adopted by Jews in several Palestinian and Babylonian cities.

Next in order is the donation of money to the charitable fund of the Community, to which no contribution should be made without the donors feeling confident that the administration is honest, prudent and capable of proper management.

Below this degree is the instance where the donor is aware to whom he is giving the alms but the recipient is unaware from whom he received them; as, e.g., the great Sages who used to go about secretly throwing money through the doors of the poor. This is quite a proper course to adopt and a great virtue where the administrators of a charitable fund are not acting fairly.

Inferior to this degree is the case where the recipient knows the identity of the donor, but not *vice versa;* as, e.g., the great Sages who used to tie sums of money in linen bundles and throw them behind their backs for poor men to pick up, so that they should not feel shame.

The next four degrees in their order are: the man who gives money to the poor before he is asked; the man who gives money to the poor after he is asked; the man who gives less than he should, but does it with good grace; and lastly, he who gives grudgingly.

8 Troubadour Love Songs

In the late twelfth century, new kinds of poetry with a distinctive set of themes began to be created at the castles and courts in France, Italy, Spain, and Germany. The poets were themselves knights or noblewomen who composed their poems to be sung or read aloud for the entertainment of fellow feudal nobles. The subject was always that of the love between man and woman.

The original inspiration for the new troubadour poetry was probably the Arab poetry of Spain and Sicily, where the theme of courtly love was developed earlier. What was revolutionary in later European poetry was its treatment of the relationship between men and women. The troubadours reversed the traditional view of men as superior and women as inferior and dependent in their relationships. They introduced what is called "courtly love," a love relationship in which the woman is the superior and dominant figure, the man inferior and dependent. The male courts the lady, paying homage to her beauty and virtue. He suffers humiliation and frustration at her will and expresses the erotic tensions that consume him.

LOVE AS JOYOUS, PAINFUL, AND HUMOROUS

The following poems were all composed by southern French troubadours. In the first selection a poet sings the praises of his beloved.

I wandered through a garden, 'twas
    filled with flowers the rarest,
And of all these brilliant blossoms
    I culled the very fairest;
So fine its shape, so sweet its scent, its
    hues so richly blent,
That heaven, I'm sure, created it itself
    to represent.
My lady is so charming, my lady is so
    meek,
Such tenderness is in her smile, such
    beauty in her cheek;
Such kisses blossom on her lip, such
    love illumines her eye—
Oh, never was there neath the stars a
    man so blest as I!
I gaze, I thrill with joy, I weep, in song
    my feelings flow—
A song of hope, delight, desire, with
    passion all aglow—
A fervent song, a pleading song, a song
    in every line—
Of thanks and praise to her who lists no
    other songs but mine.
Oh, hear me sweet! Oh, kiss me sweet!
    Oh, clasp me tenderly!
Thy beauties many, many touch, but
    none that love like me.

The following two poems tell of a lover's failure to win the affections of his beloved.

Now that the air is fresher
and the world turned green,
I shall sing once more
of the one I love and desire,
but we are so far apart
that I cannot go and witness
how my words might please her.

And nothing can console me
but death, for evil tongues
(may God curse them)
have made us part.
And alas, I so desired her
that now I moan and cry
half mad with grief.

I sing of her, yet her beauty
is greater than I can tell,
with her fresh color, lovely eyes,
and white skin, untanned
and untainted by rouge.
She is so pure and noble
that no one can speak ill of her.

But above all, one must praise,
it seems to me, her truthfulness,
her manners and her gracious speech,
for she never would betray a friend;
and I was mad to believe
what I heard tell of her
and thus cause her to be angry.

I never intended to complain;
and even now, if she so desires,
she could bring me happiness
by granting what I seek.
I cannot go on like this much longer,
for since she's been so far away
I've scarcely slept or eaten.

Love is sweet to look upon
but bitter upon parting;
one day it makes you weep
and another skip and dance,
for now I know that the more
one enters love's service,
the more fickle it becomes.

Messenger, go with Godspeed
and bring this to my lady,
for I cannot stay here much longer
and live, or be cured elsewhere,
unless I have her next to me,
naked, to kiss and embrace
within a curtained room.

I said my heart was like to break,
    And that my soul was cast,
By passion's tide, just like a wreck
    Disabled by the blast.

I swore an oath that what I felt
    Was like to turn my head;
I sighed—such sighs!—and then I knelt,
But not a word she said!

I preached of Grace in moving strain;
    I told her she was fair;
I whispered what renown she'd gain,
    By listening to my prayer.

I spoke of needle and of pole,
    And other things I'd read;
But unto all my rigmarole—
    Why not a word she said!

I prayed her then my love to test,
    To send me near or far—
I'd squelch the dragon in his den,
    I'd yoke him to my car.

I'd risk for her, as faithful knight,
    My eyes, or limbs, or head,
Being quite prepared to fool or fight—
    But not a word she said!

I argued that, if poor in cash,
    Yet I was rich in mind;
Of rivals vowed to make a hash,
    When such I chanced to find.

I knit my brows, I clenched my hand,
    I tried to wake her dread;
In quiet wise, you'll understand—
    But not a word she said!

Troubadours could also be playful. Sometimes they mocked women who labored too hard to preserve a youthful beauty.

That creature so splendid is but an old jade;
Of ointment and padding her beauty is made;
Unpainted if you had the hap to behold her,
You'd find her all wrinkles from forehead to shoulder.

What a shame for a woman who has lost all her grace
To waste thus her time in bedaubing her face!
To neglect her poor soul I am sure is not right of her,
For a body that's going to corruption in spite of her.

Sometimes they even mocked this obsession with romance.

You say the moon is all aglow,
    The nightingale a-singing—
I'd rather watch the red wine flow,
    And hear the goblets ringing.

You say 'tis sweet to hear the gale
    Creep sighing through the willows—
I'd rather hear a merry tale,
    'Mid a group of jolly fellows!

You say 'tis sweet the stars to view
    Upon the waters gleaming—
I'd rather see, 'twixt me and you
    And the post, my supper steaming.

9 Marie de France: A Female Troubadour Poet

Although little is known about her life, Marie de France is the first woman known to have written narrative poetry in the West. She was a prominent woman troubadour poet of the twelfth century, who composed literary works, particularly her *lais* (songs), which vicariously enabled women to fulfill both their emotional and intellectual needs. Her extant works—twelve *Lais,* 102 *Fables,* and *Saint Patrick's Purgatory*—were written in French some time between 1160 and 1214. Both the morals of her fables and the themes of her *lais* demonstrate that she wrote for prominent and intellectually capable people. Concerned with a human being's emotional needs, Marie writes about the internal dynamics of family life and relationships between lovers, husbands and wives, and lords and vassals. Common themes in her literature suggest that marriage restrains people and makes them sad, that the chivalric ideal necessitates sacrifice of self in behalf of one's lord, and that people inevitably suffer because of their own covetousness and conceit. However, the main message of Marie's poetry is that people have the power in their innermost selves to be emotionally free of life's cruelty and oppression.

Marie de France
Yonec
A Poem of Love, Treachery, and Vengeance

In her lai, *Yonec* (so-named for the love-child of a beautiful young woman and a noble knight), Marie describes an unnamed "girl" from a "good family" who marries an aged, jealous husband (also unnamed) who keeps her locked inside a tower for more than seven years. The following selection begins with the young woman bemoaning her fate, weeping bitterly, and wishing she had never been born. She then curses her family for forcing her to marry this man whom she suspects as having been baptized in "the river of hell." Aware of chivalry and courtly romance, she dreams about having a "handsome, courtly, brave, and valiant" lover. Within moments, a hawk flies into her chamber and becomes a handsome knight, and the young wife agrees to take him as her lover. Eventually their love is revealed to the young woman's husband by the old woman who guards the tower.

Now that I've begun these *lais*
the effort will not stop me;
every adventure that I know
I shall relate in rhyme.
My intention and my desire
is to tell you next of Yonec,
how he was born and how his father
first came to his mother.
The man who fathered Yonec
was called Muldumarec.

There once lived in Brittany
a rich man, old and ancient.
At Caerwent, he was acknowledged
and accepted as lord of the land.
The city sits on the Duelas,
which at one time was open to boats.
The man was very far along in years
but because he possessed a large fortune
he took a wife in order to have children,
who would come after him and be his heirs.
The girl who was given to the rich man
came from a good family;
she was wise and gracious [courtly] and very beautiful—
for her beauty he loved her very much.
Because she was beautiful and noble
he made every effort to guard her.
He locked her inside his tower
in a great paved chamber.
A sister of his,
who was also old and a widow, without her own lord,
he stationed with his lady
to guard her even more closely.

There were other women, I believe,
in another chamber by themselves,
but the lady never spoke to them
unless the old woman gave her permission.
So he kept her more than seven years—
they never had any children;
she never left that tower,
neither for family nor for friends.
When the lord came to sleep there
no chamberlain or porter
dared enter that room,
not even to carry a candle before the lord.
The lady lived in great sorrow,
with tears and sighs and weeping;
she lost her beauty,
as one does who cares nothing for it.
She would have preferred
death to take her quickly.

It was the beginning of April
when the birds begin their songs.
The lord arose in the morning
and made ready to go to the woods.
He had the old woman get up
and close the door behind him—
she followed his command.
The lord went off with his men.
The old woman carried a psalter
from which she intended to read the psalms.
The lady, awake and in tears,
saw the light of the sun.
She noticed that the old woman
had left the chamber.

She grieved and sighed
and wept and raged:
"I should never have been born!
My fate is very harsh.
I'm imprisoned in this tower
and I'll never leave it unless I die.
What is this jealous old man afraid of
that he keeps me so imprisoned?
He's mad, out of his senses;
always afraid of being deceived.
I can't even go to church
or hear God's service.
If I could speak to people
and enjoy myself with them
I'd be very gracious to my lord
even if I didn't want to be.
A curse on my family,
and on all the others
who gave me to this jealous man,
who married me to his body.
It's a rough rope that I pull and draw.
He'll never die—
when he should have been baptized
he was plunged instead in the river of hell;
his sinews are hard, his veins are hard,
filled with living blood.
I've often heard
that one could once find
adventures in this land
that brought relief to the unhappy.
Knights might find young girls
to their desire, noble and lovely;
and ladies find lovers
so handsome, courtly, brave, and valiant
that they could not be blamed,
and no one else would see them.
If that might be or ever was,
if that has ever happened to anyone,
God, who has power over everything,
grant me my wish in this."
When she'd finished her lament,
she saw, through a narrow window,
the shadow of a great bird.
She didn't know what it was.
It flew into the chamber;
its feet were banded; it looked like a hawk
of five or six moultings.
It alighted before the lady.
When it had been there awhile
and she'd stared hard at it,
it became a handsome and noble knight.
The lady was astonished;
her blood went cold, she trembled,
she was frightened—she covered her head.
The knight was very courteous,

he spoke first:
"Lady," he said, "don't be afraid.
The hawk is a noble bird,
although its secrets are unknown to you.
Be reassured
and accept me as your love."

The lady lay beside her love—
there was never a more beautiful couple.
When they had laughed and played
and spoken intimately,
the knight took his leave
to return to his land.
She gently begged him
to come back often.
"Lady," he said, "whenever you please,
I will be here within the hour.
But you must make certain
that we're not discovered.
This old woman will betray us,
night and day she will spy on us.
She will perceive our love,
and tell her lord about it.
If that happens,
if we are betrayed,
I won't be able to escape.
I shall die."
With that the knight departed,
leaving his love in great joy.
In the morning she rose restored;
she was happy all week.
Her body had now become precious to her,
she completely recovered her beauty.
Now she would rather remain here
than look for pleasure elsewhere.
She wanted to see her love all the time
and enjoy herself with him.
As soon as her lord departed,
night or day, early or late,
she had him all to her pleasure.
God, let their joy endure!
Because of the great joy she felt,
because she could see her love so often,
her whole appearance changed.
But her lord was clever.
In his heart he sensed
that she was not what she had been.
He suspected his sister.
He questioned her one day,
saying he was astonished
that the lady now dressed with care.
He asked her what it meant.
The old woman said she didn't know—
no one could have spoken to her,

she had no lover or friend—
it was only that she was now more willing,
to be alone than before.
His sister, too, had noticed the change.
Her lord answered:
"By my faith," he said, "I think that's so.
But you must do something for me.
In the morning, when I've gotten up
and you have shut the doors,
pretend you are going out
and leave her lying there alone.
Then hide yourself in a safe place,
watch her and find out
what it is, and where it comes from,
that gives her such great joy."
With that plan they separated.
Alas, how hard it is to protect yourself
from someone who wants to trap you,
to betray and deceive you!

The husband fashions sharp spikes of iron that mortally wound the hawk when he next comes to visit his lady-love. Now pregnant with the knight's child, the young woman leaps from her window and follows his trail of blood to a palace in another town. Before he dies, her lover gives her a magical ring that will cause her husband to forget the past and free her from her prison. He also gives her a sword to bestow on their son, Yonec, when he becomes "a brave and valiant knight." Their son will ultimately avenge his mother's betrayal and subsequent death by beheading his stepfather and becoming lord of the land.

The lady answered: "Love,
I would rather die with you
than suffer with my lord.
If I go back to him he'll kill me."
The knight reassured her,
gave her a ring,
and explained to her
that, as long as she kept it,
her lord would not remember
anything that had happened—
he would imprison her no longer.

He gave her his sword
and then made her swear
no man would ever possess it,
that she'd keep it for their son.
When the son had grown and become
a brave and valiant knight,
she would go to a festival,
taking him and her lord with her.
They would come to an abbey.
There, beside a tomb,
they would hear the story of his death,
how he was wrongfully killed.
There she would give her son the sword.
The adventure would be recited to him,
how he was born and who his father was;
then they'd see what he would do.
When he'd told her and shown her everything,
he gave her a precious robe
and told her to put it on.
Then he sent her away.
She left carrying the ring
and the sword—they comforted her.
She had not gone half a mile
from the gate of the city
when she heard the bells ring
and the mourning begin in the castle,
and in her sorrow
she fainted four times.
When she recovered from the faints
she made her way to the hill.
She entered it, passed through it,
and returned to her country.
There with her lord
she lived many days and years.
He never accused her of that deed,
never insulted or abused her.
Her son was born and nourished,
protected and cherished.
They named him Yonec.
In all the kingdom you couldn't find
one so handsome, brave, or strong,
so generous, so munificent.
When he reached the proper age,
he was made a knight.

10 The French *chansons de geste*

Medieval literature was written both in Latin, the language of learning, and in the vernacular, the traditional spoken language. The French *chansons de geste*, epic poems of heroic deeds that had first been told orally, were written in the vernacular of northern France. The poems dealt with Charlemagne's battles against the Muslims, with rebellious nobles, and with feudal warfare. The finest of these epic poems, *The Song of Roland* (La chanson de Roland), is loosely based on an actual historical event. In 778, Charlemagne invaded Spain hoping to extend his kingdom at the expense of the Saracens (Muslims). When he reached Zaragoza, south of Pamplona, Charlemagne received word of an uprising in Saxony and began his withdrawal to France. Passing back through Pamplona, he destroyed the city and ascended the Pyrenees Mountains by way of the Roncevaux Pass, where his army was ambushed. In the Battle of Roncevaux, many of Charlemagne's military leaders, including his nephew Roland, lost their lives. It was Charlemagne's greatest defeat. More than 300 years later, an anonymous author told about the disaster in a *chanson de geste* written in Old French.

The Song of Roland
CONFLICT BETWEEN CHRISTIANITY AND ISLAM

The Song of Roland presents these historical events as a classic confrontation between good and evil, between the Christian king, Charlemagne, and the Saracen king of Spain, Marsile. The poem begins with Charlemagne having conquered all of Spain except for Zaragoza, which Marsile still controls. As a peace overture, Marsile offers to convert to Christianity and to become Charlemagne's vassal if he will return with his army to Aachen. Roland counsels Charlemagne to reject the offer, but Roland's stepfather, Ganelon, argues that it would be wrong to continue to fight against a foe who seeks clemency. Roland then nominates Ganelon for the treacherous task of negotiating with Marsile. Angry at Roland, Ganelon conspires with Marsile to bring about Roland's death in battle. Ganelon manipulates the situation so that Roland is in command of the rear guard, and, as Charlemagne's army withdraws from Spain through the pass, Roland's troops are overwhelmed by the Saracens. In the following passage, the battle tide turns against Roland, his friend Count Oliver, and Archbishop Turpin.

127

Count Roland calls to Oliver:
"Comrade, sir, you will grant, I'm sure,
That the Archbishop is a very good knight.
There is no finer one on the face of the earth,
He is formidable with lance and spear."
The Count replies: "Come on, let's go help him!"
When they heard this, the Franks began striking anew.
The blows are hard and the fighting is heavy,
The Christians suffer very heavy losses.
One could see then Roland and Oliver
Striking and slashing with their swords!
The Archbishop strikes with his spear.
We have a good idea of the number they killed:
It is written in the documents and records,
The Chronicle says that there were more than four thousand.
It went well with them during four assaults,

But afterward the fifth brought them to ruin and grief.
The French knights are now all dead,
Except for sixty whom God has spared.
Before they die, they will sell their lives dearly.

128

Count Roland sees the great slaughter of his men.
He calls his companion Oliver:
"Dear sir, dear comrade, in God's name, what do you make of this?
You see so many good knights lying on the ground!
Sweet France, the fair, is to be pitied,
How impoverished she is now of such knights!
O dear King, what a shame you're not here!
Dear Oliver, how shall we do it,
How shall we break the news to him?"
Oliver said: "I don't know how to reach him.
I'd rather die than have something to blame ourselves for."

129

Roland said: "I shall sound the oliphant.
Charles, who is going through the pass, will hear it.
I give you my word that the Franks will return now."
Oliver said: "That would be dishonorable
And a reproach to all your relatives,
The shame of it would last the rest of their lives!
When I told you to, you did nothing at all,
Don't expect my consent to do it now.
If you sound the horn, it will not be a brave act.
See how bloody both your arms are!"
The Count replies: "I have struck mighty fine blows!"

130

Roland says: "Our battle is hard,
I shall sound the horn and Charles will hear it."
Oliver said: "That would not be a heroic deed!
When I told you to, comrade, you did not deign to.
If the King had been here, we would have suffered no harm.
Those who are with him over there are not to be blamed."
Oliver said: "By this beard of mine,
If I manage to see my fair sister Aida again,
You shall never lie in her arms!"

131

Roland said: "Why are you angry with me?"
The other replies: "Comrade, you brought it on yourself,
For heroism tempered with common sense is a far cry from
    madness;
Reasonableness is to be preferred to recklessness.
Frenchmen have died because of your senselessness.
We shall never again be of service to Charles.
If you had believed me, my lord would have come,
We would have fought or won (?) this battle,
King Marsile would be captured or slain.
We have come to rue your prowess, Roland!
Charlemagne will not have any help from us.
There shall never be such a man again until Judgment Day.
You will die here and France will be dishonored.
Today our loyal companionage comes to an end,
Before nightfall, our parting will be very sad."

132

The Archbishop hears them quarreling.
He urges on his horse with his pure gold spurs.
He comes up to them, he began to reprove them:
"Sir Roland and you, Sir Oliver,

In God's name I beg you, don't argue!
Sounding the horn would be of no use to us now,
Nevertheless it is best:
Let the King come and he will be able to avenge us,
The men of Spain must not return home joyful.
Our Frenchmen will dismount,
They will find us dead and cut to pieces.
They will raise us in coffins on sumpters,
They will shed tears of sorrow and pity for us.
They will bury us in hallowed ground within church walls,
Neither wolves, nor pigs, nor dogs will devour us."
Roland replies: "Well said, sir."

At this Point Roland blows the oliphant, a natural
horn made from ivory, to signal the emperor that he
and his troops need help. Charlemagne hears the
horn and, despite Ganelon's assurance that there is
no battle, he prepares to go to Roland's defense.
Oliver dies first, and then, the Archbishop. Finally,
Roland dies, just before Charlemagne arrives. When
Charlemagne finds Roland's body, he vows
vengeance. Back in Aachen, Ganelon is put on trial
for treason, found guilty, and executed by being
pulled apart by four horses. The following passage
tells of Roland's death.

135

Count Roland's mouth is bleeding,
The temple of his brain has burst.
He sounds the oliphant in agony and in pain,
Charles heard it, and his Frenchmen too.
The King said: "That horn has been blowing a long time!"
Duke Naimes replies: "A worthy knight is pouring out his
    suffering!
There is a battle, so help me.
The one who begs you to pretend you have heard nothing has
    betrayed him.
To arms, shout your battle cry,
Save your noble household:
You hear as plain as can be Roland signaling his distress!"

136

The Emperor has ordered his trumpets to be sounded.
The French dismount, they arm themselves
With hauberks, helmets, and gilded swords.
They have fine shields and long and sturdy spears,
And white, red, and blue ensigns.
All the knights of the army mount their war-horses,
They spur furiously until they are out of the pass.
They say to one another:

"If only we could see Roland before he's killed,
We would strike mighty blows with him!"
But what is the use? They have tarried too long. . . .

139

King Charles rides like fury,
His white beard is spread over his hauberk.
The knights from France all spur furiously,
They are all in a state of blind anger
For not being with Roland, the captain,
Who is fighting the Saracens of Spain.
He is so badly hurt I do not think his soul can remain in him.
God! what men, the sixty who are in his company!
No king or captain ever had finer.

140

Roland gazes at the mountains and hills.
He sees so many men from France lying dead,
He weeps over them like a noble knight:
"My lord barons, God have mercy on you!
May He grant Paradise to all your souls,
May He cause them to lie among the holy flowers!
I have never seen worthier knights than you,
You have served me constantly and for so long!
You have conquered such great nations for Charles!
The Emperor raised you, but how unfortunate the outcome!
Land of France, you are a very sweet realm,
Today made desolate by such a cruel disaster!
French knights, I see you dying for my sake:
I cannot protect or save you.
May God, who never did lie, help you!
Oliver, my friend, I must not fail you,
I shall die of sorrow if nothing else kills me.
Comrade, sir, let's go strike again!"

156

Count Roland is fighting nobly,
But his body is covered with sweat and is very hot.
He has an ache and a great pain in his head,
His temple is burst because he sounded the horn.
But he wants to know if Charles will come,
He draws the oliphant, he sounded it feebly.
The Emperor halted and listened to it.

164

Count Roland sees his peers dead
And Oliver, whom he loved so well,
He was moved with pity, he begins to weep.
His face lost all its color.
He suffered such pain that he could no longer stand,
Willy-nilly, he falls to the ground.
The Archbishop said: "You are to be pitied. worthy knight!"

165

When the Archbishop saw Roland faint,
He suffered greater anguish than ever before.
He stretched out his hand and took the oliphant.
At Roncevaux there is a running stream,
He wants to go there, he will give some water to Roland.
He turns and goes away with short, faltering steps.
He is so weak that he cannot go any farther,
He has not the strength to, he has lost too much blood.
In less time than it would take a man to cover a single acre,
His heart fails him and he falls forward.
His death is gripping him hard.

166

Count Roland recovers from his swoon,
He rises to his feet, but he is suffering great pain.
He gazes uphill and he gazes downhill:
On the green grass, beyond his companions,
He sees the noble warrior lying,
It is the Archbishop, whom God sent in his name.
The Archbishop says his confession, he gazes upward,
He has joined and raised both hands toward heaven,
And he prays God to grant him Paradise.
Charles's warrior Turpin is dead.
By fighting great battles and preaching many fine sermons,
He was always a relentless fighter against the pagans.
May God grant him his holy blessing!

167

Count Roland sees the Archbishop on the ground:
He sees his entrails spilled outside his body,
His brain is oozing out beneath his forehead.
Over his breast, on the sternum,
He has crossed his beautiful white hands.
Roland laments over him in a loud voice, as is customary in
   his land:
"Ah, noble man, high-born knight,
I commend you this day to God in His celestial Glory!

No man shall ever serve Him more willingly.
There never was such a prophet since the Apostles
To keep the Faith and to win men over.
May your soul not endure any suffering!
May it find the gate of Paradise open!"

168

Roland feels that death is near,
His brain is coming out through his ears.
He prays God to call his Peers,
And then, for his own sake, he prays the angel Gabriel.
He took the oliphant so as not to incur any blame,
And his sword Durendal with his other hand.
Where no crossbow can shoot a bolt,
He goes in the direction of Spain to a fallow field.
He climbs a hill and halts beneath two beautiful trees.
There are four blocks made of marble there.
He fell backward on the green grass,
He fainted there, for death is near.

169

The mountains are high and the trees are very high,
There are four shiny marble blocks there.
Count Roland faints on the green grass.
A Saracen is watching him all the while,
He feigns death and lies amid the others.
He smeared his body and his face with blood,
He rises to his feet and makes a dash forward.
He was well proportioned, strong, and very brave,
Through pride he embarks upon an act of fatal folly.
He seized Roland's body and his weapons,
And he said these words: "Charles's nephew is vanquished!
I shall carry this sword to Arabia."
But as the Saracen was pulling, the Count came round a bit.

170

Roland feels the Saracen stealing his sword from him,
He opened his eyes and said these words to him:
"I don't believe you're one of our men!"
He holds on to the oliphant, he does not want to part with it
    for a single moment,
And he strikes him on the helmet, whose gold is wrought
    with gems.
He smashes the steel, the head, the bones,
He knocked both his eyes out of his head,
He tumbled him over dead at his feet.
Afterward he says: "Dirty pagan, whatever possessed you
To seize me rightly or wrongly?
No one will hear of this without thinking you were mad.

My oliphant is split at the wide end now,
The crystal and the gold ornaments have fallen off."

171

Roland notices that his sight is failing him,
He rises to his feet and exerts himself to the utmost,
All color has faded from his face.
There is a dark stone in front of him,
He strikes it ten blows in bitterness and frustration.
The steel grates, but it is not smashed or nicked.
"Oh," said the Count, "Holy Mary, help me!
Oh, Durendal, noble one, you are to be pitied!
Since I am finished, I no longer have you in my care.
I have won so many battles in the field with you
And conquered so many vast lands
Over which white-bearded Charles rules!
May no turn-tail ever possess you!
A very good knight has owned you for a long time,
Never again shall there be such a sword in blessed France."

172

Roland struck the sardonyx stone,
The steel grates, but it does not break or nick.
Seeing that he cannot smash it,
He begins to lament over it to himself:
"Oh, Durendal, how beautiful you are, how clear, how
    bright!
How you shine and flash against the sun!
Charles was in the valleys of Maurienne
When God instructed him from heaven on high by His angel
To give you to a captain count:
So the great, noble king girded me with it.
With it I conquered Anjou and Brittany,
With it I conquered Poitou and Maine,
With it I conquered Normandy the free,
With it I conquered Provence and Aquitaine,
Lombardy and all Romagna;
With it I conquered Bavaria and all Flanders,
Burgundy, all Poland,
And Constantinople, which rendered homage to him,
And he does as he wishes in Saxony;
With it I conquered Scotland, . . .
And England, which he held under his jurisdiction;
With it I conquered so many countries and lands
Over which white-bearded Charles rules.
I feel sad and heavy-hearted for this sword,
I would rather die than have it remain with the pagans.
God, our Father, do not let France be dishonored in this way!"

173

Roland struck a dark stone,
He whacks off more than I can say.
The sword grates, but neither shatters nor breaks,
It rebounds upward toward heaven.
The Count, seeing that he cannot smash it,
Laments over it softly to himself:
"Oh, Durendal, how beautiful you are and how very holy!
There are many relics in the golden hilt:
Saint Peter's tooth, some of Saint Basil's blood,
Some of my lord Saint Denis's hair,
Some of Saint Mary's clothing.
It is not right for the pagans to own you,
You must be served by Christians.
May no coward ever possess you!
With you I conquered many vast lands
Over which white-bearded Charles rules,
And the Emperor is powerful and mighty as a consequence."

174

Roland feels that death is overcoming him,
It descends from his head to his heart.

He ran beneath a pine tree,
He lay down prone on the green grass.
He places his sword and (also?) his oliphant beneath him.
He turned his head toward the pagan army:
He did this because he earnestly desires
That Charles and all his men say
That the noble Count died as a conqueror.
He beats his breast in rapid succession over and over again,
He proffered his gauntlet to God for his sins.

175

Roland feels that his time is up,
He is on a steep hill, his face turned toward Spain.
He beat his breast with one hand:
"Mea culpa, Almighty God,
For my sins, great and small,
Which I committed from the time I was born
To this day when I am overtaken here!"
He offered his right gauntlet to God,
Angels from heaven descend toward him.

11 The *Iliad* of the German People

The legend of the *Nibelungenlied* (Lay of the Nibelungs),[1] which dates from the early sixth century, is based upon stories from both Scandinavia and Germany, and it is often called "the *Iliad* of the Germans." As the best expression of the heroic epic in Germany, it draws on themes from the Germanic past, especially the migration of the tribes; even Attila, leader of the Huns, who threatened both Roman and Germanic tribes during the Late Roman Empire, appears in the second part of the epic. The poem was probably first performed as a ballad by *Minnesingers* (minstrels or troubadours) along the Rhine River. Scholars assume that the first complete German text was executed sometime between 1195 and 1205. Like other epics, the *Nibelungenlied* contains traditional demonstrations of courtly graces as well as scenes typified in chivalric literature—ceremonious arrivals and departures, tournament spectacles, and sumptuous banquets—but in a much darker fashion. The *Nibelungenlied* is filled with gruesome details of death and revenge, with brutality, treachery, and greed. Although the quest for honor and loyalty to one's lord are evident in the *Nibelungenlied,* the preeminent theme is "unholy vengeance" which is carried out by Kriemhild, the Burgundian princess of Worms.

---

[1]The *Nibelungenlied* literally means the "song of the Nibelungs". According to the Germanic tradition, the Nibelungs are legendary people whose name is thought to mean "Children of the Mist." The Nibelungs, however, are never actually identified by the poet until near the end of the poem when they are equated with the Burgundians.

The *Nibelungenlied*

The story begins with Sigfrid, the son of the king of the Netherlands, who learns of Kriemhild's beauty and lively spirit and vows to marry her. At Worms he meets King Gunther, Kriemhild's brother, as well as Hagen, one of Gunther's chief vassals, who knows of Sigfrid's physical prowess, his grandiose escapades, but most important, that Sigfrid possesses the treasure of the Nibelungs. Sigfrid endears himself to the Burgundian court by demonstrating his courage, strength, and prowess in battle against the Danes, and finally meets Princess Kriemhild at the victory celebration.

The love story of Kriemhild and Sigfrid is interrupted by a shift in focus to Gunther's fascination with Brunhild, Queen of Iceland. Hearing stories of Brunhild's "vast strength and surpassing beauty" and her intention to marry any man who could defeat her in a series of athletic tests, Gunther solicits the aid of Sigfrid who agrees to help Gunther acquire Brunhild, provided he be allowed to marry Kriemhild. Although Gunther wins the contest, it is actually Sigfrid, wearing a magic cloak of invisibility, who does the deeds. This deception ultimately brings about the downfall of both Gunther and Sigfrid.

Anxious to gain the treasure of the Nibelungs, Hagen convinces King Gunther to aid in the betrayal of his brother-in-law. Feigning a desire to protect Sigfrid in battle, Hagen wins Kriemhild's confidence, and she reveals to him her husband's vulnerable spot.[2] Hagen then convinces her to sew a cross on the spot between Sigfrid's shoulder blades, and during a hunt he kills him by stabbing him in the back as he drinks from a spring.

SIXTEENTH ADVENTURE
HOW SIGFRID WAS SLAIN

Gunther and Hagen, bold, but with the face
Of false deceit, proposed a forest chase:
To hunt with sharpened spears the wild swine,
The bison and the bear—is there any sport so fine?

They took with them supplies of every kind.
Sigfrid rode, in grace and noble mind.
Beside a cooling spring he lost his life—
This was the work of Brunhild, royal Gunther's wife.

To Kriemhild's side the stalwart knight had gone.
His hunting gear and theirs was loaded on,
Ready to cross the Rhine. Never before
In all her days, had Kriemhild cause to suffer more.

He kissed his love upon her lips and cried,
"God grant I see you safe again, my bride,
And may your eyes see me. Now you must find
Diversion with your kin, I cannot stay behind."

She thought of the words she spoke in Hagen's ear
(And dared not now repeat). In pain and fear
The princess grieved that she was ever born—
Kriemhild wept, her tears unnumbered, all forlorn.

"Give up this hunt!" she cried. "Last night I dreamed
A painful thing. Two wild boars, it seemed,
Pursued my lord across a field. In sleep,
The flowers all turned red. I have my right to weep;

I fear from many hands an evil plot—
What if someone here should think he'd got
Ill use from us and turned this thought to hate?
Dear lord, I say, turn back, before it is too late."

"I'll soon return, my dear, I swear I will.
I know no persons here who wish me ill,
For all your kin are well disposed to me,
And I have always acted so that this should be."

"Oh no, my lord, I fear it can't go well.
Alas, I dreamed last night two mountains fell
On top of you, and I never saw you again.
If you should leave me now, my heart will be heavy with pain."

---

[2]The poet has Kriemhild tell Hagen the story of how Sigfrid killed a dragon (a story drawn from a much earlier Nordic myth) and bathed in its blood so that he might become invincible. As he bathed, however, a leaf from a linden tree fell between his shoulder blades, preventing the blood from touching that area.

He held his perfect wife in arms' embrace,
With lover's kiss caressed her lovely face.
He took his leave and soon he went away.
Alas, she never saw him safe beyond that day.

They rode to a certain heavy wood, in quest
Of hunt and sport, and many of the best
Were they who followed Gunther's party there.
The only ones who stayed were Gernot and Giselher.

The horses went ahead, across the Rhine,
Full laden with the hunters' bread and wine,
Their fish and meat, and other good supplies
To suit a wealthy king in full and fitting wise.

At the forest edge they had their camp site placed.
By this device the haughty hunters faced
Where game would run, there on a spacious isle.
They told the king that Sigfrid had ridden up meanwhile.

The hunters' stations now were occupied
At every major point. Lord Sigfrid cried,
That stalwart man, "And who shall show the way
To the woods and the waiting game, you lords in bold array?"

Said Hagen of Trony, "Listen, my lord, to me.
I thought the hunt today was meant to be
In Spessart and that is where I sent the wine.
We missed our drinks today; I'll not forget next time."

"Confound them," answered Sigfrid then, declaring:
"They should have brought me seven sumpters bearing
Spiced wine and mead. And failing that,
Was there no place closer to the Rhine we could have sat?"

Said Hagen of Trony, "Noble knights, my king.
Not far from here I know a cooling spring.
Do not be angry now—why not go there?"
(Counsel fraught, for many, with sorrow and grievous care).

The pang of thirst was all that Sigfrid feared.
He ordered the table that much sooner cleared,
That he might go to the hills and find the spring.
There they worked their plot—a black and faithless thing.

They placed on carts the game Sigfrid had killed
To have it carried home, and all who beheld
Granted Sigfrid honor in high degree.
(Hagen broke faith with him—and he broke it wretchedly).

As they were about to go to the linden tree
Lord Hagen said, "They're always telling me
How nothing is fast enough to keep the pace
With Sigfrid running. I wish he'd show us how he can race!"

Cried the Prince of the Low Lands, Sigmund's son:
"Find out for yourself, my friend! If you want to run
A race to the spring, all right. Whoever's faster
To the finish we shall all acknowledge master."

"Very well," said Hagen then, "let's try."
Stalwart Sigfrid made a bold reply:
"I'll first lie down in the grass before your feet."
Royal Gunther smiled, the words he heard were sweet.

Sigfrid had more to say: "I'll tell you what.
I'll carry every bit of clothes I've got,
My spear and shield, and all my hunting gear."
He put his quiver next to his sword and laced it there.

Gunther and Hagen removed their clothes and stood
In their white underwear. It did no good.
Across the clover like two wild panthers burst
The pair of running men, but Sigfrid got there first.

(In all, from many men, he won renown!)
He loosed his sword, and put his quiver down
And leaned on a linden branch his giant spear.
The splendid stranger stood by the waters flowing clear.

With perfect sense of form in everything,
He laid his shield on the ground beside the spring
And would not drink, however great his thirst
(Evil thanks he got!) till Gunther drank there first.

The spring was pure and good and cool.
Gunther bent his head above the pool
And after drinking rose and stepped away.
Ah, if Sigfrid could have done the same that day!

He paid the price for the courteous thing he did.
His sword and bow Lord Hagen took and hid
And burred back where the spear had lain before.
He looked for a certain mark on the cape that Sigfrid wore.

As Sigfrid leaned to drink, he took his aim
And hurled it through the cross. The heart-blood came
Welling from the wound, richly to spill
On Hagen's clothes. No knight has ever done so ill.

He left the spear embedded by Sigfrid's heart.
Never in all this world did Hagen start
And run so fast from any man before.
When good Lord Sigfrid knew the vicious wound he bore,

He leapt from the spring like a man out of his mind.
Up from his heart and towering out behind
Rose the shaft of the spear. His bow and sword
He sought in vain, or Hagen would have his due reward.

The wounded man could find no blade to wield,
And nothing left to fight with but his shield.
He snatched it up and after Hagen he ran—
Even thus he still caught up with Gunther's man.

Mortally wounded as he was, he hit
So hard with his shield that from the edge of it
The precious jewels spun, and the shield was shattered.
For that most splendid knight revenge was all that mattered.

Hagen stumbled and fell at Sigfrid's blows—
So violent all the island echoes rose!
Had Sigfrid sword in hand, he would have killed him.
What rage in the wounded man, as hurt and anger filled him!

The color of Sigfrid's skin had turned all pale.
He could not stand. His strength was doomed to fail;
He bore the mark of death in all his pallor.
Many lovely women later mourned his valor.

So Kriemhild's husband fell where flowers grew.
They saw the blood that left his wound burst through,
And then from bitter hurt he cursed them all,
Whose faithless plotting first designed his cruel fall.

Cried Sigfrid dying, "Cowards, knave on knave!
Is murder your reward for the help I gave?
I kept my faith with you, and so I pay!
A shame upon your race, what you have done today.

Every child that's born to you will bear
The stain of this forever. Far too unfair
Is this revenge you take for your hate of me!
You should be banned in shame from decent company."

The other knights ran up where he lay slain.
It was, for many there, a day of pain,
For he was mourned by all that ever served
A loyal cause—no more than a gallant man deserved.

Another mourned: the king of Burgundy.
The dying man looked up; "What need has he
To weep for hurt who caused it? Scorn of men
Is all it earns," said he. "Why not forget it then?"

Cried Hagen, "I don't know what you're mourning for.
Our fears are at an end. How many more
Will dare to stand against us? A fortunate hour,
I say, when I destroyed his pride and all his power!"

Cried Sigfrid, "Boasting is an easy art.
If I had seen the murder in your heart,

I should have taken care to guard my life.
I worry not so much for me as for my wife.

And God have pity that my son was born,
Whom men in later days will heap with scorn
For having kin who bear the murderer's taint.
If only I had strength!—I have a just complaint."

Said the dying man, in anguish: "Noble king,
If you intend to do a loyal thing
In all this world for any man, then take
My wife in your protection, for grace and mercy's sake.

And let it profit her that she's your sister,
As you are a well-born prince, in faith assist her.
My father and men have a long time to wait.
Never did woman's pleasure end in pain so great."

The flowers all around were wet with blood.
He fought with death but not for long—what good?
Death has always owned the sharper sword.
He had no longer strength to speak, that gallant lord.

Soon, when the warriors saw the knight was dead,
They placed him on a shield all golden red,
And then debated how they might proceed
Best to conceal the fact that Hagen did this deed.

And many spoke: "We have seen evil done.
Hide it then, and all shall speak as one
That Kriemhild's husband rode a forest lane
To hunt alone, was met by bandits there, and slain."

"I'll take him back," said Hagen. "Have no doubt:
It's all the same to me if she finds out.
She caused my lady Brunhild misery—
Now let her weep as much as she wants, for all of me!"

The treasure of the Nibelungs rightfully belongs to Kriemhild, for it is her dowry. Although she mourns for Sigfrid and blames herself for his death, Kriemhild forgives Gunther for betraying her, as well as everyone else—except Hagen, upon whom she vows revenge, which eventually leads to the destruction of the Burgundians. Once she possesses the vast treasure, Kriemhild declares that she would give it all up if she could have Sigfrid back. Instead, she begins to distribute it to rich and poor alike, for which she incurs the wrath of Hagen, who takes the treasure and sinks it in the Rhine River with the hope that he can retrieve it later.

The Late Middle Ages

During the Late Middle Ages, roughly the fourteenth and early fifteenth centuries, medieval civilization declined. In contrast to the vigor of the twelfth and thirteenth centuries, the fourteenth century was burdened by crop failures, famine, plagues, and reduced population. The church also came under attack from reformers who challenged clerical authority and questioned church teachings, from powerful kings who resisted papal interference in the political life of their kingdoms, and from political theorists who asserted that the pope had no authority to intervene in matters of state. In the city-states of Italy, a growing secularism signified a break with medieval otherworldliness and heralded the emergence of the modern outlook.

Late medieval literature evidenced both traditional Christian concerns and new literary forms and themes that pointed away from the Middle Ages. These innovations presage the Renaissance and the birth of modernity. In this respect, Dante is a pivotal figure. On the one hand, his *Divine Comedy* is profoundly medieval in its overriding concern with salvation and its creative integration of Aristotelian-Ptolemaic cosmology with the Christian viewpoint. On the other hand, Dante was also a precursor of change; he colored the traditional view of salvation with his own creative interpretation and gave a new value to vernacular literature, regarding it as a worthy companion to both classical and biblical literature. Breaking with the traditional outlook, he did not regard Latin as superior to Italian. Other writers—Francesco Petrarch, Giovanni Boccaccio, Geoffrey Chaucer, and Christine de Pizan—were influenced by Dante and also displayed a fresh spirit.

The writers of the fourteenth century whose works evidence change hardly abandoned the familiar forms of poem, romance, allegory, and dream vision, but they did transform them to fit their own purposes. Within these forms, themes appear that had not been seen since antiquity—appreciation of human talents, the value of worldly activities, and the significance of the natural love that exists between men and women. The authors often display an inner conflict: They are constrained by traditional Christian piety but also feel compelled to break the bonds of artistic convention. Thus, the literature fluctuates between the writer's desire to withdraw from the world, discipline the passions, and contemplate salvation, and the aspiration to become involved in the world and to assist in its transformation. As the literature progresses, the writers become less inhibited, the themes become less Christian and idealized, and the tone becomes more secular. Nowhere is this more evident than in the literature about women—concerning their dignity, merit, and worth. The image of women is altered in numerous literary works, in which single men and women communicate about the status and ability of women within society. The success of Christine de Pizan further illustrates the affinity for a more natural literature unaffected by piety and convention.

1 A Medieval Morality Play

Written in Middle English about 1485, *Everyman* is the best extant example of the genre of drama known as the morality play, which uses allegory to dramatize the moral struggle against evil in which every Christian is engaged. The moral themes—trust in God, do good, love mercy, and do justice—are often presented in an unduly didactic way. The plot focuses on Everyman, being stripped of all that he possesses, including family, friends, and wealth. Each character in the drama—including Fellowship, Good-Deeds, Knowledge, Beauty, Strength, and Discretion—epitomizes his or her name. The overarching theme is how every individual—Everyman—struggles, in the face of Death, to be worthy of salvation and everlasting life; but in the end, all anyone possesses is Good-Deeds—the harsh moral of the play.

Everyman

In the manner of the chorus of a Greek tragedy, the play opens with a prologue, spoken by the Messenger, who explains the plot to the audience.

PROLOGUE

MESSENGER

I pray you all give your audience,
And hear this matter with reverence,
By figure a moral play—
The *Summoming of Everyman* called it is,
That of our lives and ending shows
How transitory we be all our day.
This matter is wondrous precious,
But the intent of it is more gracious,
And sweet to bear away.
The story saith,—Man, in the beginning,
Look well, and take good heed to the ending,
Be you never so gay!
Ye think sin in the beginning full sweet,
Which in the end causeth the soul to weep,
When the body lieth in clay.
Here shall you see how Fellowship and Jollity,
And Strength, Pleasure, and Beauty,
Will fade from thee as flower in May.
For ye shall hear how our heaven's king
Calleth Everyman to a general reckoning.
Give audience, and hear what he doth say.

The audience immediately becomes aware that Everyman is nearing the end of his life and is about to be held accountable for having been enamored of the "seven deadly sins." (The seven deadly sins are pride, greed, lust, envy, gluttony, anger, and sloth.)

Subsequently, Everyman is approached by Death and is amazed to discover the meaning of such phrases as "Death giveth no warning" and the "Tide abideth no man." Death's greater function, however, is to educate Everyman into the larger issues of life and death, and at times, Death is almost sympathetic to Everyman's struggle against sin.

DEATH

I am Death, that no man dreadeth.
That every man arrests and no man spareth;
For it is God's commandment
That all to me should be obedient.

EVERYMAN

O Death, thou comest when I had thee least in mind;
In thy power it lieth me to save,
Yet of my goods will I give thee, if ye will be kind,
Yea, a thousand pound shalt thou have,
But defer this matter till another day!

DEATH

Everyman, it may not be by no way;
I set not by gold, silver, nor riches,
Nor by pope, emperor, king, duke, nor princes,
For if I would receive gifts great,
All the world I might get;
But my custom is clean contrary.
I give thee no respite. Come, do not tarry!

EVERYMAN

Alas, shall I have no longer respite?
I may say Death giveth no warning.
To think on thee it maketh my heart sick,
For all unready is my book of reckoning.
But twelve year if I might have abiding,
My counting book I would make so clear
That thy reckoning I should not need to fear.
Wherefore, Death, I pray thee, for God's mercy,
Spare me till I be provided of remedy.

DEATH

Thee availeth not to cry, weep, and pray,
But haste thee lightly that thou go the journey,
And prove thy friends if thou can.
For, know thou well, the tide abideth no man,
And in the world each living creature
For Adam's sin must die by nature.

EVERYMAN

Death, if I should this pilgrimage take,
And my reckoning surely make,
Show me, for Saint Charity,
Should I not come again shortly?

DEATH

No, Everyman. If thou be once there
Thou mayst nevermore come here,
Trust me verily.

EVERYMAN

O Gracious God, in the high seat celestial,
Have mercy on me in this my need;
Shall I have no company from this vale terrestrial
Of mine acquaintance the way to lead?

DEATH

Yea, if any be so hardy
That would go with thee and bear thee company.
Hasten to be gone to God's magnificence,
Thy reckoning to give before his presence.
What, thinkest thou thy life is given thee,
And thy worldly goods also?

EVERYMAN

I had thought so, verily.

DEATH

Nay, nay, it was but lent thee!
For as soon as thou dost go,
Another awhile shall have it and then go therefro
Even as thou hast done.
Everyman, thou art mad. Thou hast thy wits five,
And here on earth will not amend thy life,
For suddenly do I come.

EVERYMAN

O wretched caitiff,[1] whither shall I flee,
That I might escape this endless sorrow!
Now, gentle Death, spare me till to-morrow,
That I may amend me
With good advisement.

DEATH

Nay, thereto I will not consent,
Nor no man will I respite,
But to the heart suddenly I shall smite
Without any advisement.
And now out of thy sight I will me hie.
See thou make thee ready shortly,
For thou mayst say this is the day
That no man living may escape away.

DEATH withdraws.

Characters representing his friends and family—Fellowship, Kindred, Cousin, and Goods—then relate incidents of Everyman's earlier lifestyle in a universal way, carefully avoiding any indication that such behavior is unique to Everyman. Recognizing that none of these brings hope of salvation, Everyman, in despair, asks: "My Good-Deeds, where be you?" and implores her to help him. In her reply, Good-Deeds offers the assistance of her sister, Knowledge, because she is too weak to help him alone, due to Everyman's neglect of her.

EVERYMAN

O, to whom shall I make my moan
For to go with me in that heavy journey?
First Fellowship said he would with me be gone;
His words were very pleasant and gay,
But afterward he left me alone.
Then spake I to my kinsmen all in despair,
And they also gave me words fair.
They lacked no fair speaking,
But they forsook me in the ending.
Then went I to my Goods that I loved best,
In hope to have comfort, but there had I least.
For my Goods sharply did me tell
That he bringeth many into Hell.
Then of myself I was ashamed,
And so I am worthy to be blamed,
Thus may I well myself hate.
Of whom shall I now counsel take?
I think that I shall never speed
Till that I go to my Good-Deed,
But, alas, she is so weak,
That she can neither go nor speak.
Yet will I venture on her now.—
My Good-Deeds, where be you?

---

[1]A caitiff is a base, despicable person.

Enter GOOD-DEEDS.

GOOD-DEEDS
Here I lie cold in the ground.
Thy sins have me sore-bound
That I cannot stir.

EVERYMAN
O, Good-Deeds, I stand in fear;
I must pray you for counsel,
For help now would come right well.

GOOD-DEEDS
Everyman, I have understanding
That you be summoned account to make
Before Messias, of Jerusalem the King.
If you walk by me that journey I would take.

EVERYMAN
Therefore I come to you, my moan to make—
I pray you, that ye will go with me.

GOOD-DEEDS
I would full fain, but I cannot stand, verily.

EVERYMAN
Why, is there anything did you befall?

GOOD-DEEDS
Yea, sir, and I may thank you of all;
If ye had perfectly cheered me,
Your book of account now full ready would be.
Look on the books of your works and deeds—
Oh, see how they under your feet lie,
Unto your soul's heaviness.

EVERYMAN
Our Lord Jesus, help me!
For one letter here I cannot see.

GOOD-DEEDS
There is a blind reckoning in time of distress!

EVERYMAN
Good-Deeds, I pray you, help me in this need.
Or else I am for ever damned indeed.
Therefore help me to a reckoning
Before the Redeemer of all thing,
That king is, and was, and ever shall.

GOOD-DEEDS
Everyman, I am sorry for your fall,
And fain would I help you, if I were able.

EVERYMAN
Good-Deeds, your counsel I pray you give me.

GOOD-DEEDS
That shall I do verily.
Though that on my feet I may not go,
I have a sister that shall with you also,

Called Knowledge, which shall with you abide,
To help you to make that dreadful reckoning.
Enter KNOWLEDGE.

KNOWLEDGE
Everyman, I will go with thee, and be thy guide,
In utmost need to go by thy side.

For the remainder of the play, Knowledge (recognition of one's sins) is Everyman's guide. With her help, Everyman acquires new "friends"—Discretion, Strength, Five-Wits, and Beauty. Knowledge then counsels him to go to a priest and receive the sacraments. Content to stand before God on his own diminutive merits, Everyman questions Knowledge's advice, but Five-Wits admonishes him and reminds him that salvation from sin only comes from the administration of the sacraments by the priesthood of the church.

EVERYMAN
My friends, come hither and be present,
Discretion, Strength, my Five-Wits, and Beauty.
DISCRETION, STRENGTH, FIVE-WITS and BEAUTY enter.

BEAUTY
Here at your will we be all ready.
What will ye that we should do?

GOOD-DEEDS
That ye would with Everyman go,
And help him in his pilgrimage.
Advise me, will ye with him or not in that voyage?

STRENGTH
We will bring him all thither,
To his help and comfort, ye may believe me.

DISCRETION
So will we go with him all together.

EVERYMAN
Almighty God, loved mayest thou be,
I give thee laud that I have hither brought
Strength, Discretion, Beauty, and Five-Wits; I lack nought!
And my Good-Deeds, with Knowledge clear,
All stay in my company at my will here;
I desire no more to my business.

STRENGTH
And I, Strength, will stand by you in distress,
Though thou wouldest in battle fight on the ground.

FIVE-WITS
And though it were through the world round,
We will not depart for sweet nor sour.

BEAUTY
No more will I unto death's hour,
Whatsoever thereof befall.

DISCRETION
Everyman, advise you first of all,
Go with a good advisement and deliberation.
We all give you virtuous monition
That all shall be well.

EVERYMAN
My friends, hearken what I will tell.
I pray God reward you in his heavenly sphere.
Now hearken, all that be here,
For I will make my testament
Here before every one present.
In alms half my good I will give with my hands twain
In the way of charity, with good intent,
And the other half shall remain
In quiet to be returned where it ought to be.
This I do in despite of the fiend of hell,
To go quit of his peril
Ever after and this day.

KNOWLEDGE
Everyman, hearken what I say.
Go to priesthood, I advise,
And receive of him in any wise
The holy sacrament and ointment together,
Then shortly see ye turn again hither.
We will all await you here.

FIVE-WITS
Yea, Everyman, haste you that ye ready be.
There is no emperor, king, duke, nor baron,
That of God hath commission,
As hath the least priest in the world's design.
For of the blessed sacraments pure and benign,
He beareth the keys and thereof hath the cure
For man's redemption, that is ever sure;
Which God for our soul's medicine
Gave us out of his heart with great pine.
Here in this transitory life, for thee and me,
The blessed sacraments seven there be,[2]
Baptism, confirmation, with priesthood good,
And the sacrament of God's precious flesh and blood,
Marriage, the holy extreme unction, and penance;
These seven be good to have in remembrance,
Gracious sacraments of high divinity.

EVERYMAN
Fain would I receive that holy body
And meekly to my spiritual father I will go.

FIVE-WITS
Everyman, that is the best that ye can do.
God will you to salvation bring,
For priesthood exceedeth all other thing.
To us Holy Scripture they do teach,
And convert man from his sin heaven to reach;
God hath to them more power given
Than to any angel that is in heaven.
With five words he may consecrate
God's body in flesh and blood to make,
And holdeth his maker between his hands,
The priest bindeth and unbindeth all bands,
Both in earth and in heaven,
He ministers all the sacraments seven.—
Though we kissed thy feet thou wert worthy,
Thou art surgeon that cureth sin deadly.
No remedy we find that is good
But only under priesthood.
Everyman, God gave priests that dignity,
And setteth them in his stead among us to be—
Thus be they above angels in degree.

EVERYMAN departs.

As his strength wanes, Everyman asks his new friends to accompany him to the grave, but for their own reasons, each must refuse. Good-Deeds, however, offers to go with him and speaks to him about the vanity of human existence. Everyman and Good-Deeds then descend into the grave, the Angel speaks, and the drama concludes with an epilogue, spoken by the Doctor who relates the moral of the play.

EVERYMAN
I had thought surer I should have you found.

Exit STRENGTH.

He that trusteth in his Strength
She deceiveth him at the length.
Both Strength and Beauty forsaking me,
Yet they promised me fair and lovingly.

DISCRETION
Everyman, I will after Strength be gone,
As for me I will leave you alone.

EVERYMAN
Why, Discretion, will ye forsake me?

DISCRETION
Yea, in faith, I will go from thee,
For when Strength goeth before
I follow after evermore.

EVERYMAN
Yet, I pray thee, for the love of Trinity,
Look in my grave once piteously.

---

[2]The seven sacraments to which Five-Wits refers are more commonly known as follows: Baptism, Confirmation, Ordination ("priesthood good"), Eucharist ("God's precious flesh and blood"), Marriage, Last Rites ("holy the extreme unction"), and Penance.

DISCRETION
Nay, so nigh will I not come.
Farewell, every one!

Exit DISCRETION.

EVERYMAN
O all thing faileth, save God alone;
Beauty, Strength, and Discretion;
For when Death bloweth his blast
They all run from me full fast.

FIVE-WITS
Everyman, my leave now of thee I take;
I will follow the other, for here I thee forsake.

EVERYMAN
Alas! then my I wail and weep,
For I took you for my best friend.

FIVE-WITS
I will not longer thee keep.
Now farewell, and there an end.

Exit FIVE-WITS.

EVERYMAN
O Jesu, have forsaken me!

GOOD-DEEDS
Nay, Everyman, I will bide with thee,
I will not forsake thee indeed,
Thou shalt find me a good friend at need.

EVERYMAN
Gramercy, Good-Deeds, now, may I true friends see.
They have forsaken me every one.
I loved them better than my Good-Deeds alone.
Knowledge, will ye forsake me also?

KNOWLEDGE
Yea, Everyman, when ye to death do go,
But not yet for no manner of danger.

EVERYMAN
Gramercy, Knowledge, with all my heart.

KNOWLEDGE
Nay, yet I will not from hence depart,
Till I be sure where ye shall come.

EVERYMAN
Methinketh, alas, that I must be on,
To make my reckoning and debts to pay,
For I see my time is nigh spent away.
Take example, all ye that this do hear or see,
How they that I loved best do forsake me,
Except my Good-Deeds that bideth truly.

GOOD-DEEDS
All earthly things are but vanity:
Beauty, Strength, and Discretion, do man forsake,

Foolish friends and kinsmen, that fair spake,
All flee save Good-Deeds, and he am I.

EVERYMAN
Have mercy on me, God most mighty;
And stand by me, thou Mother and Maid, holy Mary.

GOOD-DEEDS
Fear not, I will speak for thee.

EVERYMAN
Here I cry God mercy.

GOOD-DEEDS
Shorten our end, and diminish our pain.
Let us go and never come again.

EVERYMAN
Into Thy hands, Lord, my soul I commend.
Receive it, Lord, that it be not lost!
As thou boughtest me, me so defend,
And rescue from the fiend's boast,
That I may appear with that blessed host
That shall be saved at the day of doom.
In manus tuas [into your hands]—of might's utmost
Forever—*commendo spiritum meum* [I command my spirit].

EVERYMAN *and* GOOD-DEEDS *enter the grave.*

KNOWLEDGE
Now hath he suffered what we all shall endure,
But Good-Deeds shall make all sure.
Now hath he made ending—
Methinketh I hear angels sing
And make great joy and melody,
Where Everyman's soul received shall be.

An ANGEL *appears.*

ANGEL
Come, excellent elect spouse to Jesu!
Hereabove thou shalt go
Because of thy singular virtue.
Now the soul is taken from the body so,
Thy reckoning is crystal-clear.
Now shalt thou into the heavenly sphere,
Unto which all ye shall come
That live well before the day of doom.

EPILOGUE

DOCTOR
This moral men may have in mind:
Ye hearers, take it of worth, old and young,
And forsake pride, for he deceiveth you in the end,
And remember Beauty, Five-Wits, Strength, and
  Discretion,
They all at the last do Everyman forsake,
Alone his Good-Deeds there doth he take.
But beware, if they be small

Before God, man hath no help at all.
No excuse may there be for Everyman—
Alas, what shall he do then?
For after death amends may no man make,
For then mercy and pity him forsake.
If his reckoning be not clear when he come,
God will say—*ite maledicti in ignem æternum.*[3]

And he that hath his account whole and sound,
High in heaven he shall be crowned,
Unto which place God bring us all thither
That we may live body and soul together.
Thereto help blessed Trinity.
Amen, say ye, for Saint Charity.
Thus endeth this moral play of Everyman.

---

[3]Go into the eternal fire, ye cursed ones.

2 Italian Vernacular Literature

During the Middle Ages, Latin was the international language of learning in the West. There were also, however, vernacular languages, that is, the language of everyday speech in each country. In Italy, the vernacular form used in the area of Florence, the Tuscan dialect, became the dominant dialect and formed the basis for modern Italian. Dante, Petrarch, and Giovanni Boccaccio (1313–1375) were the pioneers in writing literature in the Tuscan dialect. Although Boccaccio is known as a progenitor of Renaissance humanism because of his Latin writings, he is best known for his vernacular masterpiece, *The Decameron.* Many of the tales related in *The Decameron* were subsequently transformed by Geoffrey Chaucer for his *Canterbury Tales.*

Giovanni Boccaccio
The Decameron

The Decameron opens in Florence just after the bubonic plague ravaged Europe in 1348–1349. In the opening pages, Boccaccio, in striking detail, describes the effects of the disease and the fanatical fear people had of being infected.

In the year 1348 after the fruitful incarnation of the Son of God, that most beautiful of Italian cities, noble Florence, was attacked by deadly plague. It started in the East either through the influence of the heavenly bodies or because God's just anger with our wicked deeds sent it as a punishment to mortal men; and in a few years killed an innumerable quantity of people. Ceaselessly passing from place to place, it extended its miserable length over the West. Against this plague all human wisdom and foresight were vain. Orders had been given to cleanse the city of filth, the entry of any sick person was forbidden, much advice was given for keeping healthy; at the same time humble supplications were made to God by pious persons in procession, and otherwise. And yet, in the beginning of the spring of the year mentioned, its horrible results began to appear, and in a miraculous manner. The symptoms

were not the same as in the East, where a gush of blood from the nose was the plain sign of inevitable death; but it began both in men and women with certain swellings in the groin or under the armpit. They grew to the size of a small apple or an egg, more or less, and were vulgarly called tumours. In a short space of time these tumours spread from the two parts named all over the body. Soon after this the symptoms changed and black or purple spots appeared on the arms or thighs or any other part of the body, sometimes a few large ones, sometimes many little ones. These spots were a certain sign of death, just as the original tumour had been and still remained.

No doctor's advice, no medicine could overcome or alleviate this disease. An enormous number of ignorant men and women set up as doctors in addition to those who were trained. Either the disease was such that no treatment was possible or the doctors were so ignorant that they did not know what caused it, and consequently could not administer the proper remedy. In any case very few recovered; most people died within about three days of the appearance of the tumours described above, most of them without any fever or other symptoms.

The violence of this disease was such that the sick communicated it to the healthy who came near them, just as a fire catches anything dry or oily near it. And it even went further. To speak to or go near the sick brought infection and a common death to the living; and moreover, to touch the clothes or anything else the sick had touched or worn gave the disease to the person touching.

What I am about to tell now is a marvellous thing to hear; and if I and others had not seen it with our own eyes I would not dare to write it, however much I was willing to believe and whatever the good faith of the person from whom I heard it. So violent was the malignancy of this plague that it was communicated, not only from one man to another, but from the garments of a sick or dead man to animals of another species, which caught the disease in that way and very quickly died of it. One day among other occasions I saw with my own eyes (as I said just now) the rags left lying in the street of a poor man who had died of the plague; two pigs came along and, as their habit is, turned the clothes over with their snouts and then munched at them with the result that they both fell dead almost at once on the rags, as if they had been poisoned.

From these and similar or greater occurrences, such fear and fanciful notions took possession of the living that almost all of them adopted the same cruel policy, which was entirely to avoid the sick and everything belonging to them. By so doing, each one thought he would secure his own safety.

Some thought that moderate living and the avoidance of all superfluity would preserve them from the epidemic. They formed small communities, living entirely separate from everybody else. They shut themselves up in houses where there were no sick, eating the finest food and drinking the best wine very temperately, avoiding all excess, allowing no news or discussion of death and sickness, and passing the time in music and suchlike pleasures. Others thought just the opposite. They thought the sure cure for the plague was to drink and be merry, to go about singing and amusing themselves, satisfying every appetite they could, laughing and jesting at what happened. They put their words into practice, spent day and night going from tavern to tavern, drinking immoderately, or went into other people's houses, doing only those things which pleased them. This they could easily do because everyone felt doomed and had abandoned his property, so that most houses became common property and any stranger who went in made use of them as if he had owned them. And with all this bestial behaviour, they avoided the sick as much as possible.

In this suffering and misery of our city, the authority of human and divine laws almost disappeared, for, like other men, the ministers and the executors of the laws were all dead or sick or shut up with their families, so that no duties were carried out. Every man was therefore able to do as he pleased.

Many others adopted a course of life midway between the two just described. They did not restrict their victuals so much as the former, nor allow themselves to be drunken and dissolute like the latter, but satisfied their appetites moderately. They did not shut themselves up, but went about, carrying flowers or scented herbs or perfumes in their hands, in the belief that it was an excellent thing to comfort the brain with such odours; for the whole air was infected with the smell of dead bodies, of sick persons and medicines.

Others again held a still more cruel opinion, which they thought would keep them safe. They said that the only medicine against the plaguestricken was to go right away from them. Men and women, convinced of this and caring about nothing but themselves, abandoned their own city, their own houses, their dwellings, their relatives, their property, and went abroad or at least to the country round Florence, as if God's wrath in punishing men's wickedness with this plague would not follow them but strike only those who remained within the walls of the city, or as if they thought nobody in the city would remain alive and that its last hour had come.

Not everyone who adopted any of these various opinions died, nor did all escape. Some when they were still healthy had set the example of avoiding the sick and, falling ill themselves, died untended.

One citizen avoided another, hardly any neighbour troubled about others, relatives never or hardly ever visited each other. Moreover, such terror was struck into the hearts of men and women by this calamity, that brother abandoned brother, and the uncle his nephew, and the sister her brother, and very often the wife her husband. What is even worse and nearly incredible is that fathers and mothers refused to see and tend their children, as if they had not been theirs.

Thus, a multitude of sick men and women were left without any care except from the charity of friends (but these were few), or the greed of servants, though not many of these could be had even for high wages. Moreover, most of them were coarse-minded men and women, who did little more than bring the sick what they asked for or watch over them when they were dying. And very often these servants lost their lives and their earnings. Since the sick were thus abandoned by neighbours, relatives and friends, while servants were scarce, a habit sprang up which had never been heard of before. Beautiful and noble women, when they fell sick, did not scruple to take a young or old manservant, whoever he might be, and with no sort of shame, expose every part of their bodies to these men as if they had been women, for they were compelled by the necessity of their sickness to do so. This, perhaps, was a cause of looser morals in those women who survived.

In this way many people died who might have been saved if they had been looked after. Owing to the lack of attendants for the sick and the violence of the plague, such a multitude of people in the city died day and night that it was stupefying to hear of, let alone to see. From sheer necessity, then, several ancient customs were quite altered among the survivors.

The custom had been (as we still see it today), that women relatives and neighbours should gather at the house of the deceased, and there lament with the family. At the same time the men would gather at the door with the male neighbours and other citizens. Then came the clergy, few or many according to the dead person's rank; the coffin was placed on the shoulders of his friends and carried with funeral pomp of lighted candles and dirges to the church which the deceased had chosen before dying. But as the fury of the plague increased, this custom wholly or nearly disappeared, and new customs arose. Thus, people died, not only without having a number of women near them, but without a single witness. Very few indeed were honoured with the piteous laments and bitter tears of their relatives, who, on the contrary, spent their time in mirth, feasting and jesting. Even the women abandoned womanly pity and adopted this custom for their own safety. Few were they whose bodies were accompanied to church by more than ten or a dozen neighbours. Nor were these grave and honourable citizens but grave-diggers from the lowest of the people who got themselves called sextons, and performed the task for money. They took up the bier and hurried it off, not to the church chosen by the deceased but to the church nearest, preceded by four or six of the clergy with few candles and often none at all. With the aid of the grave-diggers, the clergy huddled the bodies away in any grave they could find, without giving themselves the trouble of a long or solemn burial service.

The plight of the lower and most of the middle classes was even more pitiful to behold. Most of them remained in their houses, either through poverty or in hopes of safety, and fell sick by thousands. Since they received no care and attention, almost all of them died. Many ended their lives in the streets both at night and during the day; and many others who died in their houses were only known to be dead because the neighbours smelled their decaying bodies. Dead bodies filled every corner. Most of them were treated in the same manner by the survivors, who were more concerned to get rid of their rotting bodies than moved by charity towards the dead. With the aid of porters, if they could get them, they carried the bodies out of the houses and laid them at the doors, where every morning quantities of the dead might be seen. They then were laid on biers, or as these were often lacking, on tables.

Often a single bier carried two or three bodies, and it frequently happened that a husband and wife, two or three brothers, or father and son were taken off on the same bier. It frequently happened that two priests, each carrying a cross, would go out followed by three or four biers carried by porters; and where the priests thought there was one person to bury, there would be six or eight, and often, even more. Nor were these dead honoured by tears and lighted candles and mourners, for things had reached such a pass that people cared no more for dead men than we care for dead goats. Thus it plainly appeared that what the wise had not learned to endure with patience through the few calamities of ordinary life, became a matter of indifference even to the most ignorant people through the greatness of this misfortune.

Such was the multitude of corpses brought to the churches every day and almost every hour that there was not enough consecrated ground to give them burial, especially since they wanted to bury each person in the family grave, according to the old custom. Although the cemeteries were full they were forced to dig huge trenches, where they buried the bodies by hundreds. Here they stowed them away like bales in the hold of a ship and covered them with a little earth, until the whole trench was full.

Not to pry any further into all the details of the miseries which afflicted our city, I shall add that the surrounding country was spared nothing of what befell Florence. The villages on a smaller scale, were like the city; in the fields and isolated farms the poor wretched peasants and their families were without doctors and any assistance, and perished in the highways, in their fields and houses, night and day, more like beasts than men. Just as the townsmen became dissolute and indifferent to their work and property, so the peasants, when they saw that death was upon them, entirely neglected the future fruits of their past labours both from the earth and from cattle, and thought only of enjoying what they had. Thus it happened that crows, asses, sheep, goats, pigs, fowls and even dogs, those faithful companions of man, left the farms and wandered at their will through the fields, where the wheat crops stood abandoned, unreaped and ungarnered. Many of these animals seemed endowed with reason, for, after they had pastured all day, they returned to the farms for the night of their own free will, without being driven.

Returning from the country to the city, it may be said such was the cruelty of Heaven, and perhaps in part of men, that between March and July more than one hundred thousand persons died within the walls of Florence, what between the violence of the plague and the abandonment in which the sick were left by the cowardice of the healthy. And before the plague it was not thought that the whole city held so many people.

Oh, what great palaces, how many fair houses and noble dwellings, once filled with attendants and nobles and ladies, were emptied to the meanest servant! How many famous names and vast possessions and renowned estates were left without an heir! How many gallant men and fair ladies and handsome youths, whom Galen, Hippocrates and Æsculapius themselves would have said were in perfect health, at noon dined with their relatives and friends, and at night supped with their ancestors in the next world!

After describing the effects of the disease, Boccaccio allows the plot to commence. Seven ladies and three young men, fearful of the plague, decide to flee into the country. Once there, they agree to tell stories to pass the time—each person is to tell ten tales over a ten-day period, for a total of one hundred stories. Boccaccio's stories frequently feature sensual love between men and women, and the tone is quite secular. Often the theme of love is coupled with criticism of licentious clergymen as is evident in the second tale of the eighth day, which relates how a priest arranges to have sex with a woman on a day when her husband goes into town on business.

Fair ladies, I mean to tell you a little tale about those who are constantly injuring us without our being able to injure them in the same way—I mean the priests, who have declared a Crusade against our wives, and seem to think that when they can get on one of them they have obtained forgiveness of their sins as much as if they had brought the Sultan captive from Alexandria to Avignon. We poor men of the world cannot do the like to them, although we should avenge ourselves by attacking no less eagerly the mothers, sisters, female friends and daughters of priests. So I mean to tell you about a pleasant love affair, which is not long but amusing from its conclusion; and you may at least learn from it that priests are not to be believed in everything.

In Varlungo, a village which is not far from here (as each of you knows or has heard) there was a worthy priest, most valiant of person in the service of ladies. Although he could not read much, every Sunday at the foot of an elm he comforted his parishioners with good and holy discourses. And when the male parishioners were absent, there never was a priest who more willingly visited their wives, taking them fairings and holy water and a few candle-ends, and giving them his blessing.

Now, among all his female parishioners one especially charmed him. This was one Monna Belcolore, the wife of a labourer, who went by the name of Bentivegna del Mazzo. She was a pleasant, fresh, brown-skinned, buxom peasant-girl, who knew how to grind the mill better than anyone. Moreover, she was a skilled performer on the cymbals and could sing: "The water flows in the cleft," and, waving a pocket handkerchief in her hand, dance Sellinger's Round better than any of her neighbours. All these things so charmed our priest that he was frantic about her, and rambled about all day trying to catch a glimpse of her. When he knew she was in church on Sunday morning, he lifted up his voice with a *Kyrie* or a *Sanctus* to show her what a fine singing voice he had, and brayed like an ass; whereas, if she were not there, he passed over them very hurriedly. But yet he acted in such a way that neither Bentivegna del Mazzo nor any other man observed him.

In order to become more familiar with Monna Belcolore, he was continually sending her gifts. At one time he sent her a bunch of fresh garlic bulbs, for he grew the best of anyone in the district in his garden, which he dug with his own hands; then a little basket of peas in their pods or a bunch of fresh onions or shallots. Choosing his time, he would gaze at

her in a gloomy way and heap amorous reproaches on her, while she with rustic awkwardness pretended not to notice and went her way disdainfully; so that messer priest could not come to the point.

One afternoon when the priest was sauntering along he met Bentivegna del Mazzo with a laden ass; and after joking with him, asked him where he was going. Bentivegna replied:

"Why, father, I'm going into the city on business and I'm taking these things to Ser Bonacorri da Ginestreto, who is helping me about some lawsuit where I've got to appear before the clerk to the justice of the 'Sizes."

Said the priest:

"Well done, my son, go, with my blessing, and come back soon. And if you see Lapuccio or Naldino don't forget to tell them to bring the straps for my harness."

Bentivegna said it should be done, and as he went off in the direction of Florence the priest thought that now was the time to go to Belcolore and try his luck. So, putting his best foot forward, he made no pause until he reached her cottage, which he entered, saying:

"God bless this house—who is within?"

Belcolore, who was in the hay shed, heard him and said:

"O father, you're kindly welcome. But what are you doing out in this heat?"

"So God be good to me," replied the priest. "I came to spend a little time with you, for I met your good man going into the town."

Belcolore came down and took a seat and began to sift some cabbage seed which her husband had gathered.

"Ah, Belcolore," said the priest, "must you always make me die in this way?"

Belcolore giggled, and said:

"Why, what do I do?"

"You don't do anything," said the priest, "but you won't let me do to you what I want to do and what God commands."

"Get away with you!" said Belcolore. "Priests don't do such things."

"Yes, we do," said the priest, "and better than other men. Why not? And we are better workers than other men. Do you know why? Because we only grind at harvest time. But you'll find it out for yourself if you'll only lie still and let me go."

"What good would it do me," said Belcolore, "when all you priests are as mean as you can be?"

"I don't know," said the priest. "Ask what you want. Do you want a pair of shoes or some ribbons or a piece of fine cloth, or what do you want?"

"Right you are, brother!" said Belcolore. "I don't want any of those things, but if you are so fond of me will you do me a service, and I'll do what you want?"

"Say what you want," said the priest, "and I'll gladly do it."

Then said Belcolore:

"On Saturday I have to go to Florence, to hand in the wool I have spun and to have my spinning-wheel mended. If you'll lend me five lire, which I know you have, I can take out of pawn my dark petticoat and my best girdle which I had to take to uncle, and you know that without them I can't go to church or anywhere else; and then I'll always do what you want."

"So help me God," said the priest. "I haven't them with me; but trust me, and you shall have them gladly before Saturday."

"Yes," said Belcolore, "you're all great promisers, and keep your word not at all. Do you think you can treat me like Biliuzza, who went away with nothing but promises? God's Faith, it was that sent her on the streets. If you haven't got them, go and get them."

"Ah!" said the priest, "don't make me go back home now. I see that my luck has been so good that no one else is here, and perhaps when I came back someone would be here and interrupt us. I don't know when there will be such a good chance as now."

"Ah, well!" said she. "If you want to go, go; if not, stay as you are."

The priest saw that she would not do what he wanted unless she were *salvum me fac,* and would do nothing *sine custodia;* so he said:

"I see you don't believe I would get them; to convince you I'll leave with you my cloak of Turkish cloth."

Belcolore lifted her head, and said:

"Yes? And what is your cloak worth?"

"What's it worth?" said the priest. "Why, it comes from Douai in Touai and some of our people would call it Fourai. Not a fortnight ago I paid seven lire for it to Lotto the old clothes man and made five soldi on the bargain, according to what Buglietto told me, and you know he's an expert in all such cloths."

"Oh, is it?" said Belcolore. "God help me, I should never have thought so; but give it me first."

Messer priest, who had shot his bolt, took off his cloak and gave it to her. And when she had put it away, she said:

"Father, come along to the hayloft. Nobody ever goes there."

There the priest gave her the sweetest flopping kisses and enjoyed her for a long space of time, making her a relative of the Lord God. He then departed in his cassock, as if he had been to a wedding; and returned to his church.

But when he reflected that all the candle-ends he collected in a whole year were not worth one half of five lire, he felt he had made a mistake, regretted having left his cloak behind, and began to think of some means of getting his cloak back for nothing. And since he was a very cunning fellow, he thought of a way of getting it back, which succeeded. The next day was a festival, and he sent a little boy to Monna Belcolore's house to ask her to lend him her stone mortar, because that morning Binguccio dal Poggio and Nuto Buglietti were going to dine with him and he wanted to make sauce. Belcolore sent him the mortar. And at dinner time when the priest knew Bentivegna del Mazzo and Belcolore would be eating, he sent for the parish clerk, and said:

"Take this mortar to Belcolore and say: 'The parson thanks you and will you send him back the cloak which the little boy left as a pledge?'"

The clerk went off to Belcolore's cottage with the mortar and found her at table with Bentivegna. He laid down the mortar and delivered his message. When Belcolore heard him ask for the cloak she tried to speak, but Bentivegna interrupted her angrily.

"So you take pledges from the parson, do you? By Christ, I'd like to give you a good wipe in the nose. Give it back at once, and a pox on you. And henceforth if he wants anything of ours, even the ass, don't you say 'No' to him!"

Belcolore got up grumbling and went to the chest under the bed, took out the cloak, and as she gave it to the clerk, she said:

"Say to the priest: 'Belcolore says that she prays God you may never again grind sauce in her mortar, not having done her any honour in this.'"

The clerk went off with the cloak and delivered the message to the priest, who said, laughing:

"When you see her, tell her that if she won't lend the mortar, I won't lend the pestle—tit for tat."

Bentivegna supposed his wife said these words because he had scolded her, and thought no more about them. But Belcolore was furious with the parson, and would not speak to him until vintage time. Then, after threatening to send the priest into the biggest devil's mouth, she made it up with him over new wine and hot chestnuts, and thereafter they often gorged together. Instead of the five lire the priest mended her cymbals and hung her up a large bell; and she was well satisfied.

3 An Early Masterpiece of Vernacular English

Using the framing device of Boccaccio's *Decameron*—tales within a tale—Geoffrey Chaucer (c. 1340–1400) wrote his masterpiece, *The Canterbury Tales* (after 1386), the first major work written in vernacular English. He presents thirty people assembled at the Tabard Inn who are about to embark upon a pilgrimage to the shrine of Saint Thomas à Becket, who became the Archbishop of Canterbury in 1162 and was murdered by agents of King Henry II, eight years later, as he said his evening prayers at his own altar in Canterbury Cathedral. To pass the time, each pilgrim is to tell two stories going to the shrine and two on the way back, for a total of 120 tales. (However, Chaucer only completed twenty-four of them.) As the son of a successful wine merchant, Chaucer received a good education and had an intimate understanding of the merchant class, but he spent most of his life serving members of the royal family. Chaucer's source material was drawn from ancient authors, including Virgil and Ovid; contemporary works, including the writings of Dante, Petrarch, and Boccaccio; but most important, Chaucer employed his understanding of all classes of society, about whom he had been curious all his life. Consequently, in many cases, Chaucer's characters are "caricatures"—personifying virtues and vices to which all human beings are subject—which makes the *Canterbury Tales* reminiscent of medieval morality plays (see earlier discussion of *Everyman*).

Geoffrey Chaucer
The Canterbury Tales

The following passages are taken from Chaucer's *General Prologue* in which he creates vignettes of his pilgrims, including their occupation and appearance, as they assemble at the Tabard Inn in Southwark, not far from where Chaucer lived.

[O]ne day

In Southwark, at *The Tabard,* as I lay
Ready to go on pilgrimage and start
For Canterbury, most devout at heart,
At night there came into that hostelry
Some nine and twenty in a company
Of sundry folk happening then to fall
In fellowship, and they were pilgrims all
That towards Canterbury meant to ride.
The rooms and stables of the inn were wide;
They made us easy, all was of the best.
And shortly, when the sun had gone to rest,
By speaking to them all upon the trip
I soon was one of them in fellowship
And promised to rise early and take the way
To Canterbury, as you heard me say.

But none the less, while I have time and space,
Before my story takes a further pace,
It seems a reasonable thing to say
What their condition was, the full array
Of each of them, as it appeared to me
According to profession and degree,
And what apparel they were riding in;
And at a Knight I therefore will begin.
There was a *Knight,* a most distinguished man,
Who from the day on which he first began
To ride abroad had followed chivalry,
Truth, honour, generousness and courtesy.

He had done nobly in his sovereign's war
And ridden into battle, no man more,
As well in christian as in heathen places,
And ever honoured for his noble graces. . . .
He was of sovereign value in all eyes.
And though so much distinguished, he was wise
And in his bearing modest as a maid.
He never yet a boorish thing had said
In all his life to any, come what might;
He was a true, a perfect gentle-knight. . . .
    He had his son with him, a fine young *Squire,*
A lover and cadet, a lad of fire
With locks as curly as if they had been pressed.
He was some twenty years of age, I guessed.
In stature he was of a moderate length,
With wonderful agility and strength. . . .
He was embroidered like a meadow bright
And full of freshest flowers, red and white.
Singing he was, or fluting all the day;
He was as fresh as is the month of May.
Short was his gown, the sleeves were long and wide;
He knew the way to sit a horse and ride.
He could make songs and poems and recite,
Knew how to joust and dance, to draw and write.
He loved so hotly that till dawn grew pale
He slept as little as a nightingale.
Courteous he was, lowly and serviceable,
And carved to serve his father at the table. . . .

There also was a *Nun,* a Prioress.[1]
Her way of smiling very simple and coy. . . .
Her greatest oath was only 'By St Loy!'
And she was known as Madam Eglantyne.
And well she sang a service, with a fine
Intoning through her nose, as was most seemly,
And she spoke daintily in French. . . .
She certainly was very entertaining,
Pleasant and friendly in her ways, and straining
To counterfeit a courtly kind of grace,
A stately bearing fitting to her place,
And to seem dignified in all her dealings.
As for her sympathies and tender feelings,
She was so charitably solicitous
She used to weep if she but saw a mouse
Caught in a trap, if it were dead or bleeding. . . .
She was all sentiment and tender heart.
Her veil was gathered in a seemly way,
Her nose was elegant, her eyes glass-grey;
Her mouth was very small, but soft and red,
Her forehead, certainly, was fair of spread,
Almost a span across the brows, I own;
She was indeed by no means undergrown. . . .
    A *Monk* there was, one of the finest sort
Who rode the country; hunting was his sport.
A manly man, to be an Abbot able;
Many a dainty horse he had in stable.
His bridle, when he rode, a man might hear
Jingling in a whistling wind as clear,
Aye, and as loud as does the chapel bell
Where my lord Monk was Prior of the cell. . . .
He let go by the things of yesterday
And took the modern world's more spacious way. . . .
Hunting a hare or riding at a fence
Was all his fun, he spared for no expense.
I saw his sleeves were garnished at the hand
With fine grey fur, the finest in the land,
And on his hood, to fasten it at his chin
He had a wrought-gold cunningly fashioned pin;
Into a lover's knot it seemed to pass.
His head was bald and shone like looking-glass;
So did his face, as if it had been greased.
He was a fat and personable priest;
His prominent eyeballs never seemed to settle.
They glittered like the flames beneath a kettle;
Supple his boots, his horse in fine condition.
He was a prelate fit for exhibition,
He was not pale like a tormented soul.
He liked a fat swan best, and roasted whole. . . .
    There was a *Friar,* a wanton one and merry,
A Limiter,[2] a very festive fellow.

In all Four Orders[3] there was none so mellow
So glib with gallant phrase and well-turned speech.
He'd fixed up many a marriage, giving each
Of his young women what he could afford her.
He was a noble pillar to his Order.
Highly beloved and intimate was he
With County folk within his boundary,
And city dames of honour and possessions;
For he was qualified to hear confessions,
Or so he said, with more than priestly scope;
He had a special license from the Pope.
Sweetly he heard his penitents at shrift
With pleasant absolution, for a gift.
He was an easy man in penance-giving
Where he could hope to make a decent living. . . .
    There was a *Merchant* with a forking beard
And motley dress; high on his horse he sat,
Upon his head a Flemish beaver hat
And on his feet daintily buckled boots.
He told of his opinions and pursuits
In solemn tones, and how he never lost. . . .
This estimable Merchant so had set
His wits to work, none knew he was in debt,
He was so stately in negotiation,
Loan, bargain and commercial obligation.
He was an excellent fellow all the same;
To tell the truth I do not know his name.
    An *Oxford Cleric,* still a student though,
One who had taken logic long ago,
Was there. . . .   By his bed
He preferred having twenty books in red
And black, of Aristotle's philosophy,
To having fine clothes, fiddle or psaltery. . . .
Whatever money from his friends he took
He spent on learning or another book
And prayed for them most earnestly, returning
Thanks to them thus for paying for his learning.
His only care was study, and indeed
He never spoke a word more than was need,
Formal at that, respectful in the extreme,
Short, to the point, and lofty in his theme.
The thought of moral virtue filled his speech
And he would gladly learn, and gladly teach. . . .
    There was a *Franklin*[4] with him, it appeared;
White as a daisy-petal was his beard.
A sanguine man, high-coloured and benign,
He loved a morning sop of cake in wine. . . .
His bread, his ale were finest of the fine
And no one had a better stock of wine.
His house was never short of bake-meat pies,

---

[1]A Prioress is the woman in charge of an abbey of nuns.

[2]A Limiter is a begging friar, granted a specific district in which to beg in, thus limiting his activities.

[3]The Four Orders refers to the Dominican Order, the Franciscan Order, the Carmelite Order, and the Austin Friars—all of which are mendicant friars.

[4]A Franklin is a class of landowner who is not a noble but is, nonetheless, free by virtue of his birth.

Of fish and flesh, and these in such supplies
It positively snowed with meat and drink
And all the dainties that a man could think.
According to the seasons of the year
Changes of dish were ordered to appear. . . .
As Sheriff he checked audit, every entry.
He was a model among landed gentry. . . .

A worthy *woman* from beside *Bath* city
Was with us, somewhat deaf, which was a pity. . . .
In all the parish not a dame dared stir
Towards the altar steps in front of her,
And if indeed they did, so wrath was she
As to be quite put out of charity. . . .
Bold was her face, handsome, and red in hue.
A worthy woman all her life, what's more
She'd had five husbands, all at the church door,
Apart from other company in youth;
No need just now to speak of that, forsooth.[5] . . .

A holy-minded man of good renown
There was, and poor, the *Parson* to a town,
Yet he was rich in holy thought and work.
He also was a learned man, a clerk,
Who truly knew Christ's gospel and would preach it
Devoutly to parishioners, and teach it. . . .
He stayed at home and watched over his fold
So that no wolf should make the sheep miscarry.
He was a shepherd and no mercenary.
Holy and virtuous he was, but then
Never contemptuous of sinful men,
Never disdainful, never too proud or fine,
But was discreet in teaching and benign. . . .

The *Miller* was a chap of sixteen stone,[6]
A great stout fellow big in brawn and bone.
He did well out of them, for he could go
And win the ram at any wrestling show.
His mighty mouth was like a furnace door.
A wrangler and buffoon, he had a store
Of tavern stories, filthy in the main.
His was a master-hand at stealing grain.
He felt it with his thumb and thus he knew
Its quality and took three times his due. . . .

There was a *Summoner*[7] with us in the place
Who had a fire-red cherubinnish face,[8]

---

[5]Forsooth means certainly.

[6]Sixteen stone is approximately 224 pounds.

[7]A Summoner is someone paid to "summon" a sinner to trial in a church court.

[8]Cherubinnish face refers to the cherubs of medieval art, who are generally portrayed as having faces the color of fire.

For he had carbuncles. His eyes were narrow,
He was as hot and lecherous as a sparrow.
Black, scabby brows he had, and a thin beard.
Children were afraid when he appeared. . . .
Garlic he loved, and onions too, and leeks,
And drinking strong wine till all was hazy.
Then he would shout and jabber as if crazy,
And wouldn't speak a word except in Latin. . . .

Now I have told you shortly, in a clause,
The rank, the array, the number and the cause
Of our assembly in this company. . . .
And now the time has come for me to tell
How we behaved that evening; I'll begin
After we had alighted at the Inn,
Then I'll report our journey, stage by stage,
All the remainder of our pilgrimage.
But first I beg of you, in courtesy,
Not to condemn me as unmannerly
If I speak plainly and with no concealings
And give account of all their words and dealings,
Using their very phrases as they fell.

Our *Host* gave us great welcome; everyone
Was given a place and supper was begun.
He served the finest victuals you could think,
The wine was strong and we were glad to drink.
A very striking man our Host withal,
And fit to be a marshal in a hall. . . .
"My lords," he said, "now listen for your good,
And please don't treat my notion with disdain.
This is the point. I'll make it short and plain.
Each one of you shall help to make things slip
By telling two stories on the outward trip
To Canterbury, that's what I intend,
And, on the homeward way to journey's end
Another two, tales from the days of old;
And then the man whose story is best told,
That is to say who gives the fullest measure
Of good morality and general pleasure,
He shall be given a supper, paid by all,
Here in this tavern, in this very hall,
When we come back again from Canterbury.
And in the hope to keep you bright and merry
I'll go along with you myself and ride
All at my own expense and serve as guide.
I'll be the judge, and those who won't obey
Shall pay for what we spend upon the way.
Now if you all agree to what you've heard
Tell me at once without another word,
And I will make arrangements early for it." . . .

The Nun's Priest's Tale

During the pilgrimage, the Knight interrupts the Monk's dull recital of a series of brief tragedies, and the Host calls upon him to tell another type of tale, but he refuses to do so. The Host then turns to the Nun's Priest for a new story. "The Nun's Priest's Tale," patterned after a fable by Marie de France (see page 188), is one of the most popular, captivating, and worldly beast fables ever written. The cock (Chantecleer), his hens, and the nefarious fox behave has if they were part of Homer's *Iliad* and *Odyssey*, or Virgil's *Aeneid*. Part of the joke comes from our awareness of the wide discrepancy between the description and the reality, as, for example, when the Priest tells us that the cock, walking on tiptoe, is regal or kinglike; another part comes from the shifting back and forth in tone between the seemingly serious and the plainly ridiculous, as when the hen cites a "learned authority" at one point and then recommends that the cock take a digestive of worms.

Once upon a time there was a poor old widow who lived in a small cottage beside a grove standing in a dale. This widow, since the day that she was last a wife, lived patiently a very simple life because her goods and her income were small. By handling thriftily what God sent her she supported herself and also her two daughters. She had three large sows, no more, three cows, and a sheep called Malle. Her "bower" and her "hall" in which she ate many a scanty meal were very sooty. [The words "bower" and "hall" are appropriate to the mansion or palace of a nobleman. We learn that the widow's hovel was a single room which also included the roosting place for the chickens.] She didn't need a spicy sauce; no dainty morsel passed through her throat. Her meals were appropriate to her clothing. Over-eating never made her sick. An abstemious diet was her medicine—that, and exercise and contentment at heart. Gout didn't keep her from dancing. Apoplexy didn't hurt her head. She drank no wine, neither red or white. Her table was served mostly with white and black—milk and black bread with which she found no fault, broiled bacon and, sometimes, an egg or two, for she was a sort of dairy woman.

She had a yard enclosed with dry sticks outside of which was a dry ditch. In the yard she had a cock named Chantecleer [clear singer]. No one in all the land was his equal in crowing. His voice was merrier than the merry organ played in the church on mass-days. His crowing in his "lodge" [again, upperclass] was more exact than any clock or any abbey's horologe. By nature he knew the ascension of the equinoctial [celestial equator] in that town; for each time it ascended 15 degrees he crowed; no one could indicate the hour more correctly.

His comb was redder than fine coral and battlemented like a castle wall. His bill was as black and shiny as jet. His legs and his toes were like azure; his nails whiter than the lily-flower. His feathers were colored like burnished gold.

This noble cock had in his governance seven hens to do what gave him pleasure. They were his sisters and his paramours.[1] They were wonderously like him in color. The one of them who had the most beautifully colored throat was named lovely Demoiselle Pertelote. She was courteous, discreet, meek, and companionable [words appropriate in praise of a noblewoman]. Since the day when she was seven nights old, she behaved so beautifully that she had Chantecleer's heart completely in her power. He loved her so much that all went well with him. When the bright sun arose, what a joy it was to hear them sing in sweet accord, "My beloved has gone to the country!" For in that time, as I understand it, birds and beasts knew how to talk and sing.

One dawn it happened that, as Chantecleer among all his wives sat on the porch, which was in the hall (and lovely Pertelote sat closest to him), he began to groan in his throat like a man who is sorely troubled in a dream. When Pertelote heard him roar in this way, she was aghast and said, "Dear heart, what is wrong with you that you groan like that. You are usually a good sleeper. Shame on you."

And he answered, "Madame, I pray you, don't take it amiss. By God, I dreamed right now that I was in such trouble that even now my heart is badly frightened. Now, for God's sake, interpret my dream favorably and keep my body out of a foul prison. I dreamed that I roamed up and down in our yard, and there I saw a beast, rather like a dog, who wanted to seize me and kill me. His color was between yellow and red, and his tail and both ears were tipped with black. His snout was small, and his two eyes were glowing. I still almost die from fear when I think of his looks. No doubt, this caused my groaning."

"For shame, coward," she said, "for shame. Alas, by God above, how you have lost my heart and all my love. I cannot love a coward, by my faith. For certainly, whatever any woman may say, we all desire, if it is possible, to have husbands who are brave, wise, generous, and discreet, and not a stingy man, nor a fool, nor one who is aghast at every weapon, nor a braggart, by God above! How dare you say—

---

[1] A paramour is an illicit lover.

for shame—to your beloved that anything could make you afraid? You don't have a man's heart even though you have a beard. Alas, can you be aghast of dreams? God knows, a dream is nothing but empty illusions. Dreams are caused by over-eating, and by fumes and mixtures when bodily fluids [humors] are too abundant in a person. Certainly, the dream you dreamed last night comes from a superfuity of red bile [choler]. It causes people in their dreams to dread arrows, and fires with red flames, red beasts and to fear that they will bite, also conflict and big and little whelps. In the same way the fluid melancholy [the humor black bile] causes many a man to cry out in his sleep for fear of black bears and black bulls or else black devils which want to seize them. I could tell about other humors, too, which cause distress to many a man in his sleep. But I'll pass over all that as lightly as possible."

"Consider Cato, who was so wise a man, didn't he say this: 'Pay no attention to dreams'? [Cato was the author of a Latin primer or first reading book.]

"Now, sire, when you fly down from the beams, for the love of God, take a laxative. May my soul and life be in peril if I am not giving you the best possible advice. I wouldn't lie to you in saying that on should purge yourself both of choler and melancholy. And so that you won't delay, though there is no pharmacist in this town, I myself will teach you what will be best for your health and benefit, and I will find in our yard those herbs which by nature have the power to purge you below and also above. For love of God, don't forget this: You are very choleric in your mixture of humors. Beware lest the sun in rising should find you filled with hot humors. Because, if you do, I would dare to bet a penny that you will have a tertain fever or an ague that may cause your death. For a day or two you will take digestives of worms before you take your laxatives of spurge-laurel, centaury, and fumitory, or else of hellebore, which grows there, or caper berry or gaiter berry, or pleasant herb-ivy growing in our yard. Peck them right up where they grow and eat them. Be merry, husband; dread no dream. I call tell you no more."

"Madame," he said, "Many thanks for your learned advice. But, nevertheless, concerning Lord Cato, who has such great renown for wisdom, though he told us not to dread dreams, by God, men may read in old books about many a man of more authority than Cato ever had, so help me, who say the very reverse of this advice, and who have well found by experience that dreams are significations both of joy and of tribulations which people endure in this present life. There is no need to devise arguments about this; the real proof is revealed in the event."

"One of the greatest authorities whom men read says this: Once upon a time two men, with very good intentions, went on a pilgrimage, and it so happened that they came to a town where there was such a congregation of people and so few rooms for sleeping that they couldn't find so much as a cottage in which they might both be lodged for the night. For that night they must necessarily separate. Each went to his hostelry and took such lodging as befell him. One of them was lodged far away in a yard with plow-oxen; the other was lodged well enough as was his chance or fortune which commonly governs all of us."

"It so happened that, long before day, the second man dreamed where he lay in his bed that his fellow pilgrim called to him and said, 'Alas, tonight I shall be murdered where I lie in an ox's stall. Help me, dear brother, or I'll die. In all haste, come to me'. Because of fear the man roused abruptly from his sleep, but when he was wholly awake, he turned over and took no heed. It seemed to him that his dream was only foolishness. He had the same dream a second time. In his third dream, it seemed to him that his companion came to him and said, 'I have now been slain. Look at my bloody wounds, deep and wide. Get up early in the morning, and at the west gate of the town you will see a cart load of dung in which my corpse is secretly hidden. Have that cart stopped by the authorities. To tell the truth, my gold caused me to be murdered'. And with a pitiful, pale face he told him every detail of how he had been killed. Now believe me, the man who dreamed found that his dream was entirely true, for in the morning, at daybreak, he took his way to his companion's inn, and when he came to the ox's stall, he begun to call his companion."

"The innkeeper answered him right away saying, 'Sire, your companion has gone. As soon as it was day, he went out of town'. The traveler, remembering his dream, became suspicious and went without hesitation to the town's west gate and found there a dung-cart going out as if to manure the land—a cart just like the one the dead man had described. He began boldly to cry for vengeance and justice on this felony. 'My companion was murdered during the night and lies dead in this cart. I call upon the authorities who rule this city, Harrow! [This cry—a legal one—announced to all who heard it that a crime was being committed. Everyone who heard the cry was duty bound to help capture the felon.] Here my companion lies slain.'"

"What more should I say. The people came out, overturned the cart, and found the newly murdered man in the middle of the dung."

"O blessed God, who art so just and true, thou revealest murder always. Murder will out, we see that day after day. Murder is so loathsome and abominable to God, who is so just and reasonable, that He will not suffer it to remain concealed though it may remain unknown for a year or two. Murder will out; this is my conclusion."

"And immediately the officers of the town seized the carter and the hosteler and put them to torture so that they confessed their wicked deed and were hanged by the neck."

"Thus may men see that dreams are to be feared. And indeed, in the next chapter of the same book I read—I'm not lying, so help me—that two men wanted for a certain purpose, to cross the sea to a far country. But the wind was contrary and made them stay in the city which stood on the side of a harbor. Then a few days later toward evening the wind changed and blew in exactly the way they wanted. Cheerful and glad they went to bed, determined to sail early next morning. But a great marvel happened to one of them. As he lay sleeping, he dreamed, near dawn, a wondrous dream. It seemed to him that a man stood beside his bed and commanded him to remain in the city and said to him, 'If you sail tomorrow, you will be drowned'. The traveler awoke and told his dream to his companion and begged him to give up his voyage, for that day at least. His companion, who lay by his bed side, laughed and made fun of him. 'No dream', he said, 'can so frighten me as to cause me to give up my plans. I wouldn't give a straw for your dream. Dreams are only illusions and deceits. Men dream constantly of owls and apes and many other illusions. Men dream of things that never have been nor ever will be. But since I see that you are determined to remain here and wilfully miss your tide, God knows, it makes me sorry, but still goodbye'. And thus he took his leave and went away. But before he had sailed fully half his course—I don't know why or what bad luck fell upon it, but by chance the ship's bottom split open, and man and ship sank in the sight of nearby ships which had sailed with it on the same tide."

"And, therefore, dear lovely Pertelote, from such examples you may learn that no man should be too careless about dreams, for I tell you certainly that many a dream is greatly to be feared."

"Consider the 'Life of St. Kenelm', the son of Kenulfus, the noble king of Mercia. In Kenelm's 'Life' I read that a little before he was murdered he saw his own murder in a dream. His nurse expounded to him every detail of his dream and told him to take great care against treason; but he was only seven years old and, therefore gave little importance to any dream; he was so holy at heart. By God, I'd give my shirt for you to have read this legend as I have."

"Madame Pertelote, truly, Macrobius who wrote about the 'Dream of Scipio'[2] asserts the validity of dreams and says that they are warnings of things which will be seen in the future. And, furthermore, I beg you to consider Daniel, in the Old Testament, whether he believed that dreams were illusions. Read there about Joseph, too, and you will see that dreams are sometimes—I don't say all dreams—warnings of future events. Consider Lord Pharaoh, the king of Egypt, and his baker and his butler, too, whether they didn't experience the effects of dreams. Whoever studies the histories of various kingdoms will read many wondrous things about dreams. For example, Croesus, king of Lydia, didn't he have a dream that he sat in a tree which signified that he would be hanged? Another example, Andromache, Hector's wife: The night before the day when Hector was to lose his life, she dreamed that he would be killed if he went into battle that day. She warned him but could not prevail upon him to stay. He went out to fight and was at once slain by Achilles. But that is too long a story to tell. Besides it is nearly day, and I must not remain here. But briefly, in conclusion, I say that I will have some misfortune from my dream. And further-

more, I say that I don't put any trust in laxatives because I know very well that they are poisonous. I repudiate them. I don't like them at all."

"But let's speak of pleasant things and stop all this. Madame Pertelote, by heaven, God has shown me much favor in one thing: When I see the beauty of your face, you are so scarlet red around your eyes that it makes me dread to die. It is certainly true, *In principio, mulier est hominis confusio.* [In the beginning, woman is the ruination of man]. Madame, the meaning of this Latin is: Woman is man's joy and all his happiness. For when at night I feel your soft side—even though I cannot tread you because, alas, our perch is to, narrow—I am so full of comfort and joy that I defy both dream and vision."

And with that word, they—and all his other hens—flew down from the beam because it was day. And with a cluck he began to call them because he had found a kernel of wheat which lay in the yard. He was very regal; he was no longer afraid. He feathered and trod Pertelote twenty times before it was fully daylight. He looked as if he were a grim lion as he roamed up and down on his toes: he didn't deign to set his foot to the ground. He clucks every time he finds a kernel, and all his wives run to him. Thus as royal as a prince in his great hall, I leave Chantecleer in his pasture, and later I will tell his adventure.

When March—the month the world began and in which God made man—when March was over and one day more, it happened that Chantecleer, in all his pride, his seven hens walking beside him, cast up his eyes to the bright sun which had passed through 21° and a little more in the sign of Taurus, and Chantecleer knew by nature, not by any learning, that it was the third hour of the day, he crowed with a cheerful sound and said, "The sun has climbed 21° and more in the heavens. Madame Pertelote, joy of my world, listen to the happy birds—how they sing! And look at the fresh flowers—how they bloom! My heart is full of merriment and comfort."

But suddenly a terrible thing happened to him: for happiness always turns into grief. Worldly happiness, God knows, is soon gone. And if a rhetorician really knew how to write well, he could write it in a chronicle as a most noteworthy truth. Now let everyone listen to me because this story is as true as *The Book of Lancelot de Lac,* which women admire so greatly. Now I will return to my theme.

A fox, full of crafty wickedness, who had lived in that grove for three years, on that very night (as the great vision had foretold) broke through the hedge into the yard where handsome Chantecleer and his wives were accustomed to walk. The fox lay still in a bed of cabbages, waiting for a time to fall upon Chantecleer, as eagerly as do all murderers who lie in wait to murder men.

O false murderer, lurking in your den! O, new Judas Iscariot, new Ganelon [who betrayed Charlemagne and Roland], false dissembler! O, Greek Sinon who brought Troy to utter ruin!

O, Chantecleer! May the morning be accursed on which you flew from the beam into the yard! You had been warned by your dreams that this day would be perilous for you. But

---

[2]Scipio was a Roman commander who conquered Carthage in North Africa. Cicero wrote "Scipio's Dream" in which he asserted the former greatness of the Roman Republic.

what God foreknows must be—according to the opinion of certain learned men. Any great scholar will tell you that in the universities there has been great altercation and great disputation on this subject, and it has involved a hundred thousand men. But I am not able to sift it to the bran [get down to the bare truth] as the holy doctor Augustine is able to, or Boethius, or Bishop Bradwardine—whether God's foreknowledge forces men of necessity to do a thing. By "necessity" I mean *simple necessity;* or whether I have been given free choice to do that thing or not do it, even though God foreknew it before it was done. Or whether his foreknowledge does not force it at all except by *conditional necessity.*

I don't want to have anything to do with that question. My story is about a cock, as you are about to hear, who, to his sorrow, took his wife's advice to walk in the yard on the morning when he had dreamed that dream I told you of. Women's advice is very often harmful; a woman's advice first brought mankind to woe, and made Adam leave Paradise where he had been happy and wholly at ease. But because I don't know whom I might displease if I blame the advice of women, forget it; I said it as a joke. Read the authorities where they deal with this subject, and you will learn what they say about women. These are the cock's words, not mine. I can't discern any harm in any woman.

Lovely Pertelote lies in the sun pleasantly bathing herself in the sand, and all her sisters near her. And Chantecleer freely sings more merrily than the mermaids in the sea; for *Physiologos* [*The Beastiary*] says that they sing very well and merrily. And it so happened that as Chantecleer glanced at a butterfly among the cabbages, he became aware of the fox who lay very close to the ground. He didn't in the least wish to crow then, but immediately cried out, "Cock, cock!" and startled like a man frightened to the heart; because an animal by nature desires to flee from his natural enemy if he should see him. Chantecleer, the moment he spied the fox, wanted to flee, but quickly the fox said, "Noble sire, alas, where do you want to go? Are you afraid of me? I am your friend. Indeed, I would be worse than a friend if I wanted to do any harm or injury to you. I haven't come to spy out your private affairs. But truly the only cause of my coming was to listen to you sing. My lord, your father—God bless his soul—and also your mother (bless her for her gentility) have both been in my house to my great pleasure. And certainly, sire, I would gladly please you. For when people talk about singing, I always say—may I lose my eyes if I'm lying—that, except for you, I never heard any man sing the way your father used to in the morning. Surely, all he sang was from the heart. And to make his voice stronger he would shut both his eyes very tightly, and stand on his tiptoes, and stretch his neck out until it was long and small around. And also he was so perceptive that no man anywhere could surpass him in singing or in wisdom. I have read among the verses of the book *Lord*

Burnel the Ass,[3] that there was a cock who, when he was young and ignorant, was injured in the leg by a priest's son. In revenge, the cock made the priest's son lose his benefice [appointment to a church office]. [The cock didn't wake him on the day he was to receive the office.] But certainly there is no comparison between the subtlety of this cock and the wisdom and discretion of your father. Now sing, sire, for the love of heaven, and let's see if you are able to imitate your father."

Chantecleer began to beat his wings like a man who cannot espy treachery; he was too carried away by the flattery.

Alas, O noble lords, how many false flatterers and liars are in your courts who please you much more, believe me, than any man who tells you the truth. Read *Ecclesiastes*[4] on flatterers, and beware, lords, of their treachery.

Chantecleer stood high on his toes, stretched out his neck, kept his eyes tightly closed and began to crow his very loudest crow. Lord Russell the fox immediately leapt up, grabbed Chantecleer by the neck, threw him over his back, and started to carry him off toward the woods because, as yet, no one, pursued him.

O destiny which no one can escape! Alas that Chantecleer flew down from the roost. Alas that his wife denied the significance of dreams. And all this misfortune happened on a Friday.

O Venus, goddess of pleasure, since Chantecleer was your devout worshiper and did all in his power to serve you (more for sensual delight than for procreation), how could you let him die on your day?

O Godfrey,[5] dear sovereign master [of rhetoric], when your worthy King Richard[6] was slain, how exquisitely you lamented his death. Why don't I have your skill and learning so that I could reproach Friday, as you did because your king was killed on a Friday? Then I would show you how ably I would lament for Chantecleer's fear and pain.

When Troy was captured and Pyrrhus[7] seized Priam[8] by the beard and killed him, as the *Aeneid* says, the ladies of the city never made half such a cry and lamentation as the hens of the yard made when they saw what was happening to Chantecleer. But Madame Pertelote shrieked most sovereignly, much louder than Hasdrubal's[9] wife shrieked when the Romans killed her husband and burned Carthage. She was so full of grief and despair that she rushed into the fire and burned herself with a steadfast heart. O woeful hens, you

---

[3]*Lord Burnel the Ass* is a medieval satire by Nigel Wireker (in the twelfth century) that refers to a priest who broke a cock's leg by throwing a rock at him. Consequently, the cock refused to crow on the day of the priest's ordination, thus making him late.

[4]*Ecclesiastes* is a book in the Old Testament.

[5]Godrey was an English duke who became the ruler of Jerusalem and the Christian territories following the First Crusade.

[6]King Richard, who ruled England from 1189–1199, was best known as Richard, the Lion-Heart.

[7]Pyrrhus was the son of Greek warrior, Achilles, hero of the Trojan War.

[8]Priam was King of Troy.

[9]Hasdrubal was a Roman conqueror during the Punic Wars.

cried out exactly as, when Nero[10] burned Rome, the wives of the senators cried out because their husbands had lost their lives, for Nero, though they were guiltless, had them slain.

Now, I'll return to my story.

The simple widow and her two daughters at once rushed outdoors when they heard the hens cry out in their grief. The women saw the fox going toward the grove carrying the cock away on his back; they cried, "Out! Harrow!" and "Weilawey! Look! Look! the fox," and they ran after him. Many men with staves ran with them. The dogs took up the chase—Colle, Talbot, and Garland, and also Malkyn with a distaff in her hand. There ran also the cow, the calf, and even the hogs—they were so frightened by the barking of the dogs and the shouting of the men and women that the hogs ran as if to break their hearts. They yowled like fiends in hell. The ducks cried out as if they were being killed; out of fear the geese flew over the trees; out of the hive came a swarm of bees. The noise was so hideous—surely Jack Straw [leader of the great Peasant Revolt, 1381] and all his followers never made shouts so shrill, when they were killing a Fleming as that day were made against the fox. Men brought trumpets of brass, wood, horn, and bone upon which they blew and tooted; the others shrieked and whooped. It seemed as if the heavens might fall.

Now, good men, I pray you all, listen. Behold how Fortune reverses suddenly the hope and pride of her enemy! The cock, lying upon the fox's back, though deeply frightened, spoke to the fox and said, "Sire, God help me, if I were you,

_____
[10]Nero was the Roman Emperor from A.D. 54–68, who was blamed for the great fire that destroyed much of Rome in 64.

I'd say, 'Turn back, all you proud louts! May a pestilence fall upon you! Now that I have reached the edge of the woods, the cock will stay here, and indeed I will eat him right away.'"

The fox answered, "That's just what I'll do." And as he spoke those words, the cock quickly escaped from the fox's mouth and flew immediately up to the branch of a tree.

When the fox realized that the cock was gone, he said, "Alas Chantecleer, I did you a wrong by making you afraid when I seized you and carried you out of the yard. But, sire, I didn't do it with any wicked intention. Come down, and I will tell you what I meant to do. I'll tell you the truth, God help me."

"No," said the cock, "then I would say, 'A curse on both of us', but first a curse on me, my blood, and my bones, if I let you trick me more than once. Never again with your flattery will you cause me to sing and close my eyes, for the man who wilfully closes his eyes when he should keep them open—may God never let him prosper."

"No," the fox said, "may God give great misfortune to the man who controls himself so badly that he yaks when he should shut up."

Notice well what happens when one is reckless and careless and puts his trust in flattery.

But you who think this tale is some foolishness—all about a cock and a hen, consider instead the moral lesson in the story, for St. Paul says that every thing that is written is indeed written for our instruction. Take the wheat and throw away the chaff.

And now, O God, if it be thy will, as Our Lord says, make us all good men and bring us into the bliss of heaven. Amen.

4 The Petrarchan Sonnet

Francesco Petrarca, or Petrarch (1304), was a principal figure in the emergence of the Italian Renaissance; his love for the literature of ancient Greece and Rome and his call to emulate the style of classical writers had an immense influence on Italian humanism. But for nearly a century after his death, Petrarch's reputation as an author was based on his Italian sonnets. Like Dante, for whom he expressed great admiration, Petrarch wrote poetry in the vernacular Tuscan dialect of northern Italy. A sonnet is a poem of fourteen lines expressing a single thought. The Italian sonnet, also known as the Petrarchan sonnet, consists of an octave of eight lines followed by a sextet of six lines. Petrarch's sonnets were inspired by a woman named Laura with whom he was infatuated for twenty-one years, much as Dante was by Beatrice.

Francesco Petrarch
Sonnets to Laura

In the following sonnet, Petrarch describes how he was snared by the love of Laura.

And if this be not love, what is it then?
but if it is love, God, what can love be?
if good, why mortal bitterness to me?
if ill, why is it sweetness that torments?

If willingly I burn, why these laments?
if not my will, what use can weeping be?
O living death, delightful agony,
how can you do so much where none consents?

And if I do consent, wrongly I grieve.
But such cross winds my fragile bark is blown
I drift unsteered upon the open seas:

in wisdom light, with error so weighed down
that I myself know not the thing I crave,
and burn in winter, and in summer freeze.

On the twenty-first anniversary of their first meeting, April 6, 1348, Petrarch had a presentiment of Laura's death; six weeks later, he received a letter from a friend confirming that Laura had indeed died of the plague on that very date. The following sonnet reveals how much Petrarch still misses her and longs to be with her.

My thoughts had lifted me to where she stood
whom I still seek and find on earth no more;
among the souls that the third circle bore,
she came with greater beauty and less pride.

She took my hand and said: "If hope can guide,
you will again be with me in this sphere:
for I am she who gave you so much war
and closed my day before the eventide.

No human mind can understand my bliss:
you I await and what you loved so much,
the veil I left below where now it lies."

Why did she loose my hand? why did she cease?
for at that holy and unsullied speech
I almost could have stayed in Paradise.

5 The Status of Women in Medieval Society

The precise status of a woman in medieval society differed immensely depending on the time, the place, and her class. The majority of women managed families and households, often taking part in farmwork or other crafts connected with the family livelihood. However, their legal rights, social standing, and power were inferior to those of adult males in their own families. During the High Middle Ages, the Christian church increasingly supported a patriarchal structure of authority in church and civil society that left women effectively under the domination of males, clerical and lay. Although the teachings of Aristotle about women tended to demean their status among intellectuals, several of the church's teachings recognized the inherent dignity of a woman. The church regarded marriage as a sacrament, considered adultery a sin, and subjected men and women to the same moral standards. Neither sex had any special advantage in attaining salvation.

Despite legal, social, and economic handicaps imposed upon them by males, some women successfully assumed positions of power and achievement. A few ruled kingdoms and principalities or headed convents and religious orders.

Others organized guilds; founded nunneries; practiced various crafts; served as teachers, physicians, and midwives; and operated small businesses. Some showed talent as poets, dramatists, and artists.

Jacopone da Todi
PRAISE OF THE VIRGIN MARY
"O THOU MOTHER, FOUNT OF LOVE"

The ambivalence that medieval men, particularly intellectuals, expressed toward women arose from several sources. First, medieval authors, who highly esteemed the writings of the ancient Greeks and Romans, were influenced by the hostility of classical authors toward women who did not accept their position as subordinate and inferior to men. Classical writers maintained that women were less intelligent, more carnal, and more devious than men. Second, prejudice against women was fostered by the clerical insistence that celibacy was superior to marriage (because the former made it possible to escape the distractions of the flesh and family life and concentrate on spiritual matters). Third, the Christian view of men and women as equals in the sight of God was obscured by certain scriptural texts, such as Saint Paul's "Let your women keep silence in the churches: for it is not permitted unto them to speak" (1 Corinthians 14:34); and "Wives, submit yourselves unto your own husbands, as unto the Lord" (Ephesians 5:22). This negative view of women was symbolized by the Old Testament portrait of Eve as the archetypal temptress who led Adam to sin. One medieval writer expressed it this way: "Between Adam and God in paradise there was but one woman and she had no rest until she had succeeded in banishing her husband from the garden of delights and in condemning Christ to the torments of the cross."

Countering this negative image was the New Testament picture of Mary, whose acceptance of her role as the mother of Jesus made salvation possible for all people. The highest expression of devotion to the Virgin Mary was reached in the twelfth and thirteenth centuries with the growing notion that Mary was preserved from original sin and remained free of sin throughout her life. Moreover, medieval Christians believed that Mary, by devoting her entire life to her son in his work of redemption, cooperated with him in his ministry. Therefore, as the Mother of God she was able to intercede with her son on behalf of individual Christians. The numerous artistic depictions of Mary as the Mother of God and the Queen of Heaven, as well as the multitude of churches named after the Virgin, are evidence of the popular piety that the cult of Mary generated throughout the Middle Ages.

The following poem by Italian religious poet Jacopone da Todi (1230?–1306) is a tribute to the Virgin Mary.

At the Cross her station keeping
Stood the mournful mother weeping,
  Close to Jesus to the last;
  Through her heart, His sorrow sharing,
All His bitter anguish bearing,
  Now at length the sword had passed.

O how sad and sore distressed
Was that mother highly blest
  Of the sole-begotten One!
Christ above in torment hangs:
She beneath Him holds the pangs
Of her dying glorious Son.

Is there one who would not weep
Whelmed in miseries so deep
   Christ's dear mother to behold?
Can the human heart refrain
From partaking in her pain,
   In that mother's pain untold?

Bruised, derided, cursed, defiled,
She held her tender Child
   All with bloody scourges rent;
For the sins of His own nation,
Saw Him hang in desolation,
   Till His spirit forth he sent.

O thou mother, fount of love,
Touch my spirit from above,
   Make my heart with thine accord!
Make me feel as thou hast felt;
Make my soul to glow and melt
   With the love of Christ my Lord.

Holy mother, pierce me through!
In my heart each wound renew
   Of my Saviour crucified;
Let me share with thee His pain,
Who for all my sins was slain,
   Who for me in torments died.

Let me mingle tears with thee,
Mourning Him who mourned for me,
   All the days that I may live;
By the Cross with thee to stay,
There with thee to weep and pray,
   Is all I ask of thee to give.

Virgin of all virgins blest!
Listen to my fond request:
   Let me share thy grief divine;
Let me, to my latest breath,
In my body bear the death
   Of that dying Son of thine.

Wounded with His every wound,
Steep my soul till it hath swooned
   In His very blood away;
Be to me, O virgin, nigh,
Lest in flames I burn and die
   In His awful judgment day:

Christ, when Thou shalt call me hence,
Be Thy mother my defence,
   Be Thy cross my victory
While my body here decays,
May my soul Thy goodness praise,
   Safe in paradise with Thee.

Christine de Pizan

The Book of the City of Ladies and *Joan of Arc*

In an age when most females were under the authority of men and received, at best, only an elementary education, Christine de Pizan (c. 1364–c. 1430) was an exceptional woman. She was born in Venice, and when she was five years old, her father, Tomasso de Pizzano, an astrologer, natural philosopher, and mathematician, accepted a position at the court of Charles V in France. Charles was interested in learning and education—founding the royal library, commissioning translations of scientific and classical works (including Aristotle), and redecorating the Louvre to house an eminent library.

    In 1380, when Christine was fifteen years old, she was married to Etienne de Castel, the husband her father had chosen for her. Through Etienne's position as a court secretary, Christine came into contact with educated men who introduced her to Latin prose and the works of Petrarch and Boccaccio. Charles V's untimely death in 1380 was followed by the death of her father in 1387, and, three years later, of her beloved husband. Suddenly, at the age of twenty-five, Christine found herself a widow with a daughter, two sons, a niece, and her mother to support. Seeking consolation for her grief, she began to write poetry. Learning that her poetry was well received, Christine proceeded to write courtly love poetry, as well as poems about the French court, and mythology; later, she turned her interest toward the writers of antiquity. The success of her works accorded her the patronage of such distinguished people as Philip the Bold, the Duke of Burgundy, Queen Isabella of Bavaria, the English Earl of Salisbury, and Jean, Duke of Berry.

Christine is best remembered for her extended work on the role of women in society in which she addresses such weighty issues as the ability of women to govern, their aptitude for learning, and the criminality of rape. In 1405, she authored *Cité de dames* (The Book of the City of Ladies). The structure of the book is patterned after Augustine's *City of God,* and the thematic material depends heavily on the works of Boccaccio. *The Book of the City of Ladies* is divided into three parts and describes Christine's vision of a city—founded by the goddesses Reason, Discretion, and Justice—reserved for women who have made significant contributions to society. In the following selection, Christine explains how she came to write the book as a rejoinder to those who "write such awful, damning things about women and their ways."

THE BOOK OF THE CITY OF LADIES

1. *Here begins the* Book of the City of Ladies, *the first chapter of which explains why and for what purpose the book was written.*

One day, I was sitting in my study surrounded by many books of different kinds, for it has long been my habit to engage in the pursuit of knowledge. My mind had grown weary as I had spent the day struggling with the weighty tomes of various authors whom I had been studying for some time. I looked up from my book and decided that, for once, I would put aside these difficult texts and find instead something amusing and easy to read from the works of the poets. As I searched around for some little book, I happened to chance upon a work which did not belong to me but was amongst a pile of others that had been placed in my safekeeping. I opened it up and saw from the title that it was by Matheolus.[1] With a smile, I made my choice. Although I had never read it, I knew that, unlike many other works, this one was said to be written in praise of women. Yet I had scarcely begun to read it when my dear mother called me down to supper, for it was time to eat. I put the book to one side, resolving to go back to it the following day.

The next morning, seated once more in my study as is my usual custom, I remembered my previous desire to have a look at this book by Matheolus. I picked it up again and read on a little. But, seeing the kind of immoral language and ideas it contained, the content seemed to me likely to appeal only to those who enjoy reading works of slander and to be of no use whatsoever to anyone who wished to pursue virtue or to improve their moral standards. I therefore leafed through it, read the ending, and decided to switch to some more worthy and profitable work. Yet, having looked at this book, which I considered to be of no authority, an extraordinary thought became planted in my mind which made me wonder why

on earth it was that so many men, both clerks and others, have said and continue to say and write such awful, damning things about women and their ways. I was at a loss as to how to explain it. It is not just a handful of writers who do this, nor only this Matheolus whose book is neither regarded as authoritative nor intended to be taken seriously. It is all manner of philosophers, poets and orators too numerous to mention, who all seem to speak with one voice and are unanimous in their view that female nature is wholly given up to vice.

As I mulled these ideas over in my mind again and again, I began to examine myself and my own behaviour as an example of womankind. In order to judge in all fairness and without prejudice whether what so many famous men have said about us is true, I also thought about other women I know, the many princesses and countless ladies of all different social ranks who have shared their private and personal thoughts with me. No matter which way I looked at it and no matter how much I turned the question over in my mind, I could find no evidence from my own experience to bear out such a negative view of female nature and habits. Even so, given that I could scarcely find a moral work by any author which didn't devote some chapter or paragraph to attacking the female sex, I had to accept their unfavourable opinion of women since it was unlikely that so many learned men, who seemed to be endowed with such great intelligence and insight into all things, could possibly have lied on so many different occasions. It was on the basis of this one simple argument that I was forced to conclude that, although my understanding was too crude and ill-informed to recognize the great flaws in myself and other women, these men had to be in the right. Thus I preferred to give more weight to what others said than to trust my own judgement and experience.

I dwelt on these thoughts at such length that it was as if I had sunk into a deep trance. My mind became flooded with an endless stream of names as I recalled all the authors who had written on this subject. I came to the conclusion that God had surely created a vile thing when He created woman. Indeed, I was astounded that such a fine craftsman could have

---

[1] Matheolus refers to a poem, "The Lamentations of Matheolus" (c. 1295) by Mathieu of Boulogne, that disparages women.

wished to make such an appalling object which, as these writers would have it, is like a vessel in which all the sin and evil of the world has been collected and preserved. This thought inspired such a great sense of disgust and sadness in me that I began to despise myself and the whole of my sex as an aberration in nature.

With a deep sigh, I called out to God: "Oh Lord, how can this be? Unless I commit an error of faith, I cannot doubt that you, in your infinite wisdom and perfect goodness, could make anything that wasn't good. Didn't you yourself create woman especially and then endow her with all the qualities that you wished her to have? How could you possibly have made a mistake in anything? Yet here stand women not simply accused, but already judged, sentenced and condemned! I just cannot understand this contradiction. If it is true, dear Lord God, that women are guilty of such horrors as so many men seem to say, and as you yourself have said that the testimony of two or more witnesses is conclusive, how can I doubt their word? Oh God, why wasn't I born a male so that my every desire would be to serve you, to do right in all things, and to be as perfect a creature as man claims to be? Since you chose not to show such grace to me, please pardon and forgive me, dear Lord, if I fail to serve you as well as I should, for the servant who receives fewer rewards from his lord is less obligated to him in his service."

Sick at heart, in my lament to God I uttered these and many other foolish words since I thought myself very unfortunate that He had given me a female form.

Using examples from classical antiquity, biblical history, and French history, Christine, with the help of Lady Reason and "three ladies" (symbolizing virtue), lay the foundation of the City of Ladies by figuratively "digging up" the misogynistic, disparaging, and critical remarks made about women by past writers. Reason challenges the writers, arguing that women possess the same moral and intellectual qualities as men.

---

8. *Christine explains how* Reason *instructed her and helped her to begin digging up the ground in order to lay the foundations.*

Lady Reason replied to my words, saying: "Stand up now, daughter, and without further delay let us make our way to the Field of Letters. There we will build the City of Ladies on flat, fertile ground, where fruits of all kinds flourish and fresh streams flow, a place where every good thing grows in abundance. Take the spade of your intelligence and dig deep to make a great trench all around where you see the line I have traced. I'll help to carry away the hods of earth on my shoulders."

Obeying her instructions, I jumped to my feet: thanks to the three ladies, my body felt much stronger and lighter than before. She took the lead and I followed on behind. When we came to the spot she had described, I began to excavate and

dig out the earth with the spade of my intelligence, just as she had directed me to do. The first fruit of my labours was this: "My lady, I'm remembering that image of gold being refined in the furnace that you used before to symbolize the way many male writers have launched a full-scale attack on the ways of women. I take this image to mean that the more women are criticized, the more it redounds to their glory. But please tell me exactly what it is that makes so many different authors slander women in their writings because, if I understand you correctly, they are wrong to do so. Is it Nature that makes them do this? Or, if it is out of hatred, how can you explain it?"

Reason answered my questions, saying: "My dear daughter, in order to help you see more clearly how things stand, let me carry away this first load of earth. I can tell you that, far from making them slander women, Nature does the complete opposite. There is no stronger or closer bond in the world than that which Nature, in accordance with God's wishes, creates between man and woman. Rather, there are many other different reasons which explain why men have attacked women in the past and continue to do so, including those authors whose works you have already mentioned. Some of those who criticized women did so with good intentions: they wanted to rescue men who had already fallen into the clutches of depraved and corrupt women or to prevent others from suffering the same fate, and to encourage men generally to avoid leading a lustful and sinful existence. They therefore attacked all women in order to persuade men to regard the entire sex as an abomination."

"My lady," I said, "forgive me for interrupting you. Were they right to do so, since they were acting with good intentions? Isn't it true that one's actions are judged by one's intentions?"

"You're wrong, my dear girl," she replied, "because there is no excuse for plain ignorance. If I killed you with good intentions and out of stupidity, would I be in the right? Those who have acted in this way, whoever they may be, have abused their power. Attacking one party in the belief that you are benefiting a third party is unfair. So is criticizing the nature of all women, which is completely unjustified, as I will prove to you by analogy. Condemning all women in order to help some misguided men get over their foolish behaviour is tantamount to denouncing fire, which is a vital and beneficial element, just because some people are burnt by it, or to cursing water just because some people are drowned in it. You could apply the same reasoning to all manner of things which can be put to either good or bad use. In none of these cases should you blame the thing in itself if foolish people use it unwisely. You yourself have made these points elsewhere in your writings. Those who subscribe to these opinions, whether in good or bad faith, have overstepped the mark in order to make their point. It's like somebody cutting up the whole piece of cloth in order to make himself a huge coat simply because it's not going to cost him anything and no one is going to object. It thus stops anyone else from using the material. If instead, as you yourself have rightly remarked, these writers had tried to find ways to save men from indulging in vice and from frequenting debauched women by attacking only the morals and the habits of those who were evidently guilty of such behaviour, I freely admit that they would have produced texts which were extremely useful. It's true that there's nothing worse than a woman who is dissolute and depraved: she's like a monster, a creature going against its own nature, which is to be timid, meek and pure. I can assure you that those writers who condemn the entire female sex for being sinful, when in fact there are so many women who are extremely virtuous, are not acting with my approval. They've committed a grave error, as do all those who subscribe to their views. So let us throw out these horrible, ugly, misshapen stones from your work as they have no place in your beautiful city.

"Other men have criticized women for different reasons: some because they are themselves steeped in sin, some because of a bodily impediment, some out of sheer envy, and some quite simply because they naturally take delight in slandering others. There are also some who do so because they like to flaunt their erudition: they have come across these views in books and so like to quote the authors whom they have read.

"Those who criticize the female sex because they are inherently sinful are men who have wasted their youth on dissolute behaviour and who have had affairs with many different women. These men have therefore acquired cunning through their many experiences and have grown old without repenting of their sins. Indeed, they look back with nostalgia on the appalling way they used to carry on when they were younger. Now that old age has finally caught up with them and the spirit is still willing but the flesh has grown weak, they are full of regret when they see that, for them, the 'good old days' are over and they can merely watch as younger men take over from where they have had to leave off. The only way they can release their frustration is to attack women and to try to stop others from enjoying the pleasures that they themselves used to take. You very often see old men such as these going around saying vile and disgusting things, as in the case of your Matheolus, who freely admits that he is just an impotent old man who would still like to satisfy his desires. He's an excellent example to illustrate my point as he's typical of many other similar cases.

"Yet, thank goodness, not all old men are full of depravity and rotten to the core like a leper. There are many other fine, decent ones whose wisdom and virtue have been nourished by me and whose words reflect their good character, since they speak in an honourable and sober fashion. Such men detest all kinds of wrongdoing and slander. Thus, rather than attacking and defaming individual sinners, male or female, they condemn all sins in general. Their advice to others is to avoid vice, pursue virtue and stick to the straight and narrow.

"Those men who have attacked women because of their own bodily impediments, such as impotence or a deformed limb, are all bitter and twisted in the mind. The only pleasure they have to compensate for their incapacity is to slander the female sex since it is women who bring such joy to other men. That way they are convinced that they can put others off enjoying what they themselves have never had.

"Those men who have slandered the opposite sex out of envy have usually known women who were cleverer and more virtuous than they are. Out of bitterness and spite, envious men such as these are driven to attack all women, thinking that they can thereby undermine these individuals' good reputation and excellent character, as in the case of the author of *On Philosophy* whose name I've forgotten. In this book, he goes to great lengths to argue that men should on no account praise women and that those who do so are betraying the title of his book: their doctrine is no longer 'philosophy' but 'philofolly'. However, I can assure you that it is definitely he who is the arch-exponent of 'philofolly' because of all the false reasoning and erroneous conclusions he comes out with in his book.

"As for those men who are slanderous by nature, it's not surprising if they criticize women, given that they attack everyone indiscriminately. You can take it from me that any man who wilfully slanders the female sex does so because he has an evil mind, since he's going against both reason and nature. Against reason, because he is lacking in gratitude and failing to acknowledge all the good and indispensable things that woman has done for him both in the past and still today, much more than he can ever repay her for. Against nature, in that even the birds and the beasts naturally love their mate, the female of the species. So man acts in a most unnatural way when he, a rational being, fails to love woman.

"Finally, there are those who dabble in literature and delight in mimicking even the very finest works written by authors who are greatly superior to them. They think themselves to be beyond reproach since they are merely repeating what others have already said. Believe me, this is how they set about making their defamatory remarks. Some of them scribble down any old nonsense, verse without rhyme or reason, in which they discuss the ways of women, or princes, or whoever it might be, when it is they themselves, whose habits leave much to be desired, who are most in need of moral self-improvement. Yet the common folk, who are as ignorant as they are, think that it's the best thing they've ever read."

JOAN OF ARC

Christine's final work, dated July 31, 1429, is a joyous poem about Joan of Arc's victory at Orléans and the coronation of Charles VII (1422–1461) at Rheims. Christine lauds "the Maid of Orléans" who delivered France from England, and she views Joan of Arc's triumph as a victory for womanhood.

XII

Oh, what an honor to the crown
of France, this proof divinely sent,
For by the blessings He bestows
It's clear how He approves of France:
For in the royal house of France
He finds the strongest faith—I've read
That France's Lilies never lost
Belief (but nothing's new in that!)

XIII

And you, the King of France, King Charles,
The seventh of that noble name,
Who fought a mighty war before
Good fortune came at all to you:
Do, now, observe your dignity
Exalted by the Maid, who bent
Your enemies beneath your flag
In record time (that's something new!)

XIV

And people thought that it would be
Impossible indeed for you
To ever have your country back,
For it was nearly lost; but now,
It's clearly yours; no matter who
Has done you wrong, it's yours once more,
And through the clever Maid who did
Her part therein—thanks be to God!

XXII

You, Joan, were born propitiously;
May He be blessed who gave you life!
Young maid who was ordained of God,
In you the Holy Spirit poured
His ample grace (in whom there was
And is divine munificence).
Refusing none of your requests.
Who'll grant reward enough to you?

XXIII

Could more be said about the men
And thrilling deeds of bygone times?

In Moses God who's bountiful
Instilled great moral force and grace;
Then tirelessly did he escort
God's people out of Egypt's land
By miracle. Just so have you
Saved us from ill, elected Maid!

XXIV

When I reflect upon your state,
The youthful maiden that you are,
To whom God gives the force and strength
To be the champion and the one
To suckle France upon her milk
Of peace, the sweetest nourishment,
To overthrow the rebel host:
The wonder passes Nature's work!

XXV

That is, if God, through Joshua
Performed so many miracles*
In conquering those places where
So many met defeat—a man
Of strength was Joshua. But she's
A woman—simple shepherdess—
More brave than ever man at Rome!
An easy thing for God to do!

XXVI

But as for us, we've never heard
About a marvel quite so great,
For all the heroes who have lived
In history can't measure up
In bravery against the Maid,
Who strives to rout our enemies.
It's God does that, who's guiding her
Whose courage passes that of men.

XXVII

We set great store in Gideon,†
Who was a simple laborer.
Now God caused him, the story says,
To fight, so none could hold him off,

---

*Joshua's most celebrated miracle was making the sun stand still, thus allowing him to achieve victory over the Amorites (Joshua 10: 12–14).
†Gideon was entrusted with a divinely ordained mission to deliver his country from the Midianites (Judges 6–7).

And thus he conquered everything.
Whatever word God gave to him,
The miracle was never quite
So clear as now He works for her.

XXVIII

And Esther, Judith, Deborah,*
Those ladies of enormous worth,
Through them it was that God restored
His people, who were solely pressed;
Of many others I have learned,
Courageous ladies, valiant all,
Through whom God worked his miracles.
But through the Maid He's done much more.

XXIX

By miracle has she appeared,
Divine commandment sent her here.
God's angel led her in before
The king, to bring her help to him.†
There's no illusion in her case
Because it's been indeed borne out
In council (in conclusion, then,
A thing is proved by its effect);

XXX

They questioned her most carefully
Before they would believe her words,
To priests and wise men she was led;
They searched the truth of her account
Before it might be told about
That God had sent her to the king.‡
And in recorded history
They found her destined just for this.

XXXI

The Sybil, Bede, and Merlin, too,
Five hundred years ago and more
Foresaw her in their minds,§ and as
The cure for France's plight they wrote
Of her, and of her prophesied,
Predicting that she'd bear the flag
In France's wars, as they foretold
The way of her accomplishments.

XXXII

Her life of beauty in the faith
Attests the grace of God in her,
A sign by which we place more trust
In her: Whatever she may do,
She's always keeping God before
Her eyes; she calls on Him, and serves
And supplicates in word, in deed;
And nowhere does her faith grow weak.

XXXIII

How evident it was when at
Orleans the siege was laid, for there
Her strength was first made manifest!‖
For never clearer miracle
Was seen: God helped his own, so that
The foe could help each other fight
No more than lifeless dogs might do;
Thus they were caught and put to death.

XXXIV

What honor for the female sex!
God's love for it appears quite clear,
Because the kingdom laid to waste
By all those wretched people now
Stands safe, a woman rescued it
(A hundred thousand men could not
Do that) and killed the hostile foe!
A thing beyond belief before!

*Christine not only recommends these women to Isabeau of Bavaria as models in her *Letter to the Queen of France,* but she also writes of them in *The Mutation of Fortune* and *The Book of the City of Ladies.* It is interesting to note that Jean Gerson, in his treatise on Joan of Arc, *De quadam puella,* written during the spring of 1429 in support of the supernatural nature of her mission, likewise cites these same examples.

†Reference to Joan's arrival at the dauphin's court in Chinon, probably on March 6, 1429.

‡This reference is to the interrogation and examinations to which she was subjected at Poitiers in the spring of 1429.

§For a discussion of these prophecies, see Andrew Lang, *The Maid of France* (London, 1909), pp. 32–33; 308–311.

‖The siege of Orleans was raised on May 8, 1429.

XXXV

A little girl of sixteen years
(And doesn't that pass nature's ken?)
For whom no arm's too great to bear,
She seems to have been reared to this,
So strong and resolute is she.
In front of her the enemy
Goes fleeing, not a one remains.
She acts, in sight of many eyes,

XXXVI

While ridding France of enemies,
Retaking town and castle both.
No force was ever quite so great,
If hundreds or if thousands strong!
Among our men so brave and apt
She's captain over all; such strength
No Hector or Achilles had.*
All this God does, who's guiding her.

XXXIX

Lay down, oh Englishmen, your horns,†
For you'll not bag the precious game!
Don't bring your business into France!
For your advance is stopped—a thing
You'd scarcely thought a while ago
When you were acting bellicose,
But you had not yet reached that path
Where God strikes down the arrogant.

XL

You thought you'd taken over France,
That she belonged to you by right.
But things are otherwise, false lot!
You'll beat your drums some other place,
Unless you want to have a taste
Of death, like your confederates,
Who're provender out there for wolves,
Among the furrows, lying dead.

XLI

The English will be crushed through her,
And never will they rise again
For God who wills it hears the voice
Of guiltless folk they tried to harm!
The blood of those they've killed, who'll walk
No more, cries out. God wants an end
To this; instead He has resolved
To chastise them as evil men.

XLII

In Christendom and in the Church.
She'll kindle harmony anew,‡
The faithless we have heard about,
And heretics, who lead base lives,
She will destroy, for thus it's said
In prophecy, which in advance
Could see all this; and she'll forgive
No place that vilifies God's faith.

XLIX

In regal triumph and in force
Did Charles receive the crown at Rheims,
Without a doubt, quite safe and sound,
With men-at-arms and many lords,
The year was fourteen twenty-nine,
July the seventeenth, to be
Exact, and there he stayed awhile,
A sojourn of about five days,§

L

Along with him the Virgin Maid
Then coming back across his land
No city, castle, nor small town
Resists. For whether he's despised
Or loved, and whether they are stunned
Or reassured, the citizens
Surrender. Few require attack,
So much his power makes them quail!

---

*Those who question Christine's feminism are surely overlooking these verses. It is noteworthy that she cites both biblical and pagan examples here.

†This sort of characterization of the English was common in the period of the Hundred Years' War. See C. Lenient, *La Poésie patriotique en France au moyen âge* (Paris, 1891).

‡These lines refer to the belief that Joan's mission included not only the transfer of imperial power to France, but also the restoration of the Church after the Schism. The "heretics" are apparently the Hussites, who had embarked on a campaign of revenge after the burning of John Huss in 1415.

§Christine was obviously well informed concerning these events. Accompanied by Joan, Charles arrived in Rheims on July 16 and left on July 21, 1429.

LI

Some in their foolishness believe
That they'll resist; it's pointless, though,
For in the end, whoever stands
Opposed pays for his faults to God.
It's futile. Thus they must give in,
No matter what they will. For no
Resistance can be strong enough
To last beyond the Maid's assault,

LII

Assembling in their mass they thought
They could prohibit his return
By launching a surprise attack;
But now they need no healer's balm
For one by one they've all been caught,
Opponents who are dead and gone—
Dispatched, as I have heard it said,
To either Hell or Paradise.

LIX

Alas! He's so magnanimous
He wants to pardon everyone!
And it's the Maid, obeying God,
Who causes him to act that way.
Now give yourselves, your hearts, to him,
As loyal Frenchmen ought to do!*
And when you listen to him speak,
No man will remonstrate with you.

LX

I pray to God that He'll inspire
In you the wish to act that way
So that the cruel storm of wars
We've known may be erased from thought;
And that you spend your life in peace,
The subjects of your king supreme,
So that you never give offense
To him; and may he lead you well. Amen.

---

*These lines are a final appeal to the French to heal their divisiveness and unite before the new king, a culmination that was not achieved for some time although by the end of his reign it had generally come about. The last lines of the poem also allude to division among the French.

6 The Medieval World-View

The modern world is linked in many ways to the Middle Ages. European cities, the middle class, the state system, English common law, representative institutions, universities—all had their origins in the Middle Ages. Despite these elements of continuity, the characteristic outlook of medieval people is markedly different from that of people today. Whereas science and secularism shape the modern point of view, religion was the foundation of the Middle Ages. Christian beliefs as formulated by the church made life and death purposeful and intelligible.

Medieval thinkers drew a sharp distinction between a higher, spiritual world and a lower, material world. God, the creator of the universe and the source of moral values, dwelled in the higher celestial world, an abode of perfection. The universe was organized as a hierarchy with God at the summit and hell at the other extremity. Earth, composed of base matter, stood just above hell. By believing in Christ and adhering to God's commandments as taught by the church, people could overcome their sinful nature and ascend to God's world. Sinners, on the other hand, would descend to hell, a fearful place the existence of which medieval people never doubted.

Scholastic philosophy, which sought to demonstrate through reason the truth of Christian doctrines, and the Gothic cathedral, which seemed to soar from the material world to heaven, were two great expressions of the medieval mind. A third was *The Divine Comedy* of Dante Alighieri, the greatest literary figure of the Middle Ages.

Lothario dei Segni (Pope Innocent III)
On the Misery of the Human Condition

At the center of medieval belief was the image of a perfect God and a wretched and sinful human being. God had given Adam and Eve freedom to choose; rebellious and presumptuous, they had used their freedom to disobey God. In doing so, they made evil an intrinsic part of the human personality. But God, who had not stopped loving human beings, showed them the way out of sin. God became man and died so that human beings might be saved. Men and women were weak, egocentric, and sinful. With God's grace they could overcome their sinful nature and gain salvation; without grace they were utterly helpless. A classic expression of this pessimistic view of human nature was written in the late twelfth century by an Italian canon lawyer, Lothario dei Segni (c. 1160–1216), who was later elected pope in 1198, taking the name Innocent III. His *On the Misery of the Human Condition* was enormously popular and inspired numerous rhetorical writings on the same theme as late as the seventeenth century. Scattered excerpts follow.

• For sure man was formed out of earth, conceived in guilt, born to punishment. What he does is depraved and illicit, is shameful and improper, vain and unprofitable. He will become fuel for the eternal fires, food for worms, a mass of rottenness.

I shall try to make my explanation clearer and my treatment fuller. Man was formed of dust, slime, and ashes; what is even more vile, of the filthiest seed. He was conceived from the itch of the flesh, in the heat of passion and the stench of lust, and worse yet, with the stain of sin. He was born to toil, dread, and trouble; and more wretched still, was born only to die. He commits depraved acts by which he offends God, his neighbor, and himself; shameful acts by which he defiles his name, his person, and his conscience; and vain acts by which he ignores all things important, useful, and necessary. He will become fuel for those fires which are forever hot and burn forever bright; food for the worm which forever nibbles and digests; a mass of rottenness which will forever stink and reek.

• A bird is born to fly; man is born to toil. All his days are full of toil and hardship, and at night his mind has no rest.

• How much anxiety tortures mortals! They suffer all kinds of cares, are burdened with worry, tremble and shrink with fears and terrors, are weighted down with sorrow. Their nervousness makes them depressed, and their depression makes them nervous. Rich or poor, master or slave, married or single, good and bad alike—all suffer worldly torments and are tormented by worldly vexations.

• For sudden sorrow always follows worldly joy: what begins in gaiety ends in grief. Worldly happiness is besprinkled indeed with much bitterness.

• Then, suddenly, when least expected, misfortune strikes, a calamity befalls us, disease attacks; or death, which no one can escape, carries us off.

• Men strive especially for three things: riches, pleasures, and honors. Riches lead to immorality, pleasures to shame, and honors to vanity.

• But suppose a man is lifted up high, suppose he is raised to the very peak. At once his cares grow heavy, his worries mount up, he eats less and cannot sleep. And so nature is corrupted, his spirit weakened, his sleep disturbed, his appetite lost; his strength is diminished, he loses weight. Exhausting himself, he scarcely lives half a lifetime and ends his wretched days with a more wretched death.

• Almost the whole life of mortals is full of mortal sin, so that one can scarcely find anyone who does not go astray, does not return to his own vomit and rot in his own dung. Instead they "are glad when they have done evil and rejoice in most wicked things." "Being filled with all iniquity, malice, fornication, avarice, wickedness, full of envy, murders, contention, deceit, evil, being whisperers, detractors, hateful to God, irreverent, proud, haughty, plotters of evil, disobedient to parents, foolish, dissolute, without affection, without fidelity, without mercy." This world is full of such and worse; it abounds in heretics and schismatics [Christians who reject the authority of the pope], traitors and tyrants, simonists [buyers or sellers of spiritual offices or sacred items] and hypocrites; the ambitious and the covetous, robbers and brigands, violent men, extortionists, usurers, forgers; the impious and sacreligious, the betrayers and liars, the flatterers and deceivers; gossips, tricksters, gluttons, drunkards; adulterers, incestuous men, deviates, and the dirty-minded; the lazy, the careless, the vain, the prodigal, the impetuous, the irascible, the impatient and inconstant; poisoners, fortune tellers, perjurers, cursers; men who are presumptuous and arrogant, unbelieving and desperate; and finally those ensnared in all vices together.

The Vanity of This World

The following poem, written in Latin by an unknown thirteenth-century author, expresses the medieval rejection of earthly pursuits and preoccupation with the world to come.

Why does the world war for glory that's vain?
All its successes wax only to wane;
Quickly its triumphs are frittered away,
Like vessels the potter casts out of frail clay.

As well trust to letters imprinted in ice
As trust the frail world with its treacherous device,
Its prizes a fraud and its values all wrong;
Who would put faith in its promise for long?

Rather in hardship's uncertain distress
Trust than in this world's unhappy success;
With dreams and with shadows it leads men astray,
A cheat in our work and a cheat at our play.

Where now is Samson's invincible arm,
And where is Jonathan's sweet-natured charm?
Once-famous Solomon, where now is he
Or the fair Absolom, so good to see?[1]

Whither is Caesar the great Emperor fled,
Or Croesus whose show on his table was spread?

Cicero's eloquence now is in vain;[2]
Where's Aristotle's magnificent brain?

All those great noblemen, all those past days,
All kings' achievements and all prelates' praise,
All the world's princes in all their array—
In the flash of an eye comes the end of the play.

Short is the season of all earthly fame;
Man's shadow, man's pleasure, they both are the same,
And the prizes eternal he gives in exchange
For the pleasure that leads to a land that is strange.

Food for the worms, dust and ashes, O why,
Bubble on water, be lifted so high?
Do good unto all men as long as ye may;
Ye know not your life will last after to-day.

This pride of the flesh which so dearly ye prize,
Like the flower of the grass (says the Scripture), it dies,
Or as the dry leaf which the wind whirls away,
Man's life is swept out from the light of the day.

Call not your own what one day ye may lose;
The world will take back all it gives you to use.
Let your hearts be in heaven, your thoughts in the skies;
Happy is he who the world can despise.

---

[1] In the Old Testament, Samson was the warrior hero of the Israelites; Jonathan was the son of King Saul and the loving friend of David; Solomon was the king of Israel, famous for his wisdom; and Absalom was the most beloved son of David.

[2] Croesus was a king of ancient Lydia renowed for his wealth. For Cicero, see page 100.

Dante Alighieri
The Divine Comedy

Dante Alighieri was a poet, political philosopher, soldier, and politician. Born in 1265 in Florence, Italy, he died in exile in 1321. His greatest work, *The Divine Comedy,* was composed of one hundred cantos (individual poems) and written not in Latin, the language of learning, but in the Tuscan Italian dialect of the common people. The poem is an elaborate allegory in which each character and event can be understood on two or more levels—for example, a literal description of the levels of hell and Dante's (and every Christian's) struggle to overcome a flawed human nature and to ward off worldly sin. Dante, representing all human beings, is guided through the afterworlds: hell (inferno), purgatory (purgatorio), and heaven (paradiso). The Roman poet Virgil conducts him through hell and purgatory; Beatrice, his long-dead beloved, leads him through heaven to the point where he sees God in all his glory.

Dante synthesized the various elements of the medieval outlook, and he summed up, with immense feeling, the medieval understanding of the purpose of life. The *Inferno* relates the power of God, the Father; the *Purgatorio* depicts the wisdom of Jesus as God's son; and the *Paradiso* portrays the love of the Holy Spirit. Furthermore, to illustrate the importance of the Trinity, Dante designed the *Comedy* with a strict numerological plan—each part contains 33 cantos. He chose 33 cantos for each part to correspond with the traditional belief that Jesus lived 33 years. By multiplying 33 x 3 = 99 and adding 1 canto for the introduction, the total is 100 cantos. One hundred is the square of 10, and for Dante, 10 was a perfect number because it consisted of the square of the Trinity (3), plus 1, symbolizing the triune God—God the "Three-In-One." Because the *Comedy* symbolizes the spiritual journey of every Christian who yearns for salvation but fears it will be denied because of human sinfulness, the *Comedy* later came to be better known as the "Divine Comedy."

The first canto of the *Inferno* opens on Good Friday (the day Christians traditionally associate with the crucifixion of Jesus) as Dante—the symbol for every Christian—wanders from "the True Way" and finds himself "alone in a dark wood" of error and despair. He then meets the Latin poet Virgil. In the descent through the nine concentric circles of hell, Virgil describes the nature and significance of each region through which they pass. In each section of hell, sinners are punished in proportion to their earthly sins. Over the entrance gate to hell, Dante reads these words:

> I AM THE WAY INTO THE CITY OF WOE.
> I AM THE WAY TO A FORSAKEN PEOPLE.
> I AM THE WAY INTO ETERNAL SORROW,
>
> SACRED JUSTICE MOVED MY ARCHITECT.
> I WAS RAISED HERE BY DIVINE OMNIPOTENCE,
> PRIMORDIAL LOVE AND ULTIMATE INTELLECT.
>
> ONLY THOSE ELEMENTS TIME CANNOT WEAR
> WERE MADE BEFORE ME, AND BEYOND TIME I STAND
> ABANDON ALL HOPE YE WHO ENTER HERE.

In the following selection from Canto IV, Limbo, Dante describes the first circle of hell. Dante and Virgil meet the virtuous pagans and unbaptized children who, because "they lacked Baptism's grace, which is the door of the true faith," are permitted neither to enter heaven nor to suffer in hell proper. Here they encounter the classical authors of antiquity—Homer, Horace, Ovid, and Lucan—and they pass into "a great Citadel" of reason where they meet celebrated heroes, including Hector, Aeneas, and Caesar. Finally, they are greeted by Aristotle, "the master of those who know," who is surrounded by "the great souls of philosophy," such as Thales, Heraclitus, Anaxagoras, Socrates, Hippocrates, Democritus, Plato, Diogenes, Zeno, Ptolemy, and Galen.

CIRCLE ONE: LIMBO
THE VIRTUOUS PAGANS

Dante wakes to find himself across Acheron. The Poets are now on the brink of Hell itself, which Dante conceives as a great funnel-shaped cave lying below the northern hemisphere with its bottom point at the earth's center. Around this great circular depression runs a series of ledges, each of which Dante calls a *Circle*. Each circle is assigned to the punishment of one category of sin.

As soon as Dante's strength returns, the Poets begin to cross the *First Circle*. Here they find the *Virtuous Pagans*. They were born without the light of Christ's revelation and, therefore, they cannot come into the light of God, but they are not tormented. Their only pain is that they have no hope.

Ahead of them Dante sights a great dome of light, and a voice trumpets through the darkness welcoming Virgil back, for this is his eternal place in Hell. Immediately the great Poets of all time appear—*Homer, Horace, Ovid,* and *Lucan*. They greet Virgil, and they make Dante a sixth in their company.

With them Dante enters the Citadel of Human Reason and sees before his eyes the Master Souls of Pagan Antiquity gathered on a green, and illuminated by the radiance of Human Reason. This is the highest state man can achieve without God, and the glory of it dazzles Dante, but he knows also that it is nothing compared to the glory of God.

A monstrous clap of thunder broke apart
  the swoon that stuffed my head; like one awakened
3   by violent hands, I leaped up with a start.

And having risen; rested and renewed,
  I studied out the landmarks of the gloom
6   to find my bearings there as best I could.

And I found I stood on the very brink of the valley
  called the Dolorous Abyss, the desolate chasm
9   where rolls the thunder of Hell's eternal cry,

so depthless-deep and nebulous and dim
  that stare as I might into its frightful pit
12   it gave me back no feature and no bottom.

Death-pale,* the Poet spoke: "Now let us go
  into the blind world waiting here below us.
15   I will lead the way and you will follow."

And I, sick with alarm at his new pallor,
  cried out, "How can I go this way when you
18   who are my strength in doubt turn pale with terror?"

And he: "The pain of these below us here,
  drains the color from my face for pity,
21   and leaves this pallor you mistake for fear.

Now let us go, for a long road awaits us."
  So he entered and so he led me in
24   to the first circle and ledge of the abyss.

No tortured wailing rose to greet us here
  but sounds of sighing rose from every side,
27   sending a tremor through the timeless air,

a grief breathed out of untormented sadness,
  the passive state of those who dwelled apart,
30   men, women, children—a dim and endless congress.

And the Master said to me: "You do not question†
  what souls these are that suffer here before you?
33   I wish you to know before you travel on

that these were sinless. And still their merits fail,
  for they lacked Baptism's grace, which is the door
36   of the true faith *you* were born to. Their birth fell

before the age of the Christian mysteries,
  and so they did not worship God's Trinity
39   in fullest duty. I am one of these.

For such defects are we lost, though spared the fire
  and suffering Hell in one affliction only:
42   that without hope we live on in desire."

I thought how many worthy souls there were
  suspended in that Limbo, and a weight
45   closed on my heart for what the noblest suffer.

"Instruct me, Master and most noble Sir,"
  I prayed him then, "better to understand
48   the perfect creed that conquers every error:

has any, by his own or another's merit,
  gone ever from this place to blessedness?"
51   He sensed my inner question and answered it:

---

* *death pale:* Virgil is most likely affected here by the return to his own place in Hell. "The pain of these below," then (line 19), would be the pain of his own group in Limbo (the Virtuous Pagans) rather than the total of Hell's suffering.

† *You do not question:* A master touch of characterization. Virgil's *amour propre* is a bit piqued at Dante's lack of curiosity about the position in Hell of Virgil's own kind. And it may possibly be, by allegorical extension, that Human Reason must urge the soul to question the place of reason. The allegorical point is conjectural, but such conjecture is certainly one of the effects inherent in the use of allegory; when well used, the central symbols of the allegory continue indefinitely to suggest new interpretations and shades of meaning.

"I was still new to this estate of tears
    when a Mighty One* descended here† among us,
54 crowned with the sign of His victorious years.

He took from us the shade of our first parent,
    of Abel, his pure son, of ancient Noah,
57 of Moses, the bringer of law, the obedient.

Father Abraham, David the King,
    Israel with his father and his children,
60 Rachel, the holy vessel of His blessing,

and many more He chose for elevation
    among the elect. And before these, you must know,
63 no human soul had ever won salvation."

We had not paused as he spoke, but held our road
    and passed meanwhile beyond a press of souls
66 crowded about like trees in a thick wood.

And we had not traveled far from where I woke
    when I made out a radiance before us
69 that struck away a hemisphere of dark.

We were still some distance back in the long night,
    yet near enough that I half-saw, half-sensed,
72 what quality of souls lived in that light.

"O ornament of wisdom and of art,
    what souls are these whose merit lights their way
75 even in Hell. What joy sets them apart?"

And he to me: "The signature of honor
    they left on earth is recognized in Heaven
78 and wins them ease in Hell out of God's favor."

And as he spoke a voice rang on the air:
    "Honor the Prince of Poets; the soul and glory
81 that went from us returns. He is here! He is here!"

The cry ceased and the echo passed from hearing;
    I saw four mighty presences come toward us
84 with neither joy nor sorrow in their bearing.

"Note well," my Master said as they came on,
    "that soul that leads the rest with sword in hand
87 as if he were their captain and champion.

It is Homer, singing master of the earth.
    Next after him is Horace, the satirist,
90 Ovid is third, and Lucan is the fourth.

Since all of these have part in the high name
    the voice proclaimed, calling me Prince of Poets,
93 the honor that they do me honors them."

So I saw gathered at the edge of light
    the masters of that highest school whose song
96 outsoars all others like an eagle's flight.

And after they had talked together a while,
    they turned and welcomed me most graciously,
99 at which I saw my approving Master smile.

And they honored me far beyond courtesy,
    for they included me in their own number,
102 making me sixth in that high company.‡

So we moved§ toward the light, and as we passed
    we spoke of things as well omitted here
105 as it was sweet to touch on there. At last

we reached the base of a great Citadel‖
    circled by seven towering battlements
108 and by a sweet brook flowing round them all.

---

* *a Mighty One:* Christ. His name is never directly uttered in Hell.

† *descended here:* The legend of the Harrowing of Hell is Apocryphal. It is based on I *Peter* iii, 19: "He went and preached unto the spirits in prison." The legend is that Christ in the glory of His resurrection descended into Limbo and took with Him to Heaven the first human souls to be saved. The event would, accordingly, have occurred in 33 or 34 A.D. Virgil died in 19 B.C.

‡ *making me sixth in that high company:* Merit and self-awareness of merit may well be a higher thing than modesty. An additional point Dante may well have had in mind, however, is the fact that he saw himself as one pledged to continue in his own times the classic tradition represented by these poets.

§103–105. These lines amount to a stylistic note. It is good style ('*l tacere è bello* where *bello* equals "good style") to omit this discussion, since it would digress from the subject and, moreover, his point is already made. Every great narrator tends to tell his story from climax to climax. There are times on the other hand when Dante delights in digression. (See General Note to Canto XX.)

‖ A GREAT CITADEL. The most likely allegory is that the Citadel represents philosophy (that is, human reason without the light of God) surrounded by seven walls which represent the seven liberal arts, or the seven sciences, or the seven virtues. Note that Human Reason makes a light of its own, but that it is a light in darkness and forever separated from the glory of God's light. The *sweet brook flowing* round them all has been interpreted in many ways. Clearly fundamental, however, is the fact that it divides those in the Citadel (those who wish to know) from those in the outer darkness.

This we passed over as if it were firm ground.*
    Through seven gates I entered with those sages
111   and came to a green meadow blooming round.

There with a solemn and majestic poise
    stood many people gathered in the light,
114   speaking infrequently and with muted voice.

Past that enameled green we six withdrew
    into a luminous and open height
117   from which each soul among them stood in view.

And there directly before me on the green
    the master souls of time were shown to me.
120   I glory in the glory I have seen!

Electra stood in a great company
    among whom I saw Hector and Aeneas
123   and Caesar in armor with his falcon's eye.

I saw Camilla, and the Queen Amazon
    across the field. I saw the Latin King
126   seated there with his daughter by his throne.

And the good Brutus who overthrew the Tarquin:
    Lucrezia, Julia, Marcia, and Cornelia;
129   and, by himself apart, the Saladin.

And raising my eyes a little I saw on high
    Aristotle, the master of those who know,
132   ringed by the great souls of philosophy.

All wait upon him for their honor and his.
    I saw Socrates and Plato at his side
135   before all others there. Democritus

who ascribes the world to chance, Diogenes,
    and with him there Thales, Anaxagoras,
138   Zeno, Heraclitus, Empedocles.

---

as if it were firm ground: Since Dante still has his body, and since all others in Hell are incorporeal shades, there is a recurring narrative problem in the *Inferno* (and through the rest of the *Commedia*): how does flesh act in contact with spirit? In the *Purgatorio* Dante attempts to embrace the spirit of Casella and his arms pass through him as if he were empty air. In the Third Circle, below (Canto VI, 34–36), Dante steps on some of the spirits lying in the slush and his foot passes right through them. (The original lines offer several possible readings of which I have preferred this one.) And at other times Virgil, also a spirit, picks Dante up and carries him bodily.

It is clear, too, that Dante means the spirits of Hell to be weightless. When Virgil steps into Phlegyas' bark (Canto VIII) it does not settle into the water, but it does when Dante's living body steps aboard. There is no narrative reason why Dante should not sink into the waters of this stream and Dante follows no fixed rule in dealing with such phenomena, often suiting the physical action to the allegorical need. Here, the moat probably symbolizes some requirement (The Will to Know) which he and the other poets meet without difficulty.

And I saw the wise collector and analyst—
    Dioscorides I mean. I saw Orpheus there,
141   Tully, Linus, Seneca the moralist,

Eculid the geometer, and Ptolemy,
    Hippocrates, Galen, Avicenna,
144   and Averrhoës of the Great Commentary.

I cannot count so much nobility;
    my longer theme pursues me so that often
147   the word falls short of the reality.

The company of six is reduced by four.
    My Master leads me by another road
150   away from that serenity to the roar

and trembling air of Hell. I pass from light
    into the kingdom of eternal night.

> In the lower circles of hell, Dante and Virgil experience all of hell's torments—burning sand, violent storms, darkness, and fearful monsters that whip, claw, bite, and tear sinners apart. The ninth circle, the lowest, is reserved for Lucifer and traitors. Lucifer has three faces, each a different color, and two bat-like wings. In each mouth he gnaws on the greatest traitors in history: Judas Iscariot, who betrayed Jesus, and Brutus and Cassius, who assassinated Caesar. Dante and Virgil climb over the body of Lucifer, and Dante describes how they emerge from hell after three days—symbolizing Christ's "harrowing of hell."

Canto XXXIV

NINTH CIRCLE: COCYTUS	*COMPOUND FRAUD*
ROUND FOUR: JUDECCA	*THE TREACHEROUS TO THEIR MASTERS*
THE CENTER	*SATAN*

"On march the banners of the King," Virgil begins as the Poets face the last depth. He is quoting a medieval hymn, and to it he adds the distortion and perversion of all that lies about him. "On march the banners of the King—of Hell." And there before them, in an infernal parody of Godhead, they see Satan in the distance, his great wings beating like a windmill. It is their beating that is the source of the icy wind of Cocytus, the exhalation of all evil.

All about him in the ice are strewn the sinners of the last round, *Judecca*, named for Judas Iscariot. These are the *Treacherous to Their Masters*. They lie completely sealed in the ice, twisted and distorted into every conceivable posture. It is impossible to speak to them, and the Poets move on to observe Satan.

He is fixed into the ice at the center to which flow all the rivers of guilt; and as he beats his great wings as if to escape, their icy wind only freezes him more surely into the polluted ice. In a grotesque parody of the Trinity, he has three faces, each a different color, and in each mouth he clamps a sinner whom he rips eternally with his teeth. *Judas Iscariot* is in the central mouth: *Brutus* and *Cassius* in the mouths on either side.

Having seen all, the Poets now climb through the center, grappling hand over hand down the hairy flank of Satan himself—a last supremely symbolic action—and at last, when they have passed the center of all gravity, they emerge from Hell. A long climb from the earth's center to the Mount of Purgatory awaits them, and they push on without rest, ascending along the sides of the river Lethe, till they emerge once more to see the stars of Heaven, just before dawn on Easter Sunday.

"On march the banners of the King* of Hell,"
   my Master said. "Toward us. Look straight ahead:
3   can you make him out at the core of the frozen shell?"

Like a whirling windmill seen afar at twilight,
   or when a mist has risen from the ground—
6   just such an engine rose upon my sight

stirring up such a wild and bitter wind
   I cowered for shelter at my Master's back,
9   there being no other windbreak I could find.

I stood now where the souls of the last class
   (with fear my verses tell it) were covered wholly;
12   they shone below the ice like straws in glass.

Some lie stretched out; others are fixed in place
   upright, some on their heads some on their soles;
15   another, like a bow, bends foot to face.

When we had gone so far across the ice
   that it pleased my Guide to show me the foul creature†
18   that once had worn the grace of Paradise,

he made me stop, and, stepping aside, he said:
   "Now see the face of Dis! This is the place
21   where you must arm your soul against all dread."

Do not ask, Reader, how my blood ran cold
   and my voice choked up with fear. I cannot write it:
24   this is a terror that cannot be told.

I did not die, and yet I lost life's breath:
   imagine for yourself what I became,
27   deprived at once of both my life and death.

The Emperor of the Universe of Pain
   jutted his upper chest above the ice;
30   and I am closer in size to the great mountain

the Titans make around the central pit,
   than they to his arms. Now, starting from this part,
33   imagine the whole that corresponds to it!

If he was once as beautiful as now
   he is hideous, and still turned on his Maker,
36   well may he be the source of every woe!

With what a sense of awe I saw his head
   towering above me! for it had three faces:‡
39   one was in front, and it was fiery red;

the other two, as weirdly wonderful,
   merged with it from the middle of each shoulder
42   to the point where all converged at the top of the skull;

the right was something between white and bile;
   the left was about the color one observes
45   on those who live along the banks of the Nile.

Under each head two wings rose terribly,
   their span proportioned to so gross a bird:
48   I never saw such sails upon the sea.

They were not feathers—their texture and their form
   were like a bat's wings—and he beat them so
51   that three winds blew from him in one great storm:

it is these winds that freeze all Cocytus.
   He wept from his six eyes, and down three chins
54   the tears ran mixed with bloody froth and pus.§

In every mouth he worked a broken sinner
   between his rake-like teeth. Thus he kept three
57   in eternal pain at his eternal dinner.

For the one in front the biting seemed to play
   no part at all compared to the ripping: at times
60   the whole skin of his back was flayed away.

"That soul that suffers most," explained my Guide,
   "is Judas‖ Iscariot, he who kicks his legs
63   on the fiery chin and has his head inside.

---

* *On march the banners of the King:* The hymn (*Vexilla regis prodeunt*) was written in the sixth century by Venantius Fortunatus, Bishop of Poitiers. The original celebrates the Holy Cross, and is part of the service for Good Friday to be sung at the moment of uncovering the cross.
† *the foul creature:* Satan.

‡ *three faces:* Numerous interpretations of these three faces exist. What is essential to all explanation is that they be seen as perversions of the qualities of the Trinity.
§ *bloody froth and pus:* The gore of the sinners he chews which is mixed with his slaver.
‖ *Judas:* Note how closely his punishment is patterned on that of the Simoniacs (Canto XIX).

Of the other two, who have their heads thrust forward,
    the one who dangles down from the black face
66   is Brutus: note how he writhes without a word.

And there, with the huge and sinewy arms,* is the soul
    of Cassius.—But the night is coming on†
69   and we must go, for we have seen the whole."

Then, as he bade, I clasped his neck, and he,
    watching for a moment when the wings
72   were opened wide, reached over dexterously

and seized the shaggy coat of the king demon;
    then grappling matted hair and frozen crusts
75   from one tuft to another, clambered down.

When we had reached the joint where the great thigh
    merges into the swelling of the haunch,
78   my Guide and Master, straining terribly,

turned his head to where his feet had been
    and began to grip the hair as if he were climbing;
81   so that I thought we moved toward Hell again.

"Hold fast!" my Guide said, and his breath came shrill‡
    with labor and exhaustion. "There is no way
84   but by such stairs to rise above such evil."

At last he climbed out through an opening
    in the central rock, and he seated me on the rim;
87   then joined me with a nimble backward spring.

I looked up, thinking to see Lucifer
    as I had left him, and I saw instead
90   his legs projecting high into the air.

Now let all those whose dull minds are still vexed
    by failure to understand what point it was
93   I had passed through, judge if I was perplexed.

"Get up. Up on your feet," my Master said.
    "The sun already mounts to middle tierce,§
96   and a long road and hard climbing lie ahead."

It was no hall of state we had found there,
    but a natural animal pit hollowed from rock
99   with a broken floor and a close and sunless air.

"Before I tear myself from the Abyss,"
    I said when I had risen, "O my Master,
102   explain to me my error in all this:

where is the ice? and Lucifer—how has he
    been turned from top to bottom: and how can the sun
105   have gone from night to day so suddenly?"

And he to me: "You imagine you are still
    on the other side of the center where I grasped
108   the shaggy flank of the Great Worm of Evil

which bores through the world—you *were* while I climbed
                                    down,
    but when I turned myself about, you passed
111   the point to which all gravities are drawn.

You are under the other hemisphere where you stand;
    the sky above us is the half opposed
114   to that which canopies the great dry land.

Under the midpoint of that other sky
    the Man who was born sinless and who lived
117   beyond all blemish, came to suffer and die.

You have your feet upon a little sphere
    which forms the other face of the Judecca.
120   There it is evening when it is morning here.

And this gross Fiend and Image of all Evil
    who made a stairway for us with his hide
123   is pinched and prisoned in the ice-pack still.

On this side he plunged down from heaven's height,
    and the land that spread here once hid in the sea
126   and fled North to our hemisphere for fright;

and it may be that moved by that same fear,
    the one peak‖ that still rises on this side
129   fled upward leaving this great cavern# here."

Down there, beginning at the further bound
    of Beelzebub's dim tomb, there is a space
132   not known by sight, but only by the sound

---

* *huge and sinewy arms:* The Cassius who betrayed Caesar was more generally described in terms of Shakespeare's "lean and hungry look." Another Cassius is described by Cicero (*Catiline* III) as huge and sinewy. Dante probably confused the two.

† *the night is coming on:* It is now Saturday evening.

‡ *his breath came shrill:* Cf. Canto XXIII, 85, where the fact that Dante breathes indicates to the Hypocrites that he is alive. Virgil's breathing is certainly a contradiction.

§ *middle tierce:* In the canonical day tierce is the period from about six to nine A.M. Middle tierce, therefore, is seven-thirty In going through the center point, they have gone from night to day. They have moved ahead twelve hours.

‖ *the one peak:* The Mount of Purgatory.

this great cavern: The natural animal pit of line 98. It is also "Beelzebub's dim tomb," line 131.

of a little stream* descending through the hollow
  it has eroded from the massive stone
135 in its endlessly entwining lazy flow."

My Guide and I crossed over and began
  to mount that little known and lightless road
138 to ascend into the shining world again.

He first, I second, without thought of rest
  we climbed the dark until we reached the point
141 where a round opening brought in sight the blest

and beauteous shining of the Heavenly cars.
  And we walked out once more beneath the Stars.†

As Dante and Virgil are about to reach the summit of
Mount Purgatory, Beatrice replaces Virgil as Dante's
guide. In the final canto of the *Paradiso,* Dante and
Beatrice ascend to the highest heaven, the
Empyrean, which is located beyond Saturn, the last
of the seven planets, beyond the circle of stars that
encloses the planets and above the Primum Mobile—
the outermost sphere revolving around the Earth.
Here at the summit of the universe is a realm of pure
light that radiates truth, goodness, and happiness,
where God is found. Dante glimpses the vision of
God—a mystical experience in which the aim of his
life is realized.

Little by little as my vision grew
  it penetrated further through the aura
54 of the high lamp which in Itself is true.

What then I saw is more than tongue can say.
  Our human speech is dark before the vision.
57 The ravished memory swoons and falls away.

As one who sees in dreams and wakes to find
  the emotional impression of his vision
60 still powerful while its parts fade from his mind—

just such am I, having lost nearly all
  the vision itself, while in my heart I feel
63 the sweetness of it yet distill and fall.

---

* *a little stream:* Lethe. In classical mythology, the river of forgetfulness,
from which souls drank before being born. In Dante's symbolism it
flows down from the top of Purgatory, where it washes away the memory of sin from the souls that have achieved purity. That memory it delivers to Hell, which drawn all sin to itself.
† *Stars:* As part of his total symbolism Dante ends each of the three divisions of the *Commedia* with this word. Every conclusion of the upward
soul is toward the stars. God's shining symbols of hope and virtue. It is
just before dawn of Easter Sunday that the Poets emerge—a further
symbolism.

So, in the sun, the footprints face from snow.
  On the wild wind that bore the tumbling leaves
66 the Sybil's oracles were scattered so.

O Light Supreme who doth Thyself withdraw
  so far above man's mortal understanding,
69 lend me again some glimpse of what I saw;

make Thou my tongue so eloquent it may
  of all Thy glory speak a single clue
72 to those who follow me in the world's day;

for by returning to my memory
  somewhat, and somewhat sounding in these verses,
75 Thou shalt show man more of Thy victory.

So dazzling was the splendor of that Ray,
  that I must certainly have lost my senses
78 had I, but for an instant, turned away.

And so it was, as I recall, I could
  the better bear to look, until at last
81 my vision made one with the Eternal Good.

Oh grace abounding that had made me fit
  to fix my eyes on the eternal light
84 until my vision was consumed in it!

I saw within Its depth how It conceives
  all things in a single volume bound by Love,
87 of which the universe is the scattered leaves;

substance, accident, and their relation
  so fused that all I say could do no more
90 than yield a glimpse of that bright revelation.

I think I saw the universal form
  that binds these things, for as I speak these words
93 I feel my joy swell and my spirits warm.

Twenty-five centuries since Neptune saw
  the Argo's keel have not moved all mankind,
96 recalling that adventure, to such awe

as I felt in an instant. My tranced being
  stored fixed and motionless upon that vision,
99 ever more fervent to see in the act of seeing.

Experiencing that Radiance, the spirit
  is so indrawn it is impossible
102 even to think of ever turning from It.

For the good which is the will's ultimate object
  is all subsumed in It; and, being removed,
105 all is defective which in It is perfect.

Now in my recollection of the rest
  I have less power to speak than any infant
108 wetting its tongue yet at its mother's breast;

and not because that Living Radiance bore
  more than one semblance, for It is unchanging
111 and is forever as it was before,

rather, as I grew worthier to see,
  the more I looked, the more unchanging semblance
114 appeared to change with every change in me.

Within the depthless deep and clear existence
  of that abyss of light three circles shown—
117 three in color, one in circumference:

the second from the first, rainbow from rainbow;
  the third, an exhalation of pure fire
120 equally breathed forth by the other two.

But oh how much my words miss my conception,
  which is itself so far from what I saw
123 that to call it feeble would be rank deception!

O Light Eternal fixed in Itself alone,
  by Itself alone understood, which from Itself
126 loves and glows, self-knowing and self-known;

that second aureole which shone forth in Thee,
  conceived as a reflection of the first—
129 or which appeared so to my scrutiny—

seemed in Itself of Its own coloration
  to be painted with man's image. I fixed my eyes
132 on that alone in rapturous contemplation.

Like a geometer wholly dedicated
  to squaring the circle, but who cannot find,
135 think as he may, the principle indicated—

so did I study the supernal face.
  I yearned to know just how our image merges
138 into that circle, and how it there finds place;

but mine were not the wings for such a flight.
  Yet as I wished, the truth I wished for came
141 cleaving my mind in a great flash of light.

Here my powers rest from their high fantasy,
  but already I could feel my being turned—
144 instinct and intellect balanced equally

as in a wheel whose motion nothing jars—
  by the Love that moves the Sun and the other stars.

Credits

Chapter 1

Page 2: *Epic of Gilgamesh,* translated by N.K. Sandars (Penguin Classics, 1960, Third Edition 1972). Copyright © NK Sandars, 1960, 1964, 1972. Reproduced by permission of Penguin Books Ltd. **Page 7:** From James B. Pritchard (ed.), *The Ancient Near East: A New Anthology of Texts and Pictures,* Vol. 2, pp. 151–154. Copyright © 1975 by Princeton University Press. **Page 8:** From *Babylonian and Assyrian Laws, Contracts, and Letters,* ed. C.M.W. Johns (New York: Charles Scribner's Sons, 1904), pp. 46–67 passim. **Page 11:** From *Ancient Near Eastern Texts Relating to the Old Testament,* 3/e with Supplement edited by James B. Pritchard, 1969, pp. 297–298, 100, 101, 370. Copyright © 1969 by Princeton University Press. **Page 12:** "Love Poetry" and "The Instruction of Anksheshonq," from Miriam Lichtheim, *Ancient Egyptian Literature: A Book of Readings,* Vol II. Copyright © 1973–1980 Regents of the University of California. Used by permission of the University of California Press.

Chapter 2

Page 15–25: Excerpts from the *Old Testament: Genesis, Exodus, Leviticus, Deuteronomy, Jeremiah, Job, Amos, Isaiah* from *The Holy Scriptures According to the Masoretic Text.* Philadelphia: Jewish Publication Society of America. Copyright 1917, 1955. Used by permission of the Jewish Publication Society.

Chapter 3

Page 27: From *The Iliad* by Homer, translated by E.V. Rieu (Penguin Classics, 1950). Copyright © Estate of E.V. Rieu, 1946. Reproduced by permission of Penguin Books Ltd. **Page 33:** From *Works and Days/The Poems of Hesiod,* translated with introduction and comments by R. M. Frazer University of Oklahoma Press, 1983. Copyright 1983 by the University of Oklahoma Press, Norman, Publishing Division of the University. All rights reserved. **Page 35:** "The Pursuit of Excellence" by Pindar, translated by H.D.F. Kitto in *The Greeks.* Revised Edition. (Penguin Books, 1951. Revised edition 1957). Copyright © H.D.F. Kitto, 1951, 1957. **Page 36:** *Antigone,* from *Three Theban Plays* by Sophocles, translated by Robert Fagles. Translation copyright © 1982 by Robert Fagles. **Page 36:** From *The History of the Peloponnesian War* by Thucydides, translated by Rex Warner (Penguin Classics, 1954). Translation © Rex Warner, 1954. Reproduced by permission of Penguin Books Ltd. **Page 38:** Sappho poems #21, 32, 40 and 78, from Josephine Balmer, *Sappho: Poems and Fragments* (Newcastle upon Tyne: Bloodaxe Books, Ltd, 1992). Reprinted by permission of Bloodaxe Books Ltd. **Page 39:** Sappho poem about Cleis, from Sappho "A Girl," in *The Oxford Book of Greek Verse in Translation,* T.F. Higham and C.M. Bowra, eds. (Oxford, Clarendon Press, 1938). Reprinted by permission of Oxford University Press. **Page 39:** *Sappho: A New Translation,* one Fragment #32 "Virginity O my virginity!" translated by Mary Barnard. Copyright © 1958 The Regents of the University of California; © renewed 1986 Mary Barnard. Used by permission of the University of California Press. **Page 40, 61:** From *Three Thebian Plays: Antigone, Oedipus The King, and Oedipus at Colonus* by Sophocles, edited by Theodore Howard Banks, copyright © 1956 by Oxford University Press, Inc. Used by permission of Oxford University Press, Inc. **Page 65:** Aeschylus, "The Persians," from Aeschylus, The Persians: A Translations and Commentary by Anthony J. Podlecki , 1970. Used by permission of Gerald Duckworth & Co. Ltd. **Page 67:** From *The Medea,* translated by Rex Warner in Euripides, Vol. 3 of Richard Lattimore, *The Complete Greek Tragedies,* p. 101, 96. Copyright © 1959 by The Bodley Head. **Page 67:** From *Lysistrata,* copyright © 1991 by Ivan R. Dee, Inc., translation copyright © 1991 by Nicholas Rudall. **Page 70:** From *The Trial and Death of Socrates,* trans. F.J. Church (London, Macmillan, 1880), pp. 37–41, 50–53, 56–57. **Page 73:** Plato *The Republic of Plato,* tranlsated by F. M. Cornford, (NY: Oxford University Press, 1941). Reprinted by permission of Oxford University Press. **Page 77:** Plato "Phaedo" from *Phaedo,* translated by David Gallop (Oxford: Clarendon Press, 1975). Reprinted by permissions of Oxford University Press. **Page 79:** From *The Oxford Translation of Aristotle,* edited by W.D. Ross. Copyright © 1925. **Page 79:** Aristotle, *The Politics,* translated by T.A. Sinclair, revised by Trevor J. Saunders. Copyright © 1962 by the Estate of T.A. Sinclair, revised translation copyright © 1981 by Trevor J. Saunders.

Chapter 4

Page 86: Daniel, *First Maccabees, Second Maccabees,* (Wilmington: Michael Glazier, 1981; Collegeville: The Liturgical Press, 1990). **Page 87:** From *Philo, Volume IV,* Loeb Classical Library Volume L 261, translated by F.H. Colson and G.H. Whitaker, Cambridge, Mass.: Harvard University Press, 1932, and from *Philo, Volume VII,* Loeb Classical Library Volume L 320, translated by F.H. Colson, Cambridge, Mass.: Harvard University Press, 1937. The Loeb Classical Library ® is a registered trademark of the President and Fellows of Harvard College. **Page 89:** From *Epicurus: The Extant Remains,* translated by Cyril Bailey, pp. 53, 83, 85, 89, 97, 101, 115, 117, 119. Copyright © 1926. **Page 90:** Longus, " Hellenistic Romance" *Daphnis, and Chloe with 42 colous plates after the lithographs by Marc Chagall,* translated by Paul Turner (Munchen, Germany: Prestel-Verlag, 1994), pp. 16, 17, 20, 22, 25, 28, 98, 146–147, 150. Copyright Prestel-Verlag, Munich-New York, 1994. Copyright Paul Turner, 1956, 1968, 1989. This edition is published in association with Penguin Books Ltd. The moral rights of the author have been asserted. Reproduced by permission of Penguin Books Ltd. **Page 93:** Apollonius of Rhodes, "Agonautica" from Fowler, Barbara Hughes, ed. *Hellenistic Poetry.* © 1990. Reprinted by permission of The University of Wisconsin Press.

Chapter 5

Page 98: *Lucretius.* Translated by Anthony M. Esolen. *On the Nature of Things: De rerum natura.* pp. 26–27, 191–193. Copyright The Johns Hopkins University Press, All Rights Reserved. Published 1995. Reprinted with permission of The Johns Hopkins University Press. **Page 100:** From *Selected Works* by Cicero, translated by Michael Grant (Penguin Classics 1960, second revised edition 1971) copyright © Michael Grant 1960, 1965, 1971. Reproduced by permission of Penguin Books Ltd. **Page 101:** Reprinted by permission of the publishers and the Trustees of the Loeb Classical Library from *Seneca: Volume I,* Loeb Classical Library Vol. L 214, translated by John W. Basore, pp. 209, 211, 213, Cambridge, Mass.: Harvard University Press, 1928. The Loeb Classical Library ® is a registered trademark of the President and Fellows of Harvard College. **Page 103:** From *Meditations* by Marcus Aurelius, translated by Maxwell Staniforth (Penguin Classics, 1964) copyright © Maxwell Staniforth, 1964. Reproduced by permission of Penguin Books Ltd. **Page 104:** Reprinted by permission of the publishers and the Trustees of the Loeb Classical Library from *Catullus,* Loeb Classical Library Colume L 6, translated by F. W. Cornish, pp. 5, 53–54, Cambridge, Mass.: Harvard University Press, 1913, Revised 1950, 1962. The Loeb Classical Library ® is a registered trademark of the President and Fellows of Harvard College. **Page 105:** From *The Aeneid by Virgil,* translated by Robert Fitzgerald, copyright © 1980, 1982, 1983 by Robert Fitzgerald. Used by permission of Random House, Inc. **Page 110:** Horace, *The Odes and Epodes of Horace,* edited by Joseph P. Clancy. Copyright © 1960 by University of Chicago Press. Reprinted with permission. **Page 111:** From *The Epic Poems* by Ovid, translated by Peter Green, (Penguin Classics, 1982). Copyright © Peter Green, 1982. Reproduce by permission of Penguin Books Ltd. **Page 115:** Adapted from *The Satires of Juvenal,* translated by Hubert Creekmore (New York: The New American Library, 1963).

Chapter 6

Page 118: From *The New Jerusalem Bible,* copyright © 1985 by Doubleday, a division of Random House, Inc. and Darton, Longman, & Todd, Ltd. Used by permission of Doubleday, a division of Random House, Inc. **Page 121:**